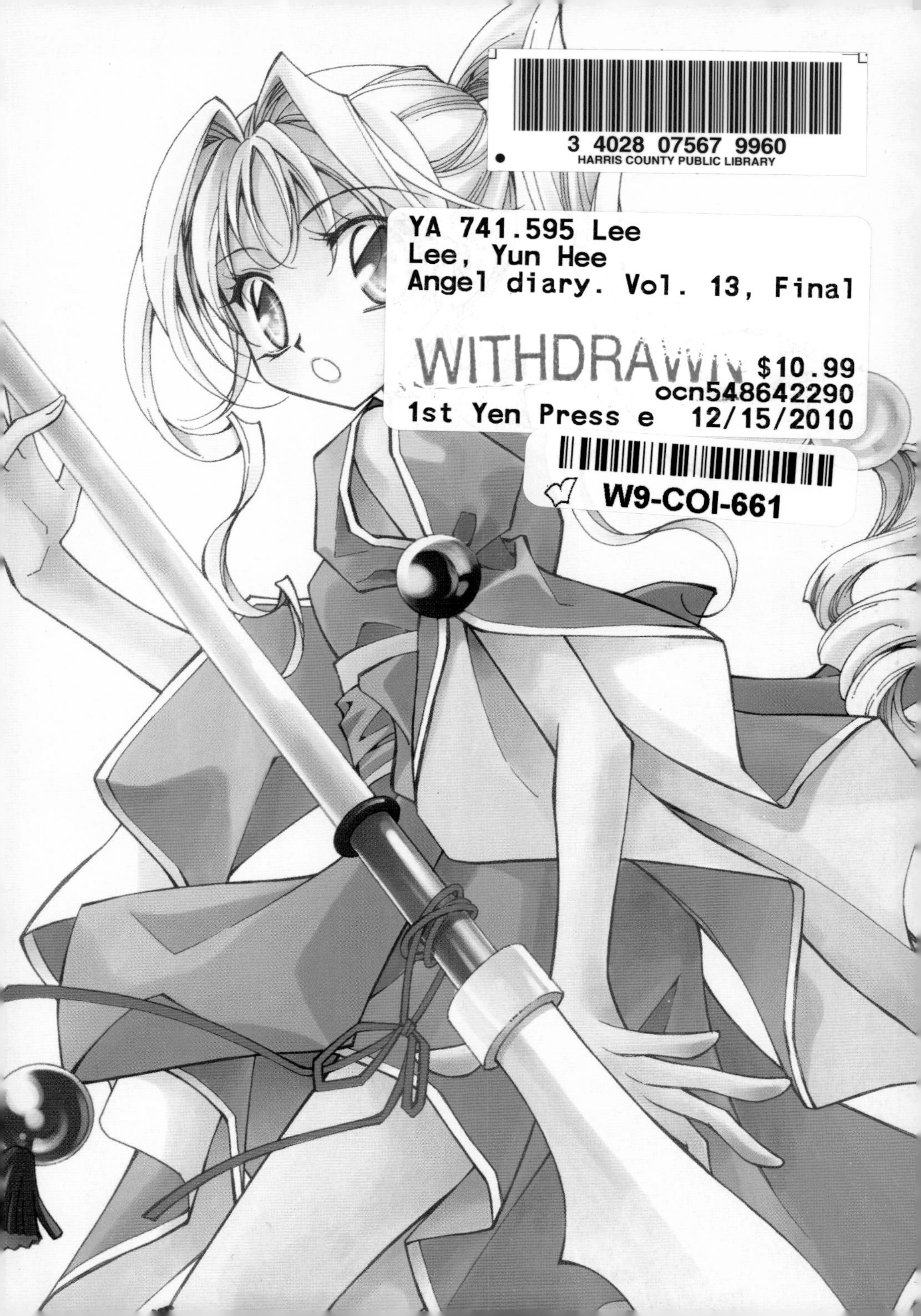

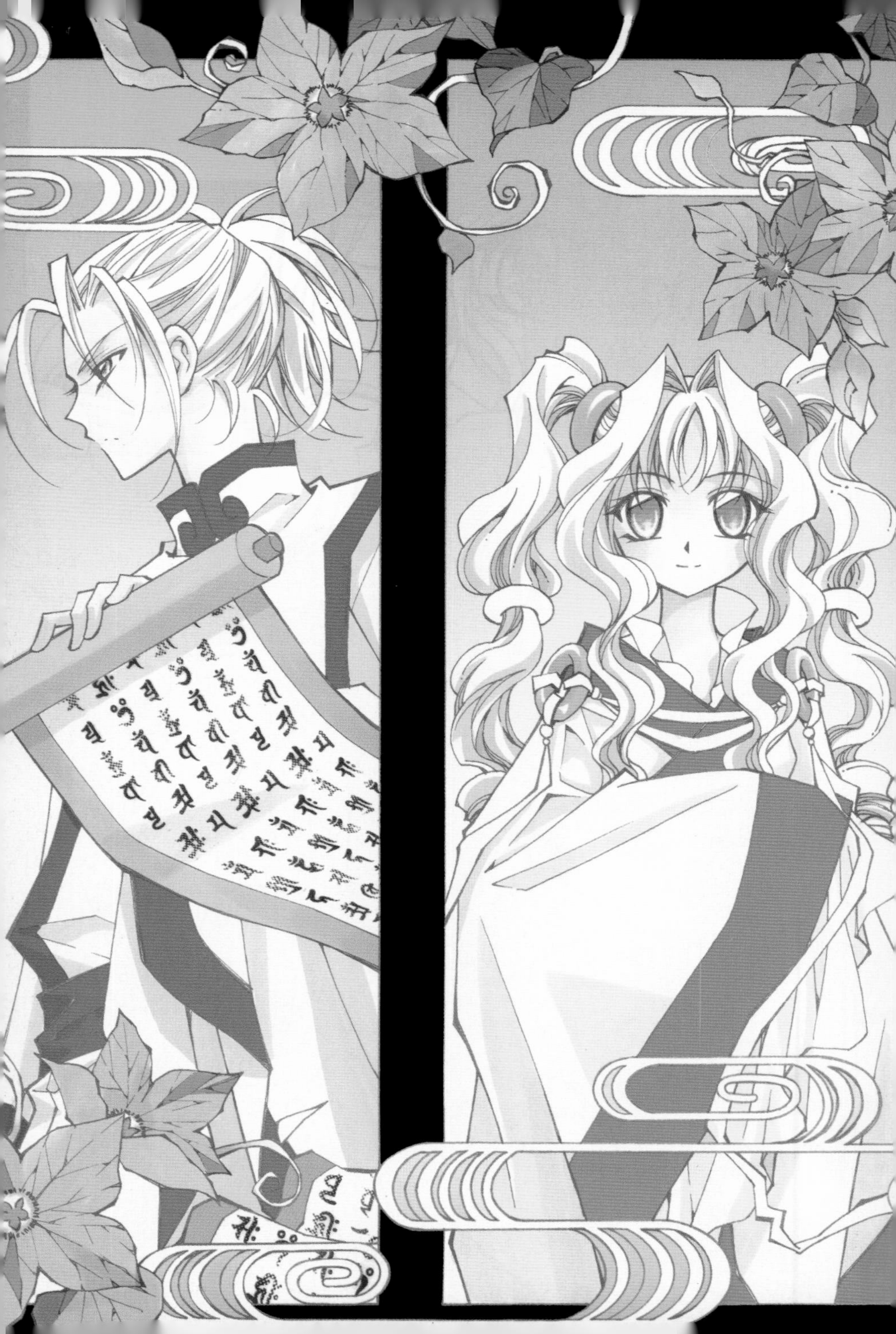

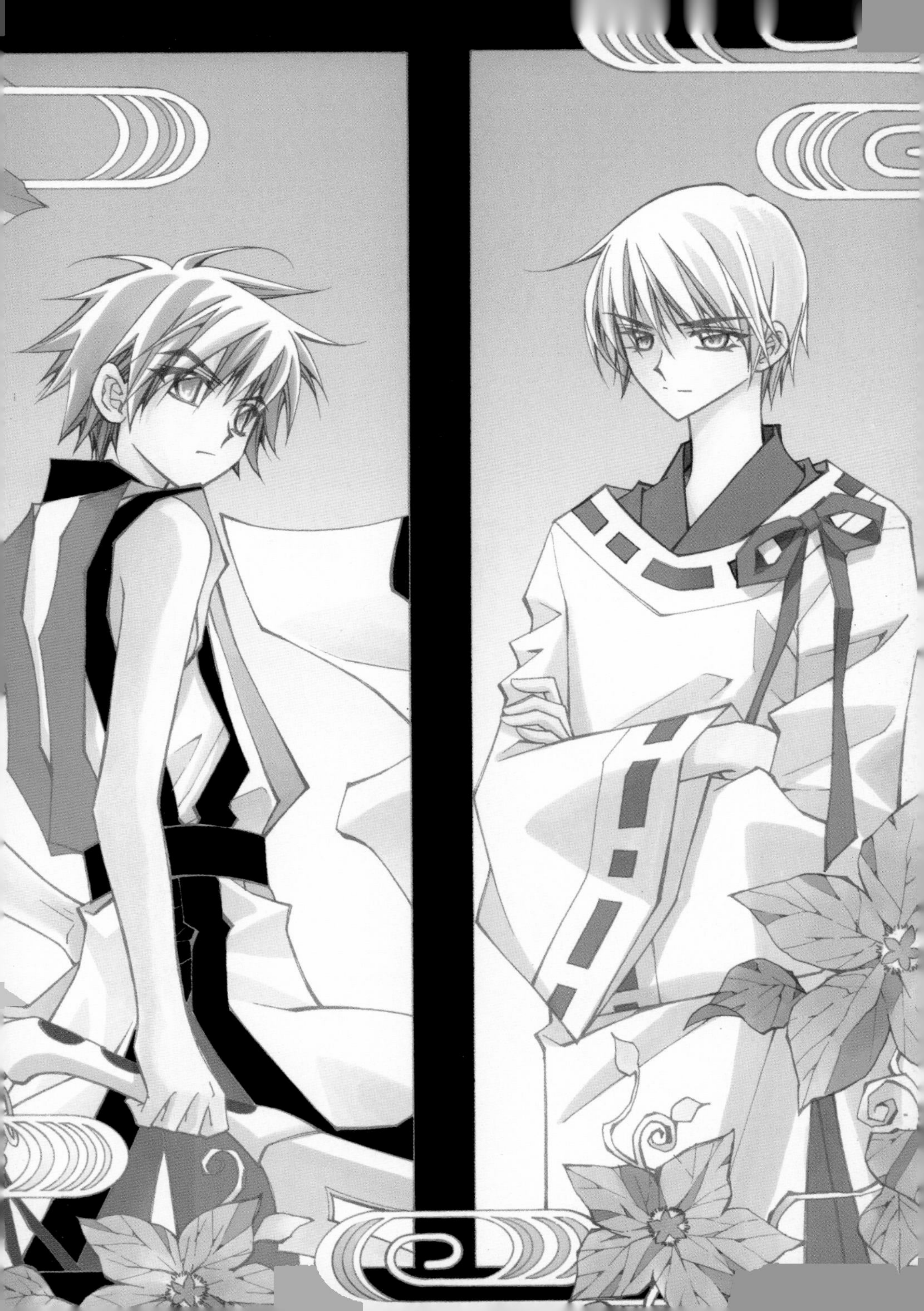

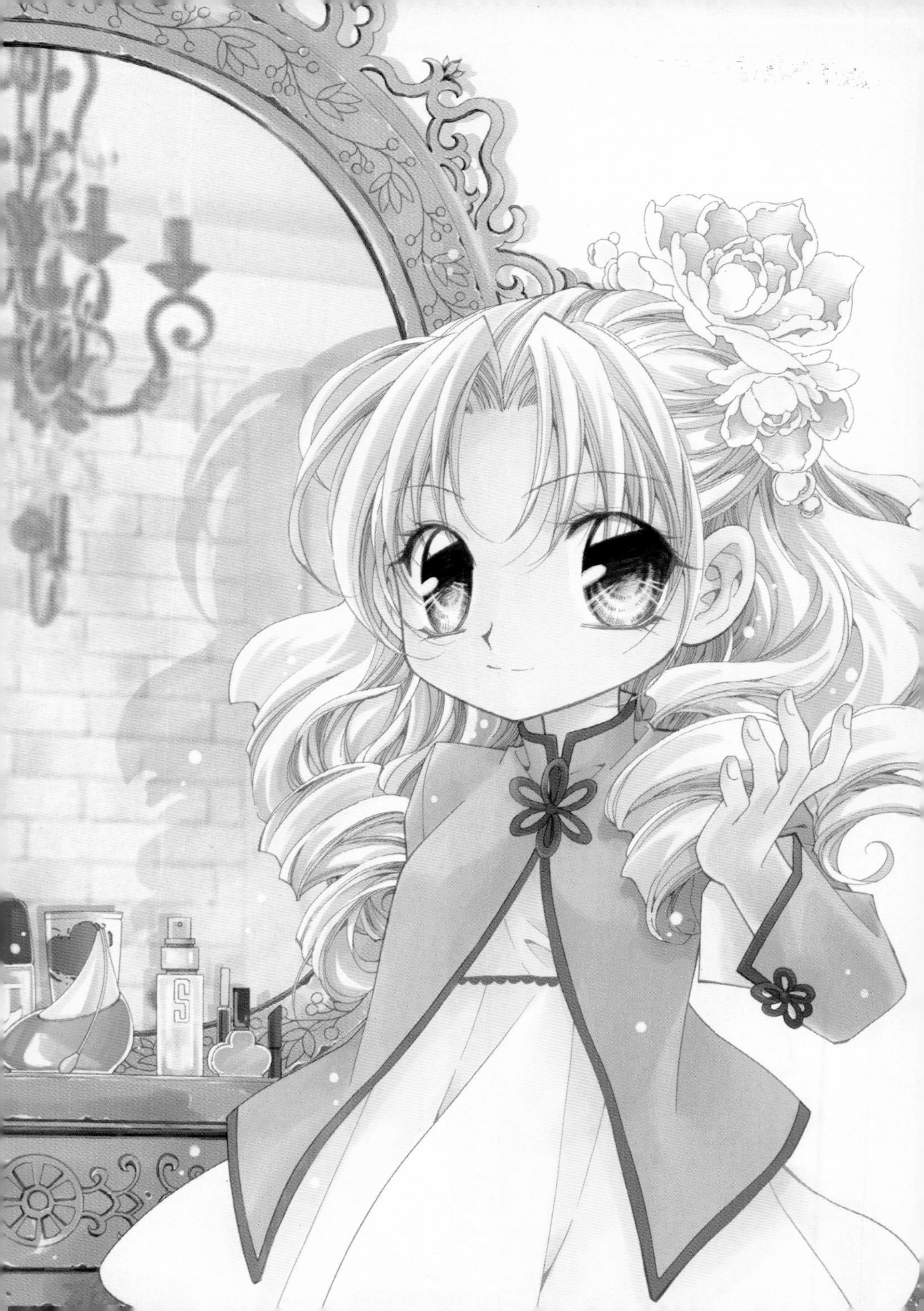

Angel Diary

vol. 13
FINAL

Kara · Lee YunHee

Yen
Press

• A WORD FROM THE CREATORS •

THIS IS REALLY THE CONCLUSION. MANY THINGS HAPPENED WHILE
WE WORKED ON *ANGEL DIARY*. THERE WAS EVEN A WHOLE YEAR
WHEN THE SERIES WAS DISCONTINUED. IT'S TRUE WHAT THEY SAY,
YOU DO CARE MORE FOR THE TROUBLESOME CHILD. WE WISH WE
COULD KEEP TELLING YOU MORE STORIES OF THIS WORLD, BUT IT'S
TIME TO SAY FAREWELL TO BOTH IT AND THE CHARACTERS IN IT,
OUR KIDS. EVEN THOUGH THEY'RE LEAVING, I'M SURE THEY'LL FIND
A HAPPY NEW LIFE SOMEWHERE ELSE. WE WOULD LIKE TO THANK
SEOUL CULTURAL PUBLISHERS FOR GIVING US THE CHANCE TO
FINISH OUR TALE. AND WE WOULD ALSO LIKE TO THANK THE
READERS WHO HUNG ON TO THIS SERIES UNTIL
THE VERY END. GOOD-BYE.

BY *KARA*

HELLO. THIS IS THE LAST TIME I'LL BE WRITING A NOTE FOR *ANGEL
DIARY*. AT LAST, WE'VE COME TO VOLUME 13, THE FINALE. SO MUCH
TIME HAS PASSED WHILE WE WORKED ON THESE THIRTEEN BOOKS.
I HADN'T THOUGHT ABOUT THIS BEFORE, BUT ONE OF THE *ANGEL
DIARY* READERS I KNOW WAS IN JUNIOR HIGH WHEN WE STARTED,
AND NOW SHE'S PREPARING FOR HER UNIVERSITY ENTRANCE EXAM.
THANKS TO THE READERS WHO'VE STUCK WITH *ANGEL DIARY* FOR
SUCH A LONG TIME. THE SERIES WAS ABLE TO HAVE A COMPLETE
STORY ALL BECAUSE OF YOU. THOUGH THERE ARE SOME EXTRA STO-
RIES HERE, I WANTED TO WRITE MORE STORIES ABOUT THE DIFFER-
ENT CHARACTERS. I STILL FEEL LIKE WHAT'S HERE IS NOT ENOUGH.
IF I KEEP FLESHING OUT ALL THE LITTLE THINGS LIKE I WANT, WE'LL
NEVER BE DONE, SO I MUST END IT HERE. THANK YOU SO MUCH FOR
CARING, LOVING, AND WAITING FOR *ANGEL DIARY*. LET'S MEET
AGAIN IN A DIFFERENT BOOK.

BY *YUNHEE LEE*

CONTENTS

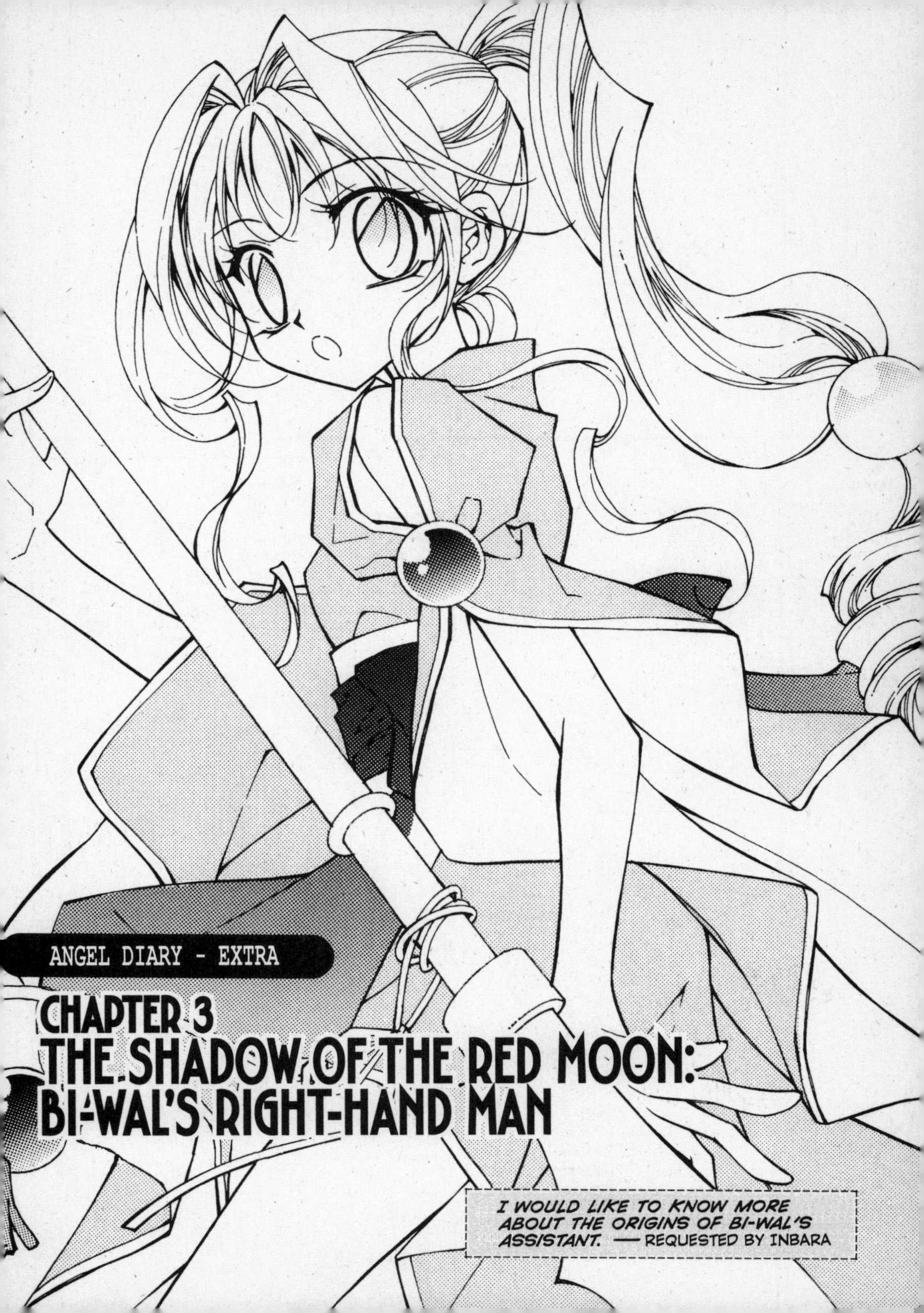
ANGEL DIARY - EXTRA
CHAPTER 3
THE SHADOW OF THE RED MOON:
BI-WAL'S RIGHT-HAND MAN
I WOULD LIKE TO KNOW MORE ABOUT THE ORIGINS OF BI-WAL'S ASSISTANT. —REQUESTED BY INBARA

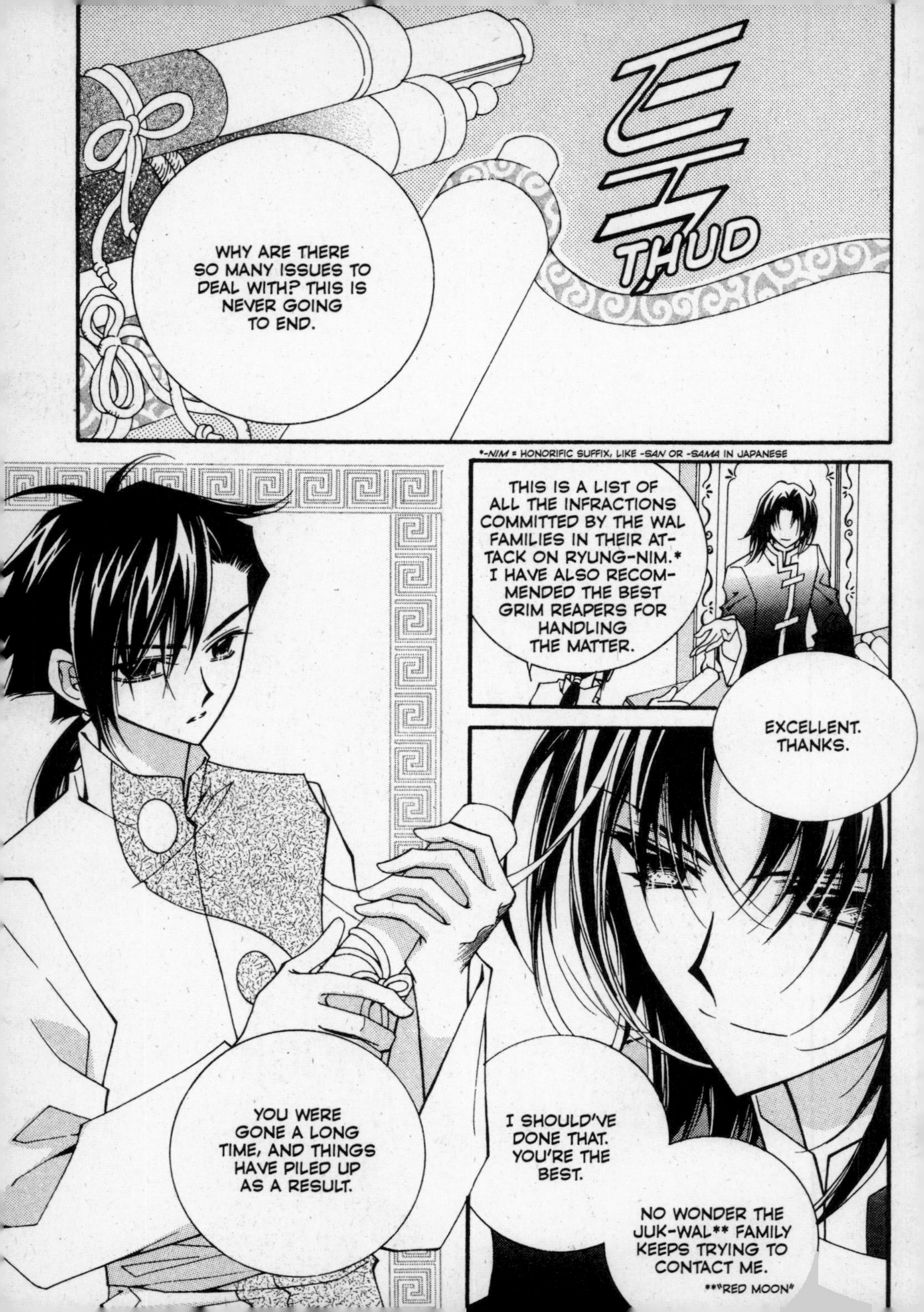
THUD
WHY ARE THERE SO MANY ISSUES TO DEAL WITH? THIS IS NEVER GOING TO END.
YOU WERE GONE A LONG TIME, AND THINGS HAVE PILED UP AS A RESULT.
THIS IS A LIST OF ALL THE INFRACTIONS COMMITTED BY THE WAL FAMILIES IN THEIR ATTACK ON RYUNG-NIM.* I HAVE ALSO RECOMMENDED THE BEST GRIM REAPERS FOR HANDLING THE MATTER.
EXCELLENT. THANKS.
I SHOULD'VE DONE THAT. YOU'RE THE BEST.
NO WONDER THE JUK-WAL** FAMILY KEEPS TRYING TO CONTACT ME.

*-*NIM* = HONORIFIC SUFFIX, LIKE -*SAN* OR -*SAMA* IN JAPANESE

**"RED MOON"

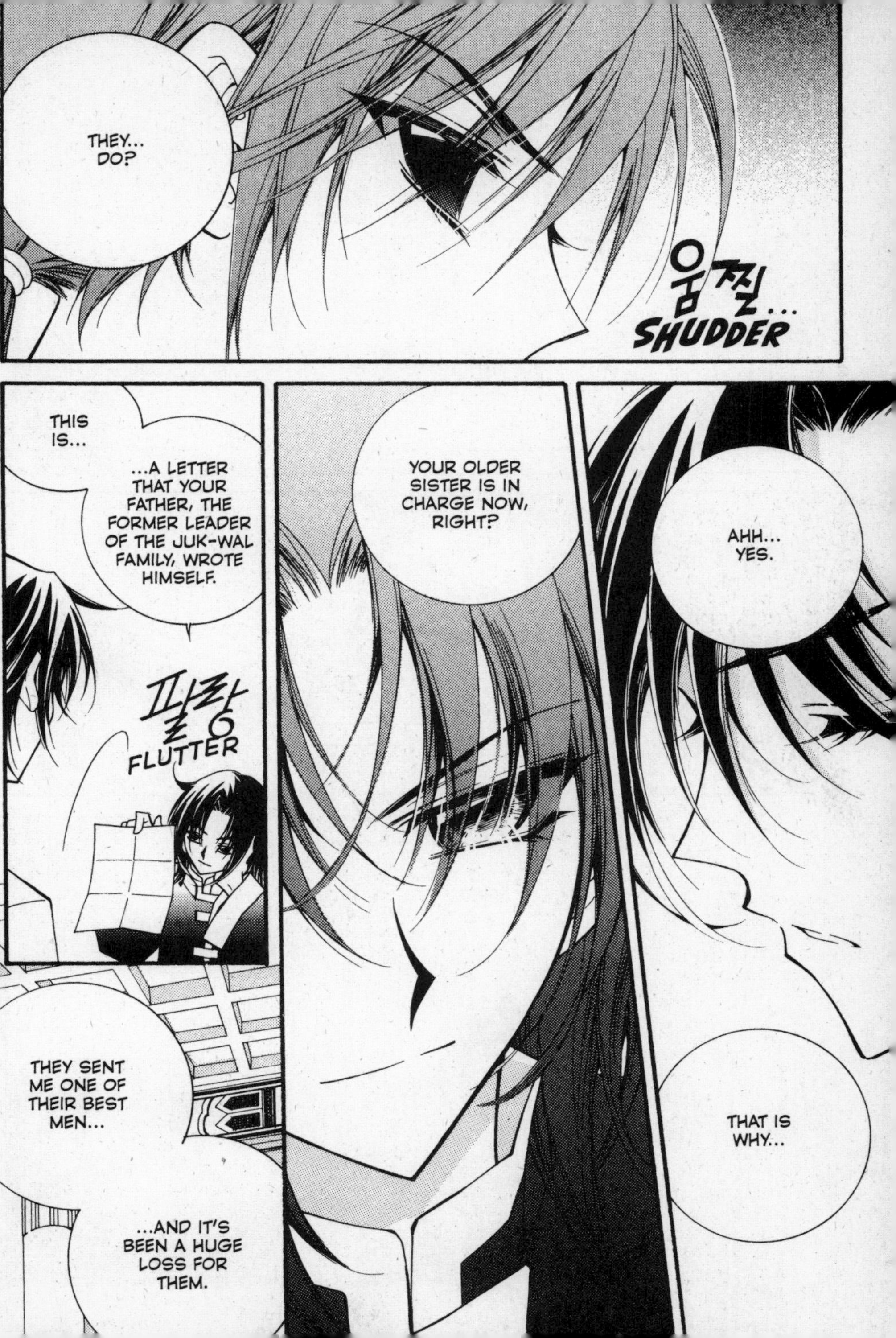
THEY... DO?
움찔...
SHUDDER
THIS IS...
...A LETTER THAT YOUR FATHER, THE FORMER LEADER OF THE JUK-WAL FAMILY, WROTE HIMSELF.
팔랑
FLUTTER
THEY SENT ME ONE OF THEIR BEST MEN...
...AND IT'S BEEN A HUGE LOSS FOR THEM.
YOUR OLDER SISTER IS IN CHARGE NOW, RIGHT?
AHH... YES.
THAT IS WHY...

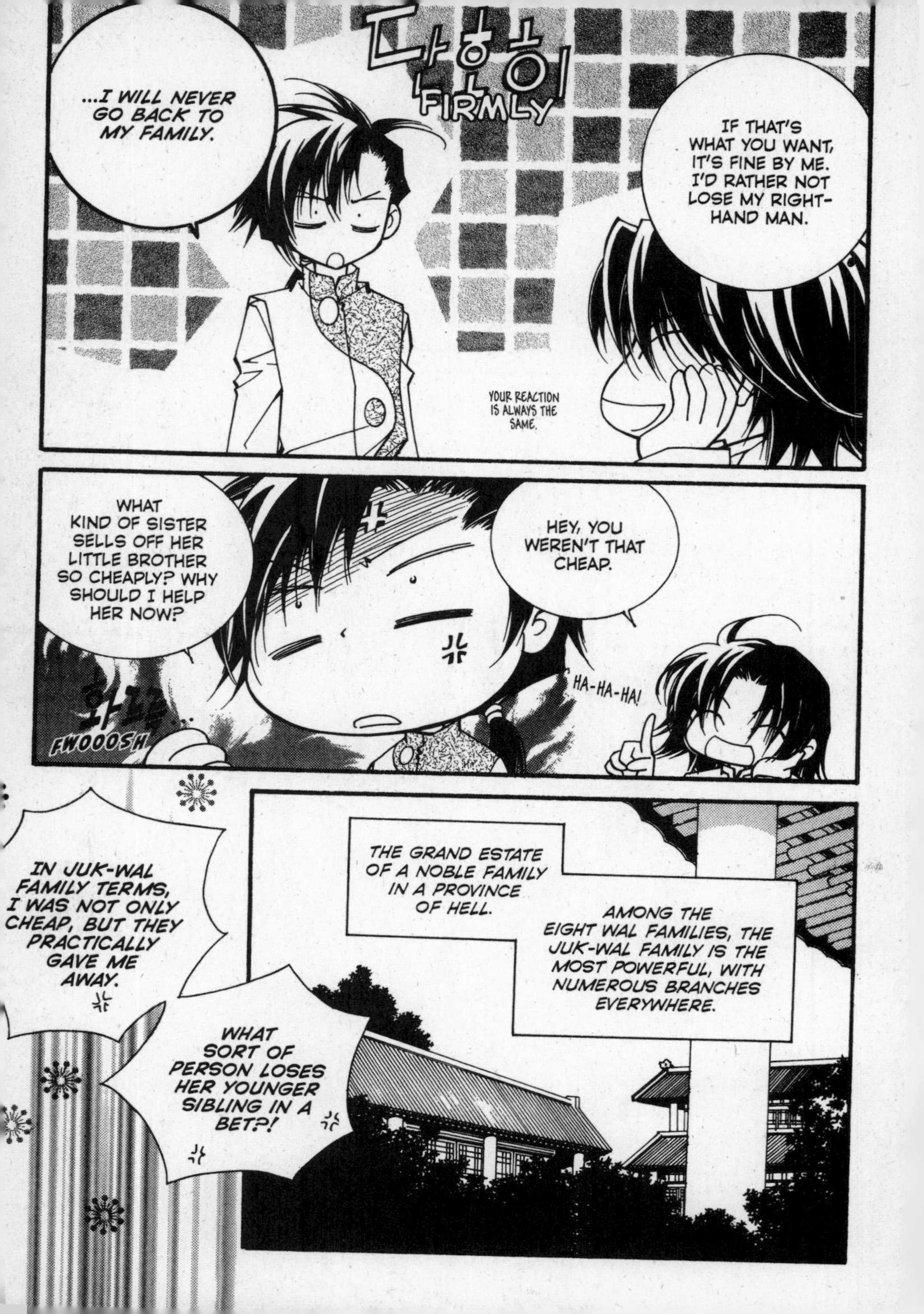
...I WILL NEVER GO BACK TO MY FAMILY.
단호히
FIRMLY
IF THAT'S WHAT YOU WANT, IT'S FINE BY ME. I'D RATHER NOT LOSE MY RIGHT-HAND MAN.
YOUR REACTION IS ALWAYS THE SAME.
WHAT KIND OF SISTER SELLS OFF HER LITTLE BROTHER SO CHEAPLY? WHY SHOULD I HELP HER NOW?
HEY, YOU WEREN'T THAT CHEAP.
HA-HA-HA!
FWOOOSH
IN JUK-WAL FAMILY TERMS, I WAS NOT ONLY CHEAP, BUT THEY PRACTICALLY GAVE ME AWAY.
WHAT SORT OF PERSON LOSES HER YOUNGER SIBLING IN A BET?!
THE GRAND ESTATE OF A NOBLE FAMILY IN A PROVINCE OF HELL.
AMONG THE EIGHT WAL FAMILIES, THE JUK-WAL FAMILY IS THE MOST POWERFUL, WITH NUMEROUS BRANCHES EVERYWHERE.

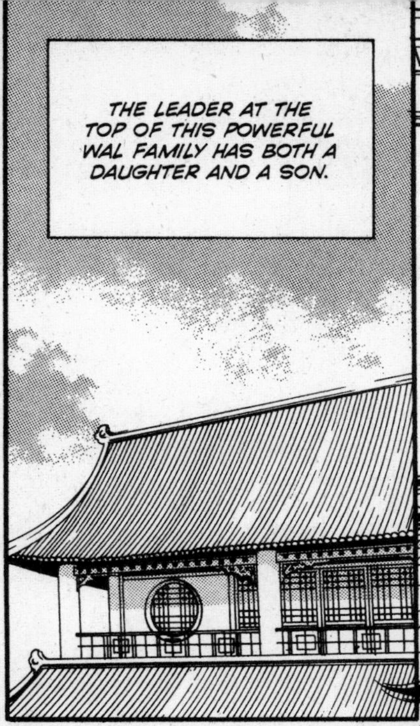
THE LEADER AT THE TOP OF THIS POWERFUL WAL FAMILY HAS BOTH A DAUGHTER AND A SON.
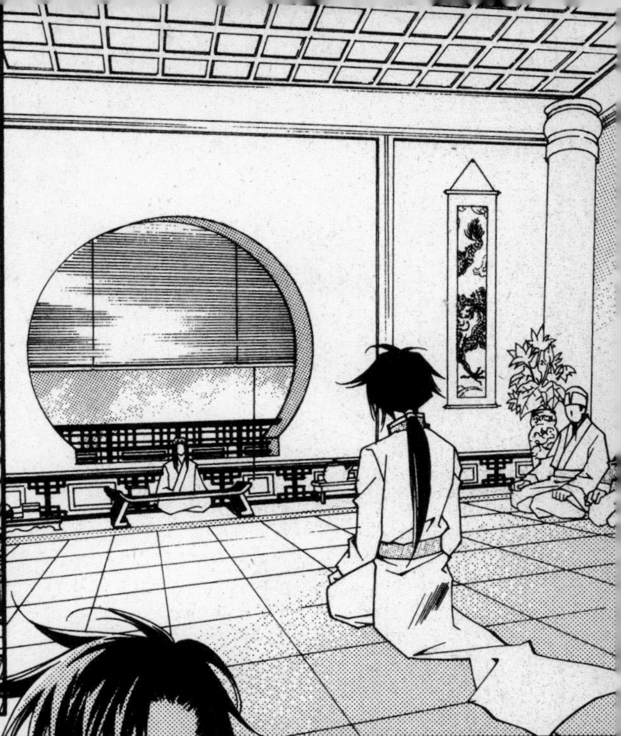
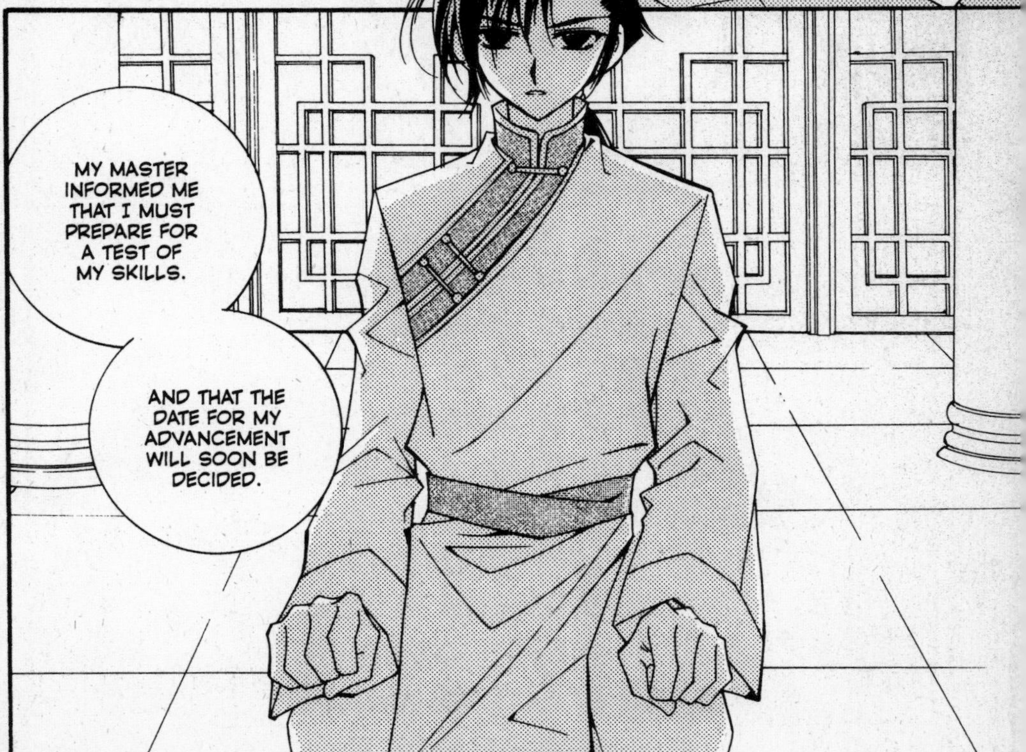
MY MASTER INFORMED ME THAT I MUST PREPARE FOR A TEST OF MY SKILLS.
AND THAT THE DATE FOR MY ADVANCEMENT WILL SOON BE DECIDED.

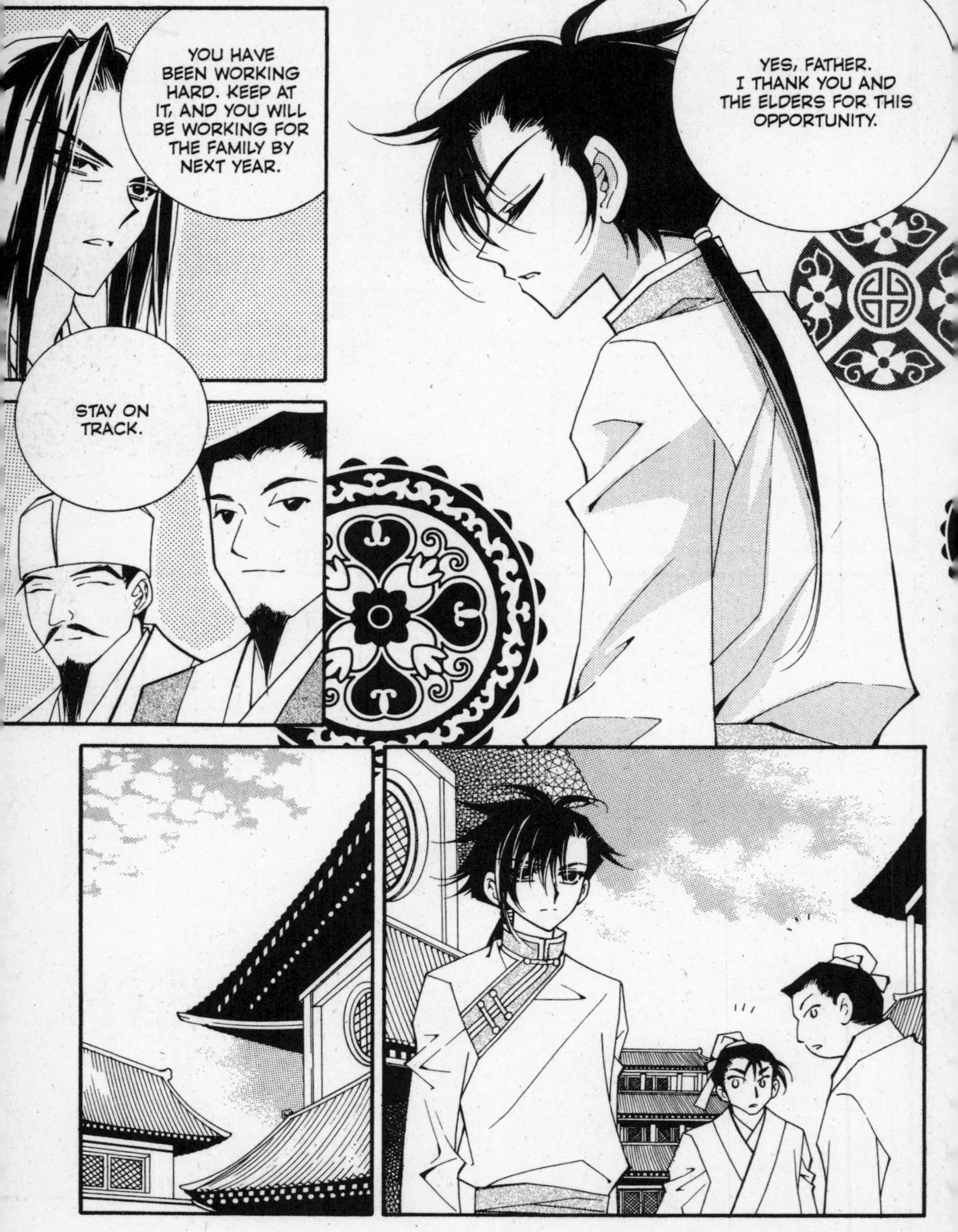
YOU HAVE BEEN WORKING HARD. KEEP AT IT, AND YOU WILL BE WORKING FOR THE FAMILY BY NEXT YEAR.
YES, FATHER. I THANK YOU AND THE ELDERS FOR THIS OPPORTUNITY.
STAY ON TRACK.

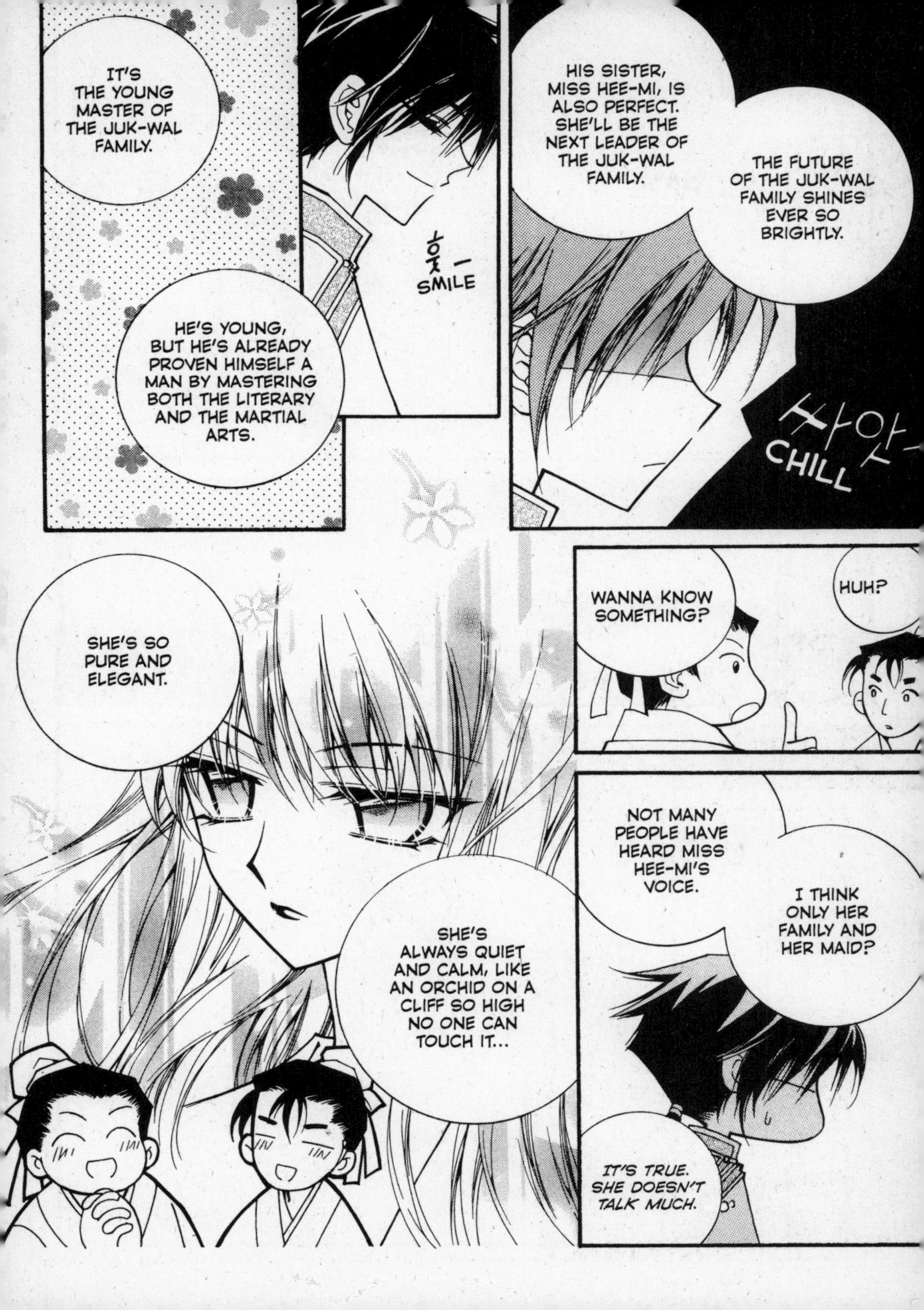
IT'S THE YOUNG MASTER OF THE JUK-WAL FAMILY.
SMILE
HE'S YOUNG, BUT HE'S ALREADY PROVEN HIMSELF A MAN BY MASTERING BOTH THE LITERARY AND THE MARTIAL ARTS.
HIS SISTER, MISS HEE-MI, IS ALSO PERFECT. SHE'LL BE THE NEXT LEADER OF THE JUK-WAL FAMILY.
THE FUTURE OF THE JUK-WAL FAMILY SHINES EVER SO BRIGHTLY.
CHILL
SHE'S SO PURE AND ELEGANT.
SHE'S ALWAYS QUIET AND CALM, LIKE AN ORCHID ON A CLIFF SO HIGH NO ONE CAN TOUCH IT...
WANNA KNOW SOMETHING?
HUH?
NOT MANY PEOPLE HAVE HEARD MISS HEE-MI'S VOICE.
I THINK ONLY HER FAMILY AND HER MAID?
IT'S TRUE. SHE DOESN'T TALK MUCH.

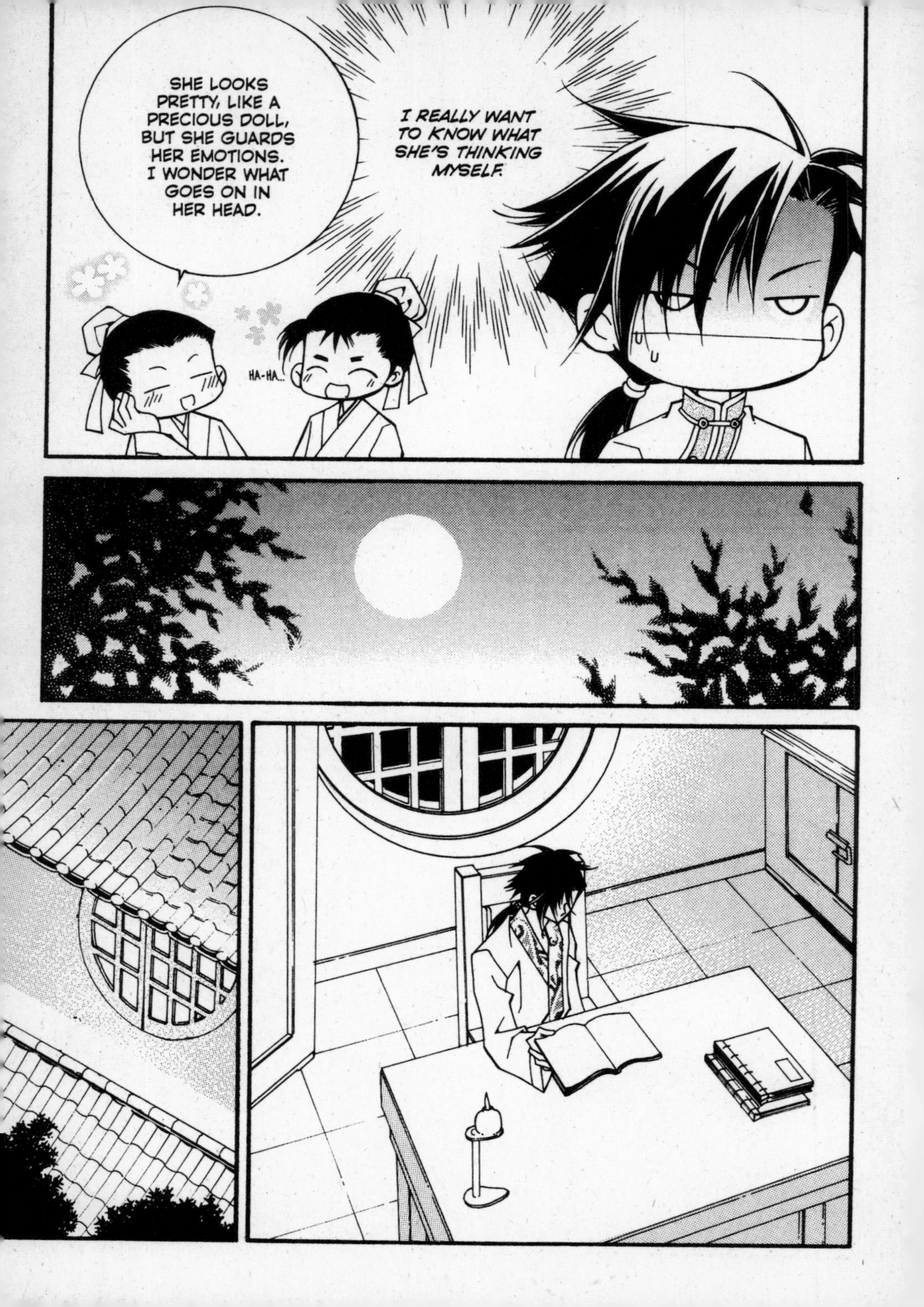
SHE LOOKS PRETTY, LIKE A PRECIOUS DOLL, BUT SHE GUARDS HER EMOTIONS. I WONDER WHAT GOES ON IN HER HEAD.
I REALLY WANT TO KNOW WHAT SHE'S THINKING MYSELF.
HA-HA...

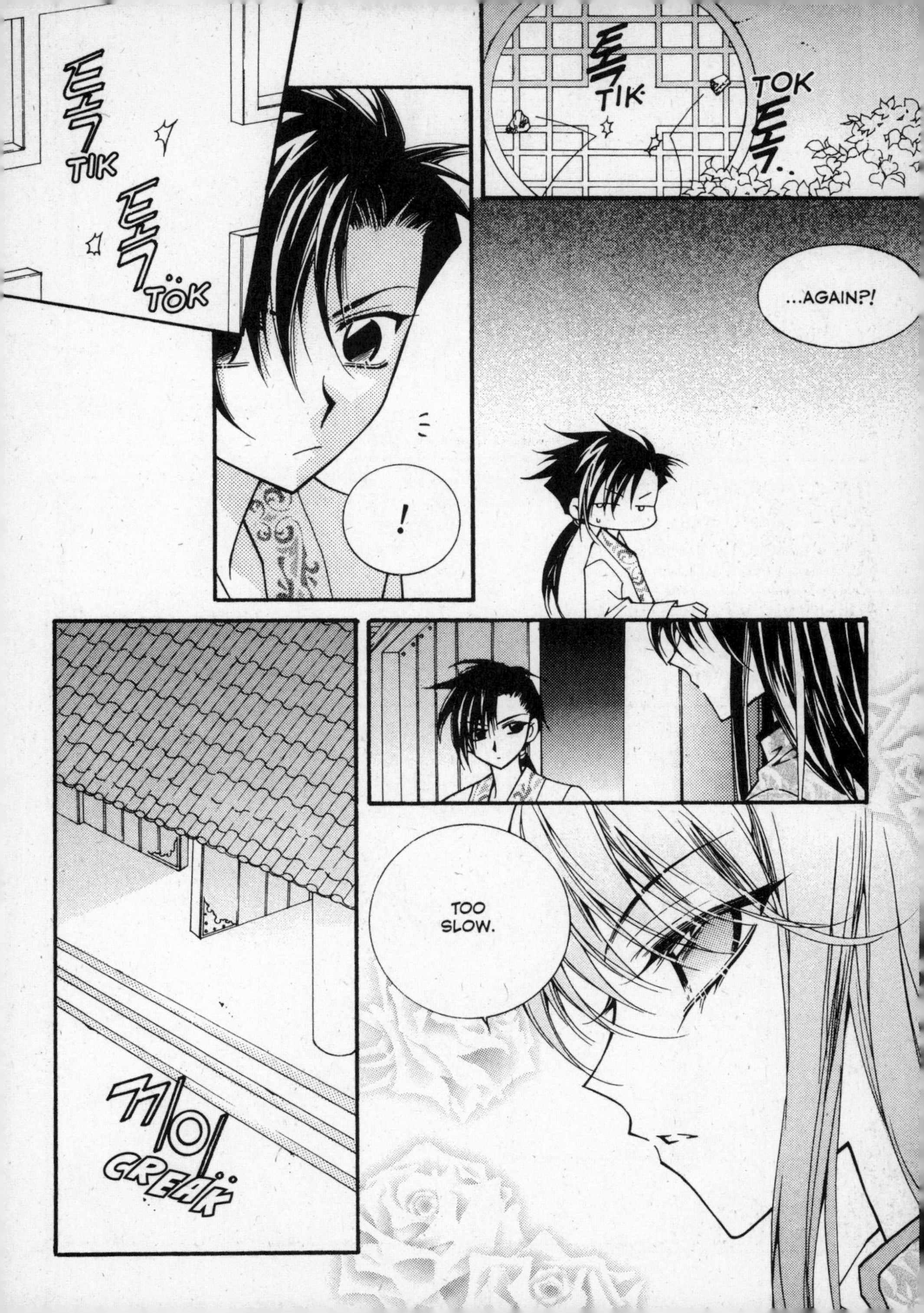

톡
TIK
톡
TÖK
!
톡
TIK·
TOK
톡...
...AGAIN?!
끼이
CREAK
TOO SLOW.

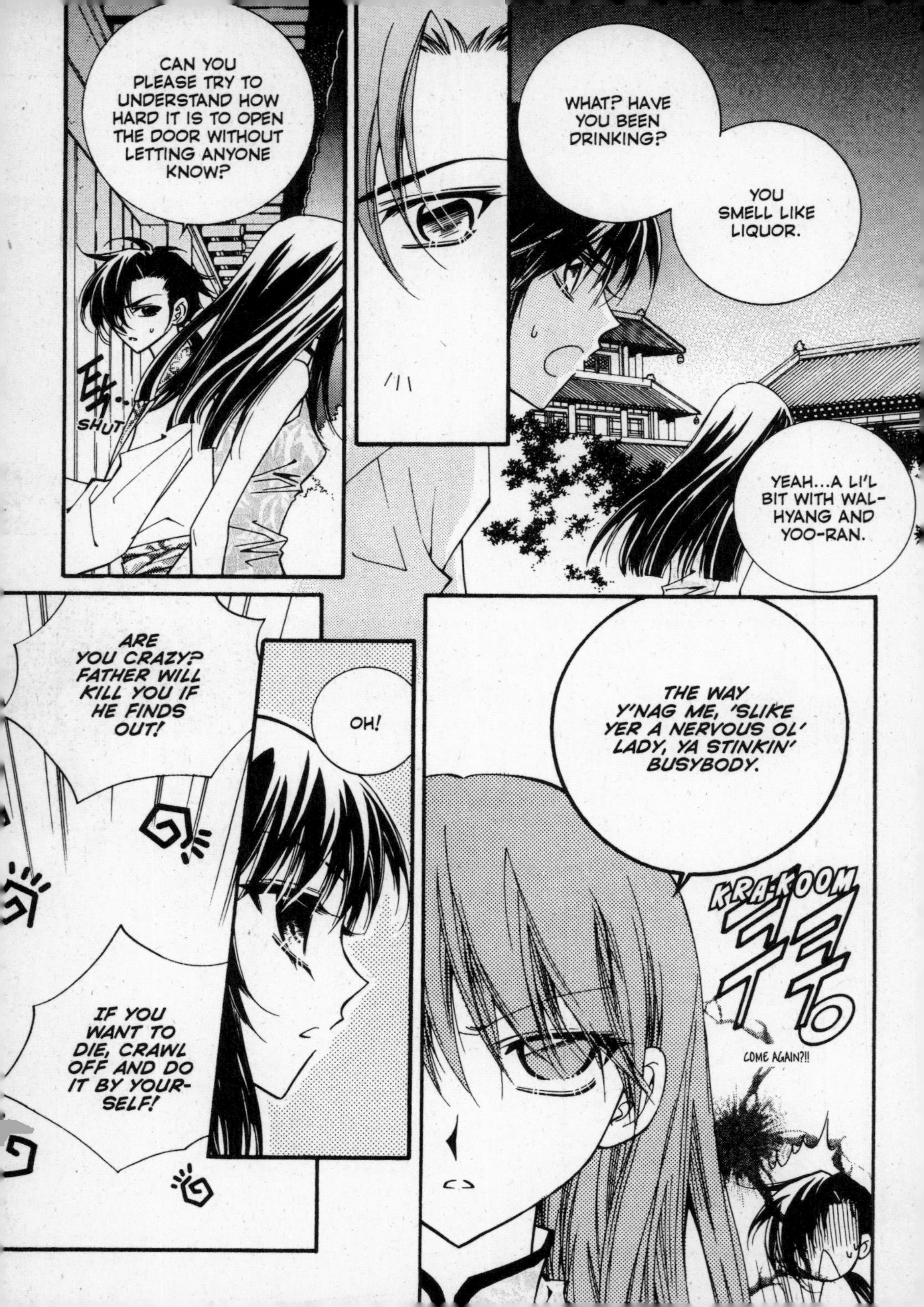
CAN YOU PLEASE TRY TO UNDERSTAND HOW HARD IT IS TO OPEN THE DOOR WITHOUT LETTING ANYONE KNOW?
SHUT
WHAT? HAVE YOU BEEN DRINKING?
YOU SMELL LIKE LIQUOR.
YEAH...A LI'L BIT WITH WAL-HYANG AND YOO-RAN.
ARE YOU CRAZY? FATHER WILL KILL YOU IF HE FINDS OUT!
IF YOU WANT TO DIE, CRAWL OFF AND DO IT BY YOUR-SELF!
OH!
THE WAY Y'NAG ME, 'SLIKE YER A NERVOUS OL' LADY, YA STINKIN' BUSYBODY.
KRA-KOOM
COME AGAIN?!!

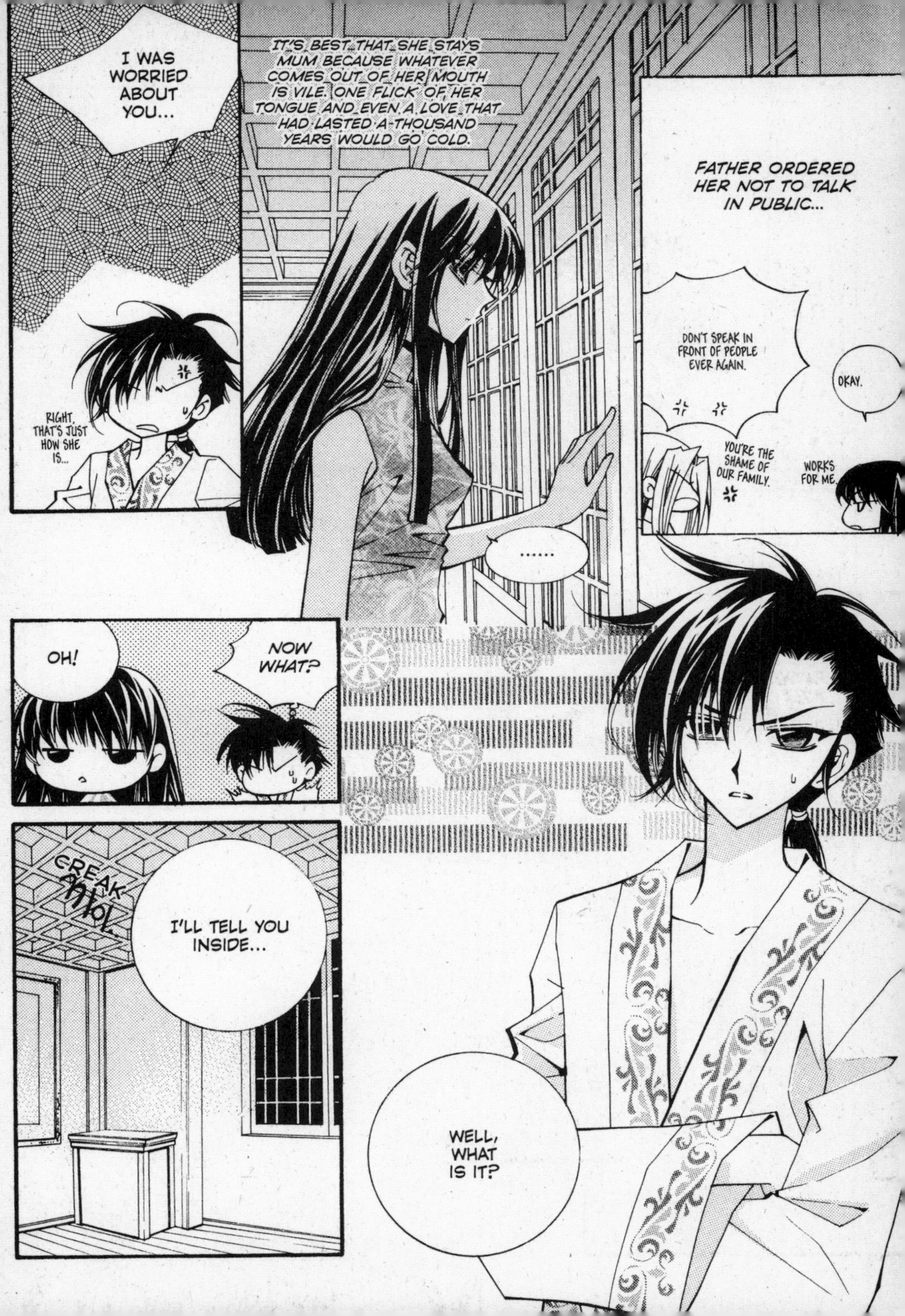
I WAS WORRIED ABOUT YOU...
RIGHT, THAT'S JUST HOW SHE IS...
IT'S BEST THAT SHE STAYS MUM BECAUSE WHATEVER COMES OUT OF HER MOUTH IS VILE. ONE FLICK OF HER TONGUE AND EVEN A LOVE THAT HAD LASTED A THOUSAND YEARS WOULD GO COLD.
......
FATHER ORDERED HER NOT TO TALK IN PUBLIC...
DON'T SPEAK IN FRONT OF PEOPLE EVER AGAIN.
OKAY.
YOU'RE THE SHAME OF OUR FAMILY.
WORKS FOR ME.
OH!
NOW WHAT?
CREAK
I'LL TELL YOU INSIDE...
WELL, WHAT IS IT?

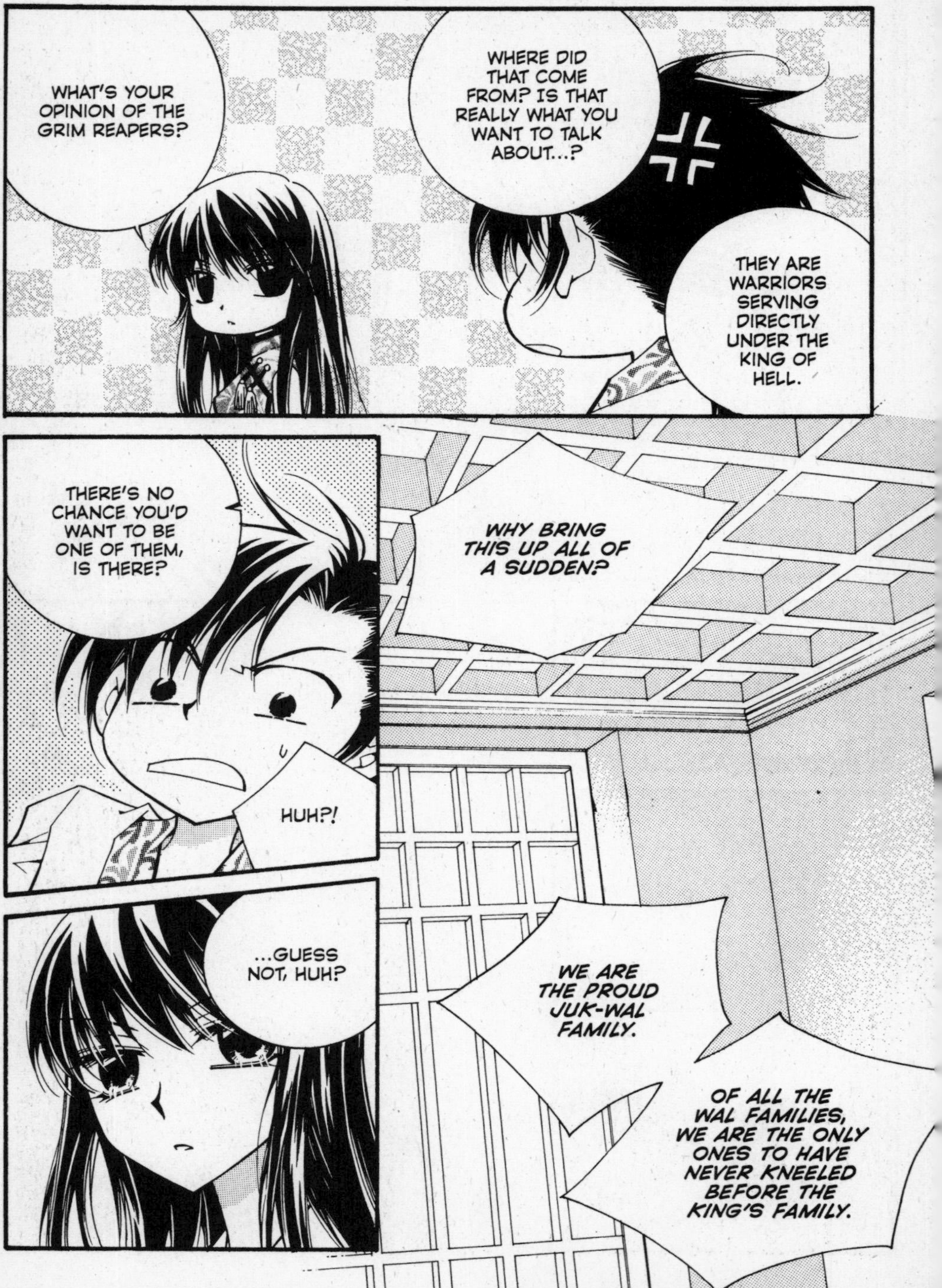
WHAT'S YOUR OPINION OF THE GRIM REAPERS?
WHERE DID THAT COME FROM? IS THAT REALLY WHAT YOU WANT TO TALK ABOUT...?
THEY ARE WARRIORS SERVING DIRECTLY UNDER THE KING OF HELL.
THERE'S NO CHANCE YOU'D WANT TO BE ONE OF THEM, IS THERE?
HUH?!
...GUESS NOT, HUH?
WHY BRING THIS UP ALL OF A SUDDEN?
WE ARE THE PROUD JUK-WAL FAMILY.
OF ALL THE WAL FAMILIES, WE ARE THE ONLY ONES TO HAVE NEVER KNEELED BEFORE THE KING'S FAMILY.

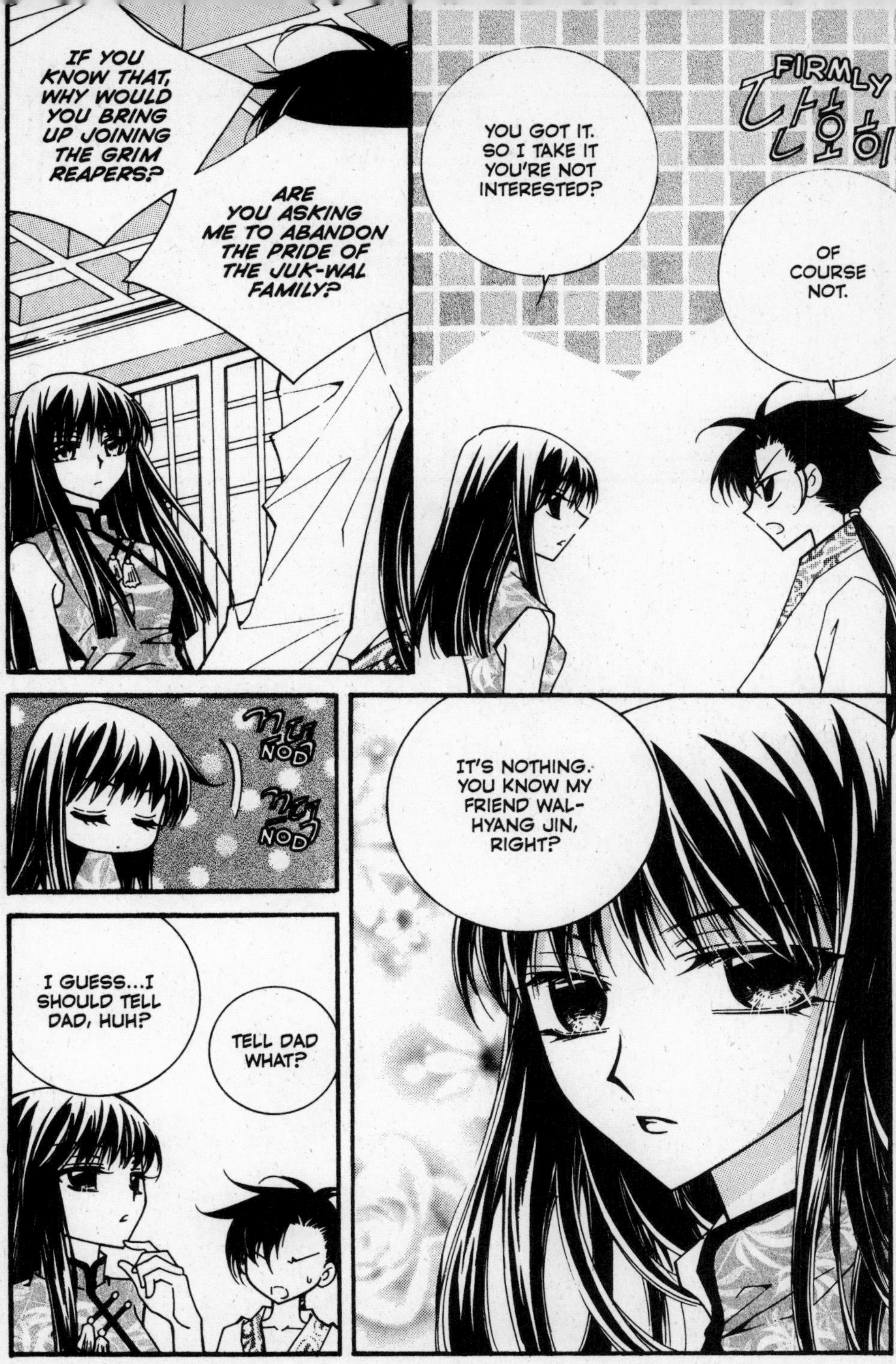
IF YOU KNOW THAT, WHY WOULD YOU BRING UP JOINING THE GRIM REAPERS?
ARE YOU ASKING ME TO ABANDON THE PRIDE OF THE JUK-WAL FAMILY?
YOU GOT IT. SO I TAKE IT YOU'RE NOT INTERESTED?
FIRMLY 단호히
OF COURSE NOT.
NOD
NOD
I GUESS...I SHOULD TELL DAD, HUH?
TELL DAD WHAT?
IT'S NOTHING. YOU KNOW MY FRIEND WAL-HYANG JIN, RIGHT?

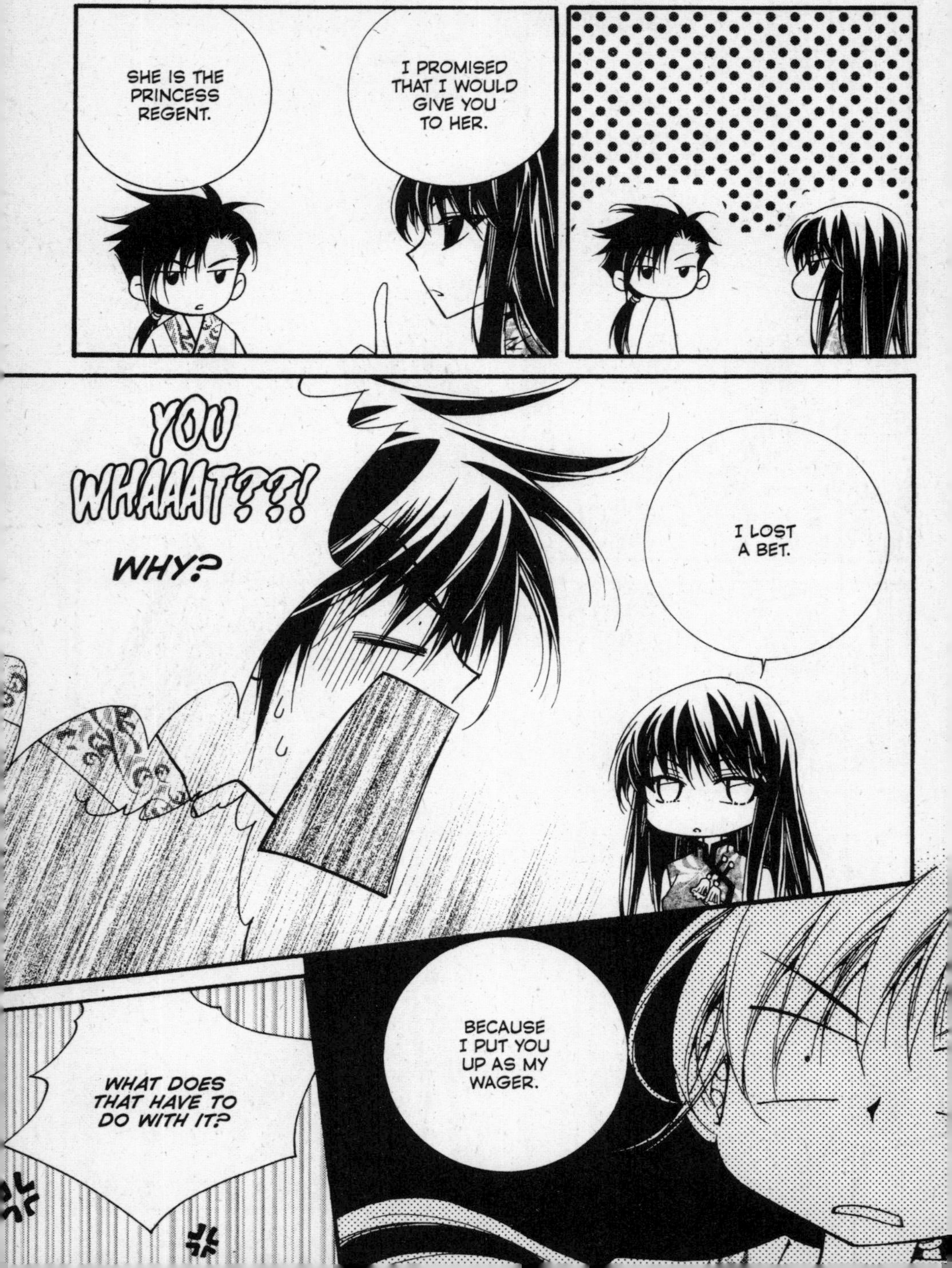
SHE IS THE PRINCESS REGENT.
I PROMISED THAT I WOULD GIVE YOU TO HER.
YOU WHAAAT???!
WHY?
I LOST A BET.
WHAT DOES THAT HAVE TO DO WITH IT?
BECAUSE I PUT YOU UP AS MY WAGER.

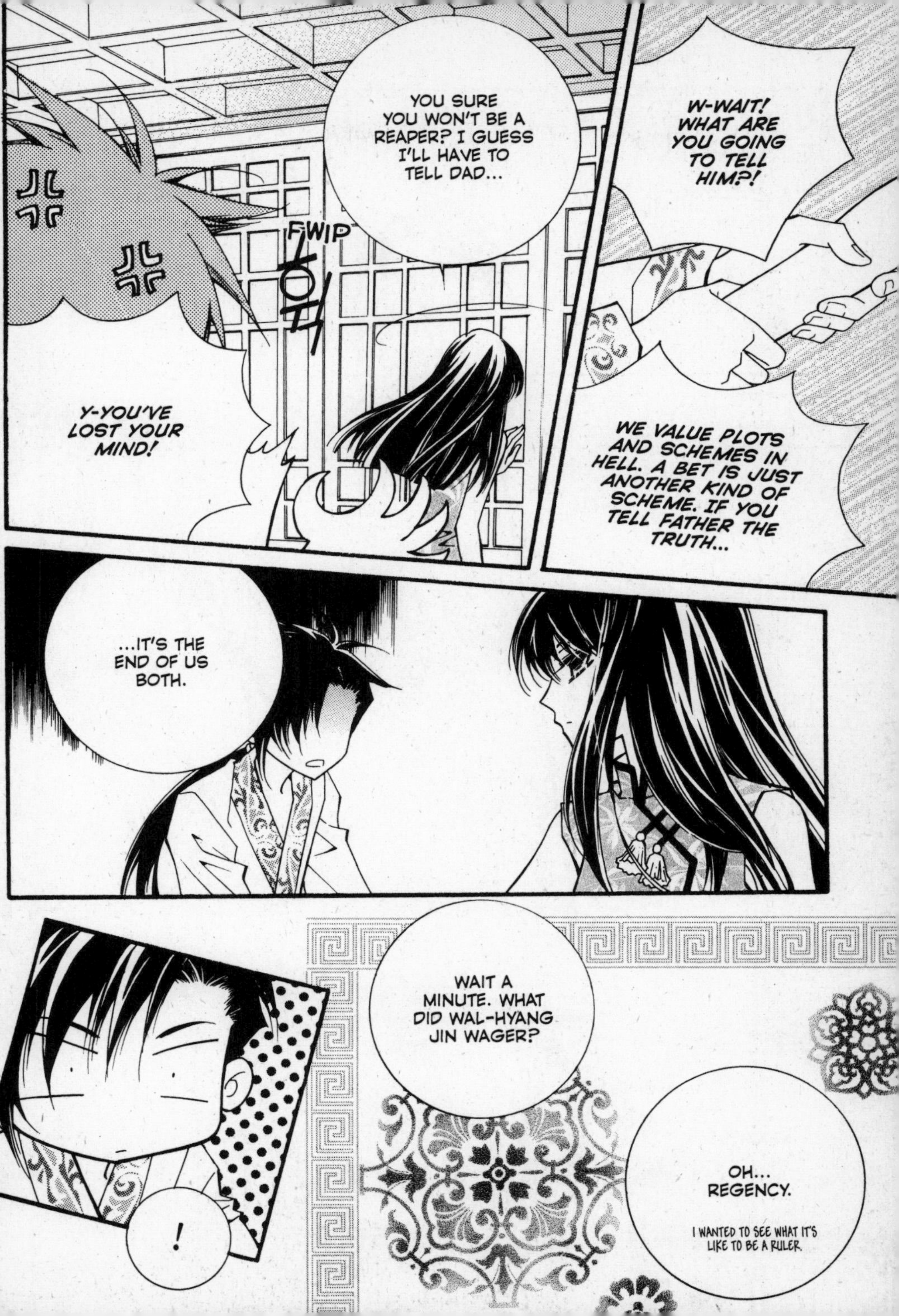
YOU SURE YOU WON'T BE A REAPER? I GUESS I'LL HAVE TO TELL DAD...
FWIP
Y-YOU'VE LOST YOUR MIND!
W-WAIT! WHAT ARE YOU GOING TO TELL HIM?!
WE VALUE PLOTS AND SCHEMES IN HELL. A BET IS JUST ANOTHER KIND OF SCHEME. IF YOU TELL FATHER THE TRUTH...
...IT'S THE END OF US BOTH.
!
WAIT A MINUTE. WHAT DID WAL-HYANG JIN WAGER?
OH... REGENCY.
I WANTED TO SEE WHAT IT'S LIKE TO BE A RULER.

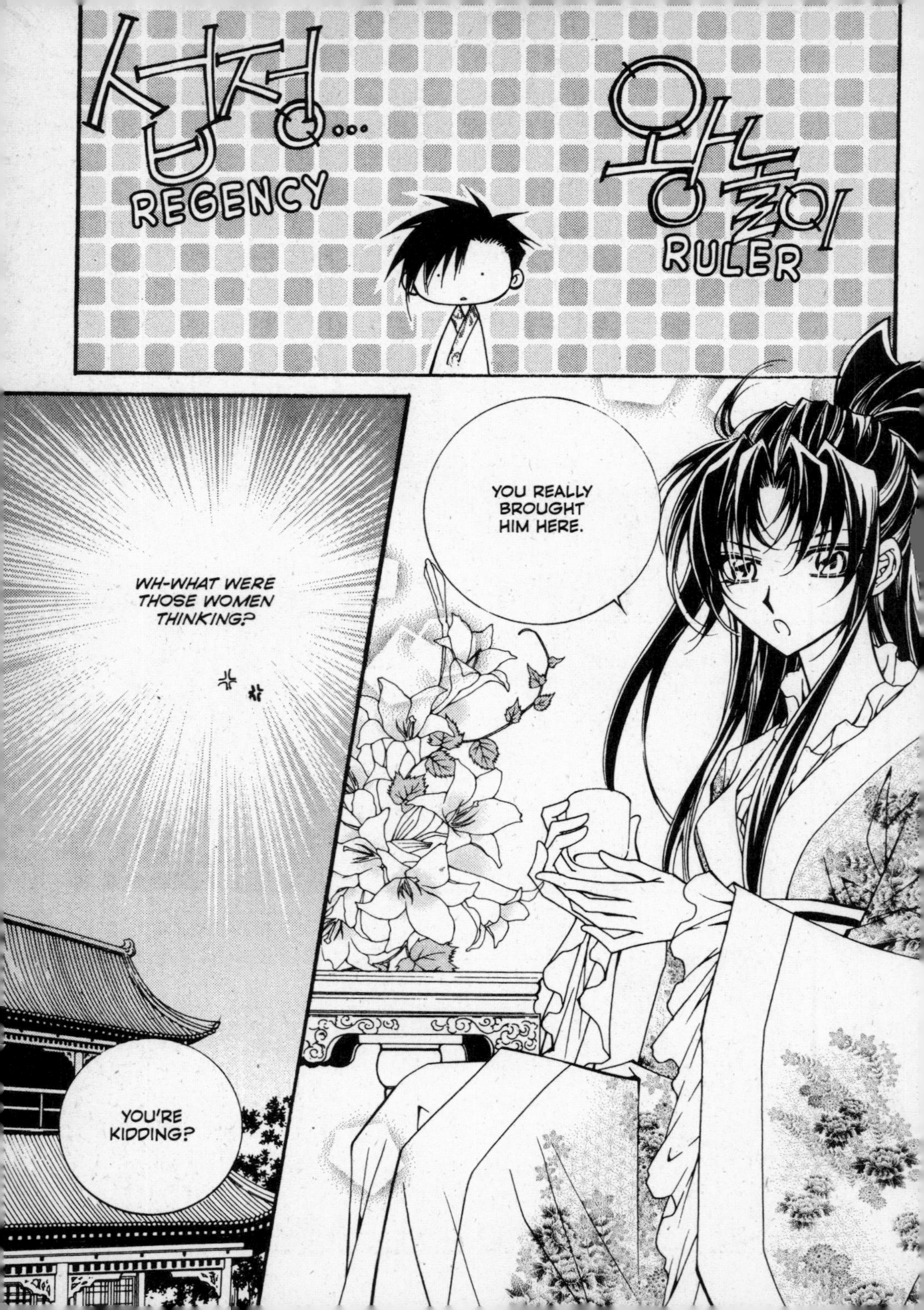
섭정...
REGENCY
RULER
WH-WHAT WERE THOSE WOMEN THINKING?
YOU'RE KIDDING?
YOU REALLY BROUGHT HIM HERE.

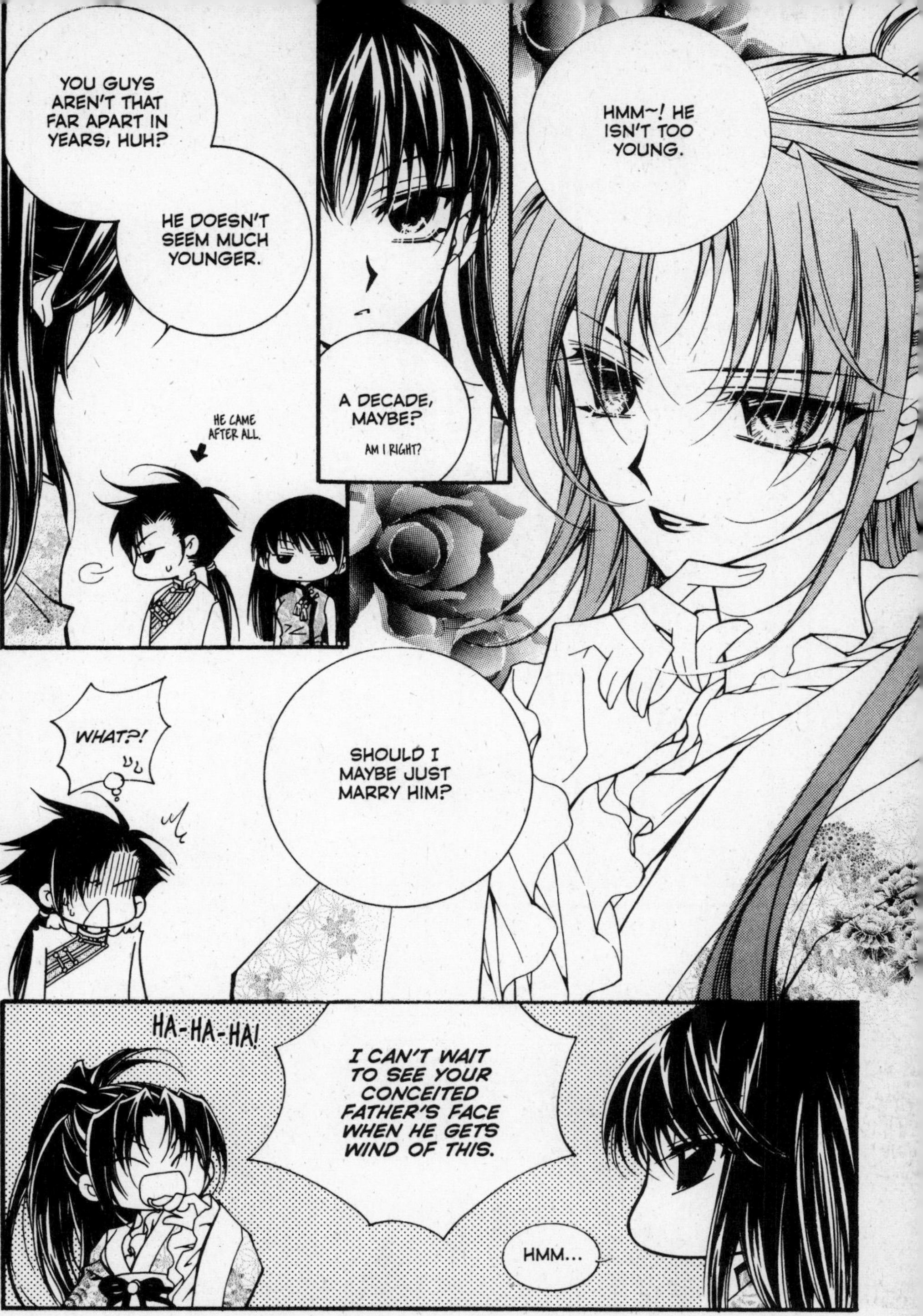
YOU GUYS AREN'T THAT FAR APART IN YEARS, HUH?
HE DOESN'T SEEM MUCH YOUNGER.
HE CAME AFTER ALL.
A DECADE, MAYBE?
AM I RIGHT?
HMM~! HE ISN'T TOO YOUNG.
WHAT?!
SHOULD I MAYBE JUST MARRY HIM?
HA-HA-HA!
I CAN'T WAIT TO SEE YOUR CONCEITED FATHER'S FACE WHEN HE GETS WIND OF THIS.
HMM...

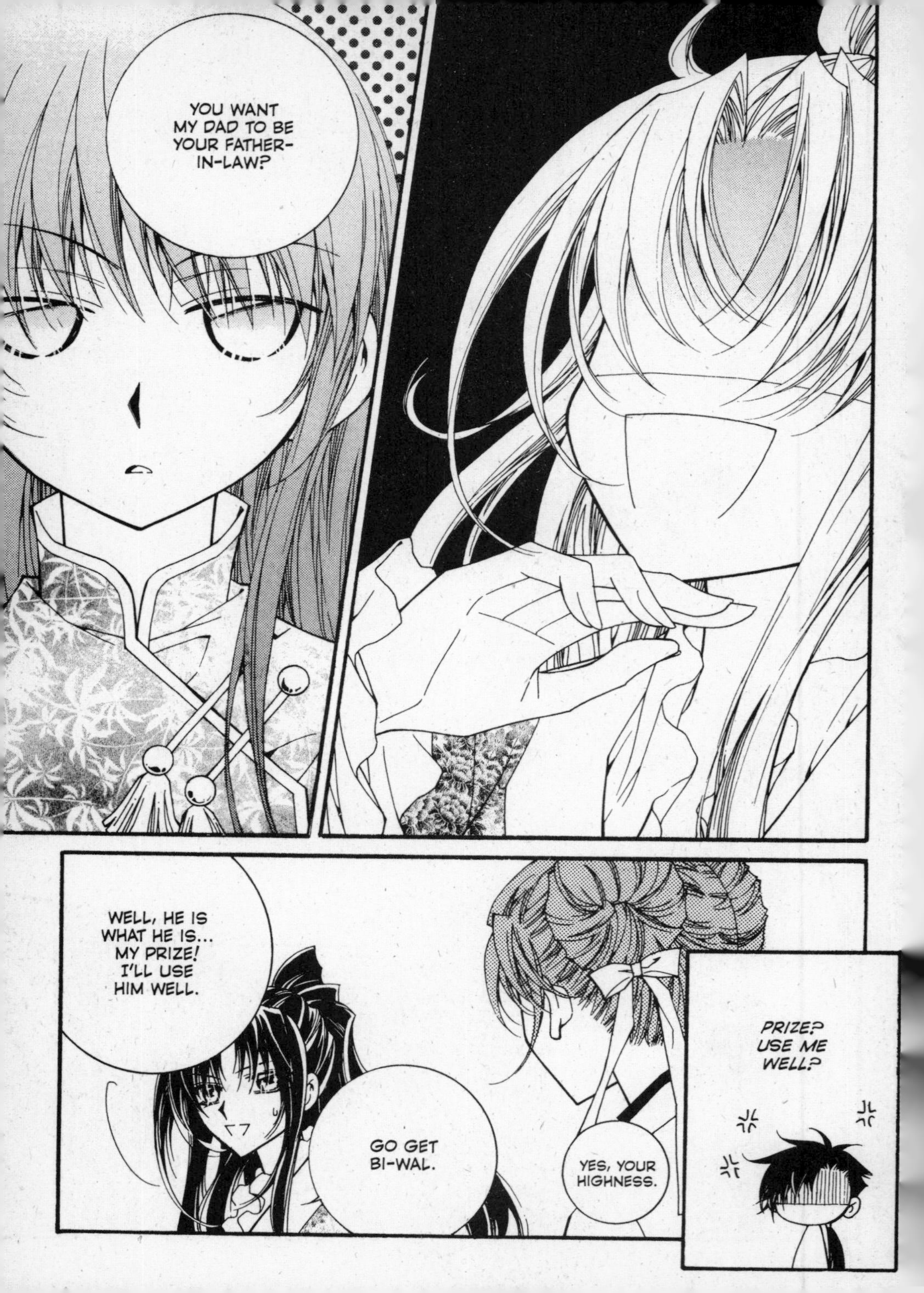
YOU WANT MY DAD TO BE YOUR FATHER-IN-LAW?
WELL, HE IS WHAT HE IS... MY PRIZE! I'LL USE HIM WELL.
GO GET BI-WAL.
YES, YOUR HIGHNESS.
PRIZE? USE ME WELL?

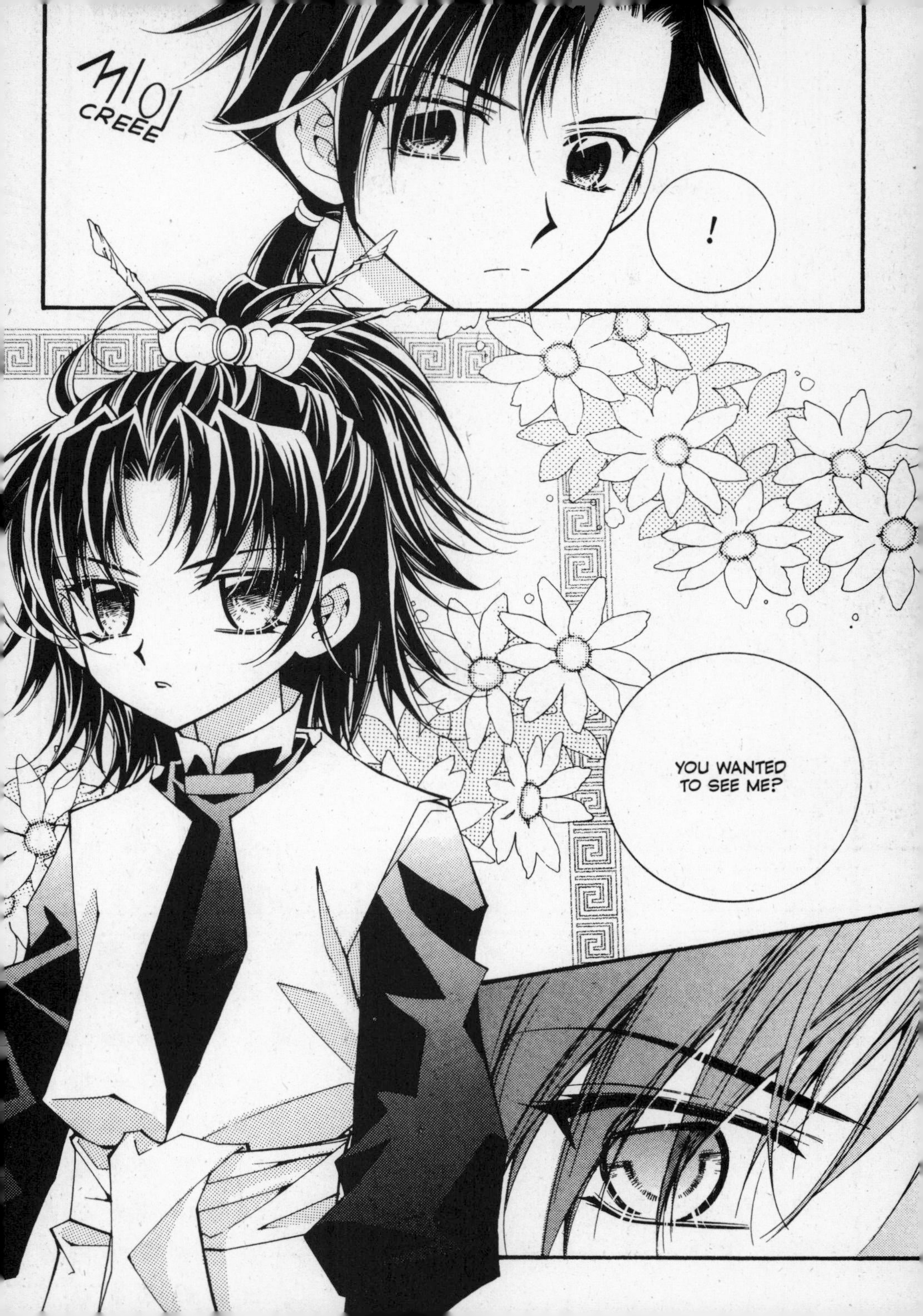
CREEE
!
YOU WANTED TO SEE ME?

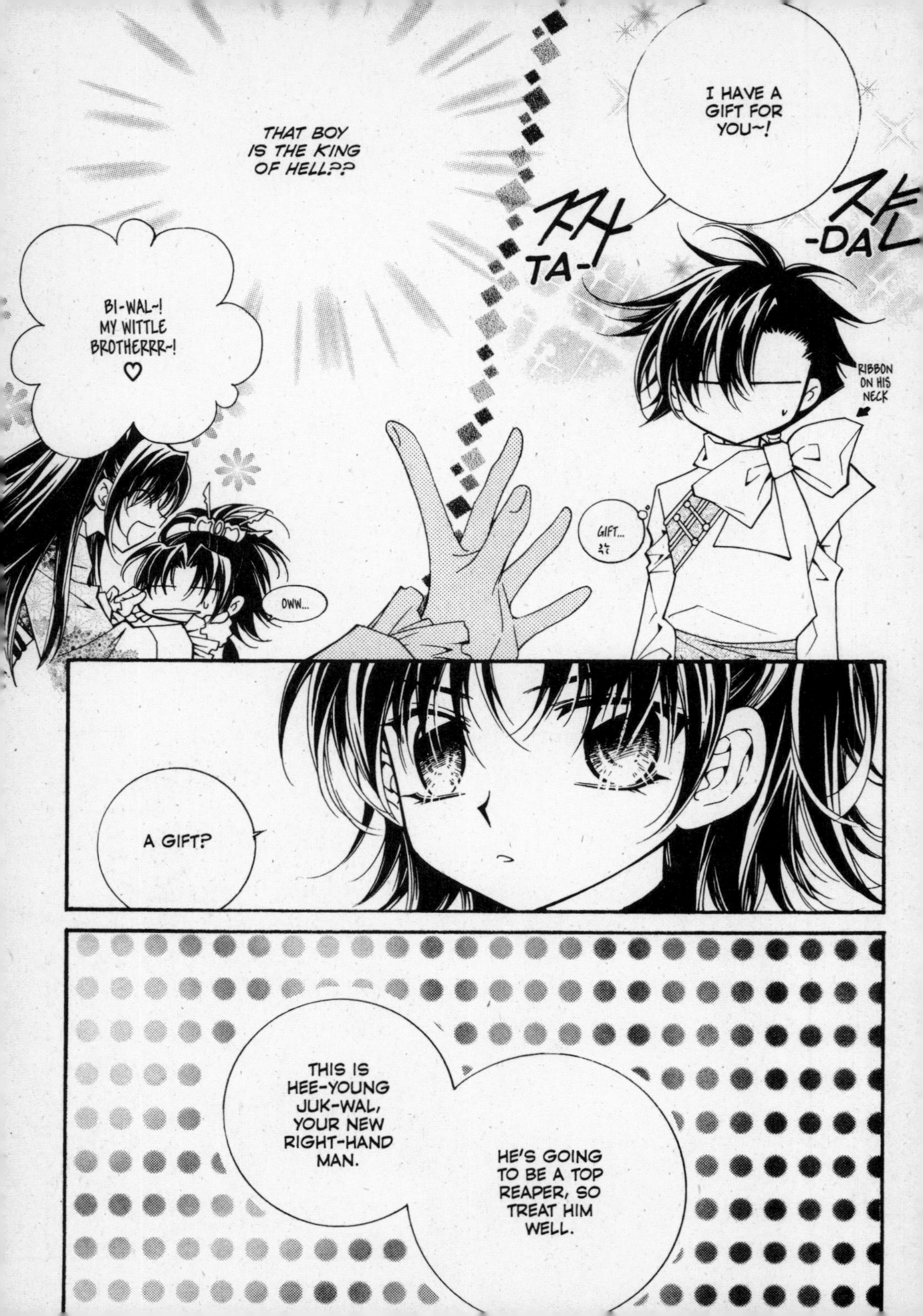
THAT BOY IS THE KING OF HELL??
I HAVE A GIFT FOR YOU~!
BI-WAL~! MY WITTLE BROTHERRR~! ♡
TA-
-DAL
RIBBON ON HIS NECK
GIFT...
OWW...
A GIFT?
THIS IS HEE-YOUNG JUK-WAL, YOUR NEW RIGHT-HAND MAN.
HE'S GOING TO BE A TOP REAPER, SO TREAT HIM WELL.

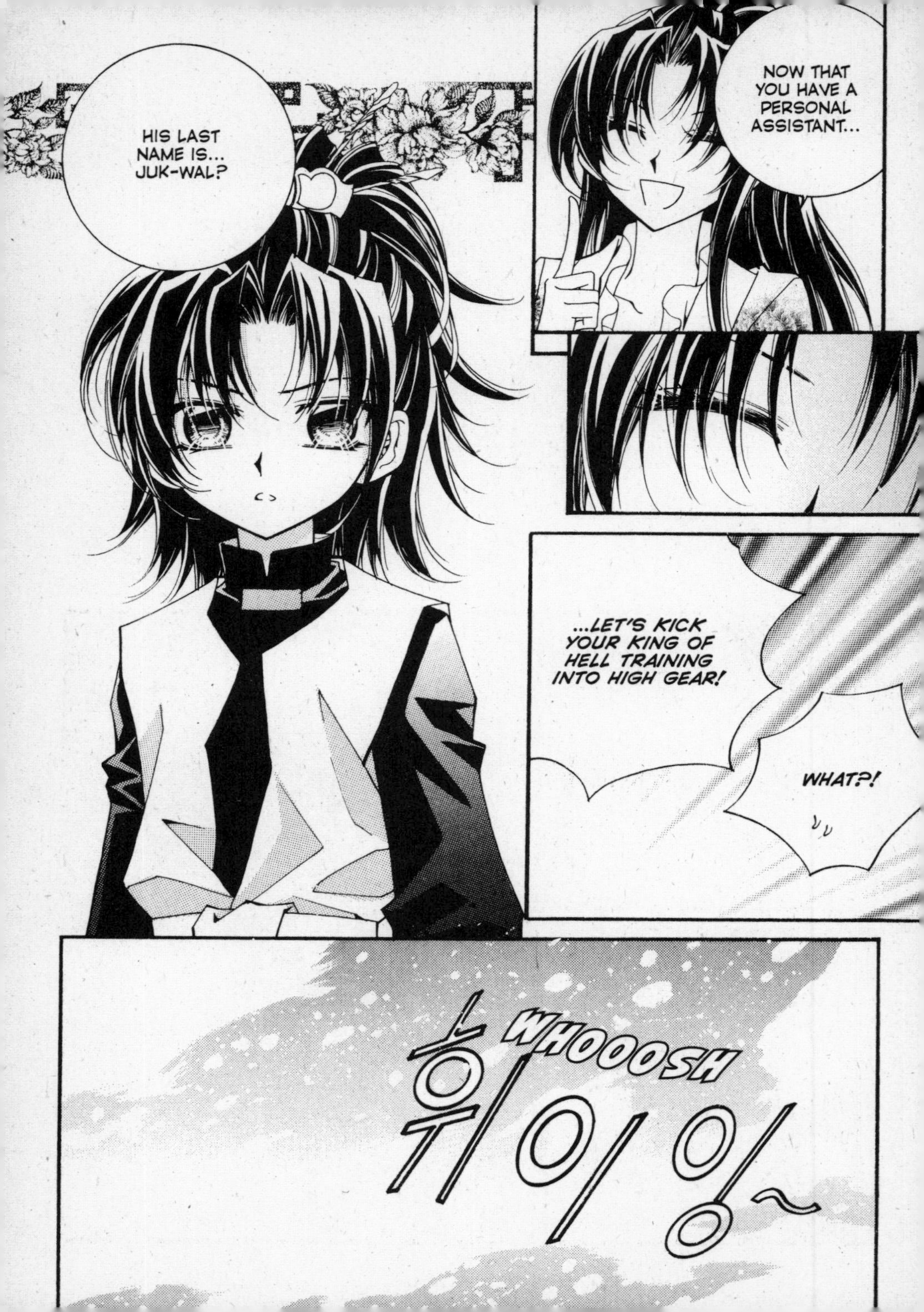
HIS LAST NAME IS... JUK-WAL?
NOW THAT YOU HAVE A PERSONAL ASSISTANT...
...LET'S KICK YOUR KING OF HELL TRAINING INTO HIGH GEAR!
WHAT?!
WHOOOSH
휘이잉~

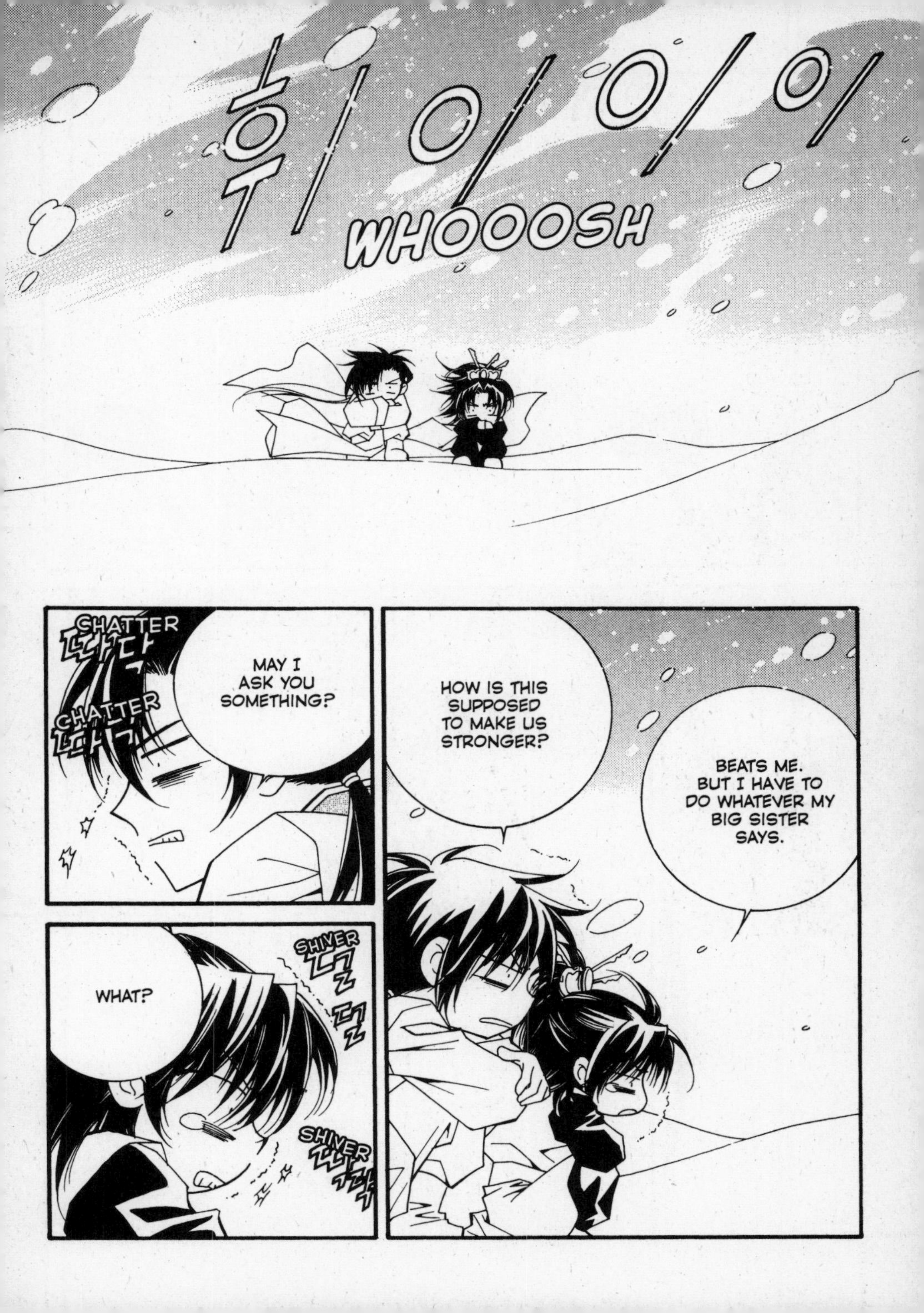
휘이이익
WHOOOSH
CHATTER
CHATTER
MAY I ASK YOU SOMETHING?
SHIVER
SHIVER
WHAT?
HOW IS THIS SUPPOSED TO MAKE US STRONGER?
BEATS ME. BUT I HAVE TO DO WHATEVER MY BIG SISTER SAYS.

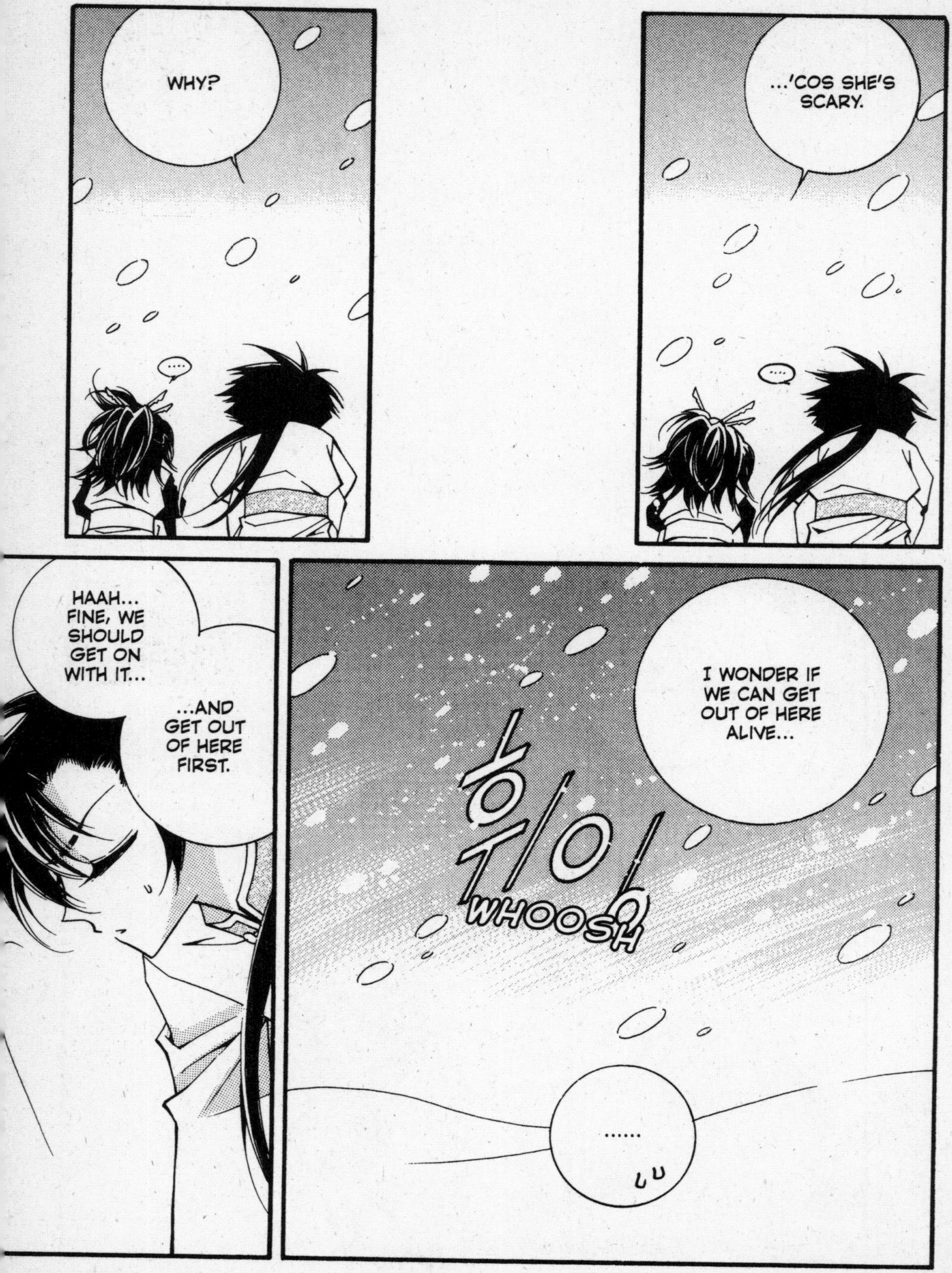
WHY?
....
...'COS SHE'S SCARY.
....
HAAH... FINE, WE SHOULD GET ON WITH IT...
...AND GET OUT OF HERE FIRST.
I WONDER IF WE CAN GET OUT OF HERE ALIVE...
WHOOSH
......

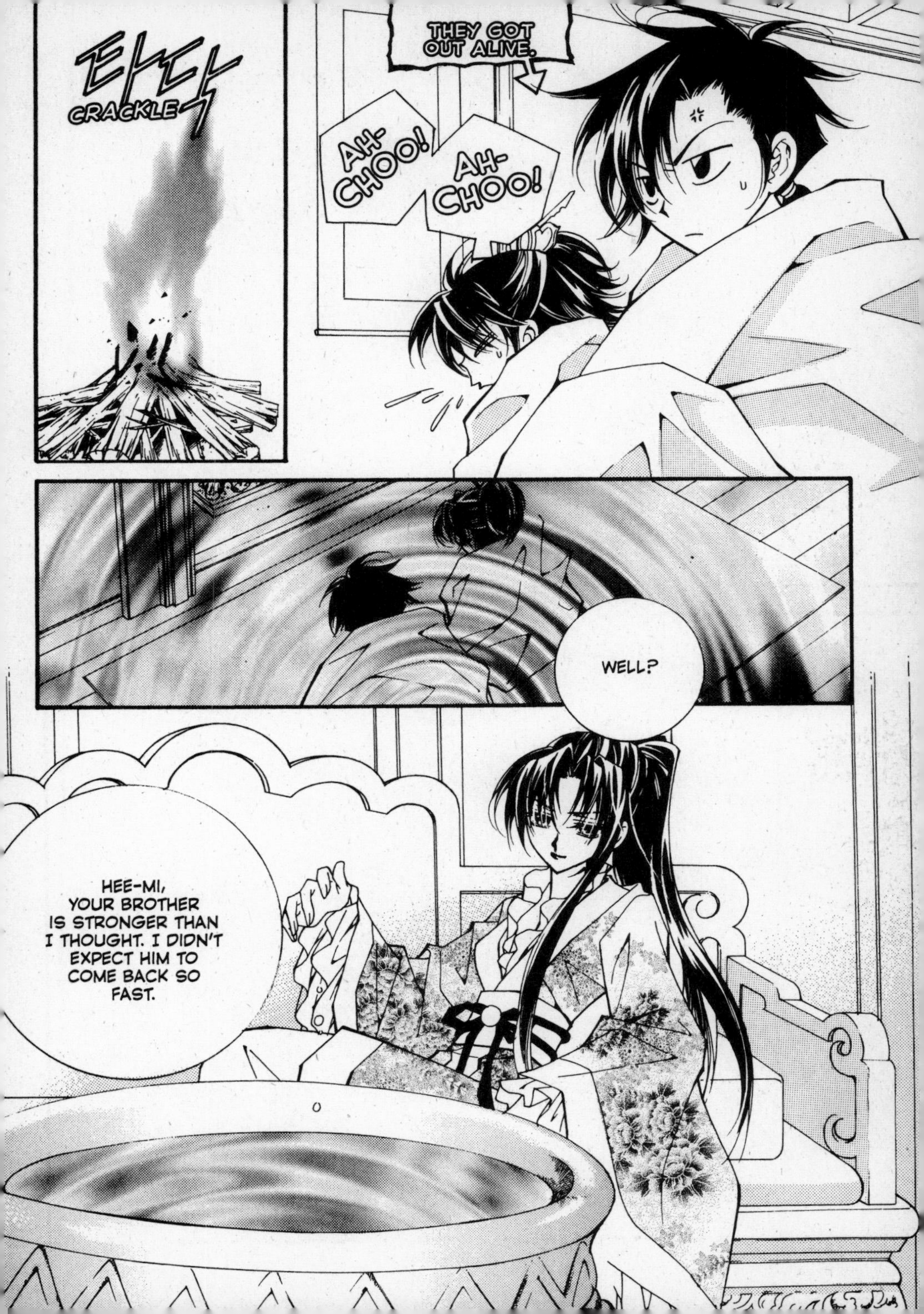

CRACKLE
THEY GOT OUT ALIVE.
AH-CHOO!
AH-CHOO!
WELL?
HEE-MI, YOUR BROTHER IS STRONGER THAN I THOUGHT. I DIDN'T EXPECT HIM TO COME BACK SO FAST.

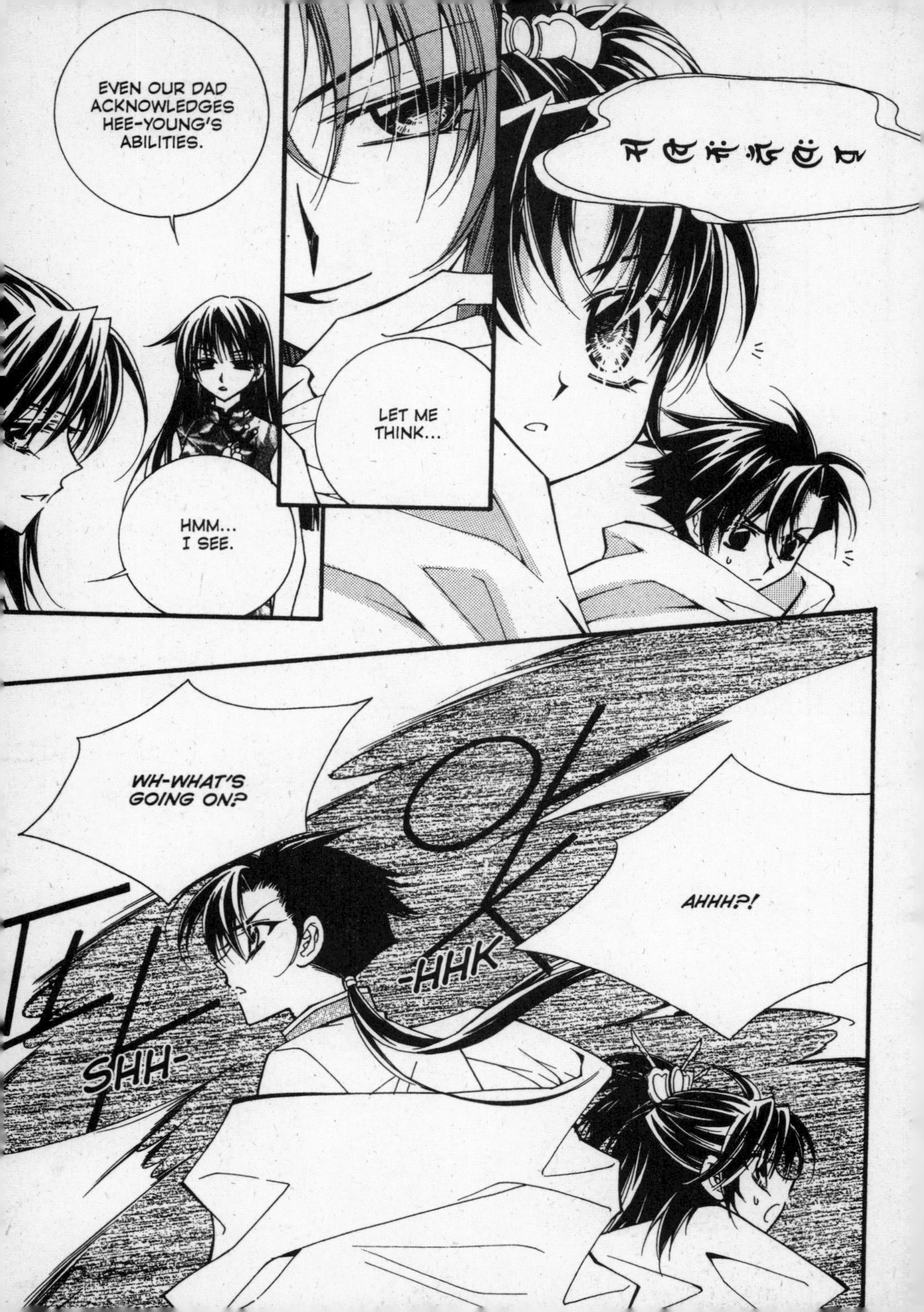
EVEN OUR DAD ACKNOWLEDGES HEE-YOUNG'S ABILITIES.
HMM... I SEE.
LET ME THINK...
WH-WHAT'S GOING ON?
AHHH?!
-HHK
SHH-

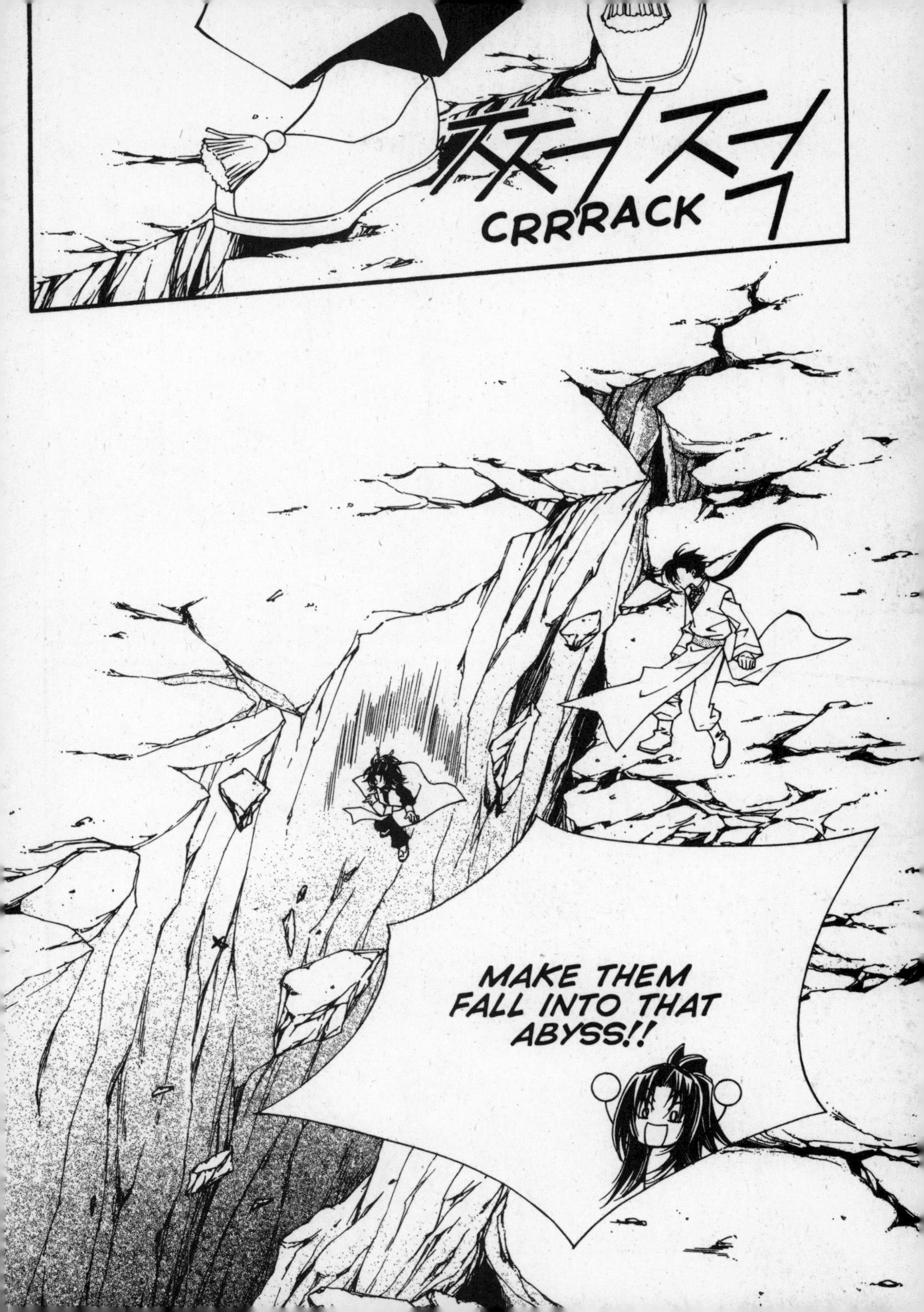
CRRRACK
MAKE THEM FALL INTO THAT ABYSS!!

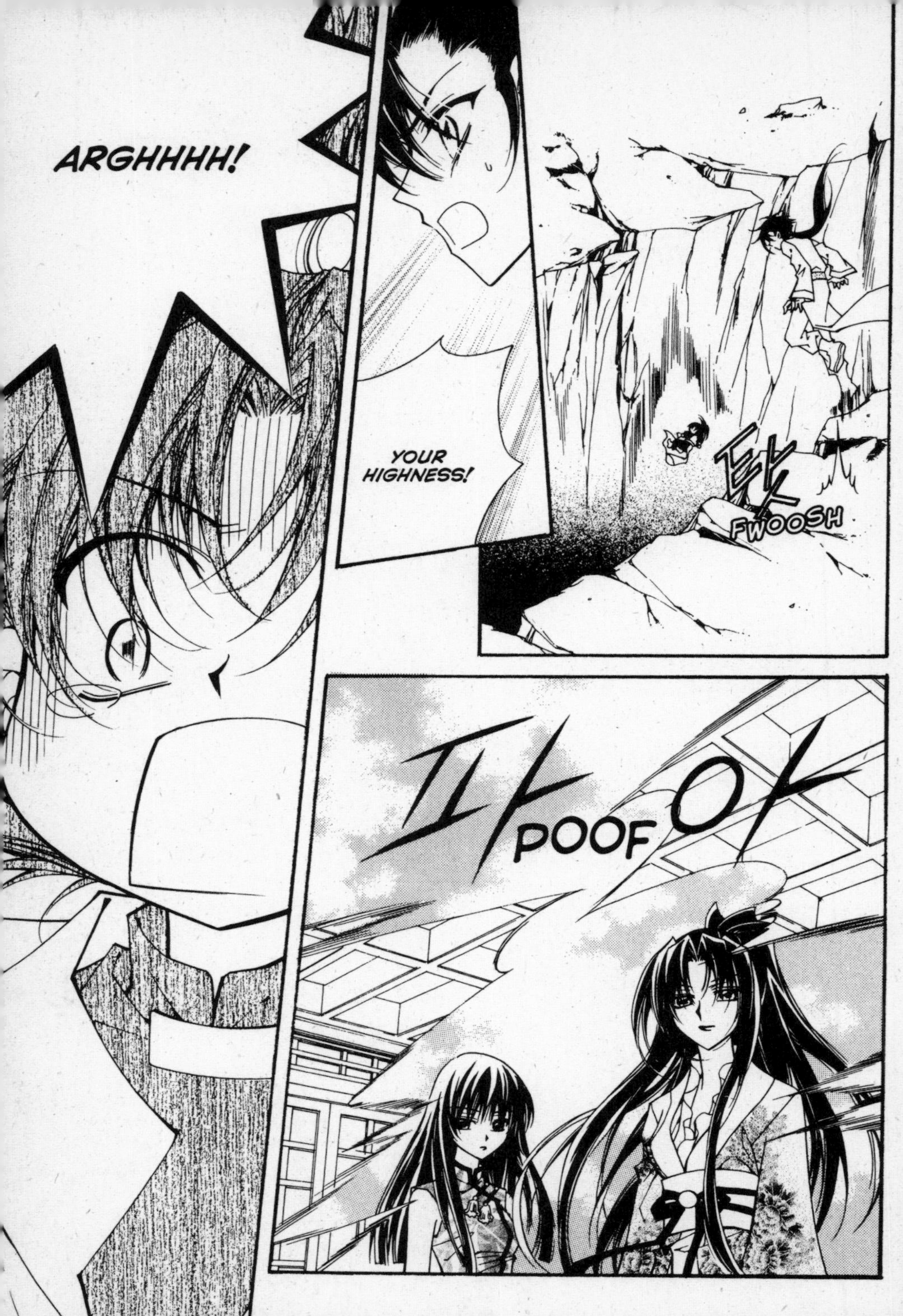
ARGHHHH!
YOUR HIGHNESS!
FWOOSH
POOF

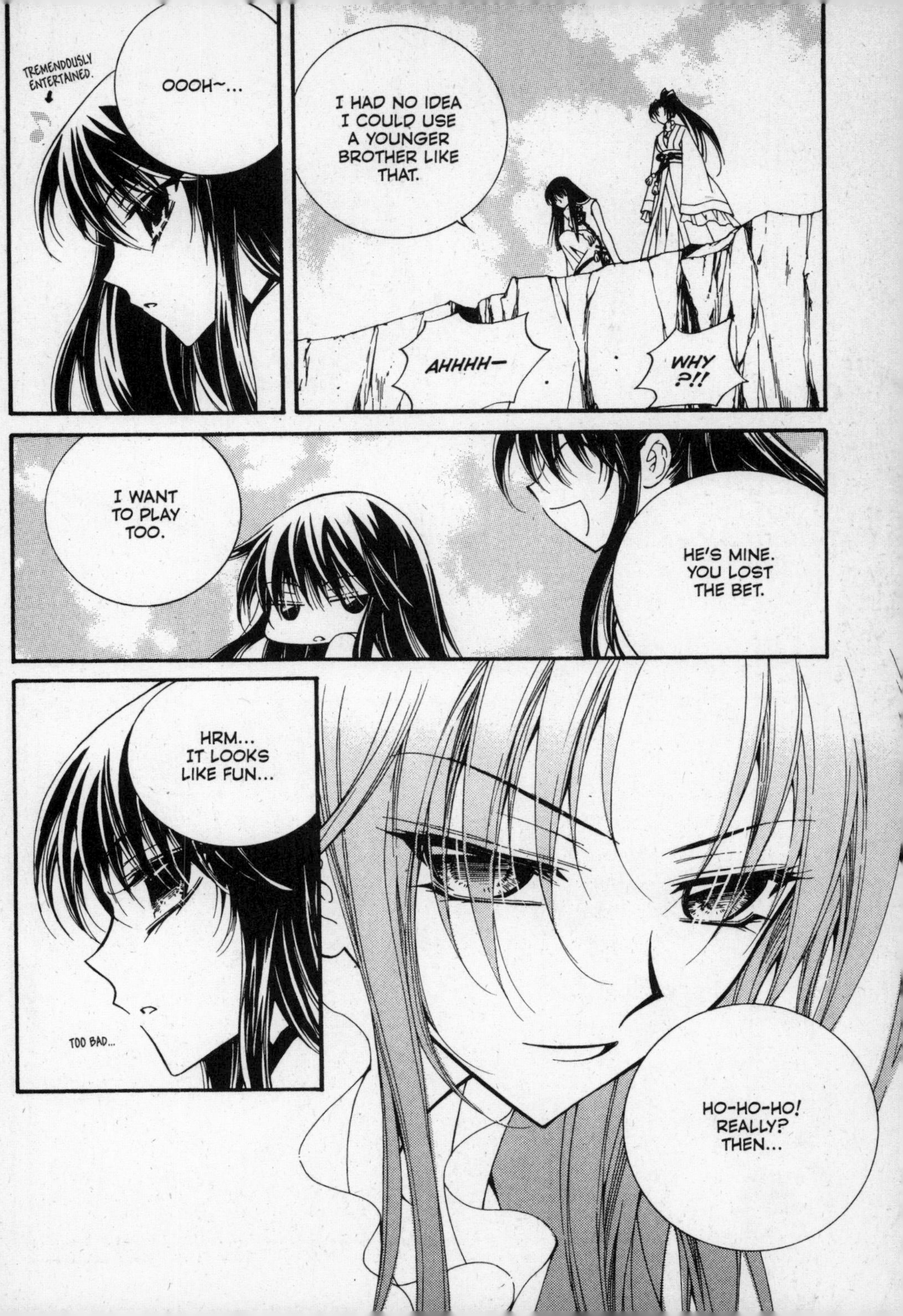
TREMENDOUSLY ENTERTAINED.
OOOH~...
I HAD NO IDEA I COULD USE A YOUNGER BROTHER LIKE THAT.
AHHHH—
WHY ?!!
I WANT TO PLAY TOO.
HE'S MINE. YOU LOST THE BET.
HRM... IT LOOKS LIKE FUN...
TOO BAD...
HO-HO-HO! REALLY? THEN...

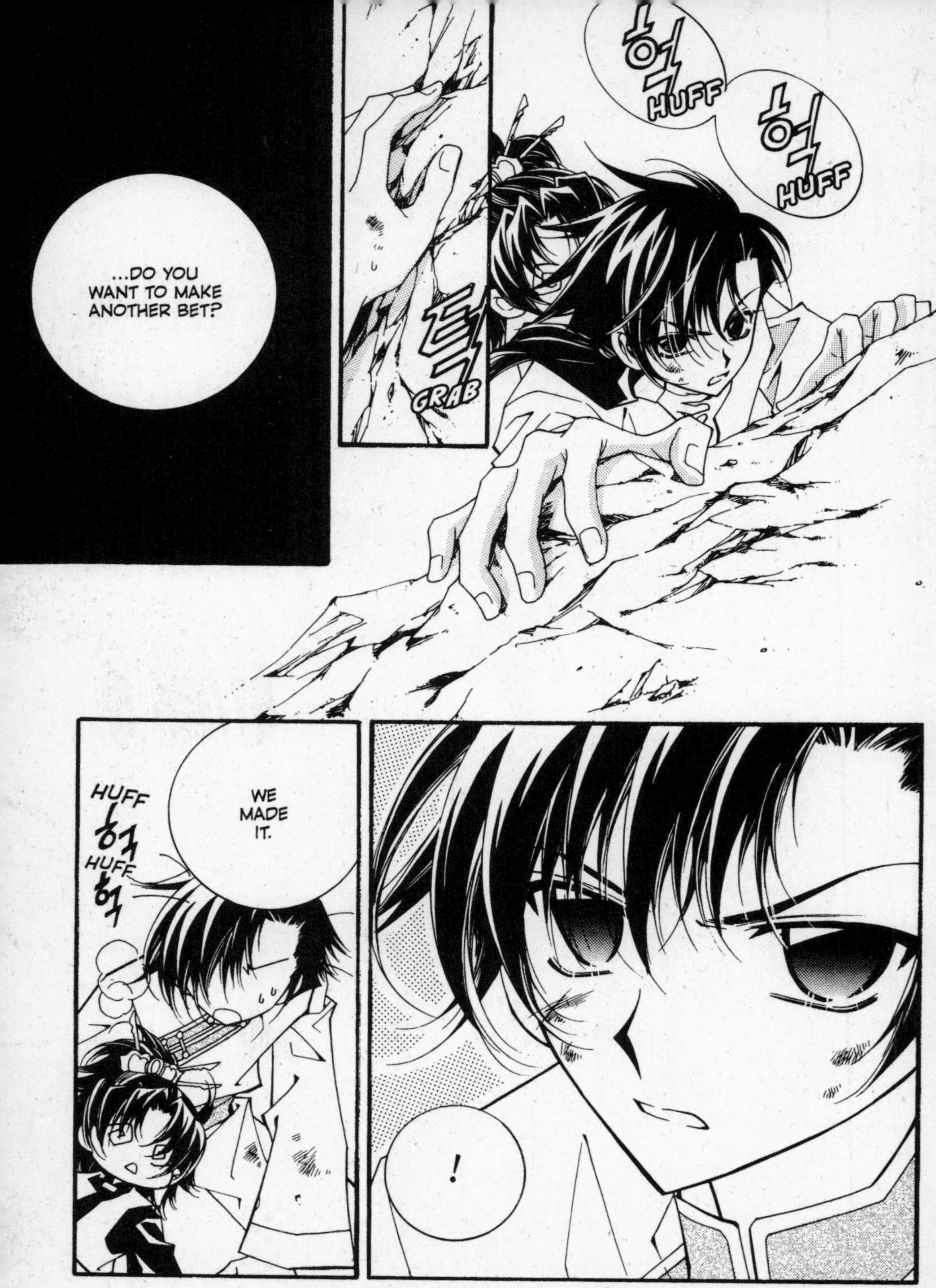

...DO YOU WANT TO MAKE ANOTHER BET?
GRAB
헉 HUFF
헉 HUFF
HUFF 헉
HUFF 헉
WE MADE IT.
!

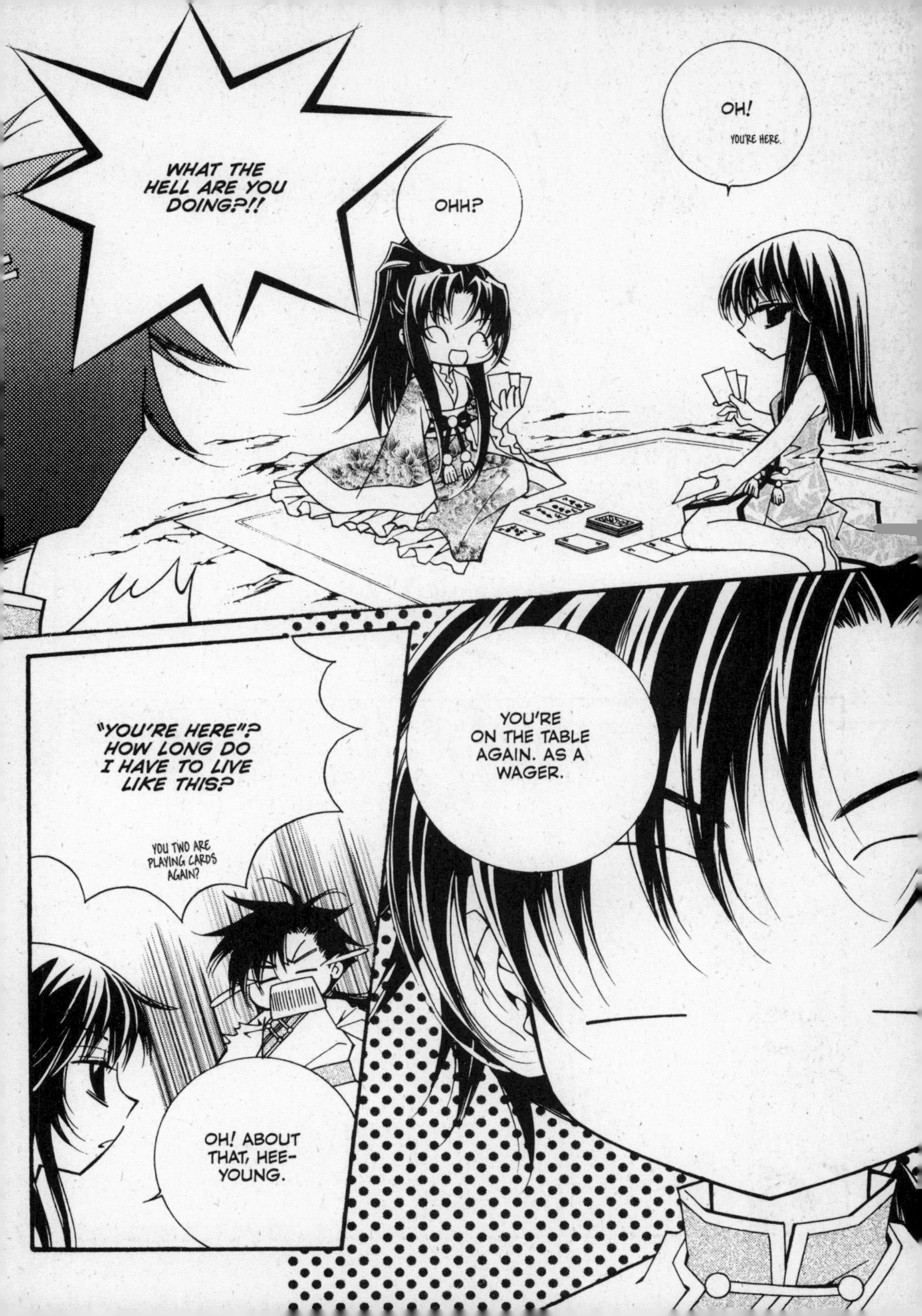
WHAT THE HELL ARE YOU DOING?!!
OHH?
OH!
YOU'RE HERE.
"YOU'RE HERE"? HOW LONG DO I HAVE TO LIVE LIKE THIS?
YOU TWO ARE PLAYING CARDS AGAIN?
OH! ABOUT THAT, HEE-YOUNG.
YOU'RE ON THE TABLE AGAIN. AS A WAGER.

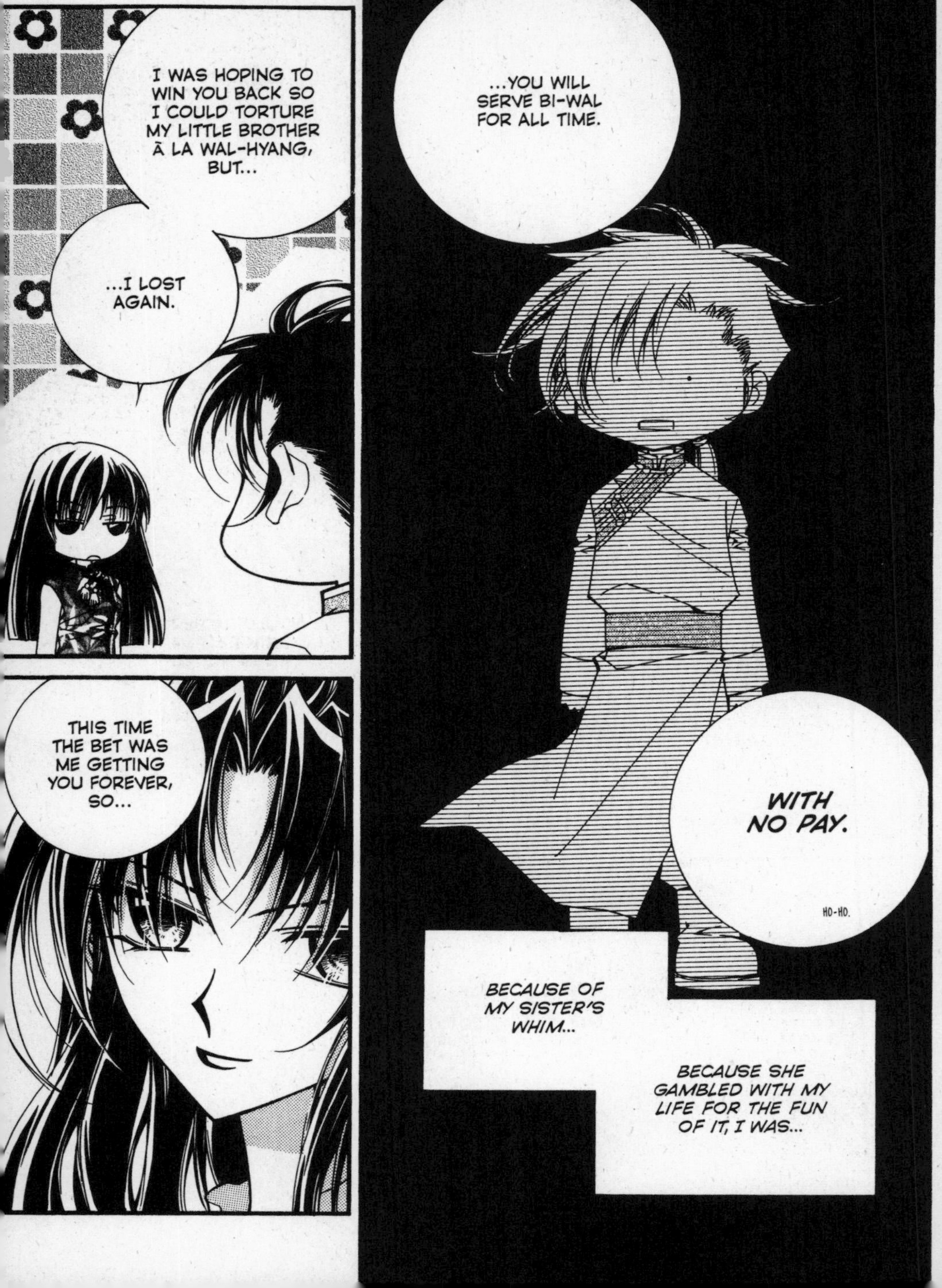
I WAS HOPING TO WIN YOU BACK SO I COULD TORTURE MY LITTLE BROTHER Ã LA WAL-HYANG, BUT...
...I LOST AGAIN.
THIS TIME THE BET WAS ME GETTING YOU FOREVER, SO...
...YOU WILL SERVE BI-WAL FOR ALL TIME.
WITH NO PAY.
HO-HO.
BECAUSE OF MY SISTER'S WHIM...
BECAUSE SHE GAMBLED WITH MY LIFE FOR THE FUN OF IT, I WAS...

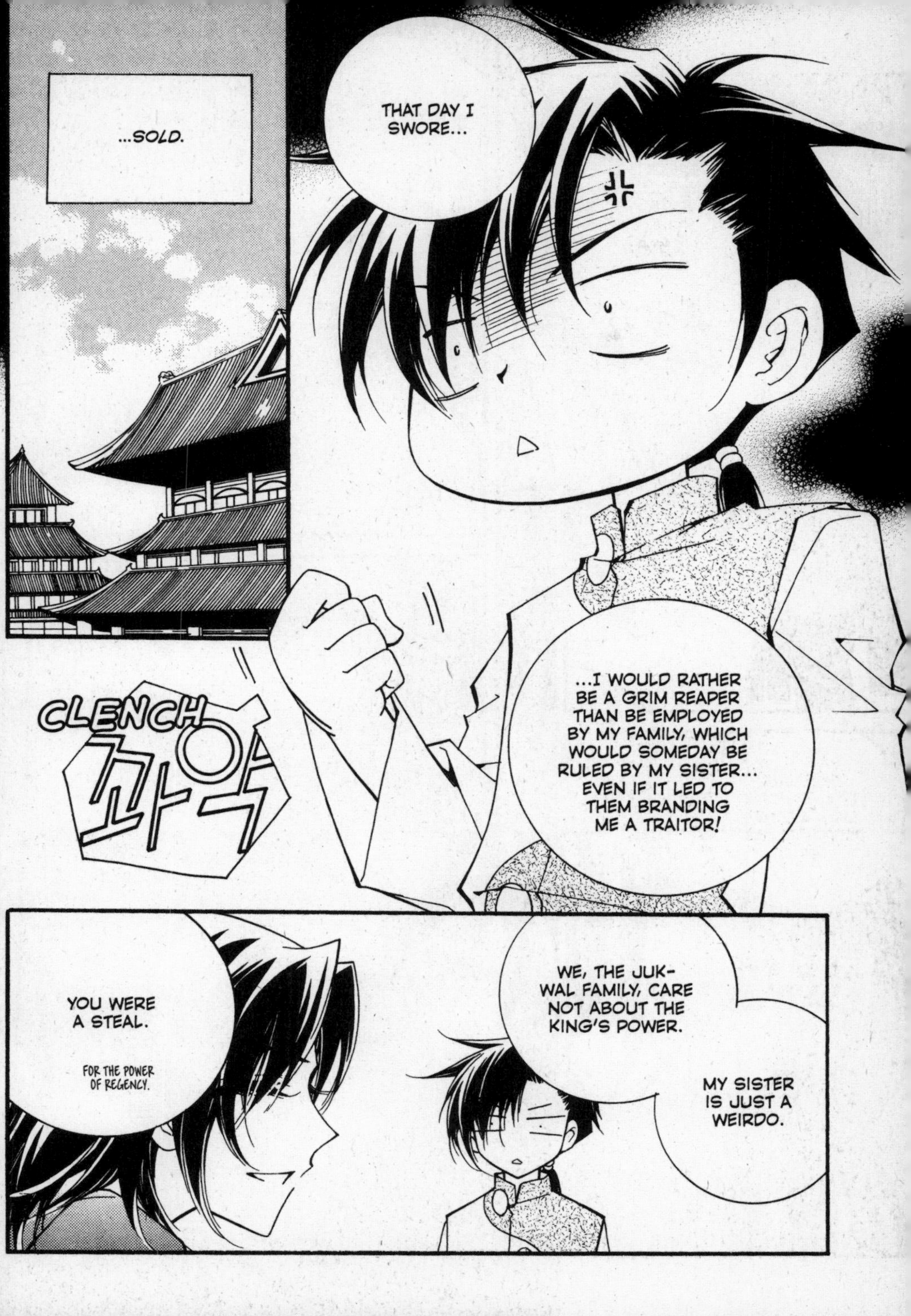
...SOLD.
THAT DAY I SWORE...
CLENCH
...I WOULD RATHER BE A GRIM REAPER THAN BE EMPLOYED BY MY FAMILY, WHICH WOULD SOMEDAY BE RULED BY MY SISTER... EVEN IF IT LED TO THEM BRANDING ME A TRAITOR!
YOU WERE A STEAL.
FOR THE POWER OF REGENCY.
WE, THE JUK-WAL FAMILY, CARE NOT ABOUT THE KING'S POWER.
MY SISTER IS JUST A WEIRDO.

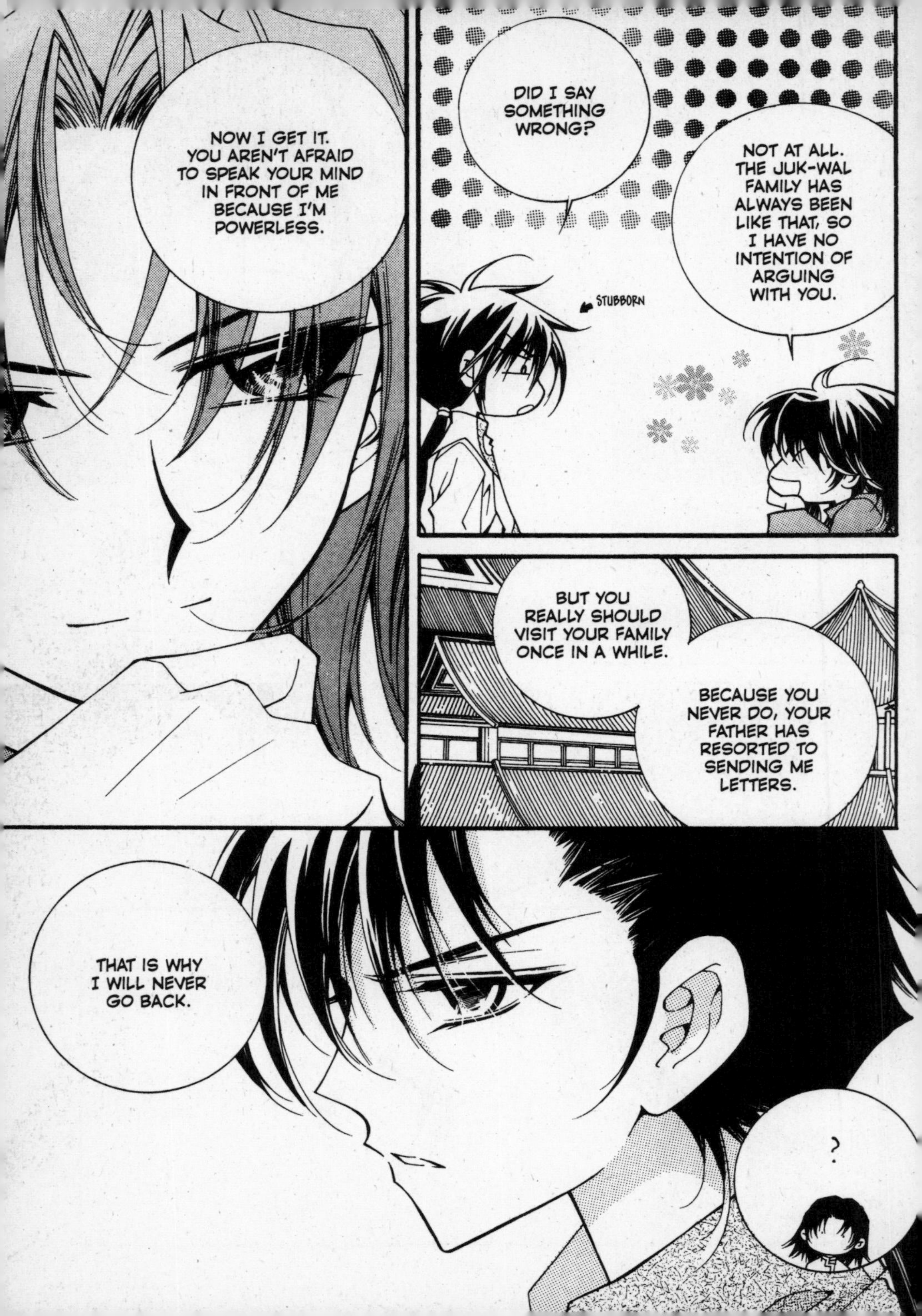
NOW I GET IT. YOU AREN'T AFRAID TO SPEAK YOUR MIND IN FRONT OF ME BECAUSE I'M POWERLESS.
DID I SAY SOMETHING WRONG?
STUBBORN
NOT AT ALL. THE JUK-WAL FAMILY HAS ALWAYS BEEN LIKE THAT, SO I HAVE NO INTENTION OF ARGUING WITH YOU.
BUT YOU REALLY SHOULD VISIT YOUR FAMILY ONCE IN A WHILE.
BECAUSE YOU NEVER DO, YOUR FATHER HAS RESORTED TO SENDING ME LETTERS.
THAT IS WHY I WILL NEVER GO BACK.
?

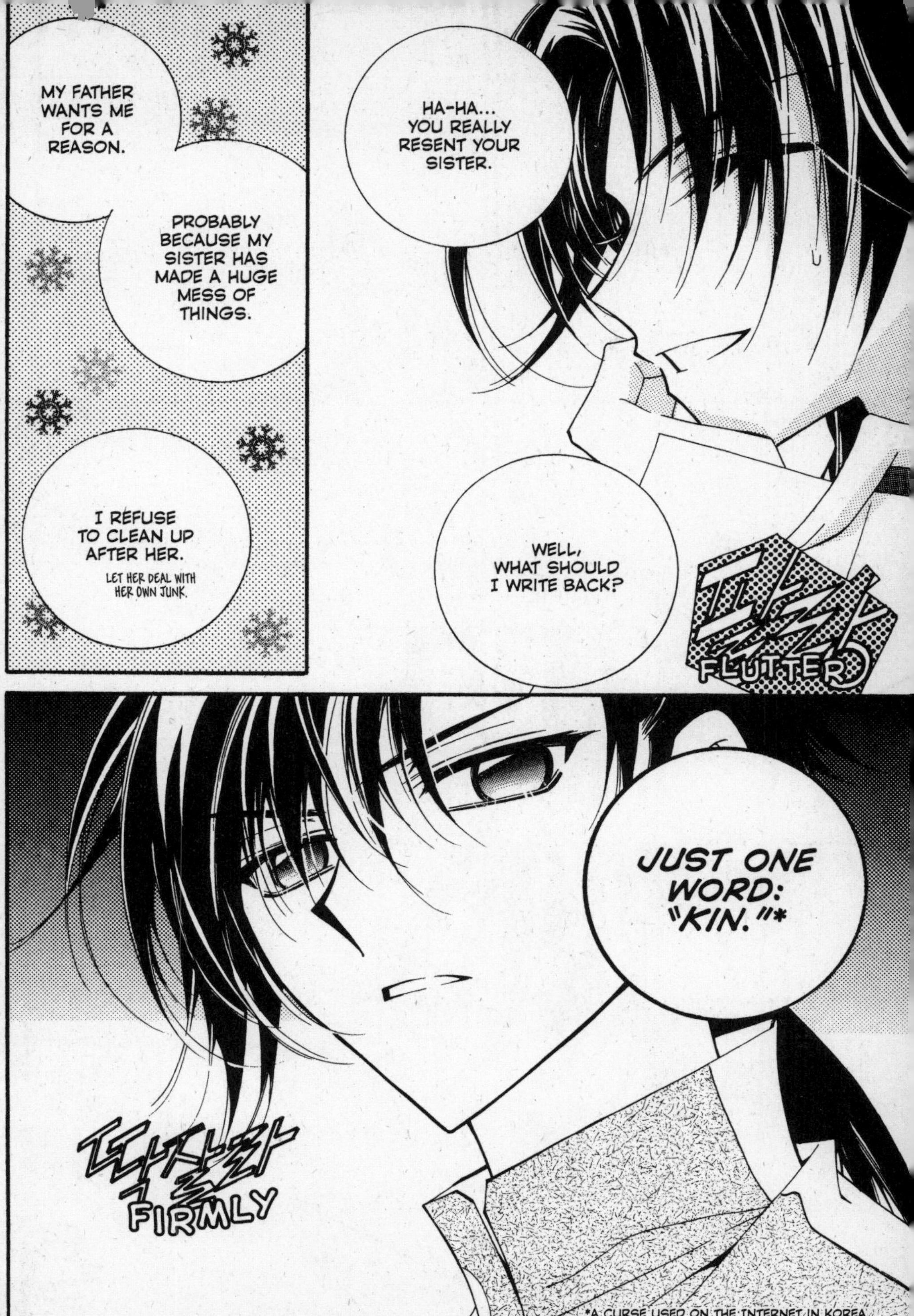
MY FATHER WANTS ME FOR A REASON.
PROBABLY BECAUSE MY SISTER HAS MADE A HUGE MESS OF THINGS.
I REFUSE TO CLEAN UP AFTER HER.
LET HER DEAL WITH HER OWN JUNK.
HA-HA... YOU REALLY RESENT YOUR SISTER.
WELL, WHAT SHOULD I WRITE BACK?
FLUTTER
JUST ONE WORD: "KIN."*
FIRMLY

*A CURSE USED ON THE INTERNET IN KOREA

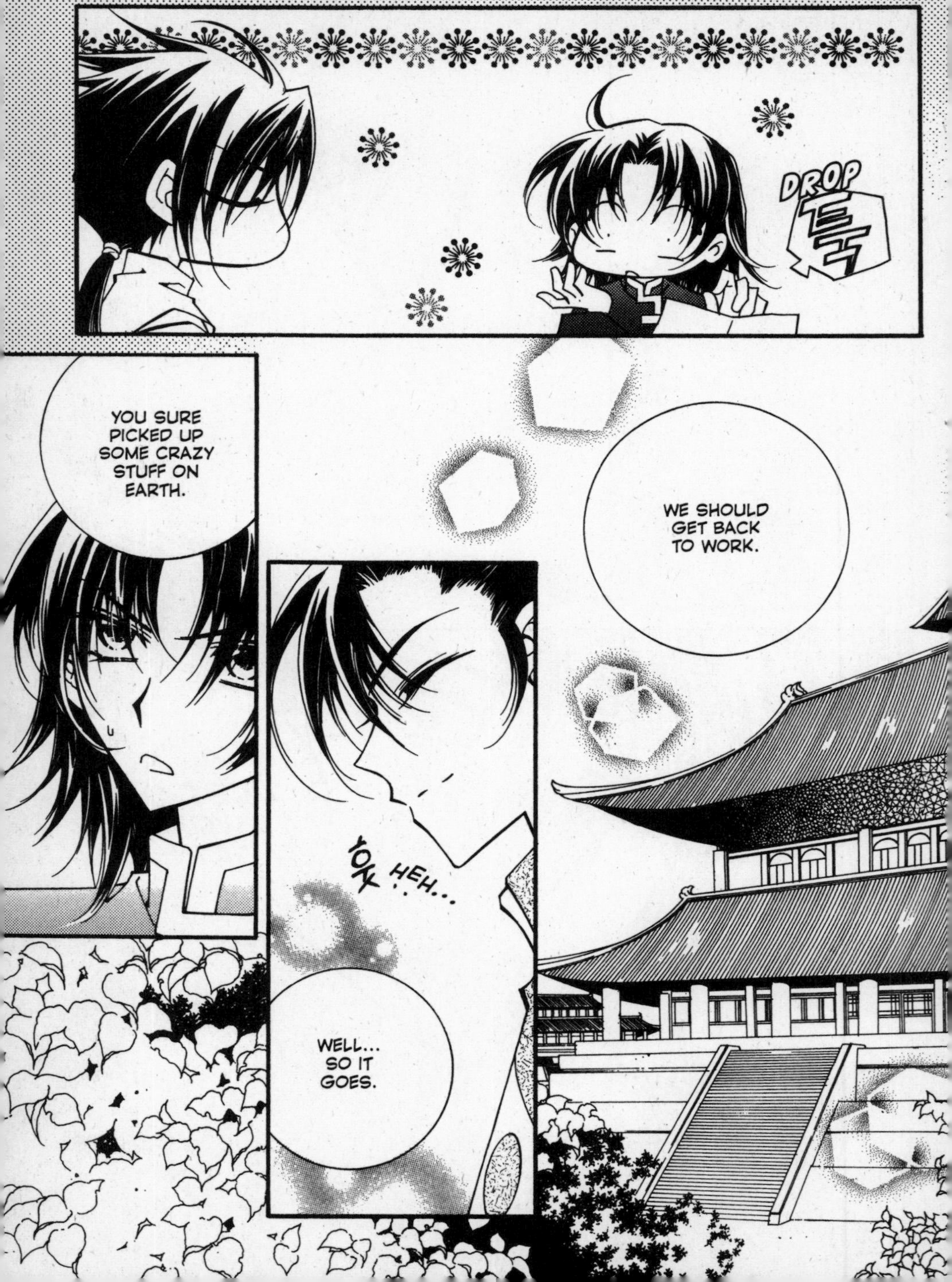
DROP
YOU SURE PICKED UP SOME CRAZY STUFF ON EARTH.
YOK
HEH...
WELL... SO IT GOES.
WE SHOULD GET BACK TO WORK.

ANGEL DIARY - EXTRA

CHAPTER 4
WHO MADE HER THAT WAY?: AH-HIN'S STORY

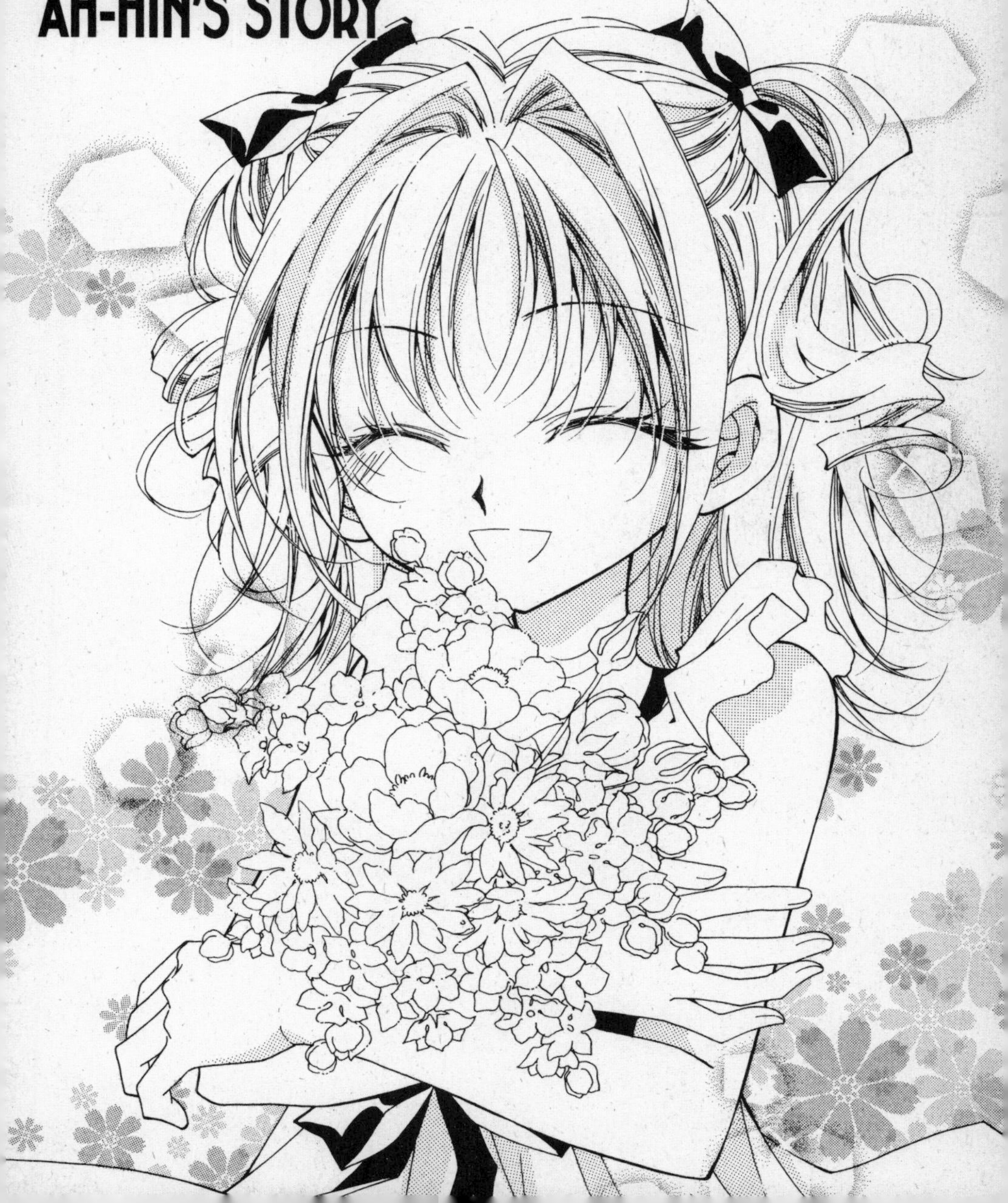

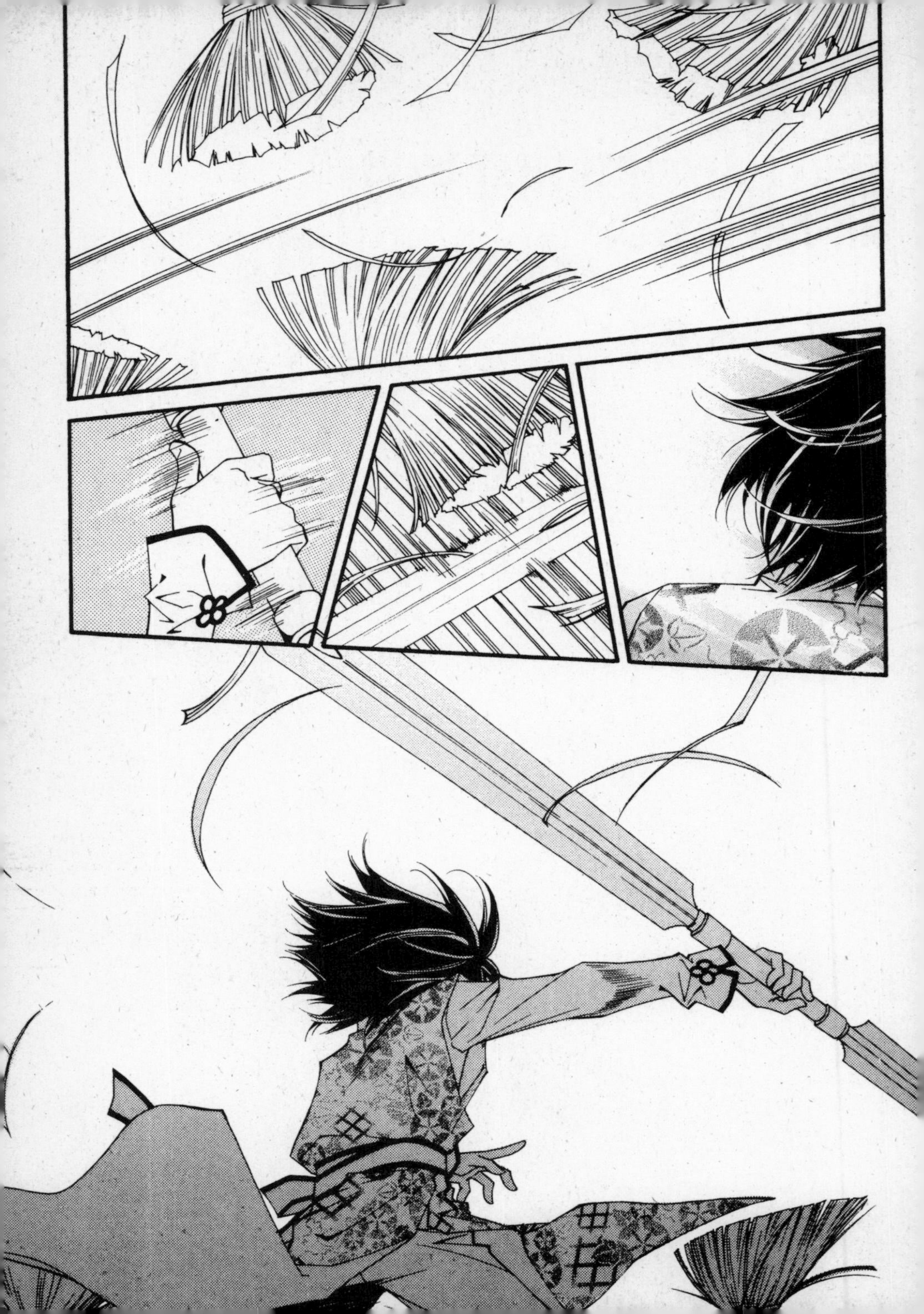

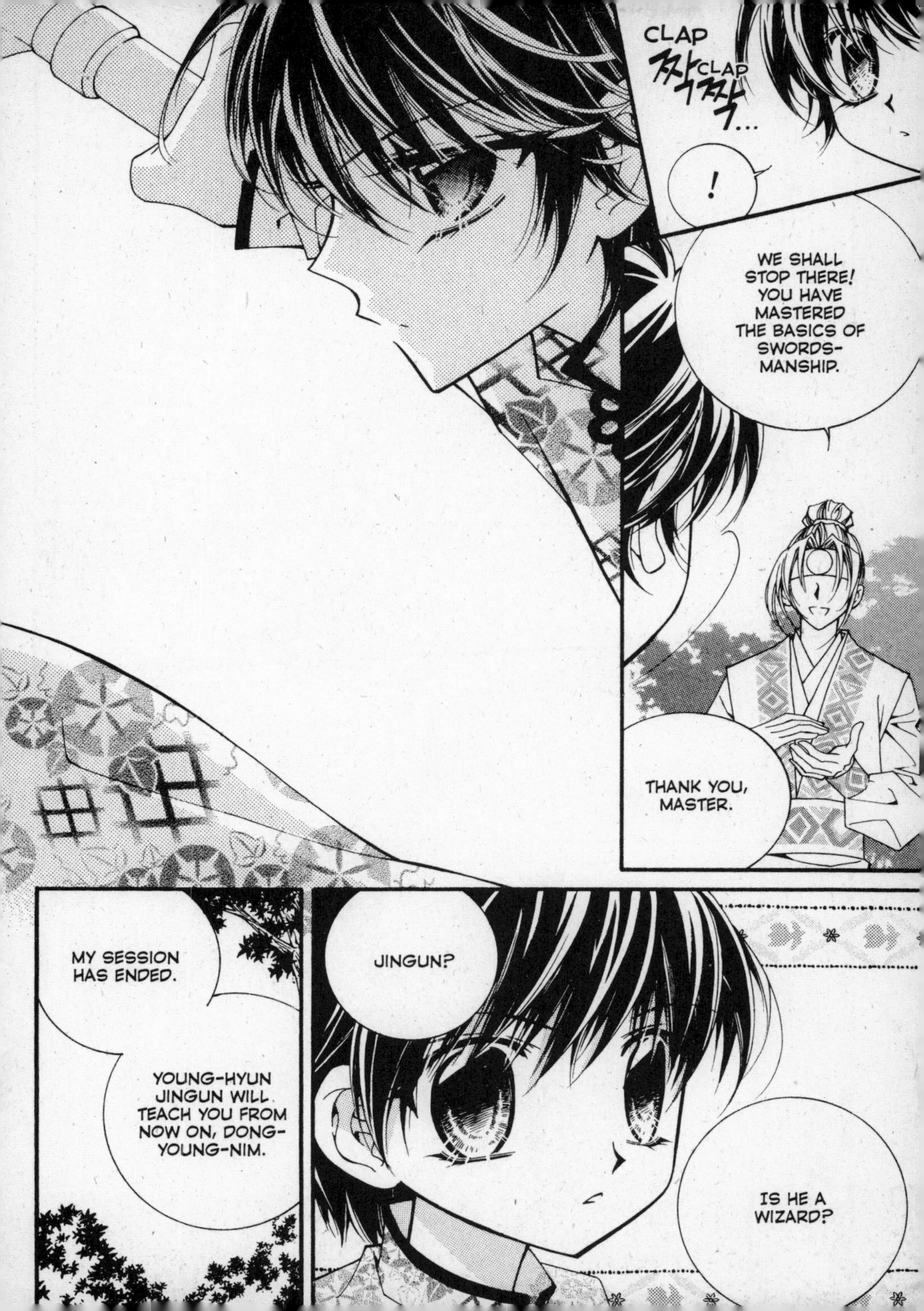
CLAP
짝짝...
CLAP
!
WE SHALL STOP THERE! YOU HAVE MASTERED THE BASICS OF SWORDS-MANSHIP.
THANK YOU, MASTER.
MY SESSION HAS ENDED.
YOUNG-HYUN JINGUN WILL TEACH YOU FROM NOW ON, DONG-YOUNG-NIM.
JINGUN?
IS HE A WIZARD?

HE CAME TO HEAVEN TO TEACH THE SUCCESSOR OF THE WHITE TIGER.

HE IS THE MASTER OF THE NEXT WHITE TIGER?

I DISCUSSED YOU, THE WINTER GENERAL, WITH HIM, AND HE AGREED TO TEACH YOU AS WELL.

THE NEXT WHITE TIGER WILL BE PART OF THE CLASS TOO.

YOU CAN ONLY IMPROVE YOUR SKILLS BY PRACTICING WITH AN OPPONENT.

I HOPE YOU PRACTICE HARD AND BECOME THE BEST WARRIOR IN HEAVEN. THEN...

......

THE SUCCESSOR OF THE WHITE TIGER?

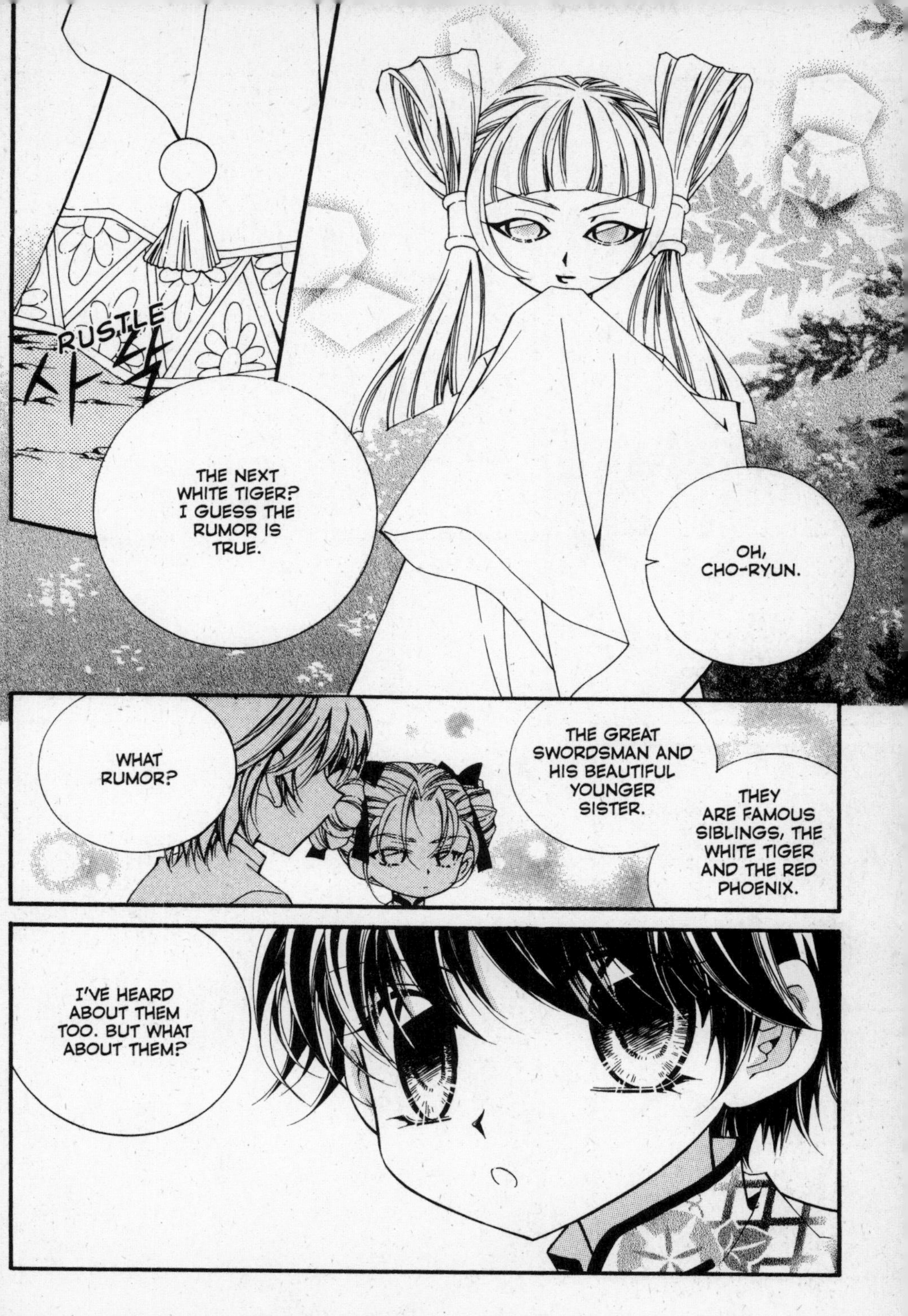
RUSTLE
사落
THE NEXT WHITE TIGER? I GUESS THE RUMOR IS TRUE.
OH, CHO-RYUN.
WHAT RUMOR?
THE GREAT SWORDSMAN AND HIS BEAUTIFUL YOUNGER SISTER.
THEY ARE FAMOUS SIBLINGS, THE WHITE TIGER AND THE RED PHOENIX.
I'VE HEARD ABOUT THEM TOO. BUT WHAT ABOUT THEM?

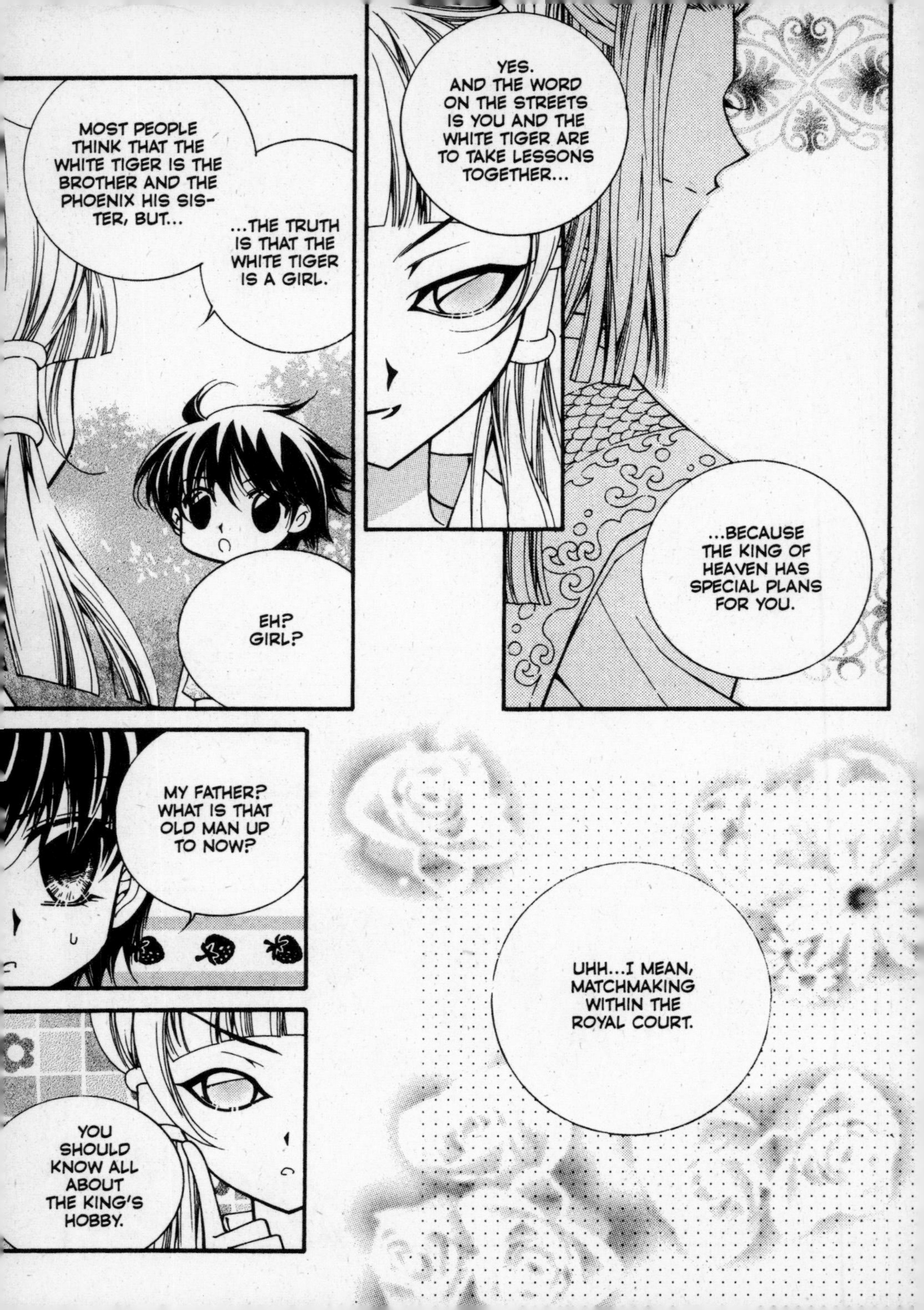
MOST PEOPLE THINK THAT THE WHITE TIGER IS THE BROTHER AND THE PHOENIX HIS SIS-TER, BUT...
...THE TRUTH IS THAT THE WHITE TIGER IS A GIRL.
EH? GIRL?
YES. AND THE WORD ON THE STREETS IS YOU AND THE WHITE TIGER ARE TO TAKE LESSONS TOGETHER...
...BECAUSE THE KING OF HEAVEN HAS SPECIAL PLANS FOR YOU.
MY FATHER? WHAT IS THAT OLD MAN UP TO NOW?
YOU SHOULD KNOW ALL ABOUT THE KING'S HOBBY.
UHH...I MEAN, MATCHMAKING WITHIN THE ROYAL COURT.

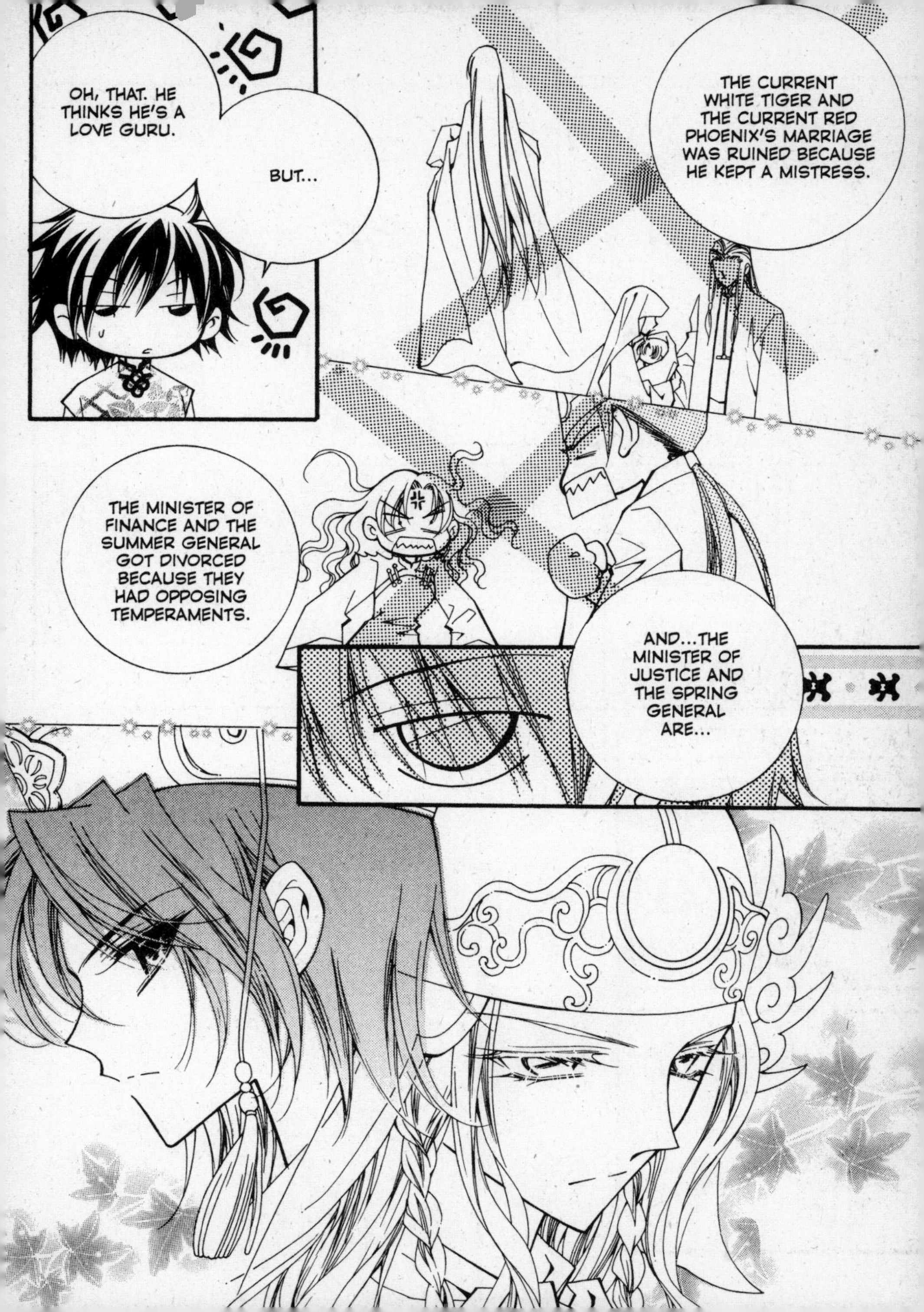
OH, THAT. HE THINKS HE'S A LOVE GURU.
BUT...
THE CURRENT WHITE TIGER AND THE CURRENT RED PHOENIX'S MARRIAGE WAS RUINED BECAUSE HE KEPT A MISTRESS.
THE MINISTER OF FINANCE AND THE SUMMER GENERAL GOT DIVORCED BECAUSE THEY HAD OPPOSING TEMPERAMENTS.
AND...THE MINISTER OF JUSTICE AND THE SPRING GENERAL ARE...

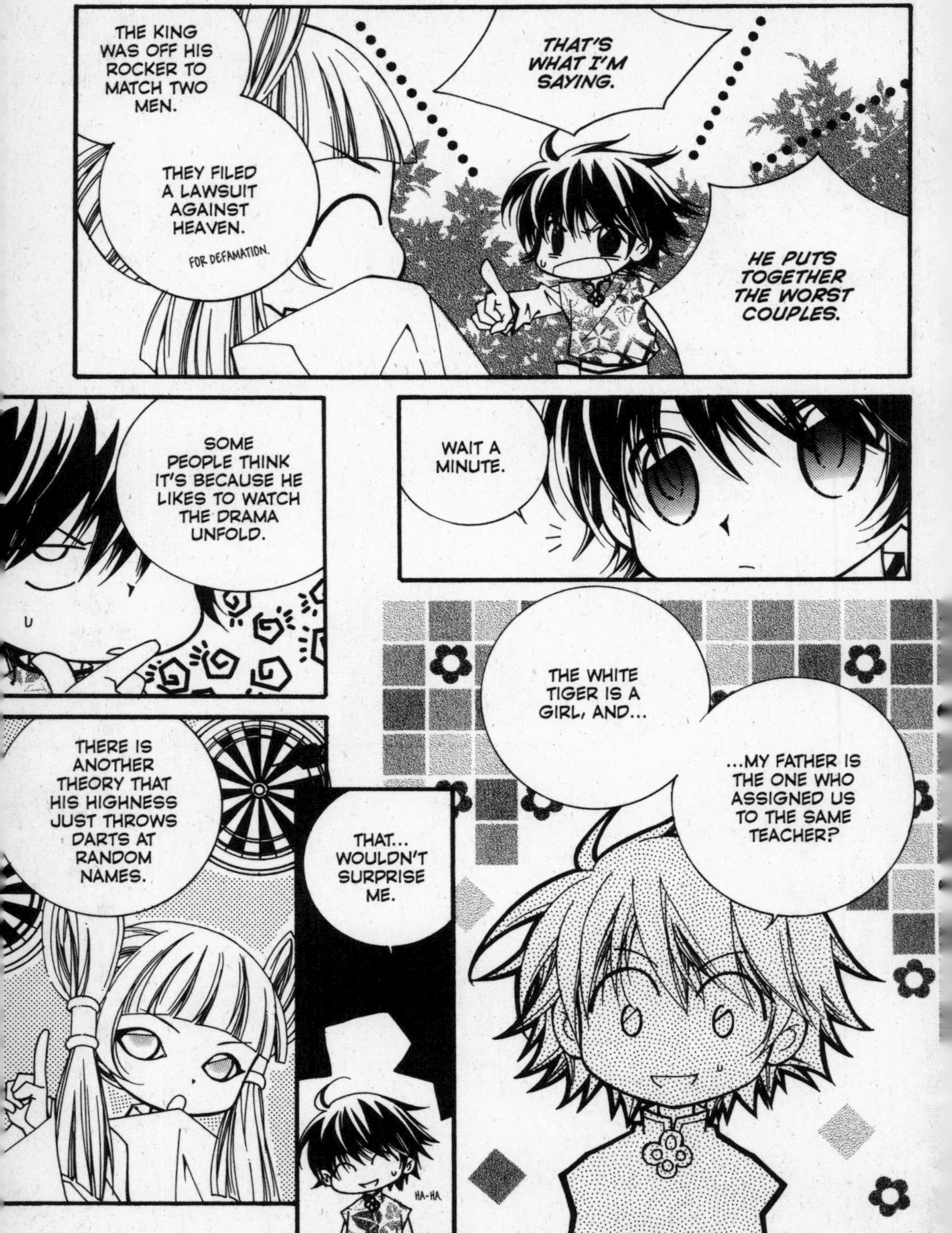
THE KING WAS OFF HIS ROCKER TO MATCH TWO MEN.
THAT'S WHAT I'M SAYING.
THEY FILED A LAWSUIT AGAINST HEAVEN.
FOR DEFAMATION.
HE PUTS TOGETHER THE WORST COUPLES.
SOME PEOPLE THINK IT'S BECAUSE HE LIKES TO WATCH THE DRAMA UNFOLD.
WAIT A MINUTE.
THERE IS ANOTHER THEORY THAT HIS HIGHNESS JUST THROWS DARTS AT RANDOM NAMES.
THAT... WOULDN'T SURPRISE ME.
HA-HA.
THE WHITE TIGER IS A GIRL, AND...
...MY FATHER IS THE ONE WHO ASSIGNED US TO THE SAME TEACHER?

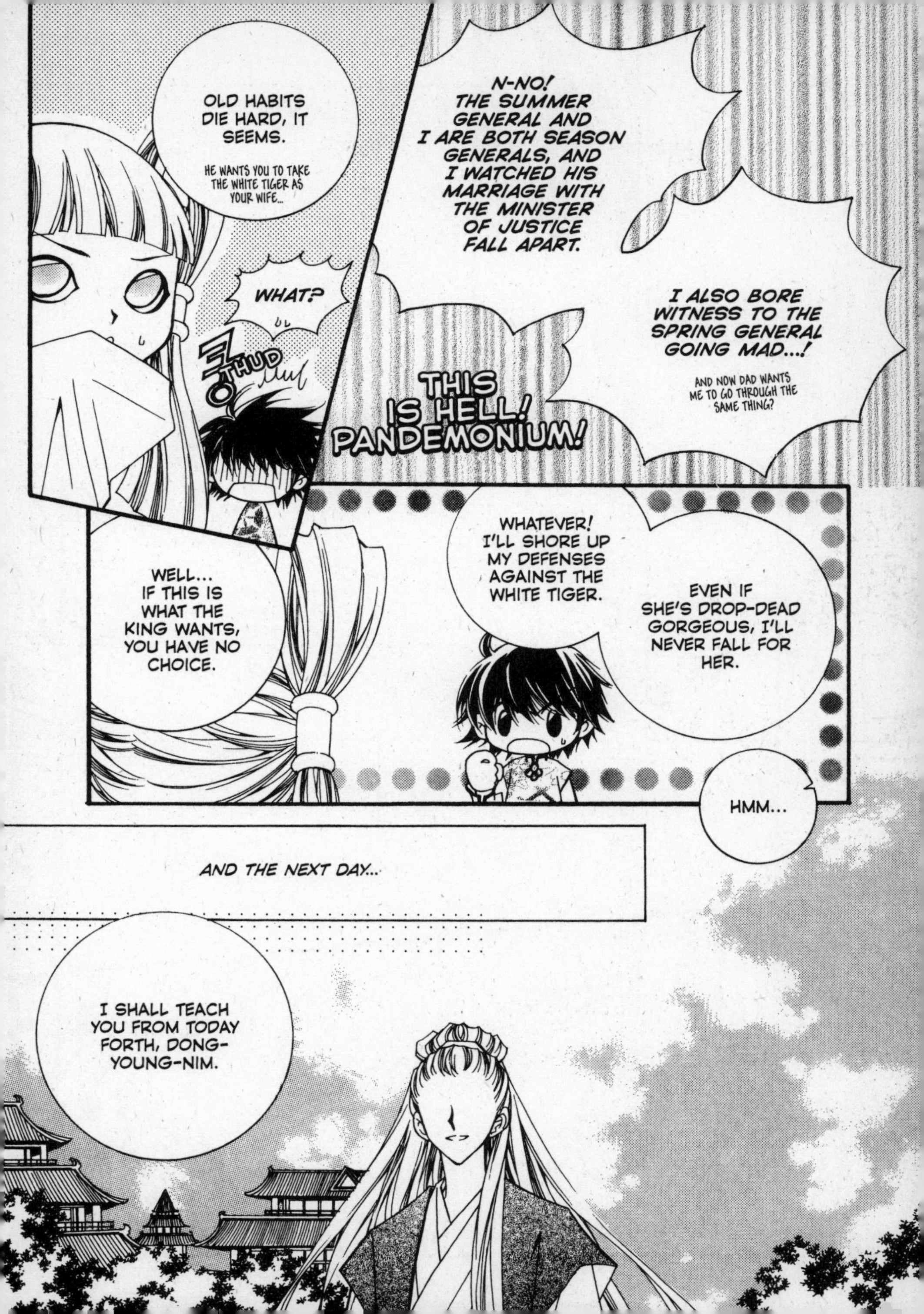
OLD HABITS DIE HARD, IT SEEMS.
HE WANTS YOU TO TAKE THE WHITE TIGER AS YOUR WIFE...
WHAT?
THUD
N-NO! THE SUMMER GENERAL AND I ARE BOTH SEASON GENERALS, AND I WATCHED HIS MARRIAGE WITH THE MINISTER OF JUSTICE FALL APART.
THIS IS HELL! PANDEMONIUM!
I ALSO BORE WITNESS TO THE SPRING GENERAL GOING MAD...!
AND NOW DAD WANTS ME TO GO THROUGH THE SAME THING?
WELL... IF THIS IS WHAT THE KING WANTS, YOU HAVE NO CHOICE.
WHATEVER! I'LL SHORE UP MY DEFENSES AGAINST THE WHITE TIGER.
EVEN IF SHE'S DROP-DEAD GORGEOUS, I'LL NEVER FALL FOR HER.
HMM...
AND THE NEXT DAY...
I SHALL TEACH YOU FROM TODAY FORTH, DONG-YOUNG-NIM.

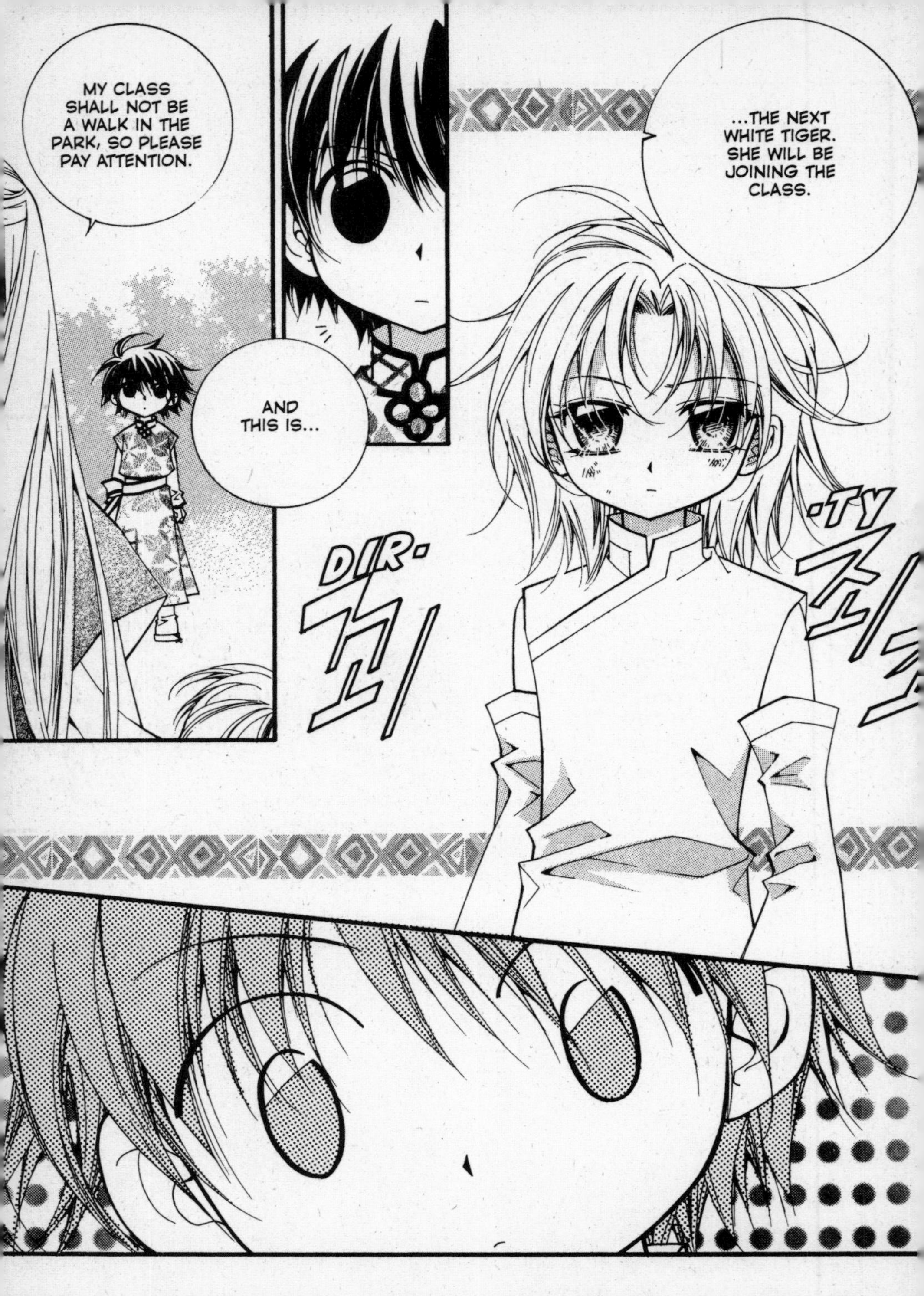
MY CLASS SHALL NOT BE A WALK IN THE PARK, SO PLEASE PAY ATTENTION.
AND THIS IS...
...THE NEXT WHITE TIGER. SHE WILL BE JOINING THE CLASS.
DIR-
-TY

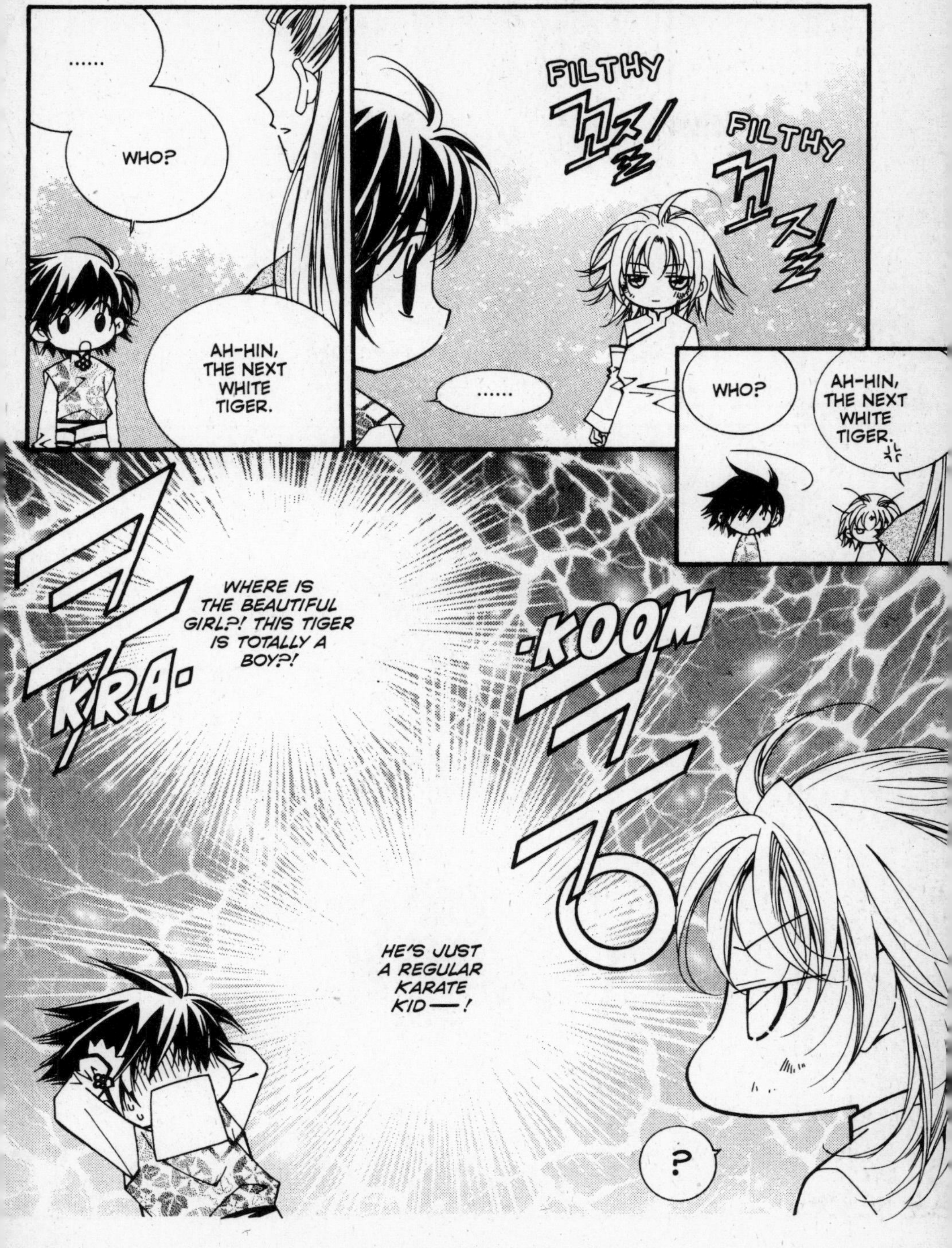

......
WHO?
AH-HIN, THE NEXT WHITE TIGER.
FILTHY
FILTHY
......
WHO?
AH-HIN, THE NEXT WHITE TIGER.
KRA-
WHERE IS THE BEAUTIFUL GIRL?! THIS TIGER IS TOTALLY A BOY?!
-KOOM
HE'S JUST A REGULAR KARATE KID—!
?

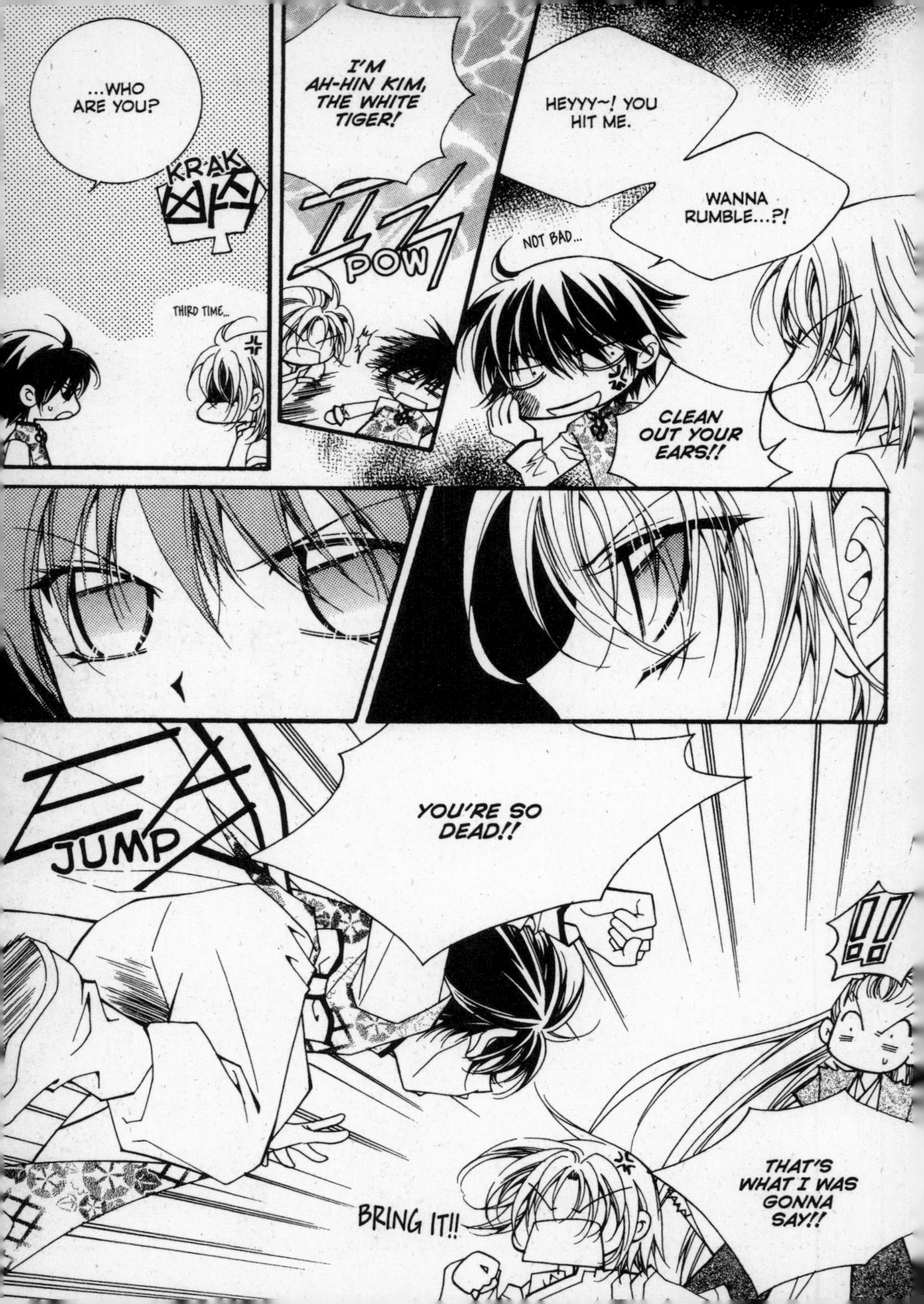
...WHO ARE YOU?
KRAK
THIRD TIME...
I'M AH-HIN KIM, THE WHITE TIGER!
POW
HEYYY~! YOU HIT ME.
WANNA RUMBLE...?!
NOT BAD...
CLEAN OUT YOUR EARS!!
JUMP
YOU'RE SO DEAD!!
BRING IT!!
THAT'S WHAT I WAS GONNA SAY!!

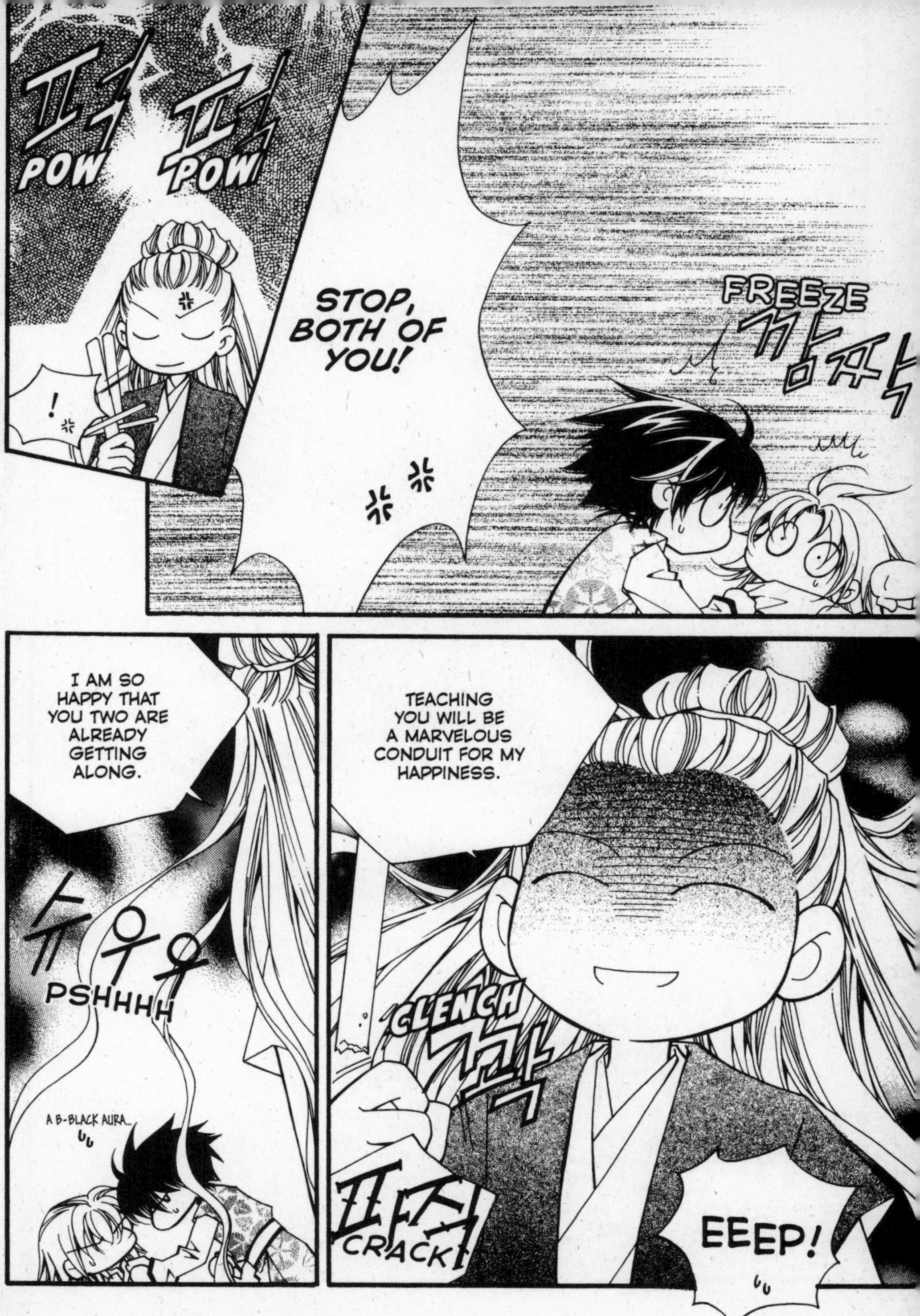
POW
POW
!
STOP, BOTH OF YOU!
FREEZE
I AM SO HAPPY THAT YOU TWO ARE ALREADY GETTING ALONG.
PSHHHH
A B-BLACK AURA...
TEACHING YOU WILL BE A MARVELOUS CONDUIT FOR MY HAPPINESS.
CLENCH
CRACK
EEEP!

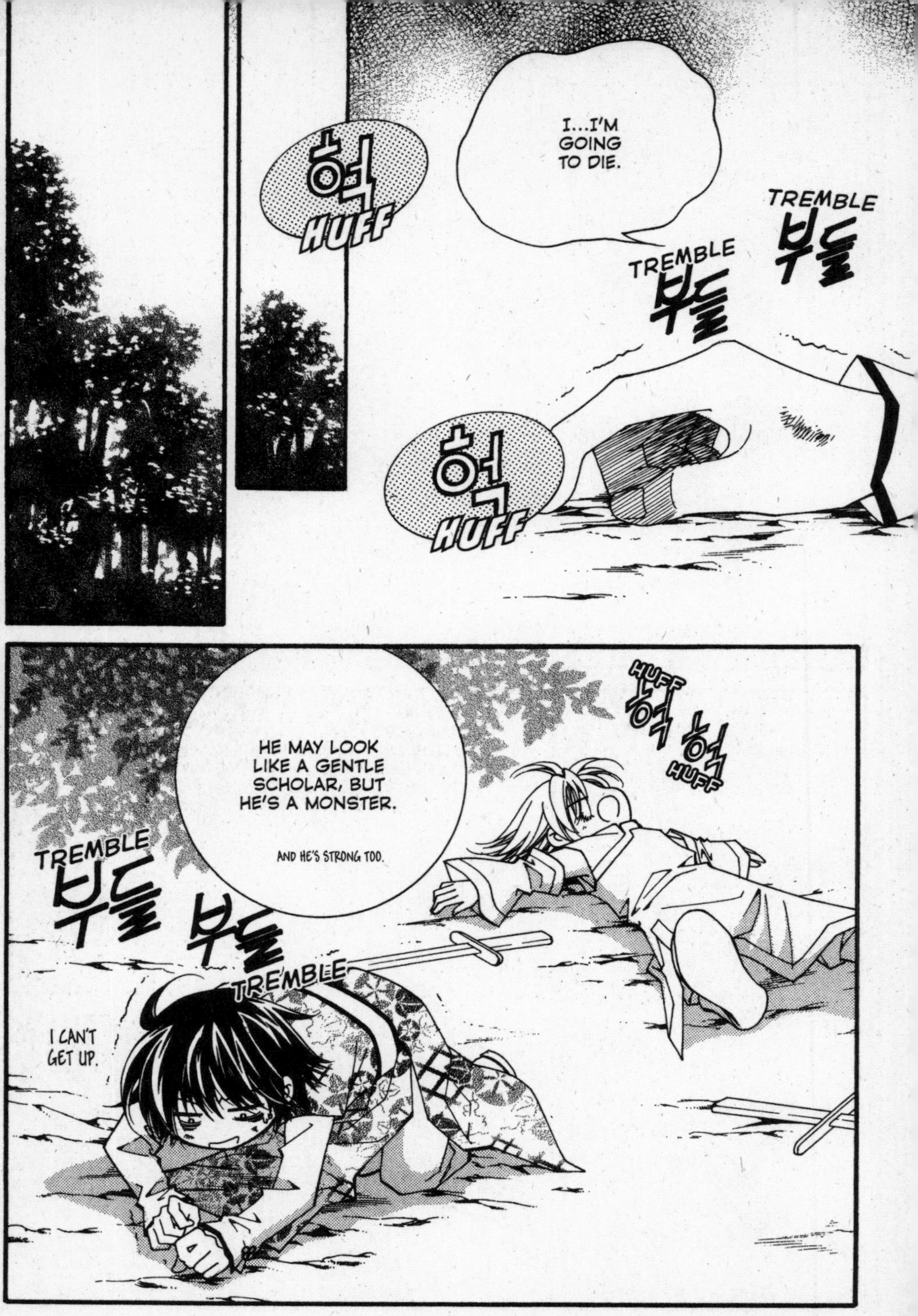
헉
HUFF
I...I'M GOING TO DIE.
TREMBLE
부들
TREMBLE
부들
헉
HUFF
HE MAY LOOK LIKE A GENTLE SCHOLAR, BUT HE'S A MONSTER.
AND HE'S STRONG TOO.
HUFF
헉 헉
HUFF
TREMBLE
부들 부들
TREMBLE
I CAN'T GET UP.

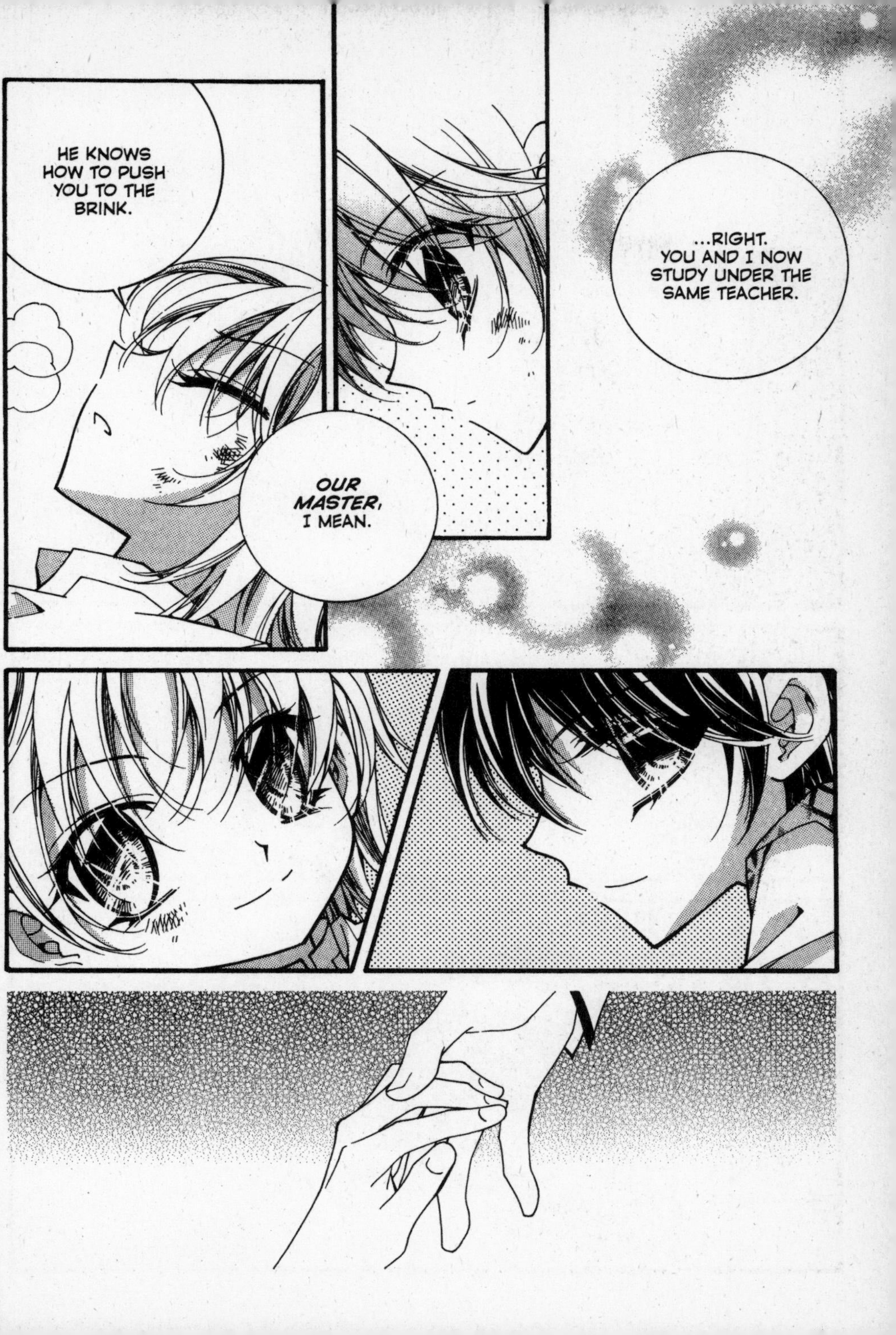
HE KNOWS HOW TO PUSH YOU TO THE BRINK.
OUR MASTER, I MEAN.
...RIGHT. YOU AND I NOW STUDY UNDER THE SAME TEACHER.

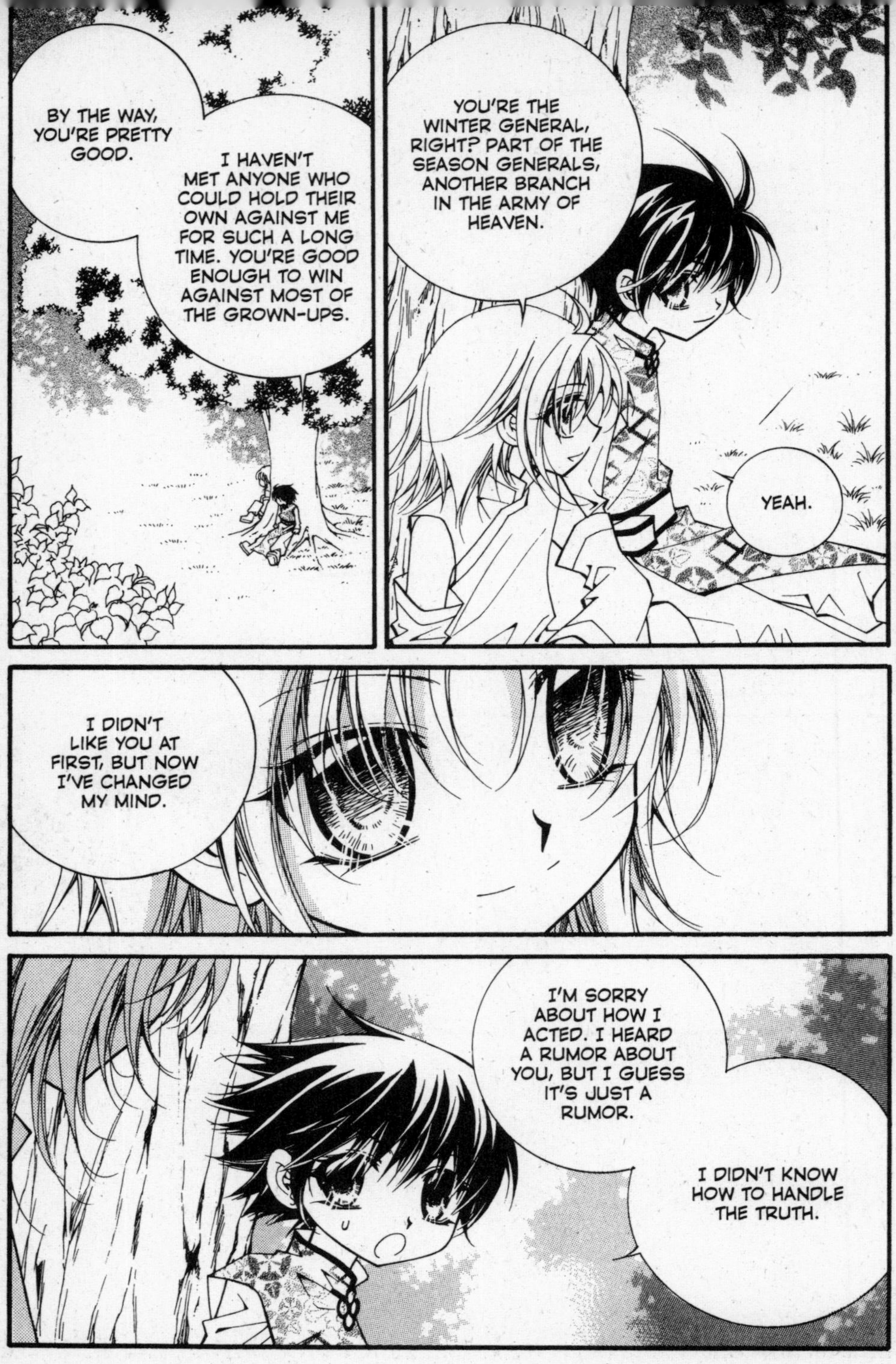
BY THE WAY, YOU'RE PRETTY GOOD.
I HAVEN'T MET ANYONE WHO COULD HOLD THEIR OWN AGAINST ME FOR SUCH A LONG TIME. YOU'RE GOOD ENOUGH TO WIN AGAINST MOST OF THE GROWN-UPS.
YOU'RE THE WINTER GENERAL, RIGHT? PART OF THE SEASON GENERALS, ANOTHER BRANCH IN THE ARMY OF HEAVEN.
YEAH.
I DIDN'T LIKE YOU AT FIRST, BUT NOW I'VE CHANGED MY MIND.
I'M SORRY ABOUT HOW I ACTED. I HEARD A RUMOR ABOUT YOU, BUT I GUESS IT'S JUST A RUMOR.
I DIDN'T KNOW HOW TO HANDLE THE TRUTH.

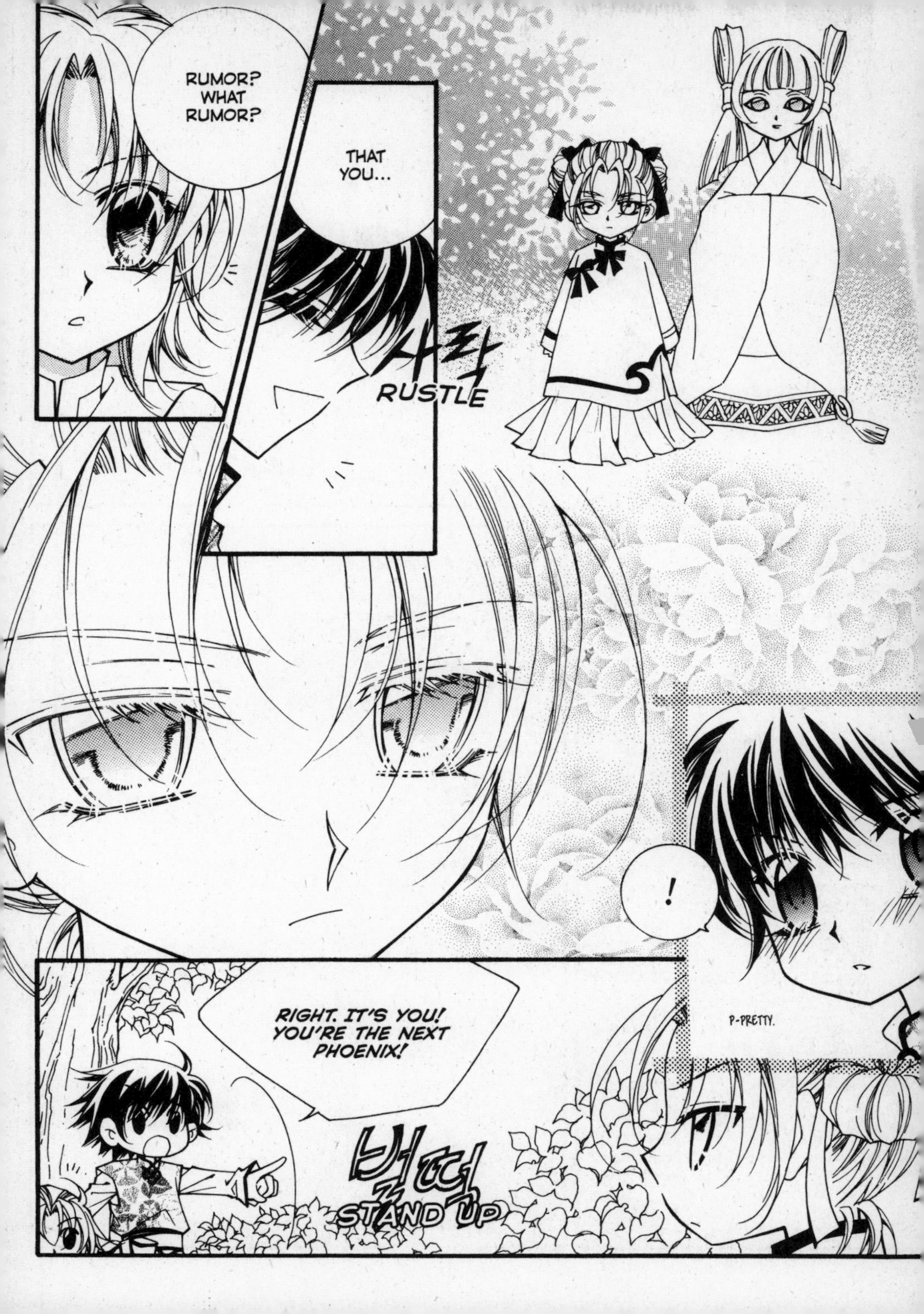

RUMOR? WHAT RUMOR?
THAT YOU...
RUSTLE
!
P-PRETTY.
RIGHT. IT'S YOU! YOU'RE THE NEXT PHOENIX!
벌떡
STAND UP

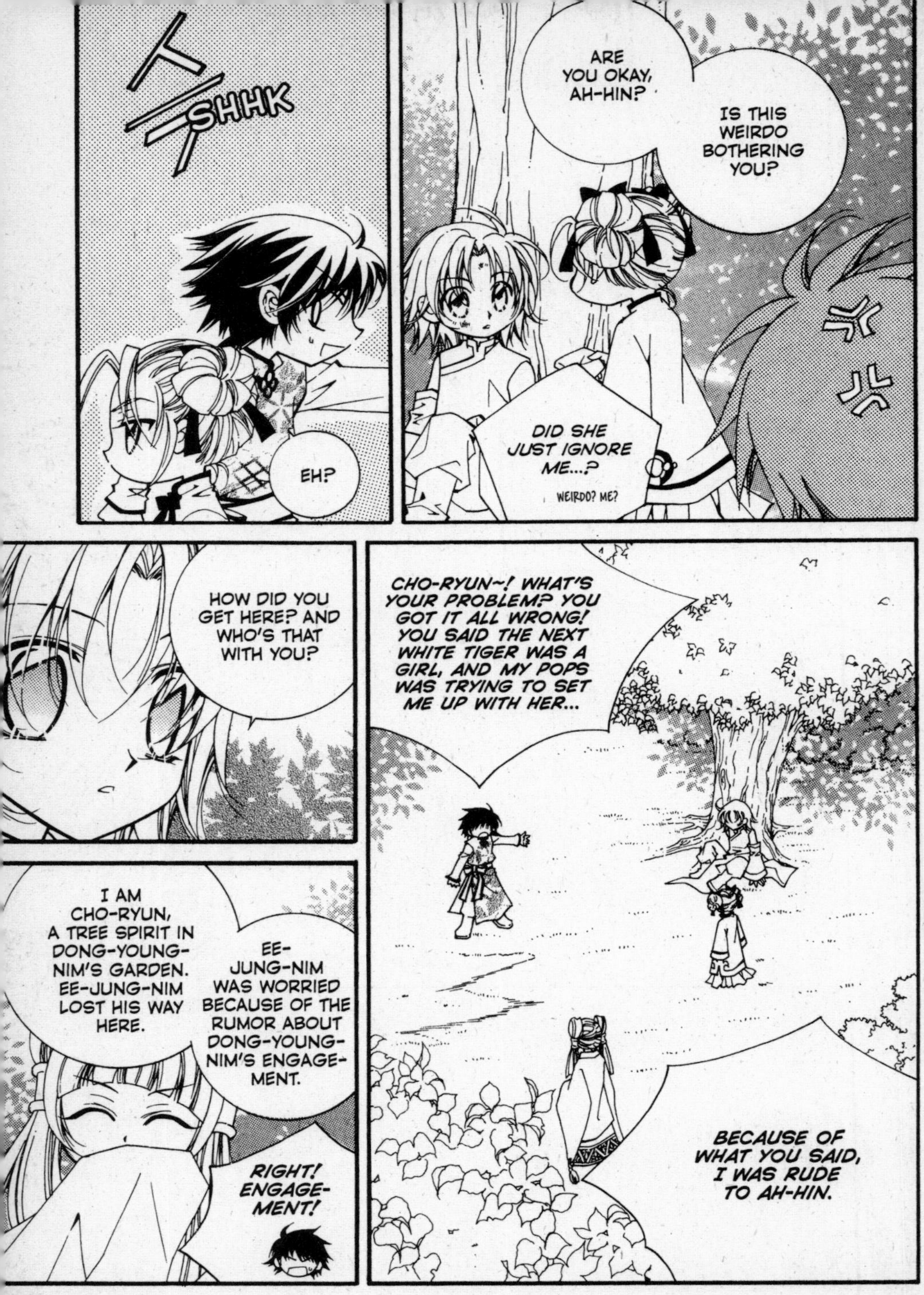
SHHK
EH?
ARE YOU OKAY, AH-HIN?
IS THIS WEIRDO BOTHERING YOU?
DID SHE JUST IGNORE ME...?
WEIRDO? ME?
HOW DID YOU GET HERE? AND WHO'S THAT WITH YOU?
I AM CHO-RYUN, A TREE SPIRIT IN DONG-YOUNG-NIM'S GARDEN. EE-JUNG-NIM LOST HIS WAY HERE.
EE-JUNG-NIM WAS WORRIED BECAUSE OF THE RUMOR ABOUT DONG-YOUNG-NIM'S ENGAGEMENT.
RIGHT! ENGAGEMENT!
CHO-RYUN~! WHAT'S YOUR PROBLEM? YOU GOT IT ALL WRONG! YOU SAID THE NEXT WHITE TIGER WAS A GIRL, AND MY POPS WAS TRYING TO SET ME UP WITH HER...
BECAUSE OF WHAT YOU SAID, I WAS RUDE TO AH-HIN.

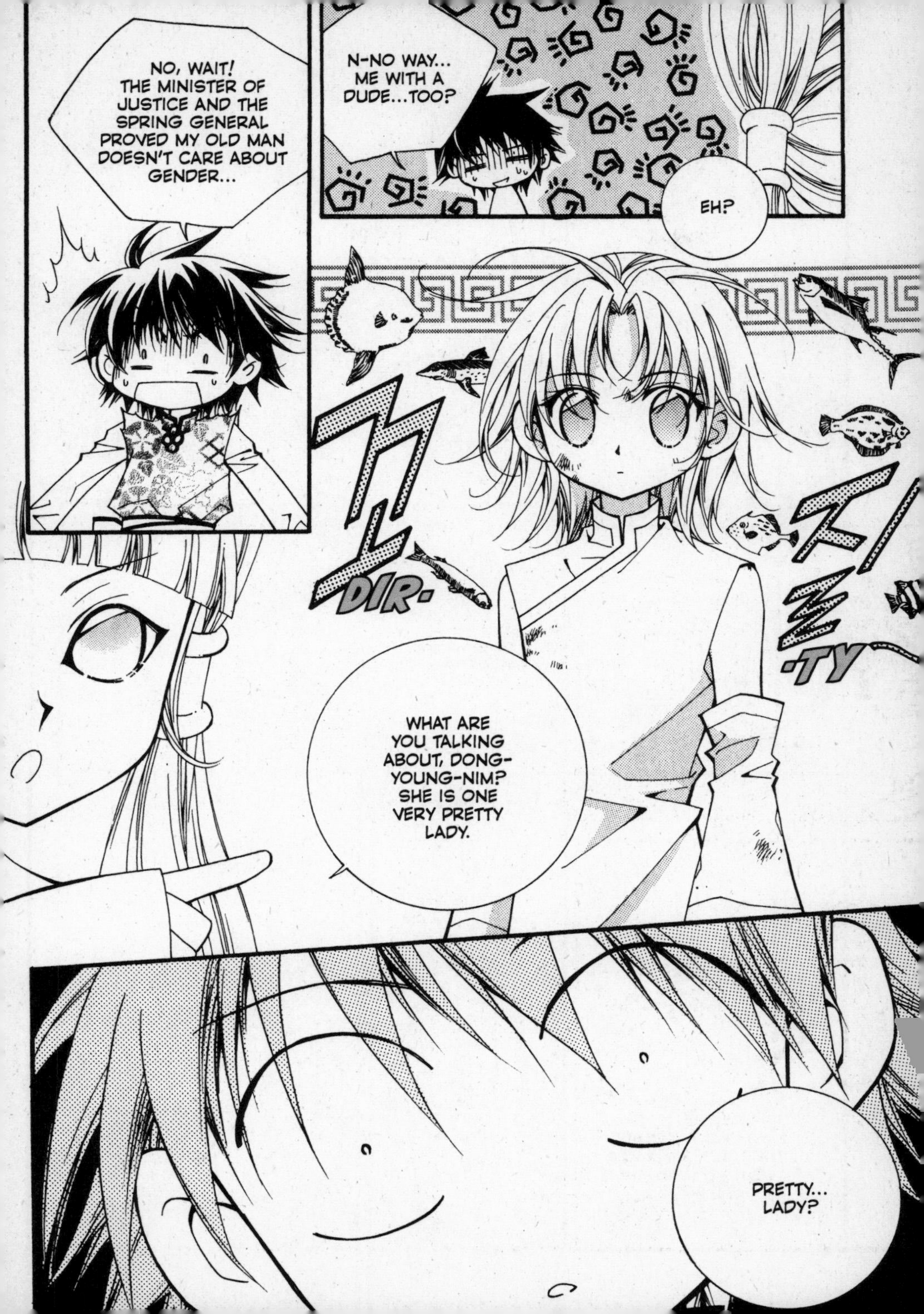

NO, WAIT! THE MINISTER OF JUSTICE AND THE SPRING GENERAL PROVED MY OLD MAN DOESN'T CARE ABOUT GENDER...
N-NO WAY... ME WITH A DUDE...TOO?
EH?
DIR-
-TY
WHAT ARE YOU TALKING ABOUT, DONG-YOUNG-NIM? SHE IS ONE VERY PRETTY LADY.
PRETTY... LADY?

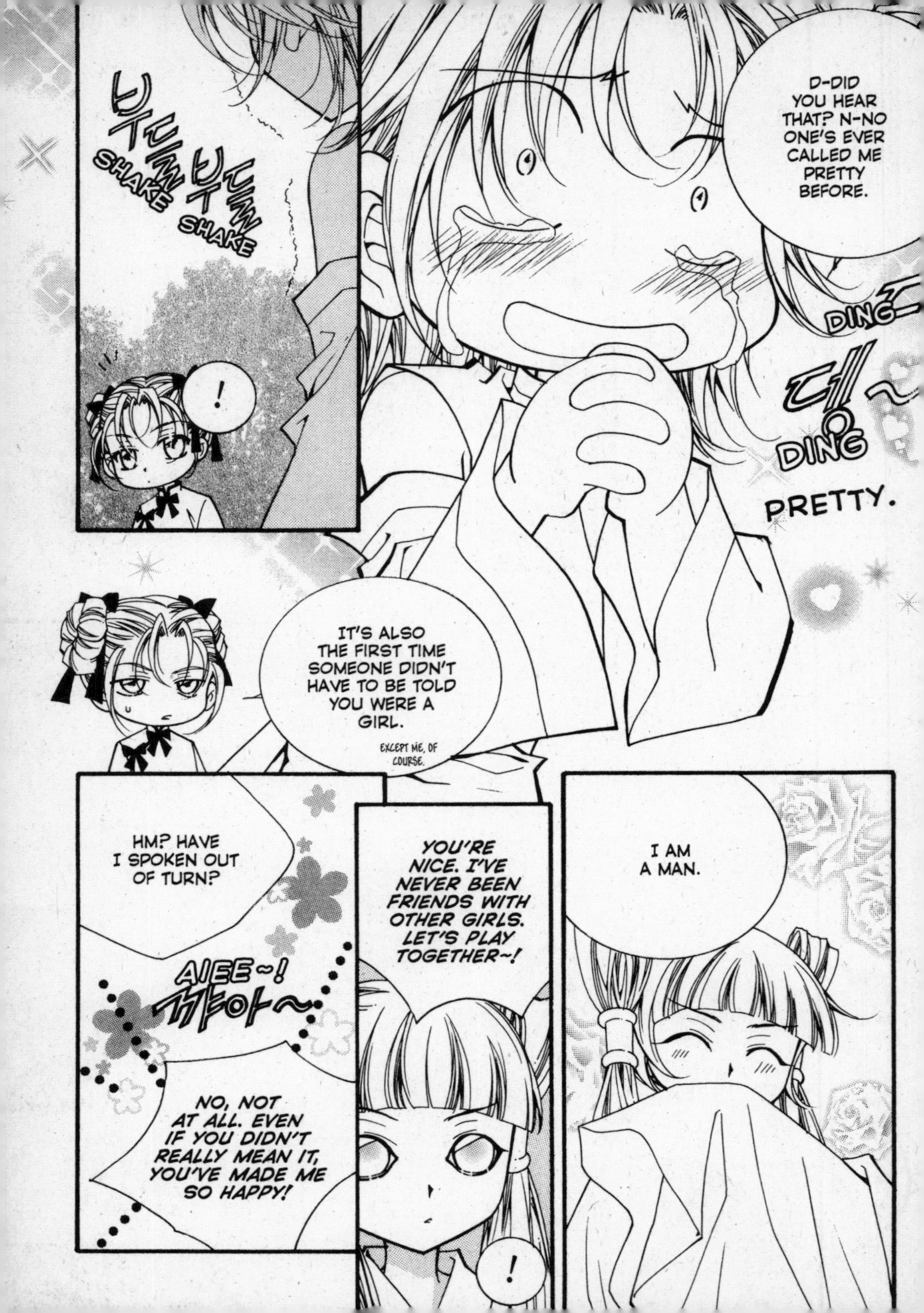
SHAKE SHAKE
!
D-DID YOU HEAR THAT? N-NO ONE'S EVER CALLED ME PRETTY BEFORE.
DING DING
PRETTY.
IT'S ALSO THE FIRST TIME SOMEONE DIDN'T HAVE TO BE TOLD YOU WERE A GIRL.
EXCEPT ME, OF COURSE.
HM? HAVE I SPOKEN OUT OF TURN?
AIEE~!
NO, NOT AT ALL. EVEN IF YOU DIDN'T REALLY MEAN IT, YOU'VE MADE ME SO HAPPY!
YOU'RE NICE. I'VE NEVER BEEN FRIENDS WITH OTHER GIRLS. LET'S PLAY TOGETHER~!
!
I AM A MAN.

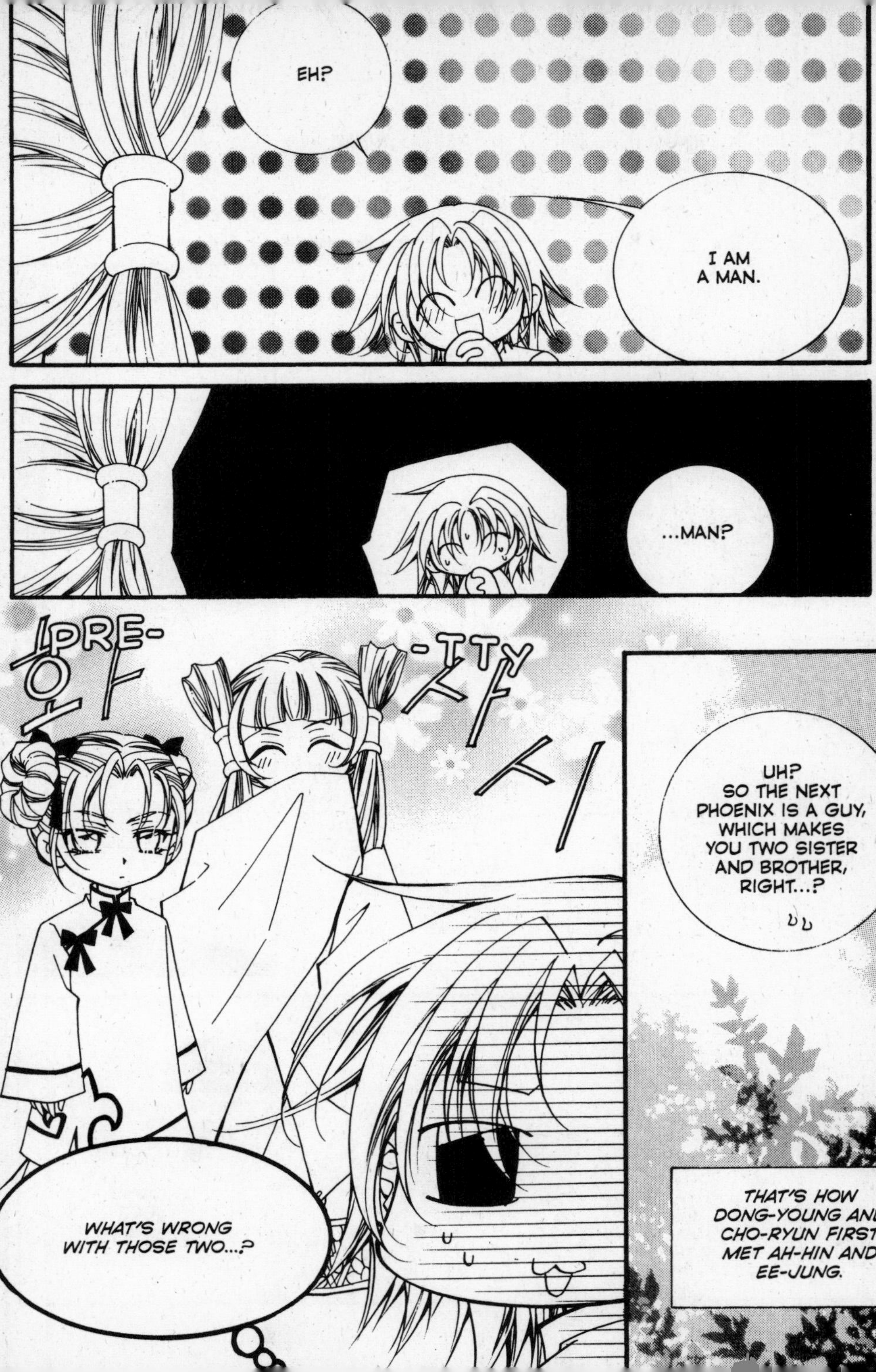
EH?
I AM A MAN.
...MAN?
PRE- -TTY
WHAT'S WRONG WITH THOSE TWO...?
UH? SO THE NEXT PHOENIX IS A GUY, WHICH MAKES YOU TWO SISTER AND BROTHER, RIGHT...?
THAT'S HOW DONG-YOUNG AND CHO-RYUN FIRST MET AH-HIN AND EE-JUNG.

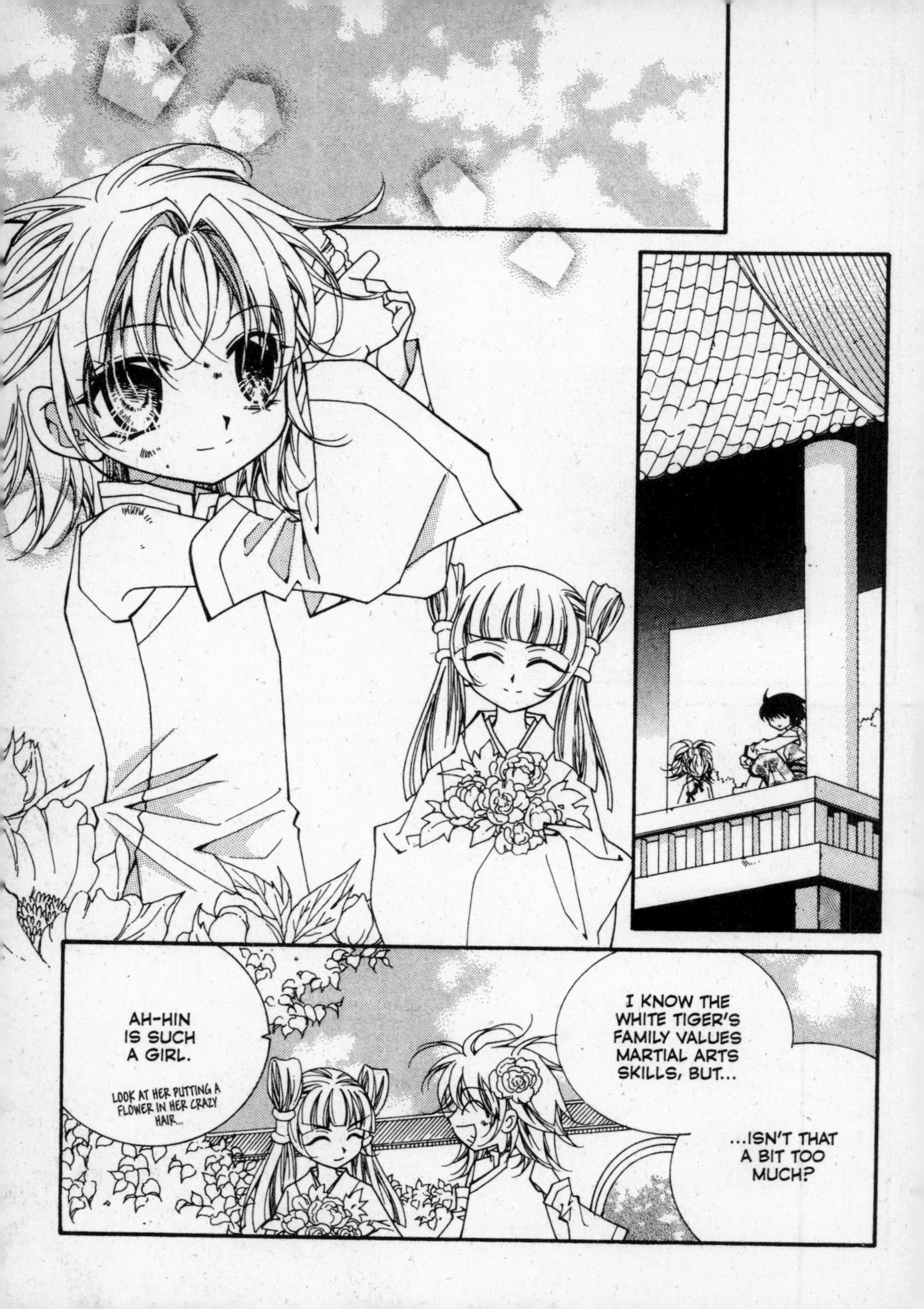
AH-HIN IS SUCH A GIRL.
LOOK AT HER PUTTING A FLOWER IN HER CRAZY HAIR...
I KNOW THE WHITE TIGER'S FAMILY VALUES MARTIAL ARTS SKILLS, BUT...
...ISN'T THAT A BIT TOO MUCH?

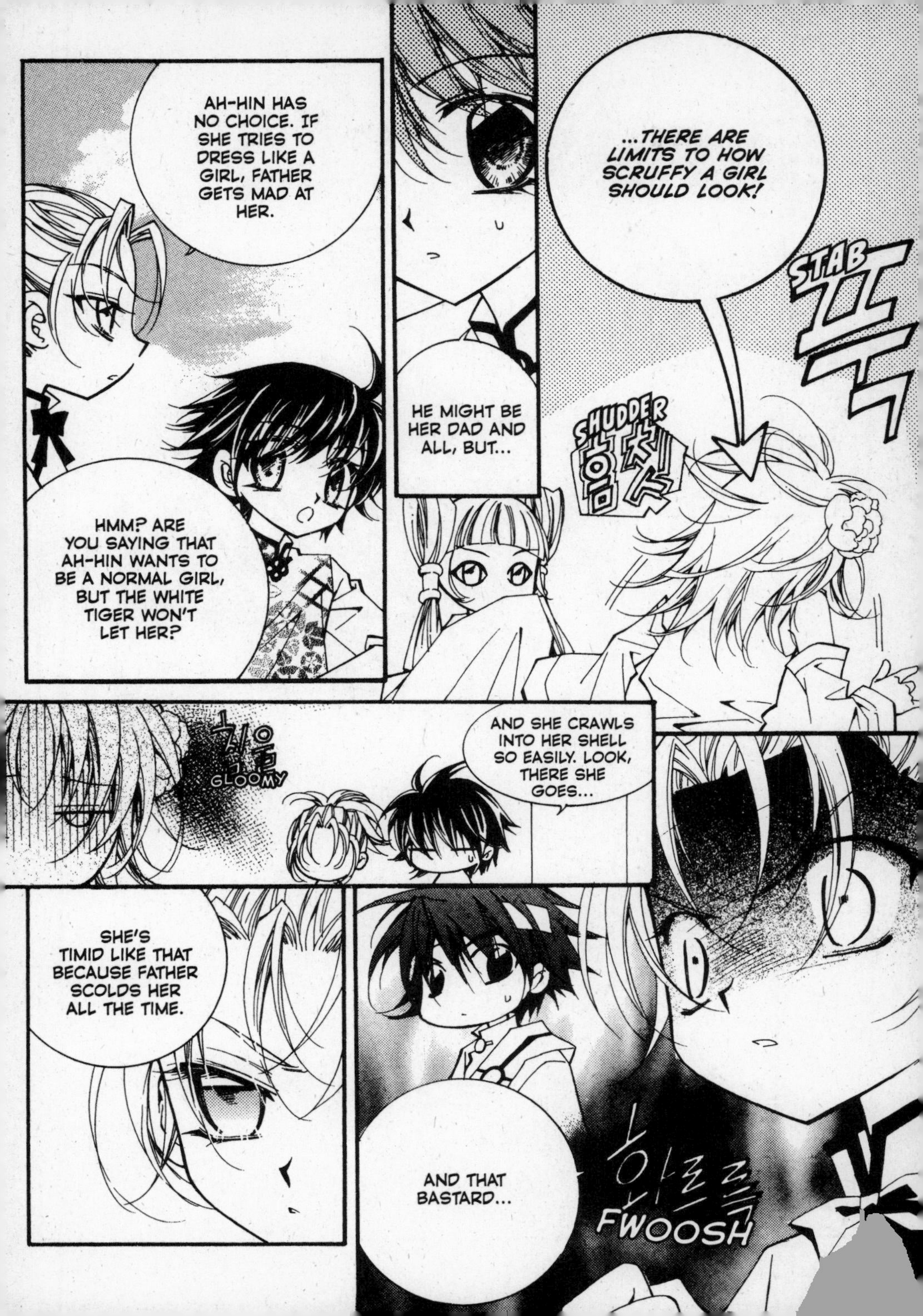
AH-HIN HAS NO CHOICE. IF SHE TRIES TO DRESS LIKE A GIRL, FATHER GETS MAD AT HER.
HMM? ARE YOU SAYING THAT AH-HIN WANTS TO BE A NORMAL GIRL, BUT THE WHITE TIGER WON'T LET HER?
HE MIGHT BE HER DAD AND ALL, BUT...
...THERE ARE LIMITS TO HOW SCRUFFY A GIRL SHOULD LOOK!
STAB
SHUDDER
GLOOMY
AND SHE CRAWLS INTO HER SHELL SO EASILY. LOOK, THERE SHE GOES...
SHE'S TIMID LIKE THAT BECAUSE FATHER SCOLDS HER ALL THE TIME.
AND THAT BASTARD...
FWOOSH

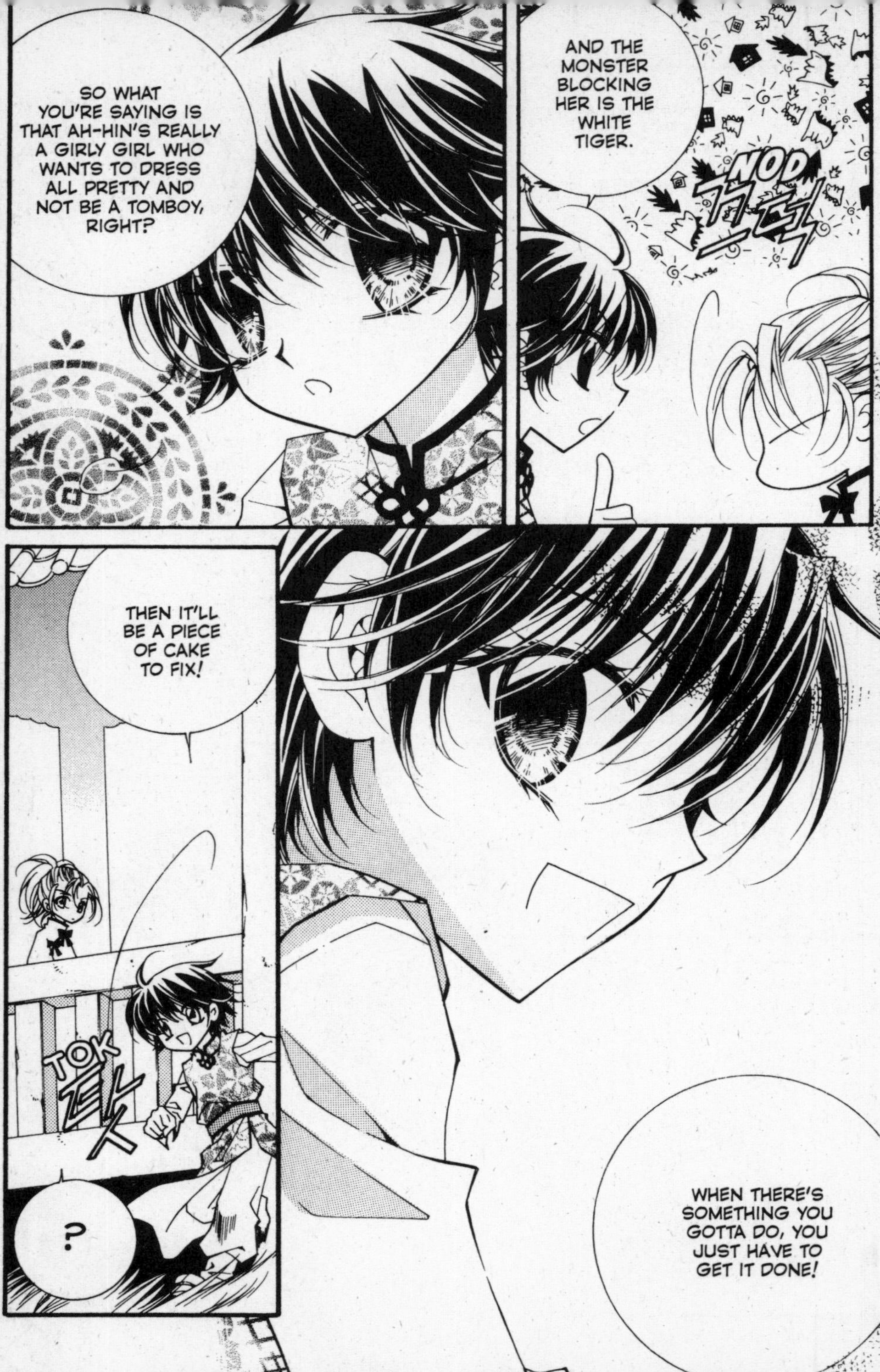
SO WHAT YOU'RE SAYING IS THAT AH-HIN'S REALLY A GIRLY GIRL WHO WANTS TO DRESS ALL PRETTY AND NOT BE A TOMBOY, RIGHT?
AND THE MONSTER BLOCKING HER IS THE WHITE TIGER.
NOD
THEN IT'LL BE A PIECE OF CAKE TO FIX!
TOK
?
WHEN THERE'S SOMETHING YOU GOTTA DO, YOU JUST HAVE TO GET IT DONE!

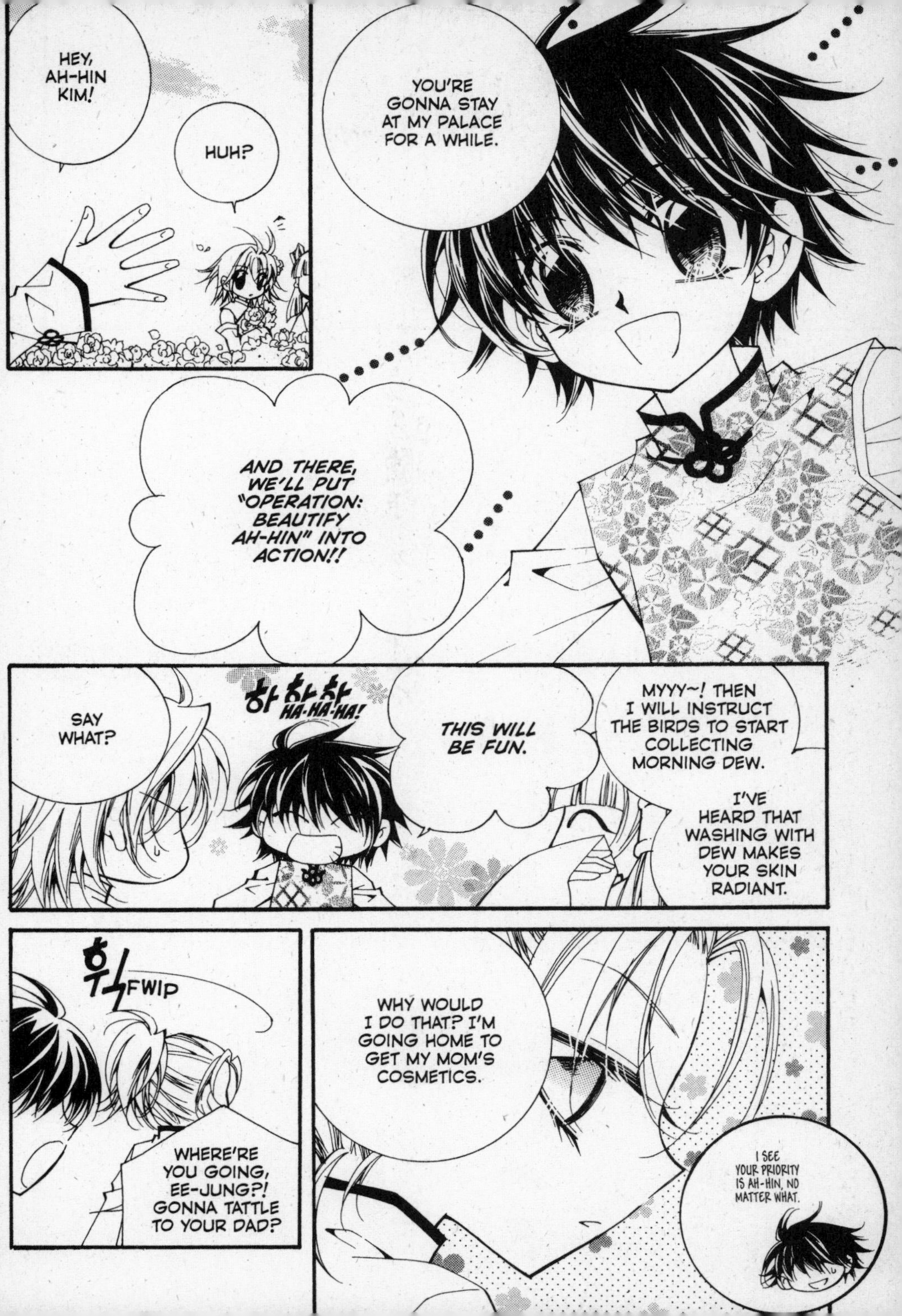
HEY, AH-HIN KIM!
HUH?
YOU'RE GONNA STAY AT MY PALACE FOR A WHILE.
AND THERE, WE'LL PUT "OPERATION: BEAUTIFY AH-HIN" INTO ACTION!!
SAY WHAT?
하하하
HA-HA-HA!
THIS WILL BE FUN.
MYYY~! THEN I WILL INSTRUCT THE BIRDS TO START COLLECTING MORNING DEW.
I'VE HEARD THAT WASHING WITH DEW MAKES YOUR SKIN RADIANT.
휙
FWIP
WHERE'RE YOU GOING, EE-JUNG?! GONNA TATTLE TO YOUR DAD?
WHY WOULD I DO THAT? I'M GOING HOME TO GET MY MOM'S COSMETICS.
I SEE YOUR PRIORITY IS AH-HIN, NO MATTER WHAT.

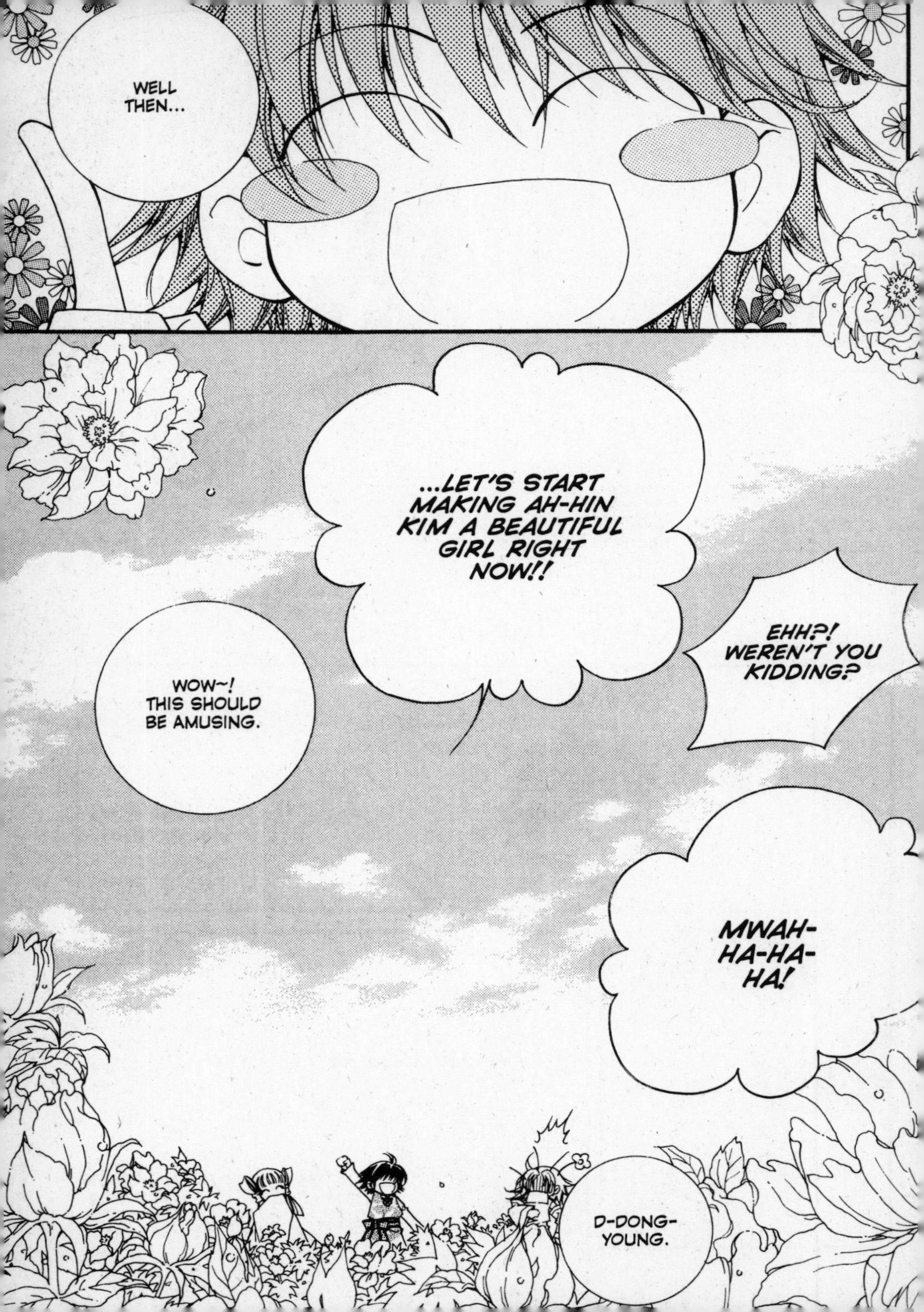
WELL THEN...
...LET'S START MAKING AH-HIN KIM A BEAUTIFUL GIRL RIGHT NOW!!
WOW~! THIS SHOULD BE AMUSING.
EHH?! WEREN'T YOU KIDDING?
MWAH-HA-HA-HA!
D-DONG-YOUNG.

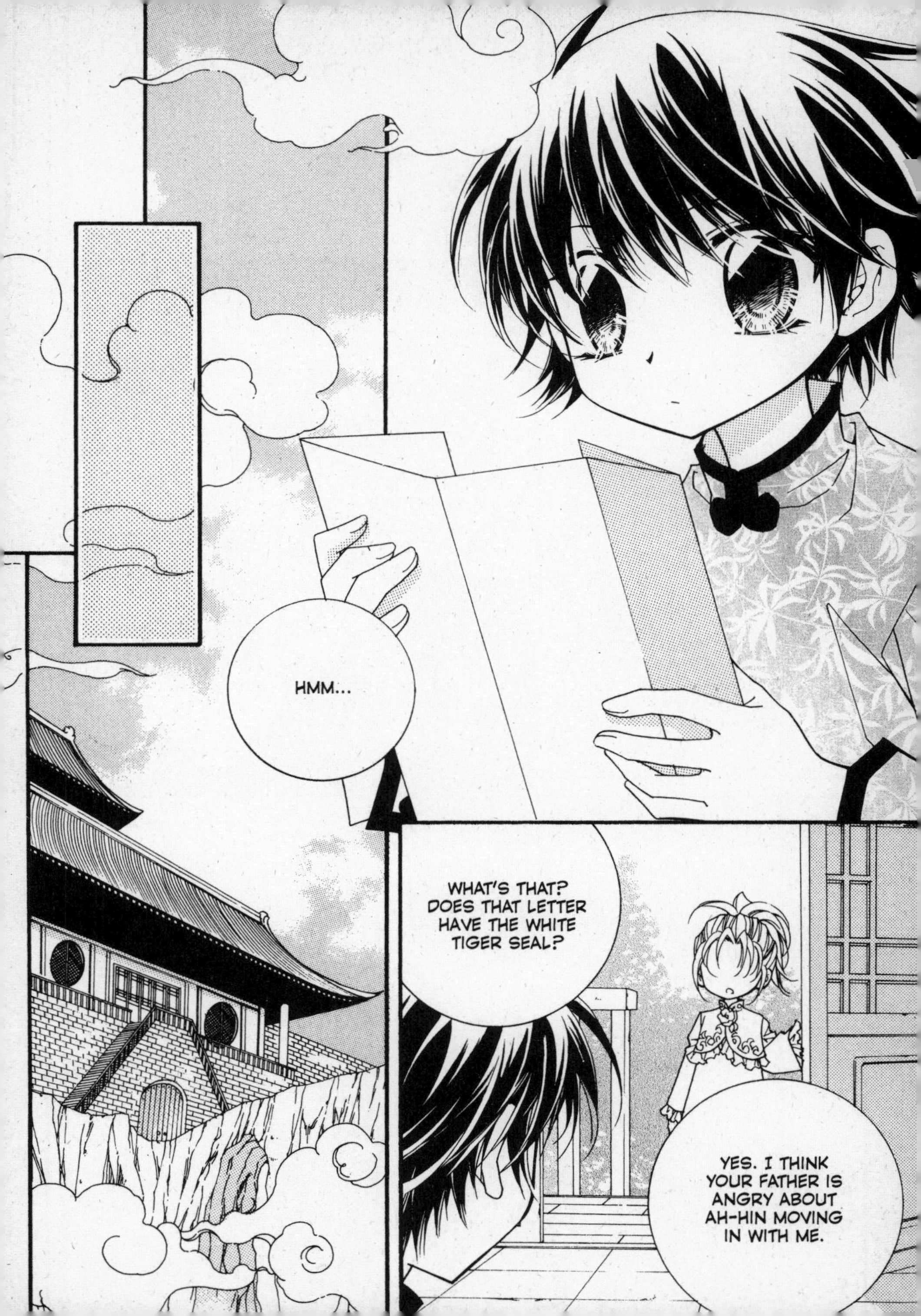
HMM...
WHAT'S THAT? DOES THAT LETTER HAVE THE WHITE TIGER SEAL?
YES. I THINK YOUR FATHER IS ANGRY ABOUT AH-HIN MOVING IN WITH ME.

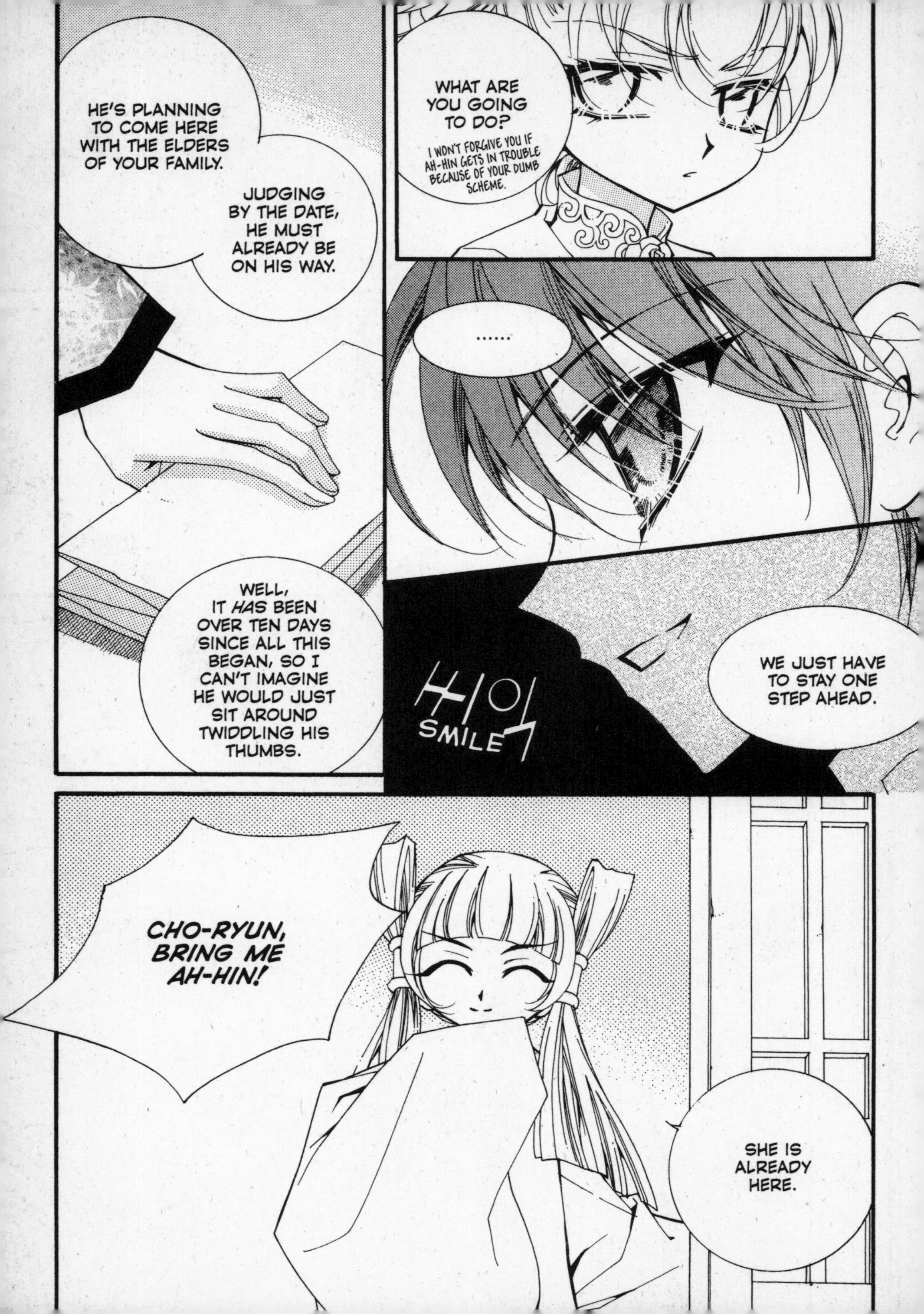
HE'S PLANNING TO COME HERE WITH THE ELDERS OF YOUR FAMILY.
JUDGING BY THE DATE, HE MUST ALREADY BE ON HIS WAY.
WHAT ARE YOU GOING TO DO?
I WON'T FORGIVE YOU IF AH-HIN GETS IN TROUBLE BECAUSE OF YOUR DUMB SCHEME.
......
WELL, IT *HAS* BEEN OVER TEN DAYS SINCE ALL THIS BEGAN, SO I CAN'T IMAGINE HE WOULD JUST SIT AROUND TWIDDLING HIS THUMBS.
SMILE
WE JUST HAVE TO STAY ONE STEP AHEAD.
CHO-RYUN, BRING ME AH-HIN!
SHE IS ALREADY HERE.

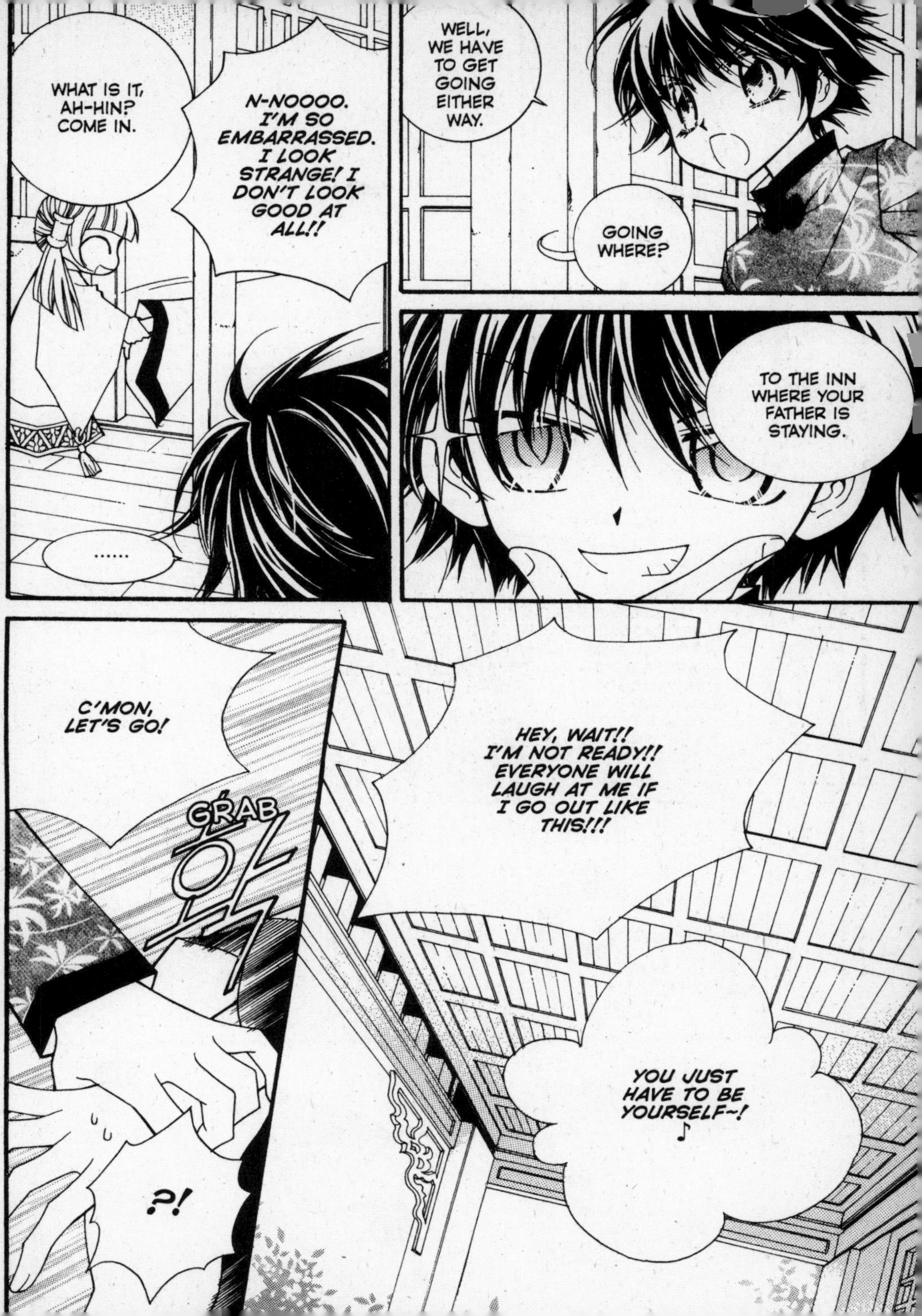
WHAT IS IT, AH-HIN? COME IN.
N-NOOOO. I'M SO EMBARRASSED. I LOOK STRANGE! I DON'T LOOK GOOD AT ALL!!
......
WELL, WE HAVE TO GET GOING EITHER WAY.
GOING WHERE?
TO THE INN WHERE YOUR FATHER IS STAYING.
C'MON, LET'S GO!
GRAB
?!
HEY, WAIT!! I'M NOT READY!! EVERYONE WILL LAUGH AT ME IF I GO OUT LIKE THIS!!!
YOU JUST HAVE TO BE YOURSELF~! ♪

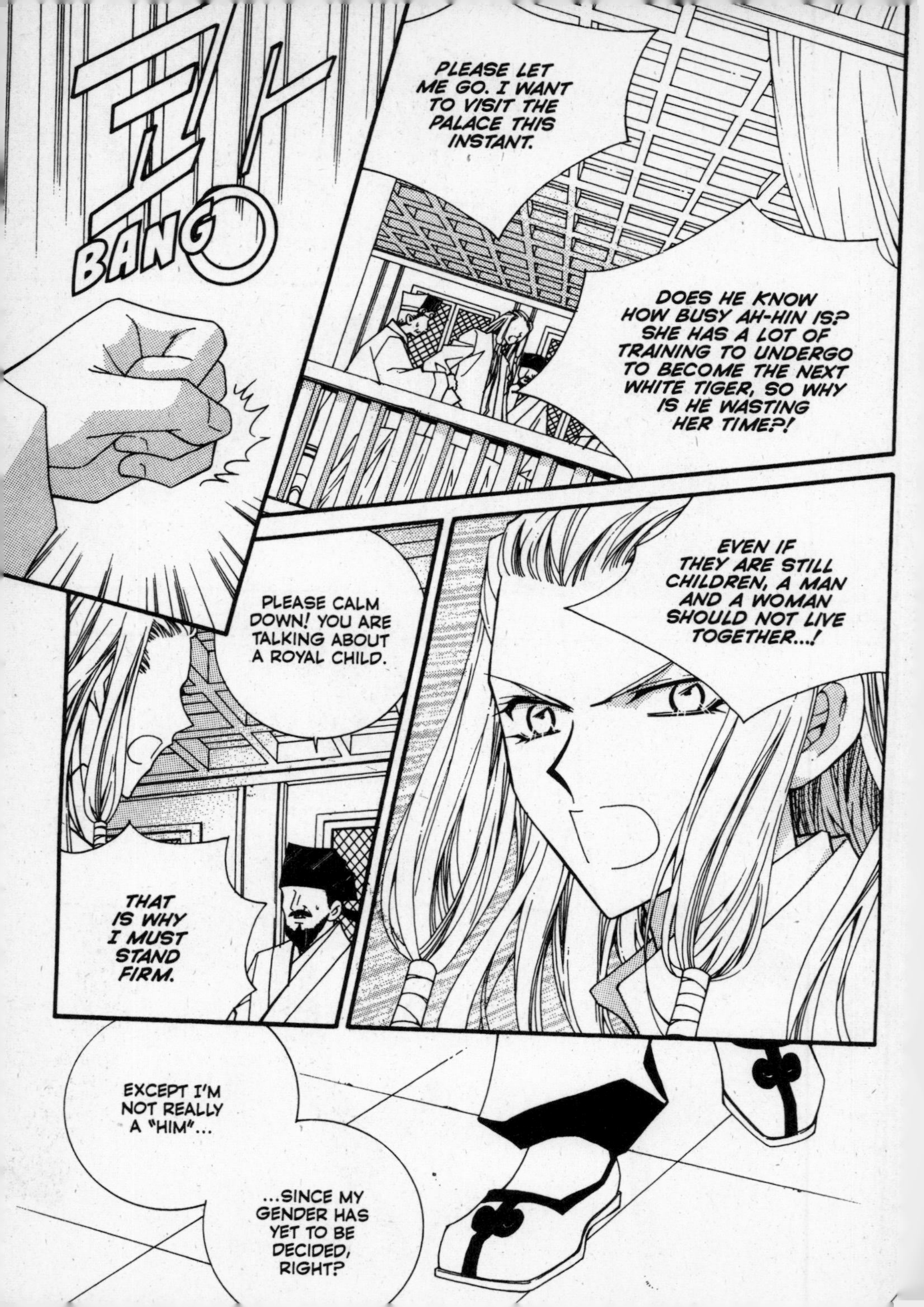
BANG
PLEASE LET ME GO. I WANT TO VISIT THE PALACE THIS INSTANT.
DOES HE KNOW HOW BUSY AH-HIN IS? SHE HAS A LOT OF TRAINING TO UNDERGO TO BECOME THE NEXT WHITE TIGER, SO WHY IS HE WASTING HER TIME?!
PLEASE CALM DOWN! YOU ARE TALKING ABOUT A ROYAL CHILD.
THAT IS WHY I MUST STAND FIRM.
EVEN IF THEY ARE STILL CHILDREN, A MAN AND A WOMAN SHOULD NOT LIVE TOGETHER...!
EXCEPT I'M NOT REALLY A "HIM"...
...SINCE MY GENDER HAS YET TO BE DECIDED, RIGHT?

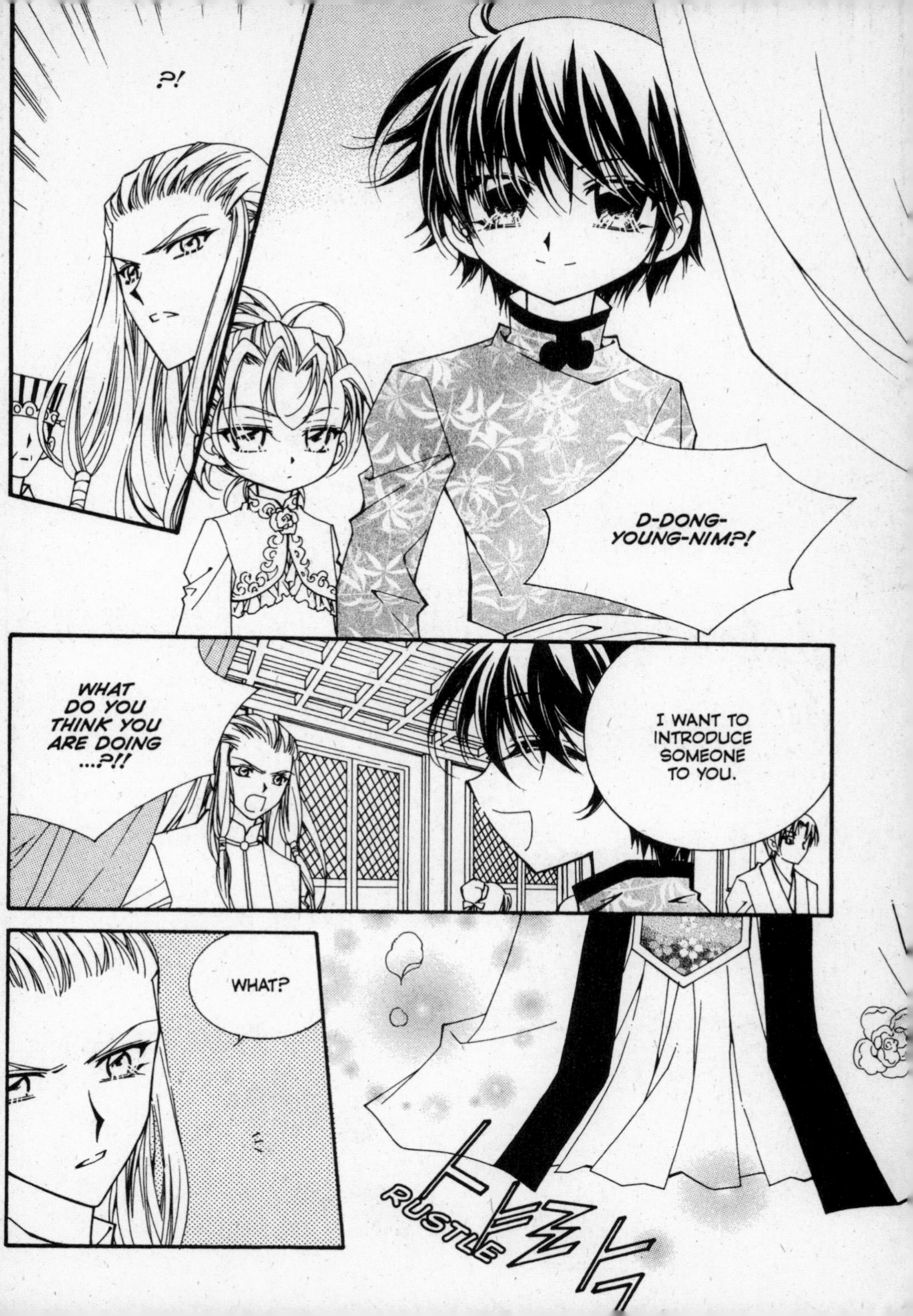
?!
D-DONG-YOUNG-NIM?!
WHAT DO YOU THINK YOU ARE DOING ...?!!
I WANT TO INTRODUCE SOMEONE TO YOU.
WHAT?
RUSTLE

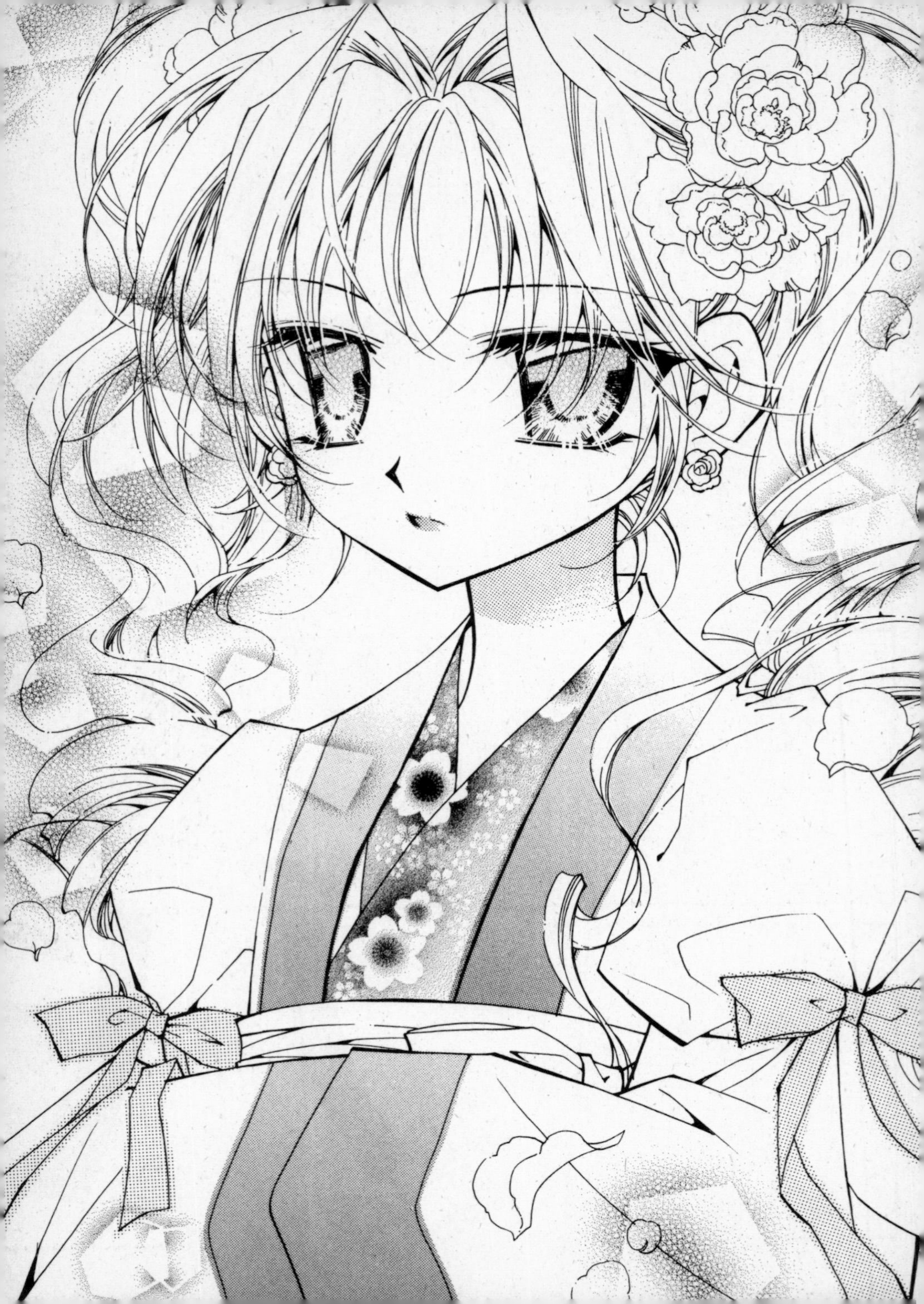

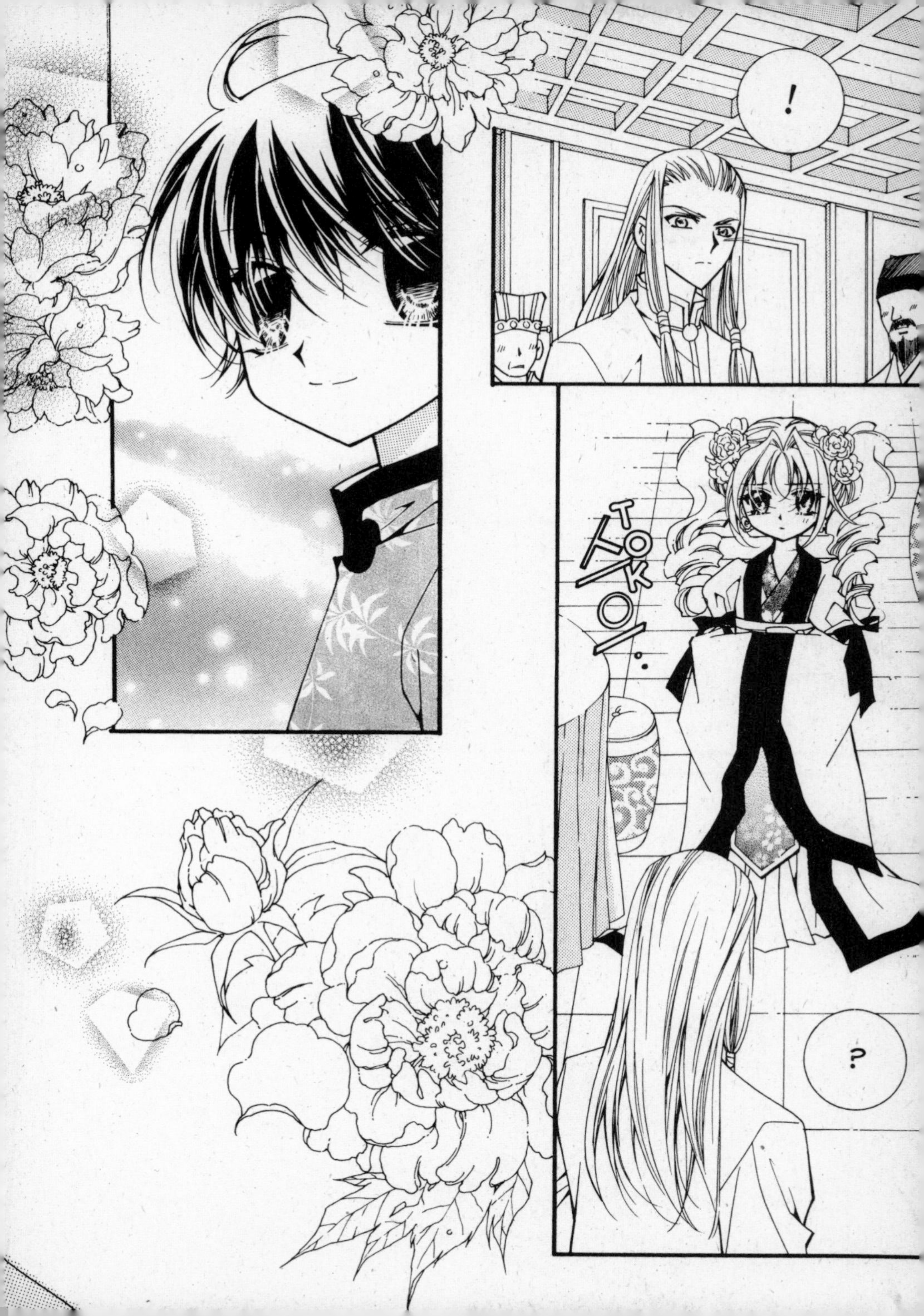
!
TOKO TOKO...
?

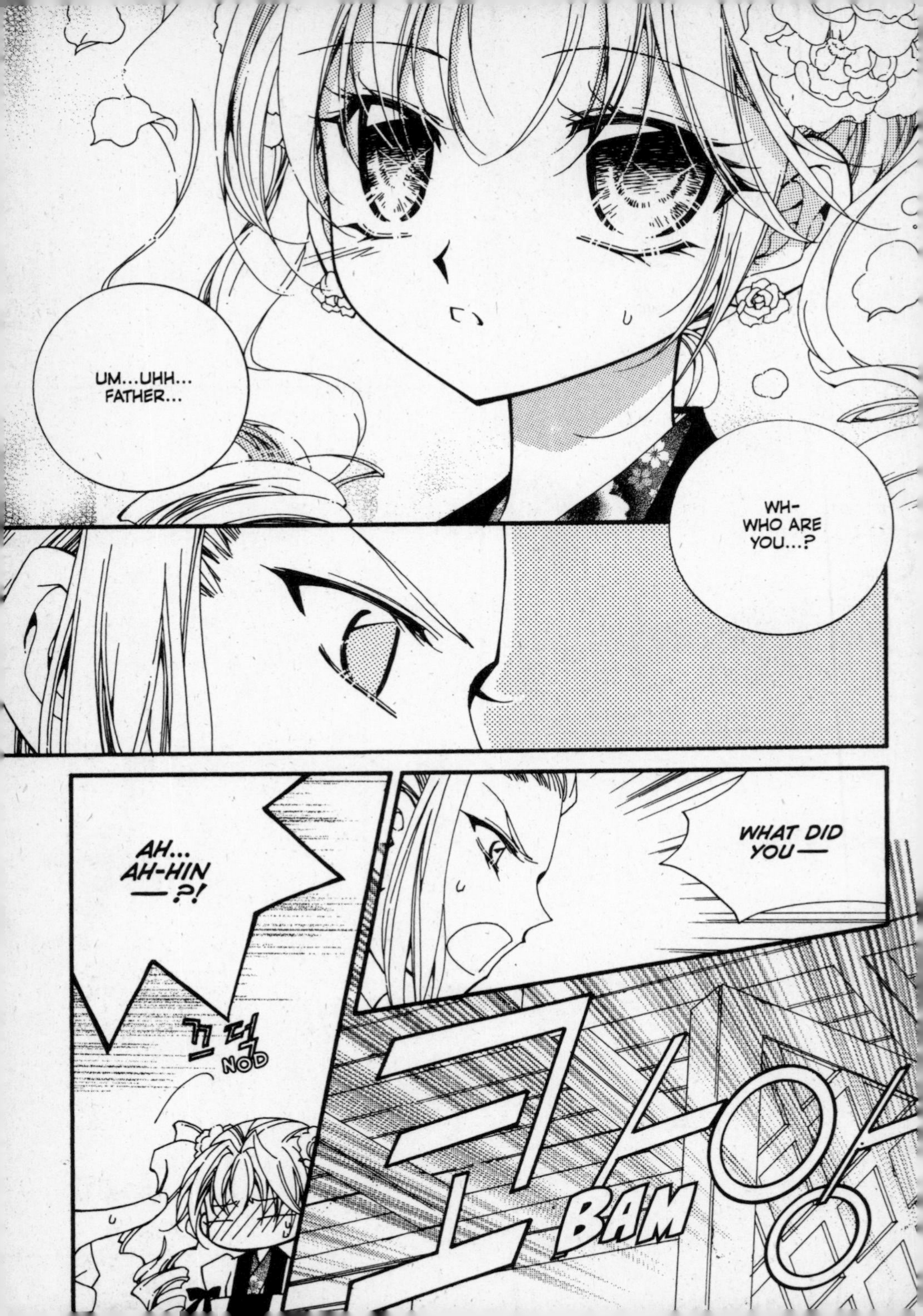
UM...UHH... FATHER...
WH- WHO ARE YOU...?
AH... AH-HIN —?!
WHAT DID YOU—
끄덕
NOD
BAM

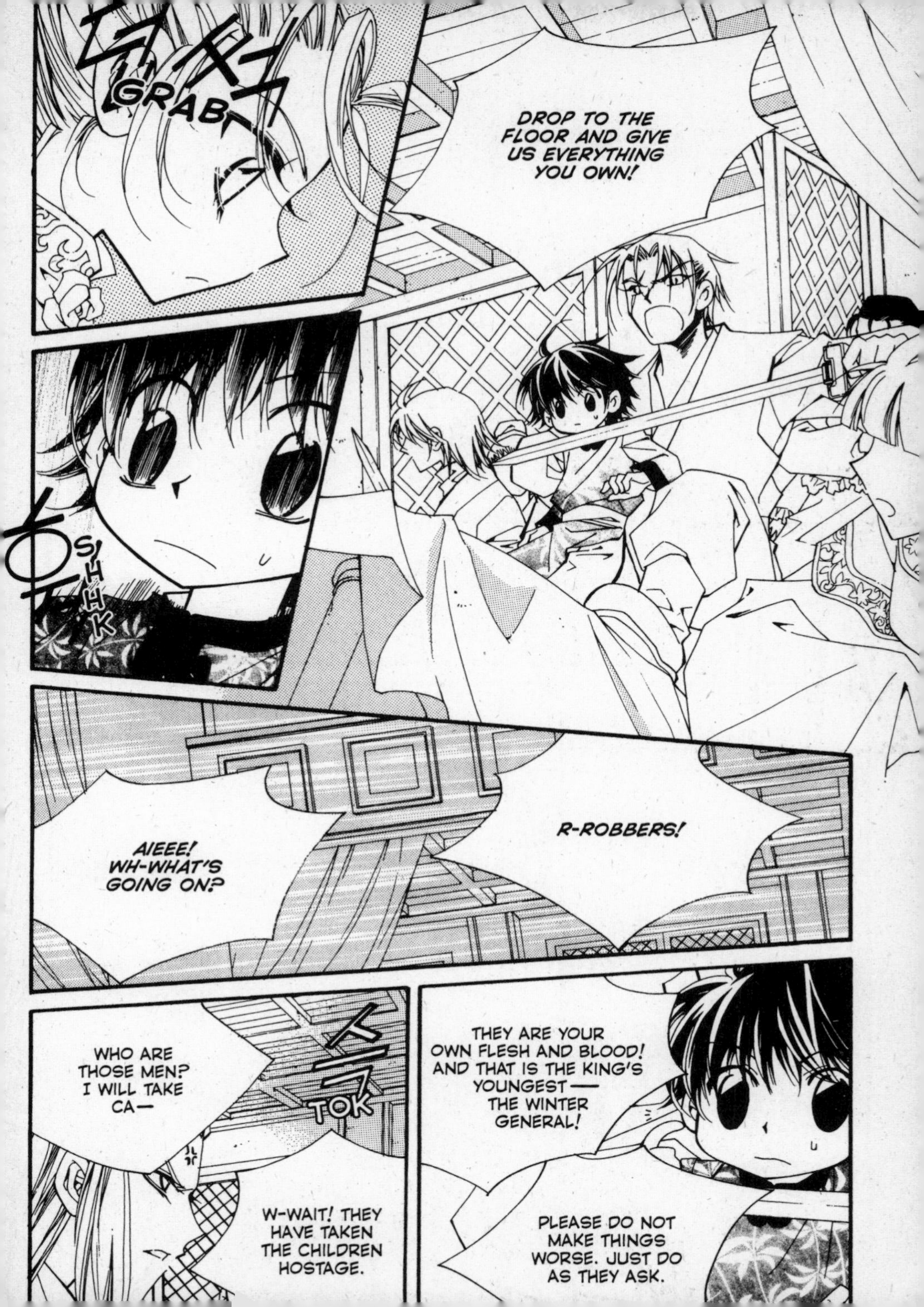
GRAB
DROP TO THE FLOOR AND GIVE US EVERYTHING YOU OWN!
SHHK
AIEEE! WH-WHAT'S GOING ON?
R-ROBBERS!
WHO ARE THOSE MEN? I WILL TAKE CA—
TOK
W-WAIT! THEY HAVE TAKEN THE CHILDREN HOSTAGE.
THEY ARE YOUR OWN FLESH AND BLOOD! AND THAT IS THE KING'S YOUNGEST— THE WINTER GENERAL!
PLEASE DO NOT MAKE THINGS WORSE. JUST DO AS THEY ASK.

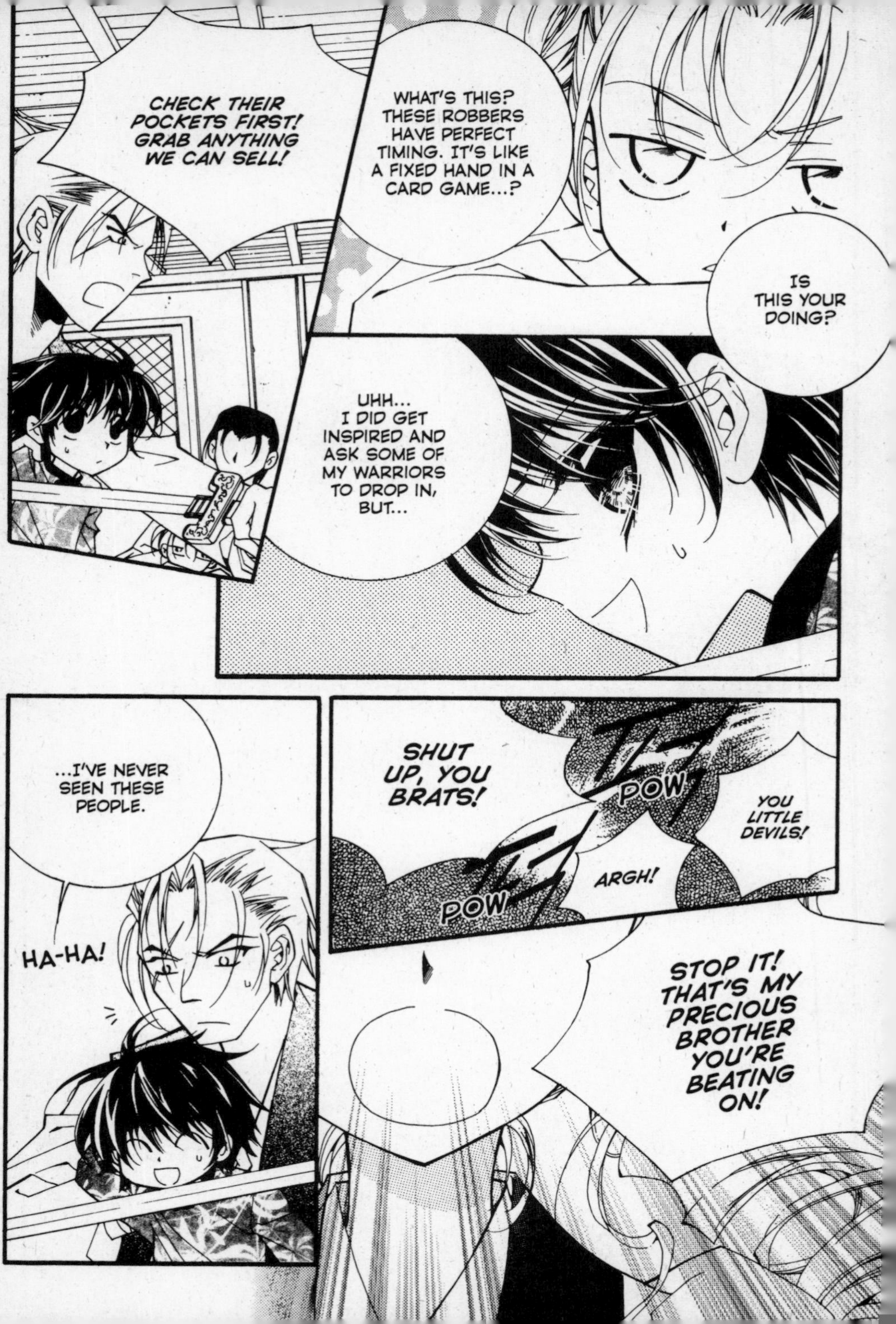
WHAT'S THIS? THESE ROBBERS HAVE PERFECT TIMING. IT'S LIKE A FIXED HAND IN A CARD GAME...?
IS THIS YOUR DOING?
CHECK THEIR POCKETS FIRST! GRAB ANYTHING WE CAN SELL!
UHH... I DID GET INSPIRED AND ASK SOME OF MY WARRIORS TO DROP IN, BUT...
YOU LITTLE DEVILS!
SHUT UP, YOU BRATS!
POW
POW
ARGH!
STOP IT! THAT'S MY PRECIOUS BROTHER YOU'RE BEATING ON!
...I'VE NEVER SEEN THESE PEOPLE.
HA-HA!

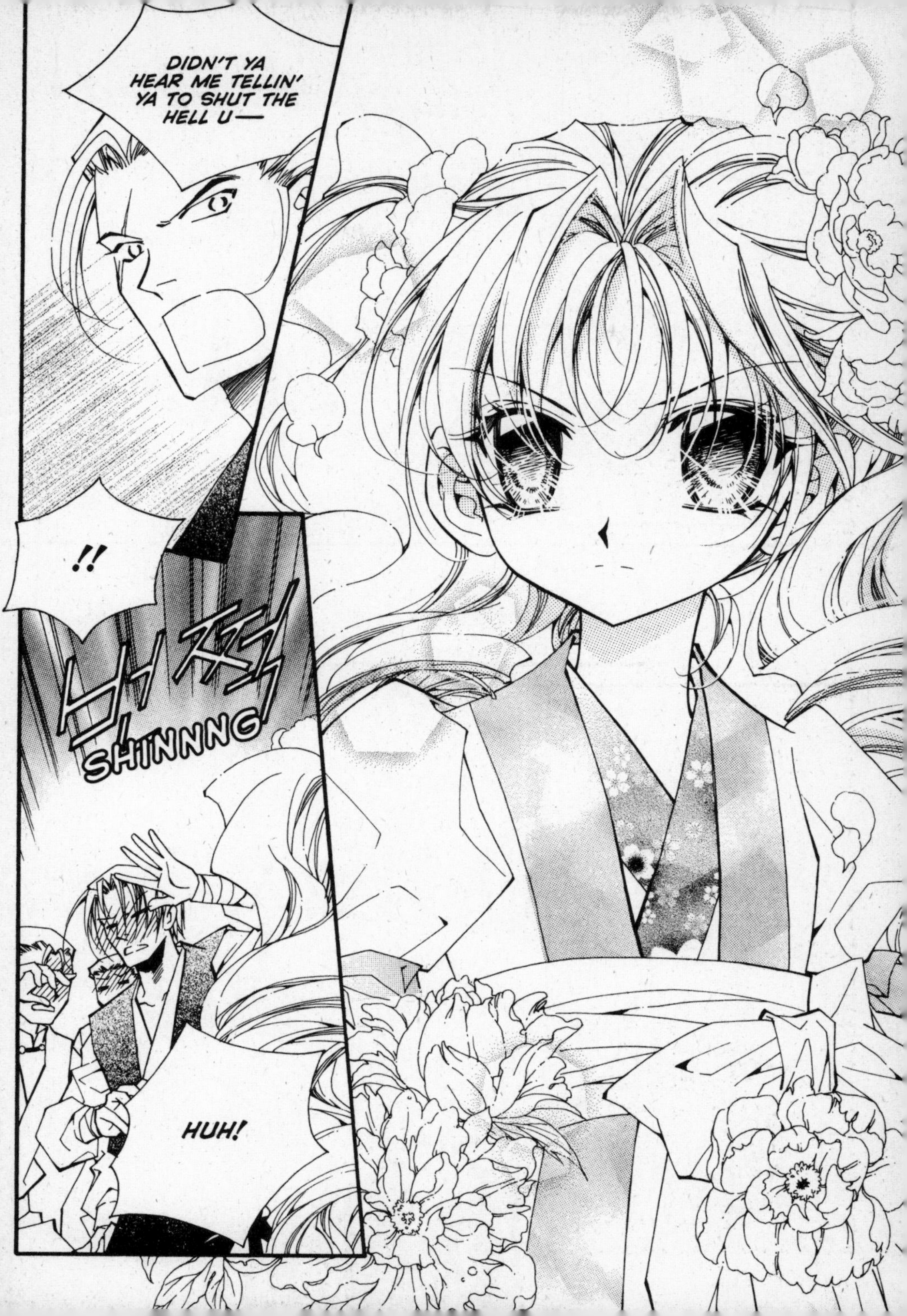
DIDN'T YA HEAR ME TELLIN' YA TO SHUT THE HELL U—
!!
번쩍
SHINNNG
HUH!

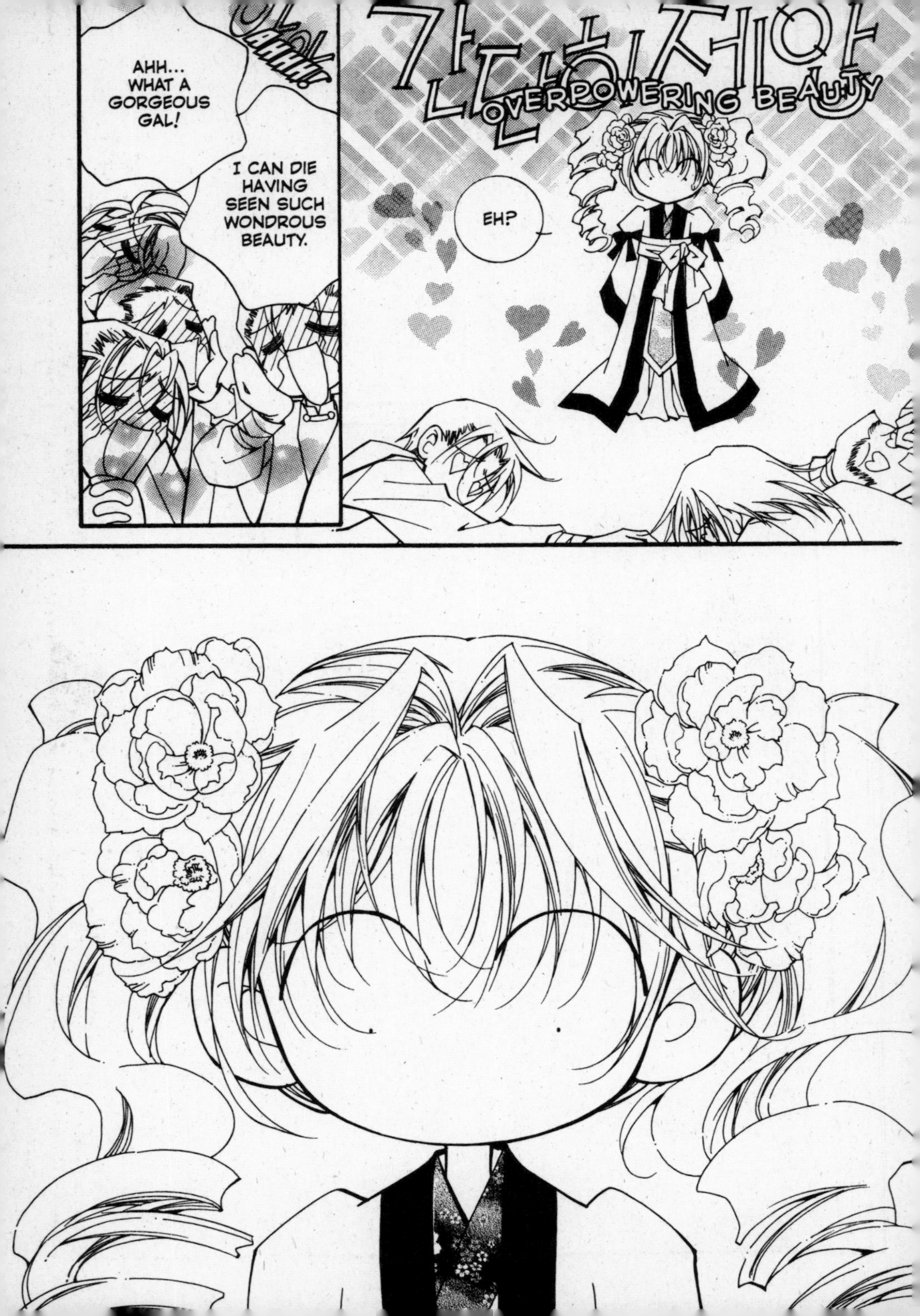
UAHHH!
AHH... WHAT A GORGEOUS GAL!
I CAN DIE HAVING SEEN SUCH WONDROUS BEAUTY.
OVERPOWERING BEAUTY
EH?

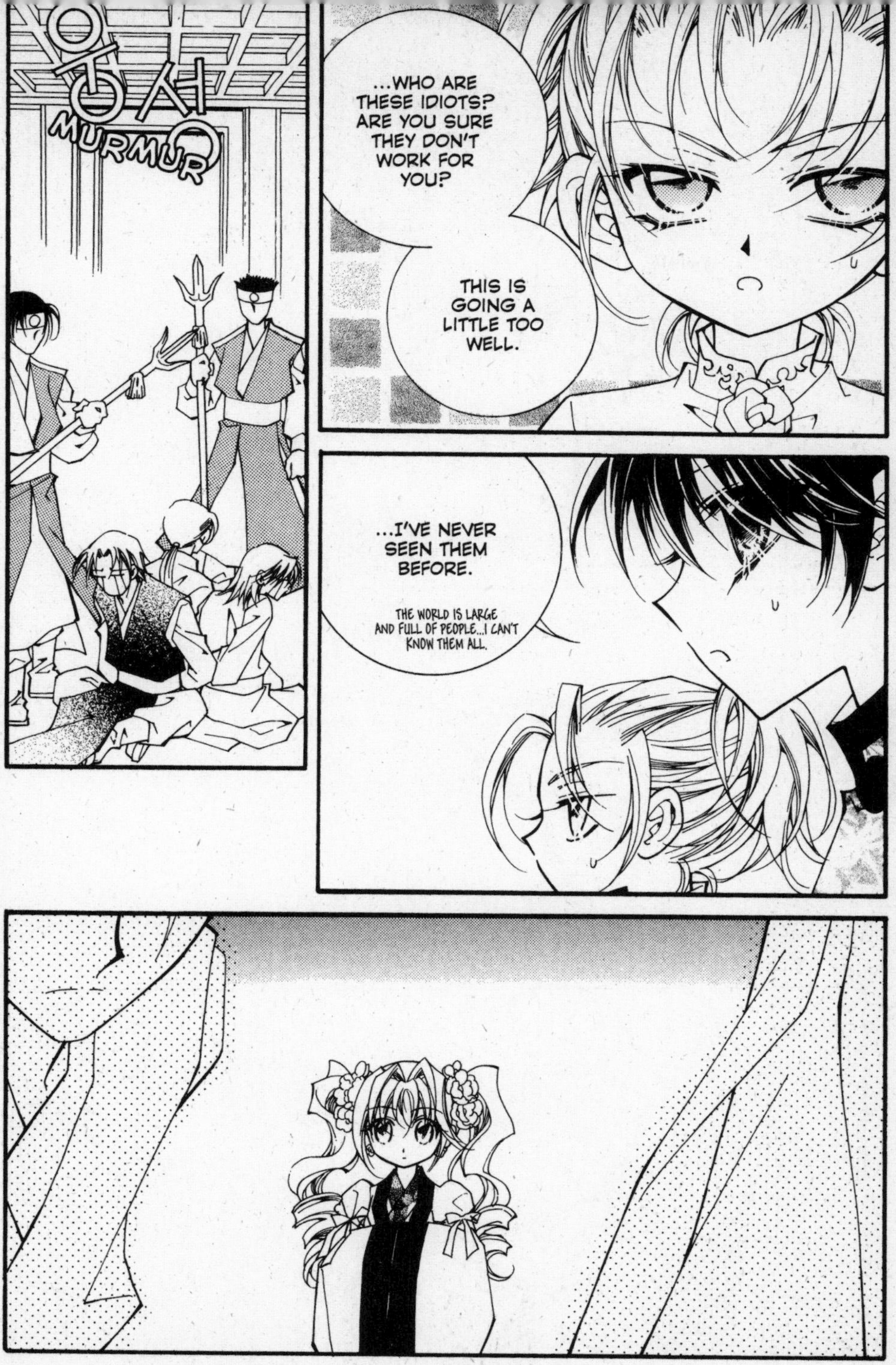

웅성
MURMUR
...WHO ARE THESE IDIOTS? ARE YOU SURE THEY DON'T WORK FOR YOU?
THIS IS GOING A LITTLE TOO WELL.
...I'VE NEVER SEEN THEM BEFORE.
THE WORLD IS LARGE AND FULL OF PEOPLE...I CAN'T KNOW THEM ALL.

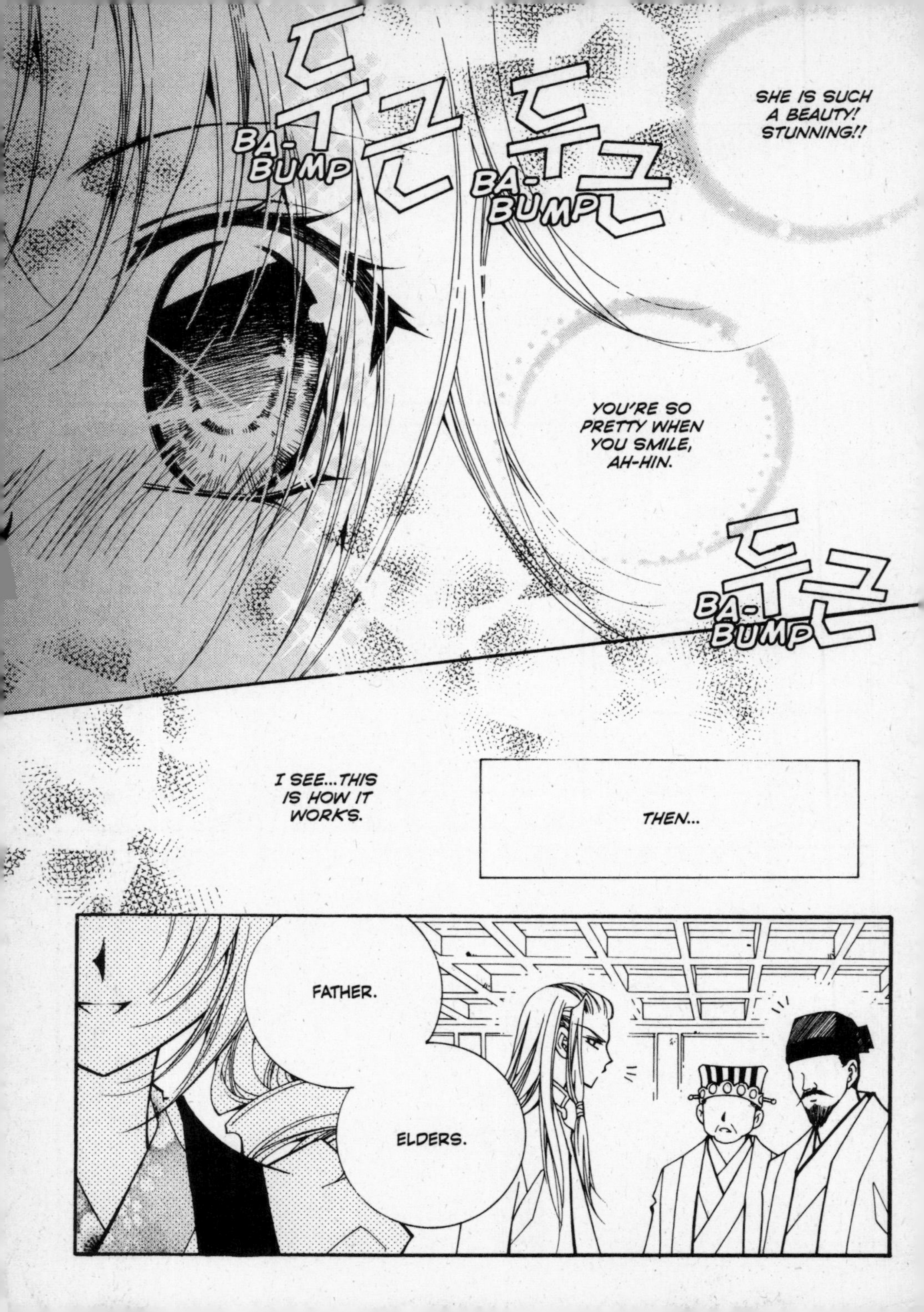

BA-BUMP
BA-BUMP
SHE IS SUCH A BEAUTY! STUNNING!!
YOU'RE SO PRETTY WHEN YOU SMILE, AH-HIN.
BA-BUMP
I SEE...THIS IS HOW IT WORKS.
THEN...
FATHER.
ELDERS.

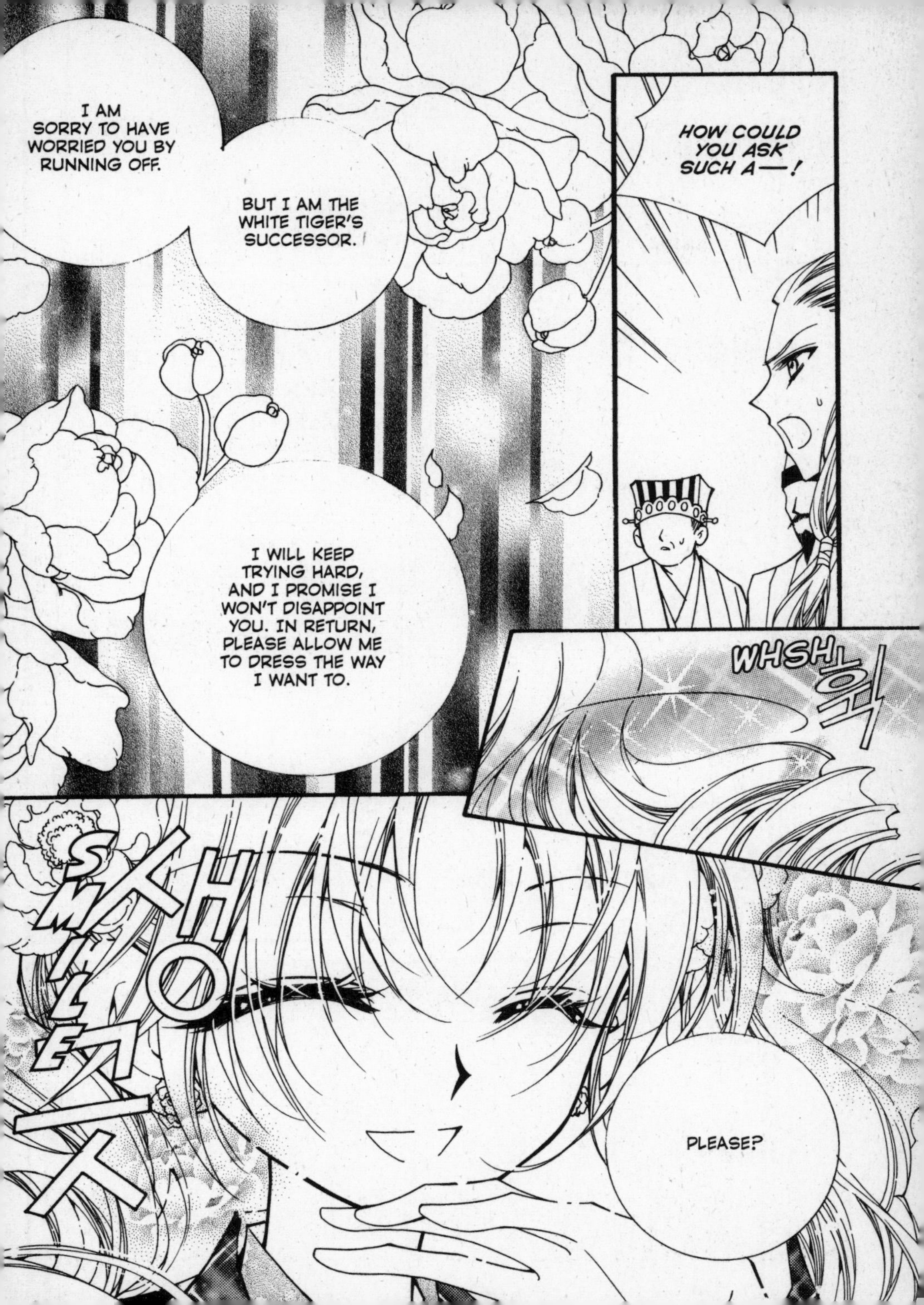
I AM SORRY TO HAVE WORRIED YOU BY RUNNING OFF.
BUT I AM THE WHITE TIGER'S SUCCESSOR.
I WILL KEEP TRYING HARD, AND I PROMISE I WON'T DISAPPOINT YOU. IN RETURN, PLEASE ALLOW ME TO DRESS THE WAY I WANT TO.
HOW COULD YOU ASK SUCH A—!
WHSH
SMILE
PLEASE?

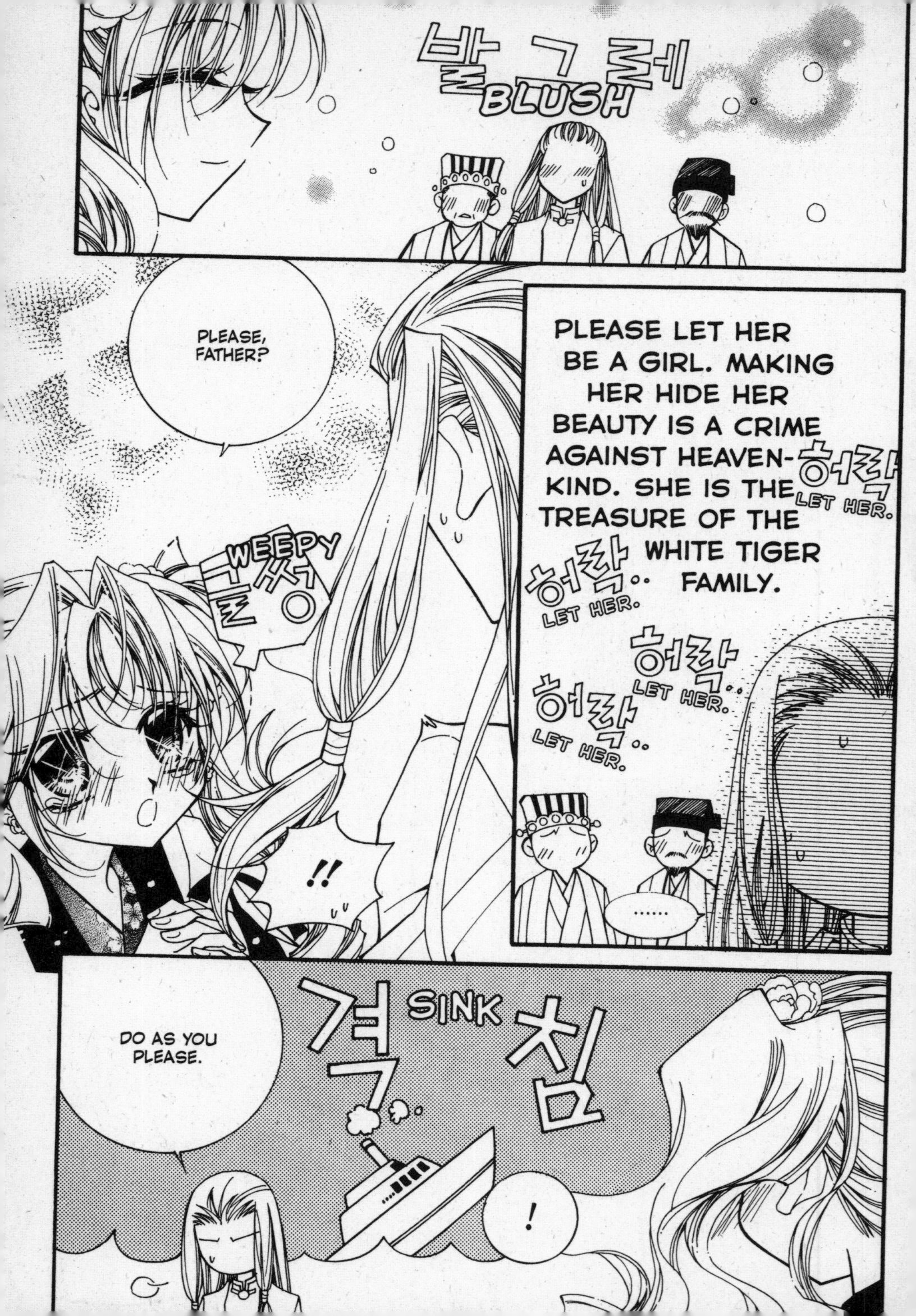

발그레
BLUSH
PLEASE, FATHER?
글썽
WEEPY
!!
PLEASE LET HER BE A GIRL. MAKING HER HIDE HER BEAUTY IS A CRIME AGAINST HEAVEN-KIND. SHE IS THE TREASURE OF THE WHITE TIGER FAMILY.
허락
LET HER.
허락..
LET HER.
허락..
LET HER.
허락..
LET HER.
......
DO AS YOU PLEASE.
격침
SINK
!

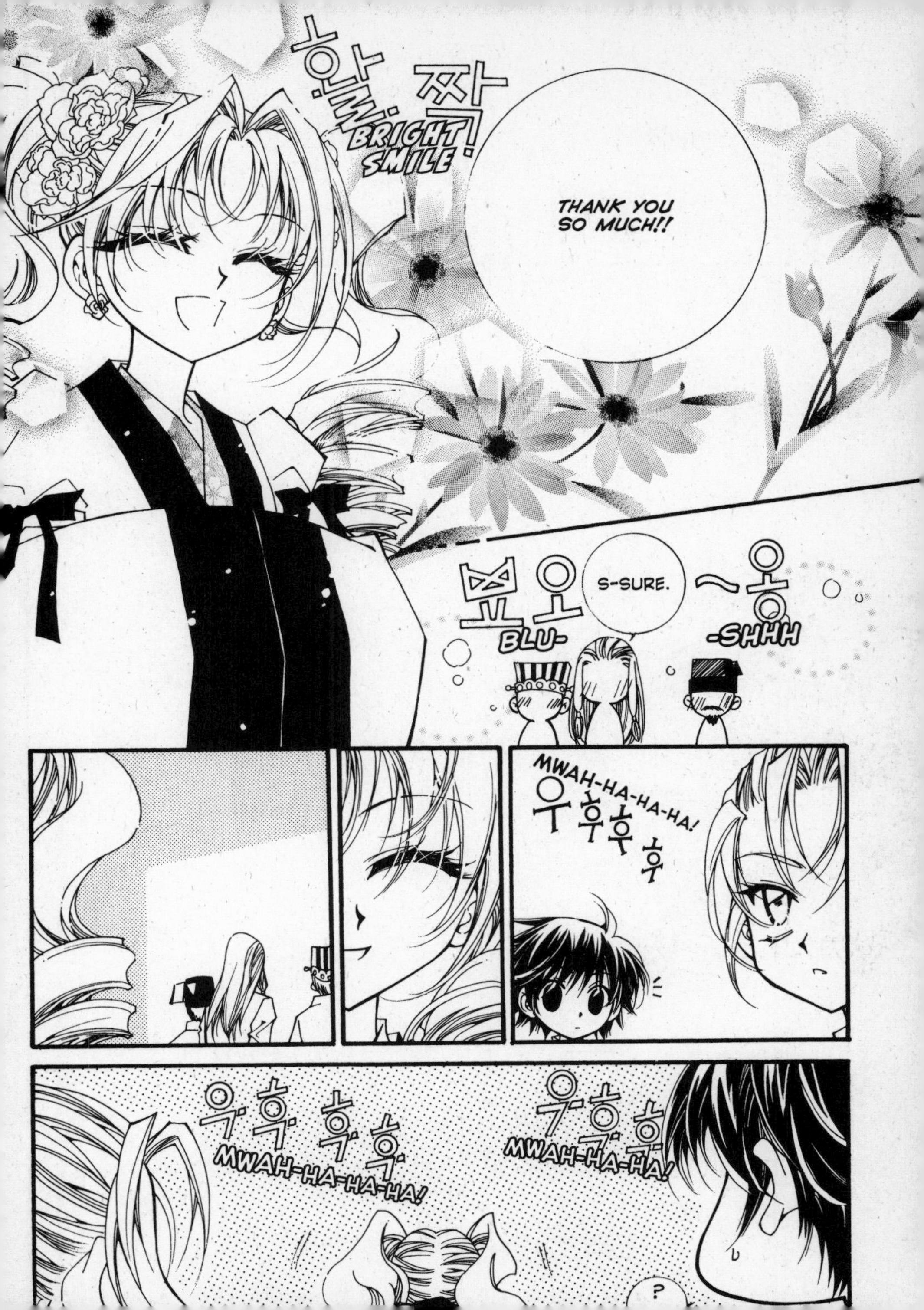
활짝
BRIGHT SMILE
THANK YOU SO MUCH!!
뽀오~옹
BLU- -SHHH
S-SURE.
우후후 후
MWAH-HA-HA-HA!
우후 후후
MWAH-HA-HA-HA!
우후후
MWAH-HA-HA!
?

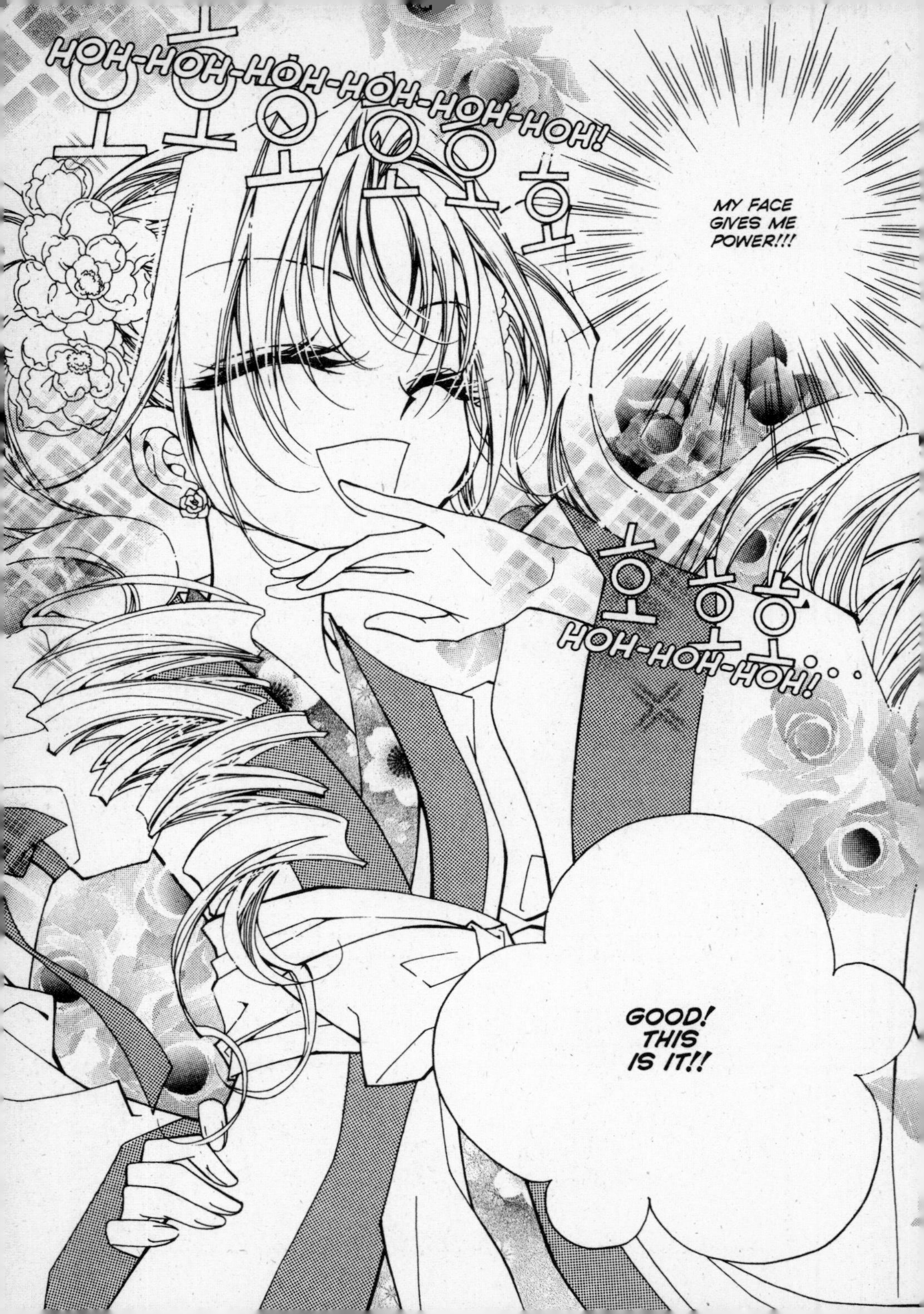

호호호호호호
HOH-HOH-HOH-HOH-HOH-HOH!
MY FACE GIVES ME POWER!!!
호호호
HOH-HOH-HOH!
GOOD! THIS IS IT!!

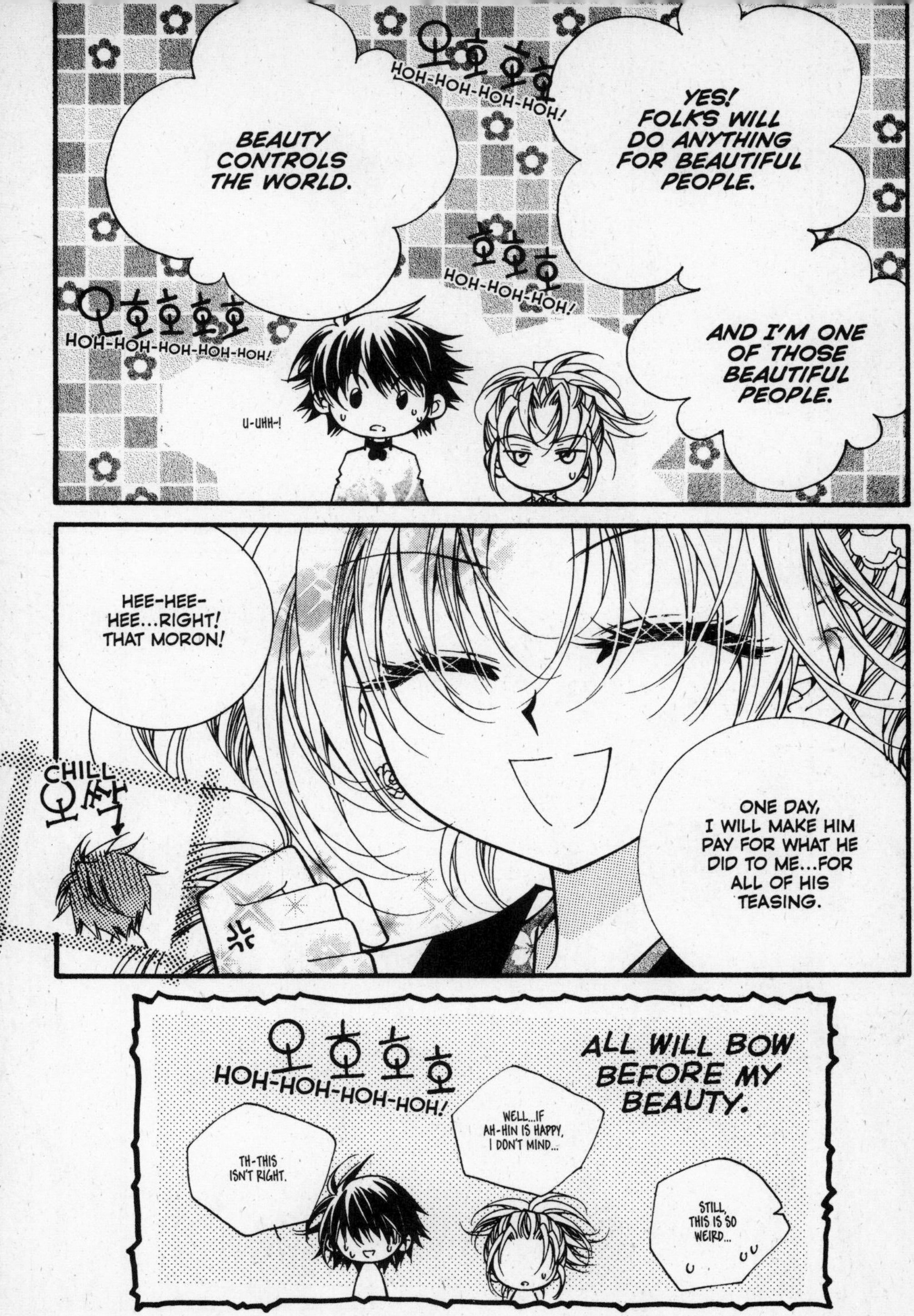
오호호호
HOH-HOH-HOH-HOH!
BEAUTY CONTROLS THE WORLD.
YES! FOLKS WILL DO ANYTHING FOR BEAUTIFUL PEOPLE.
호호호
HOH-HOH-HOH!
오호호호호
HOH-HOH-HOH-HOH-HOH!
U-UHH-!
AND I'M ONE OF THOSE BEAUTIFUL PEOPLE.
HEE-HEE-HEE...RIGHT! THAT MORON!
CHILL
오싹
ONE DAY, I WILL MAKE HIM PAY FOR WHAT HE DID TO ME...FOR ALL OF HIS TEASING.
오호호호
HOH-HOH-HOH-HOH!
ALL WILL BOW BEFORE MY BEAUTY.
TH-THIS ISN'T RIGHT.
WELL...IF AH-HIN IS HAPPY, I DON'T MIND...
STILL, THIS IS SO WEIRD...

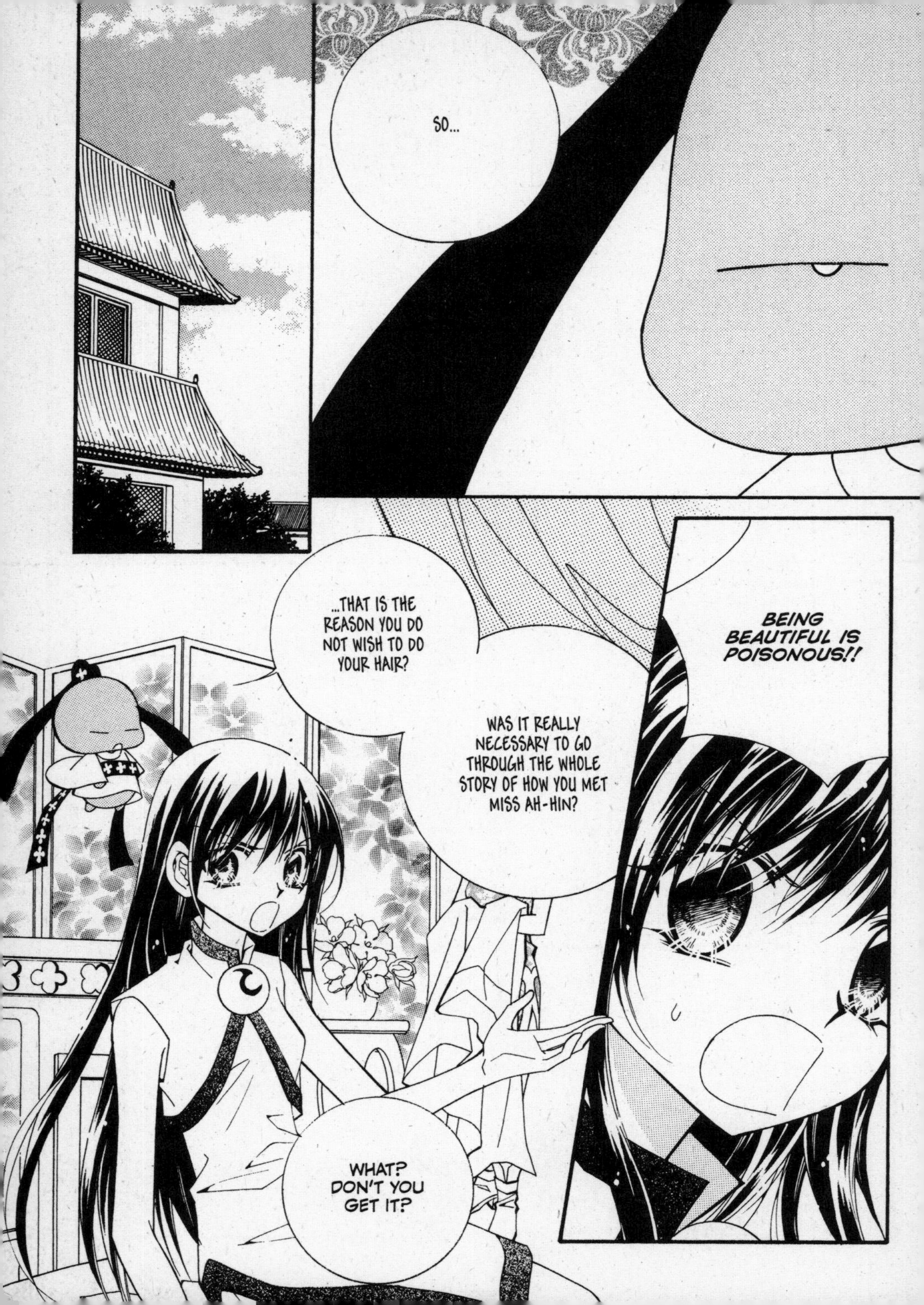
SO...
...THAT IS THE REASON YOU DO NOT WISH TO DO YOUR HAIR?
WAS IT REALLY NECESSARY TO GO THROUGH THE WHOLE STORY OF HOW YOU MET MISS AH-HIN?
WHAT? DON'T YOU GET IT?
BEING BEAUTIFUL IS POISONOUS!!

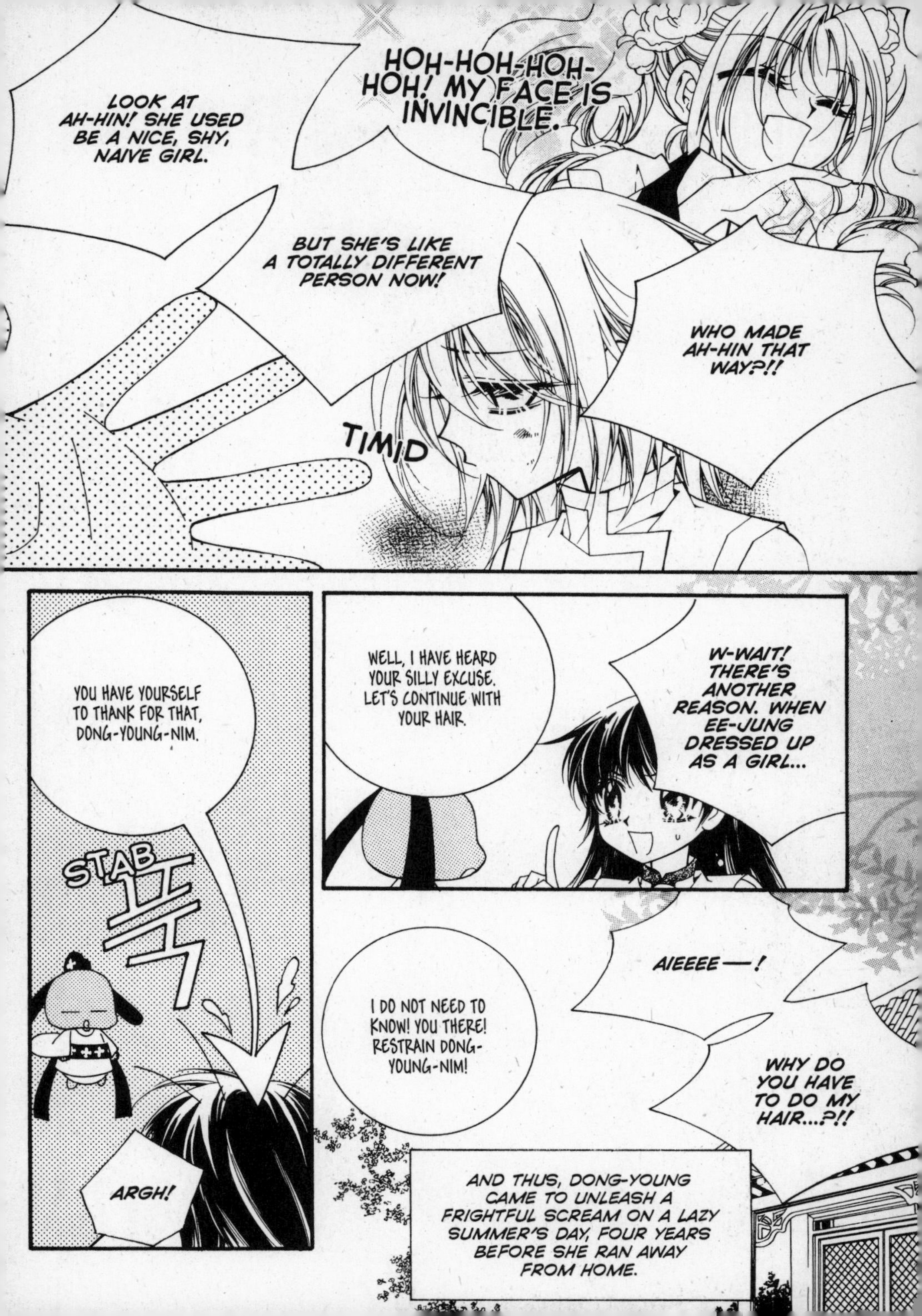
HOH-HOH-HOH-HOH! MY FACE IS INVINCIBLE.
LOOK AT AH-HIN! SHE USED BE A NICE, SHY, NAIVE GIRL.
BUT SHE'S LIKE A TOTALLY DIFFERENT PERSON NOW!
WHO MADE AH-HIN THAT WAY?!!
TIMID
W-WAIT! THERE'S ANOTHER REASON. WHEN EE-JUNG DRESSED UP AS A GIRL...
WELL, I HAVE HEARD YOUR SILLY EXCUSE. LET'S CONTINUE WITH YOUR HAIR.
YOU HAVE YOURSELF TO THANK FOR THAT, DONG-YOUNG-NIM.
STAB
AIEEEE—!
I DO NOT NEED TO KNOW! YOU THERE! RESTRAIN DONG-YOUNG-NIM!
WHY DO YOU HAVE TO DO MY HAIR...?!!
ARGH!
AND THUS, DONG-YOUNG CAME TO UNLEASH A FRIGHTFUL SCREAM ON A LAZY SUMMER'S DAY, FOUR YEARS BEFORE SHE RAN AWAY FROM HOME.

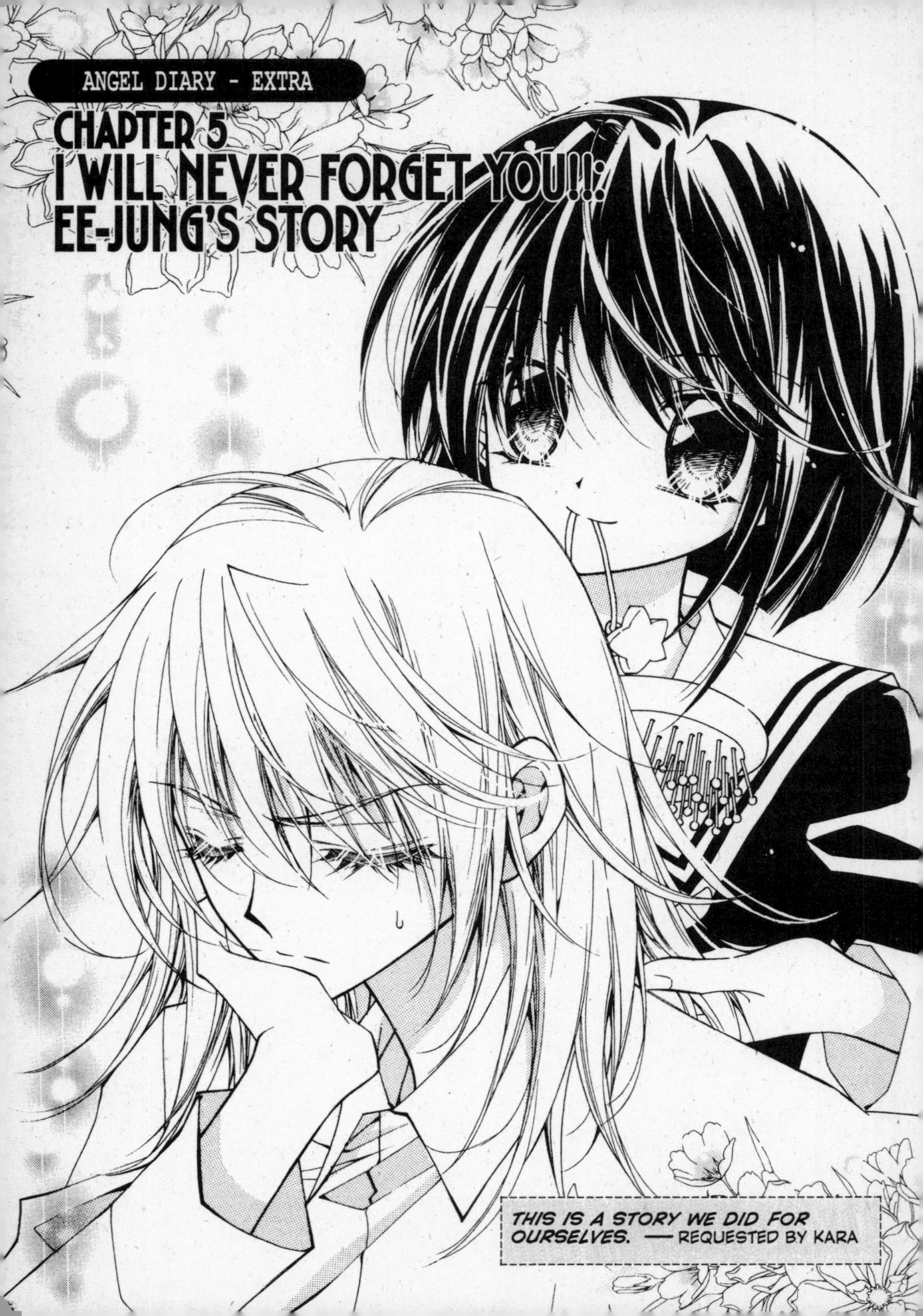
ANGEL DIARY - EXTRA
CHAPTER 5
I WILL NEVER FORGET YOU!!: EE-JUNG'S STORY
THIS IS A STORY WE DID FOR OURSELVES. — REQUESTED BY KARA

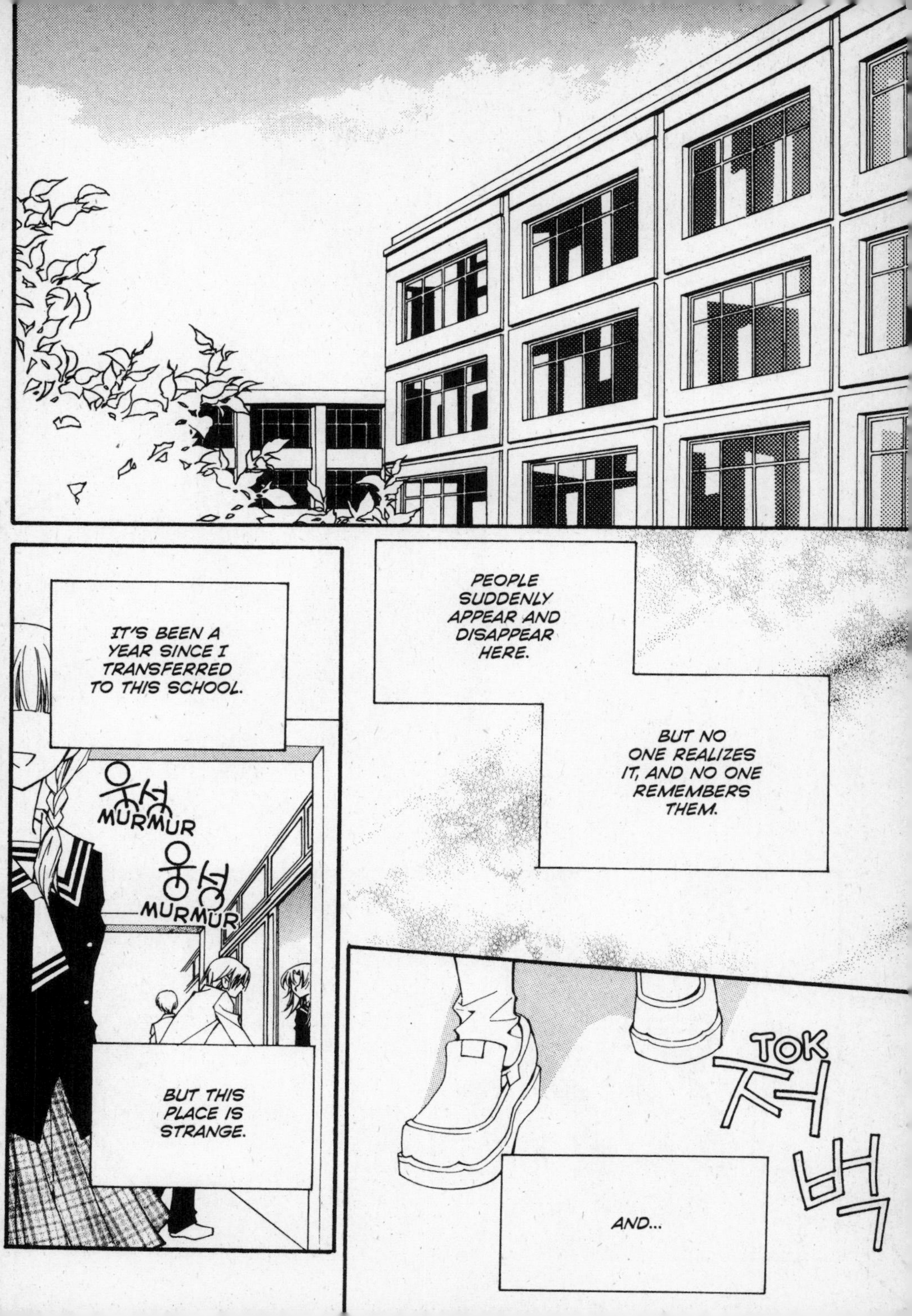
IT'S BEEN A YEAR SINCE I TRANSFERRED TO THIS SCHOOL.
MURMUR
MURMUR
BUT THIS PLACE IS STRANGE.
PEOPLE SUDDENLY APPEAR AND DISAPPEAR HERE.
BUT NO ONE REALIZES IT, AND NO ONE REMEMBERS THEM.
TOK
AND...

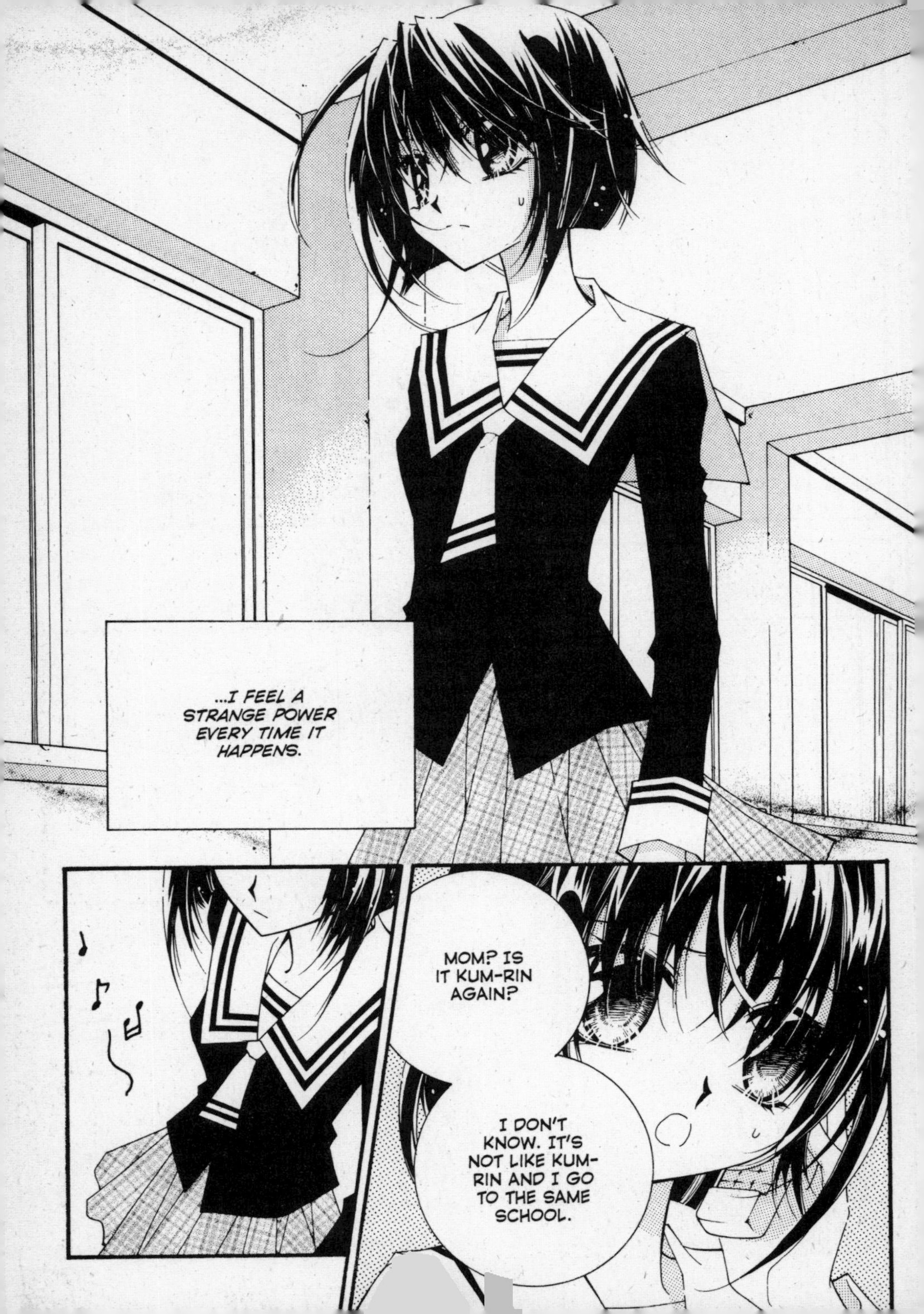
...I FEEL A STRANGE POWER EVERY TIME IT HAPPENS.
MOM? IS IT KUM-RIN AGAIN?
I DON'T KNOW. IT'S NOT LIKE KUM-RIN AND I GO TO THE SAME SCHOOL.

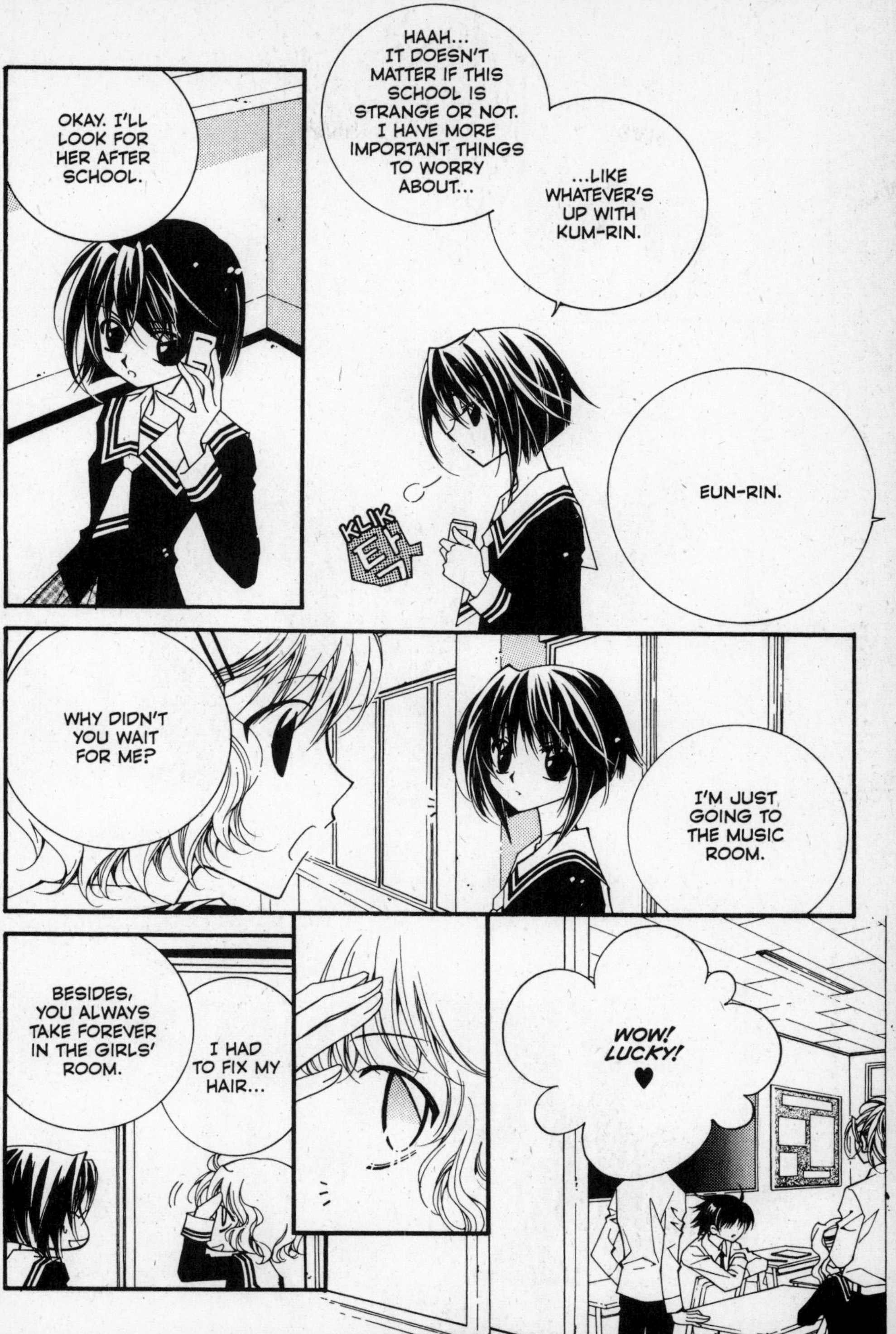
OKAY. I'LL LOOK FOR HER AFTER SCHOOL.
HAAH... IT DOESN'T MATTER IF THIS SCHOOL IS STRANGE OR NOT. I HAVE MORE IMPORTANT THINGS TO WORRY ABOUT...
...LIKE WHATEVER'S UP WITH KUM-RIN.
KLIK
EUN-RIN.
WHY DIDN'T YOU WAIT FOR ME?
I'M JUST GOING TO THE MUSIC ROOM.
BESIDES, YOU ALWAYS TAKE FOREVER IN THE GIRLS' ROOM.
I HAD TO FIX MY HAIR...
WOW! LUCKY! ♥

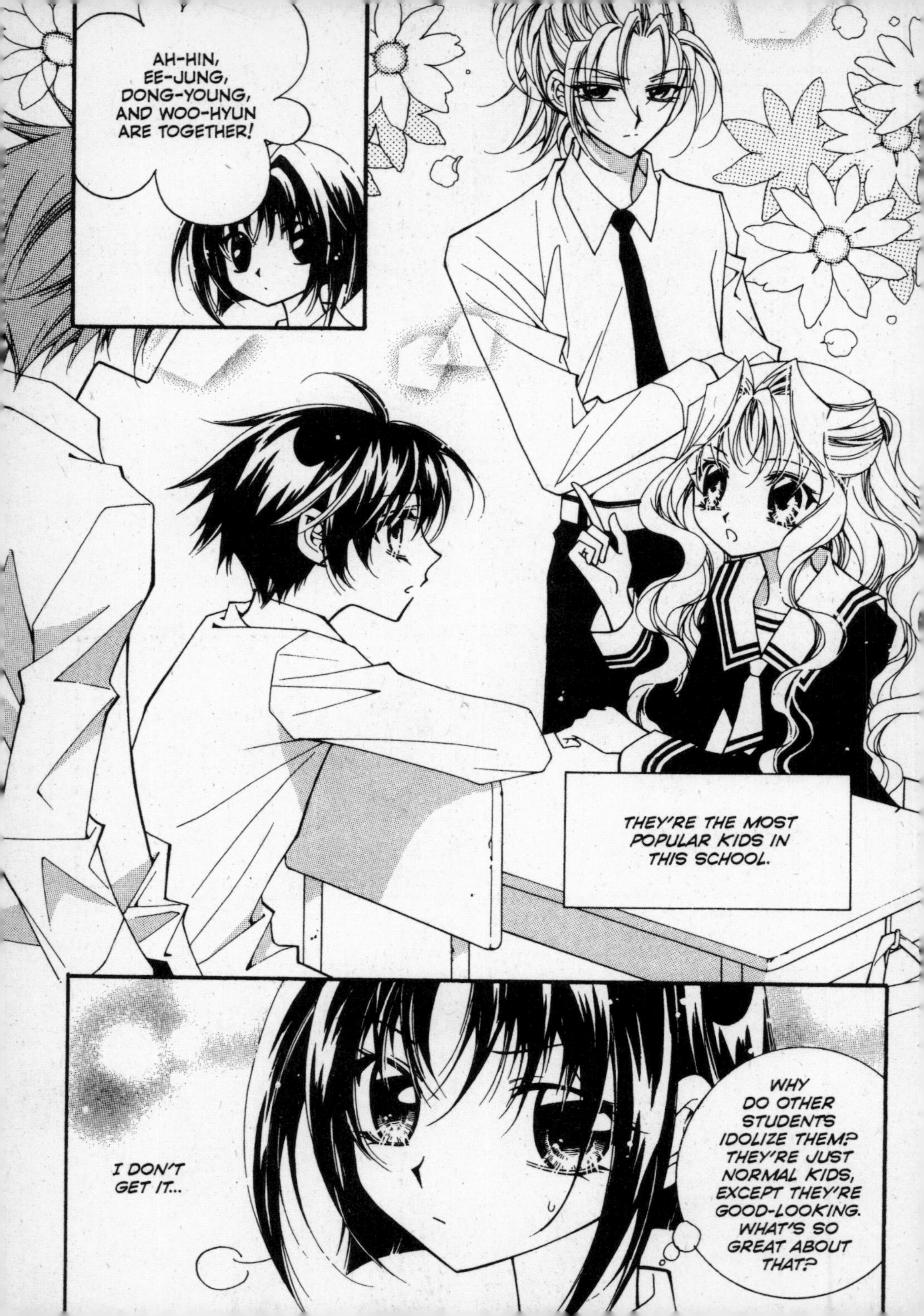
AH-HIN, EE-JUNG, DONG-YOUNG, AND WOO-HYUN ARE TOGETHER!
THEY'RE THE MOST POPULAR KIDS IN THIS SCHOOL.
I DON'T GET IT...
WHY DO OTHER STUDENTS IDOLIZE THEM? THEY'RE JUST NORMAL KIDS, EXCEPT THEY'RE GOOD-LOOKING. WHAT'S SO GREAT ABOUT THAT?

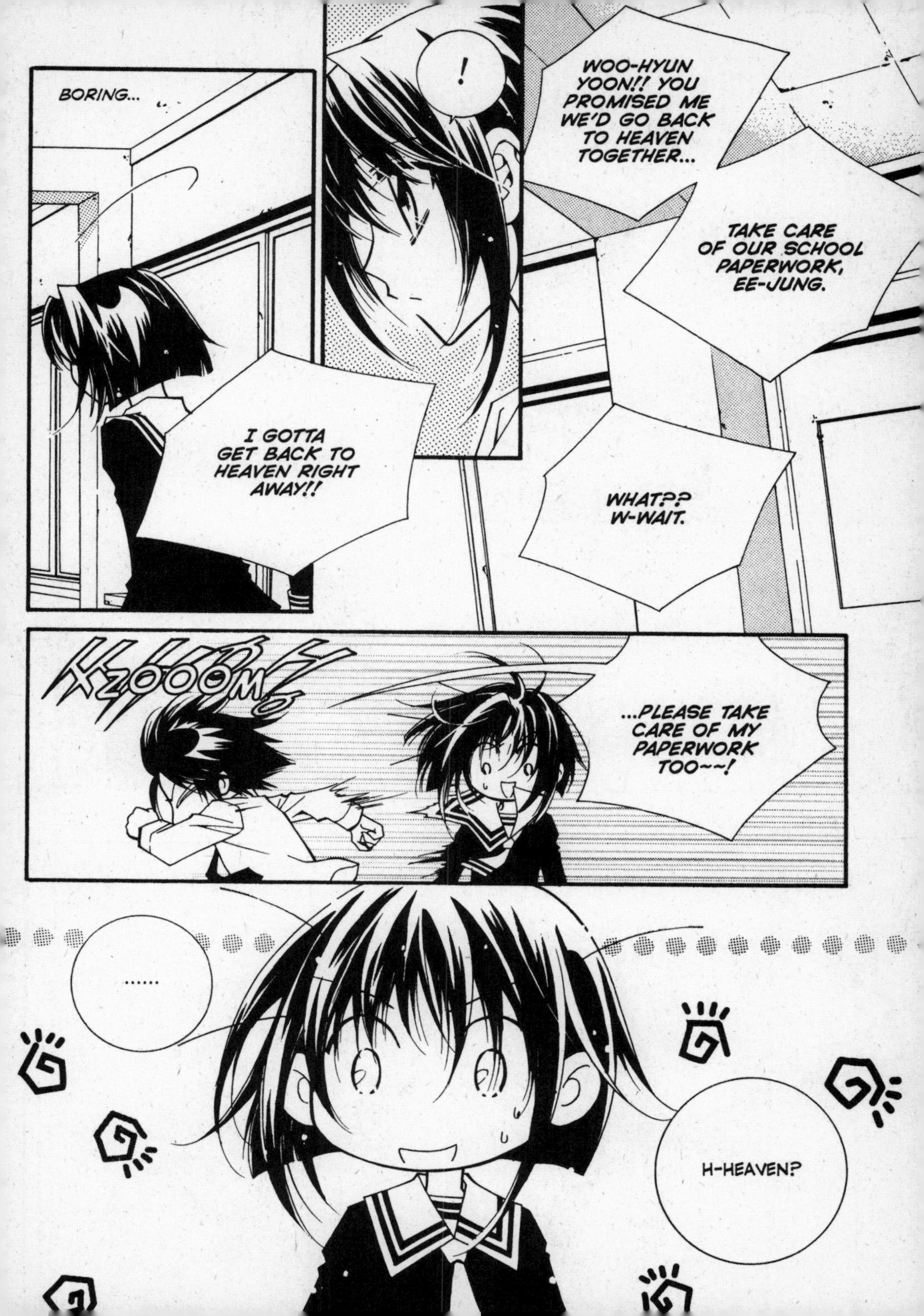
BORING...
I GOTTA GET BACK TO HEAVEN RIGHT AWAY!!
!
WOO-HYUN YOON!! YOU PROMISED ME WE'D GO BACK TO HEAVEN TOGETHER...
TAKE CARE OF OUR SCHOOL PAPERWORK, EE-JUNG.
WHAT?? W-WAIT.
ZOOOM
...PLEASE TAKE CARE OF MY PAPERWORK TOO~~!
......
H-HEAVEN?

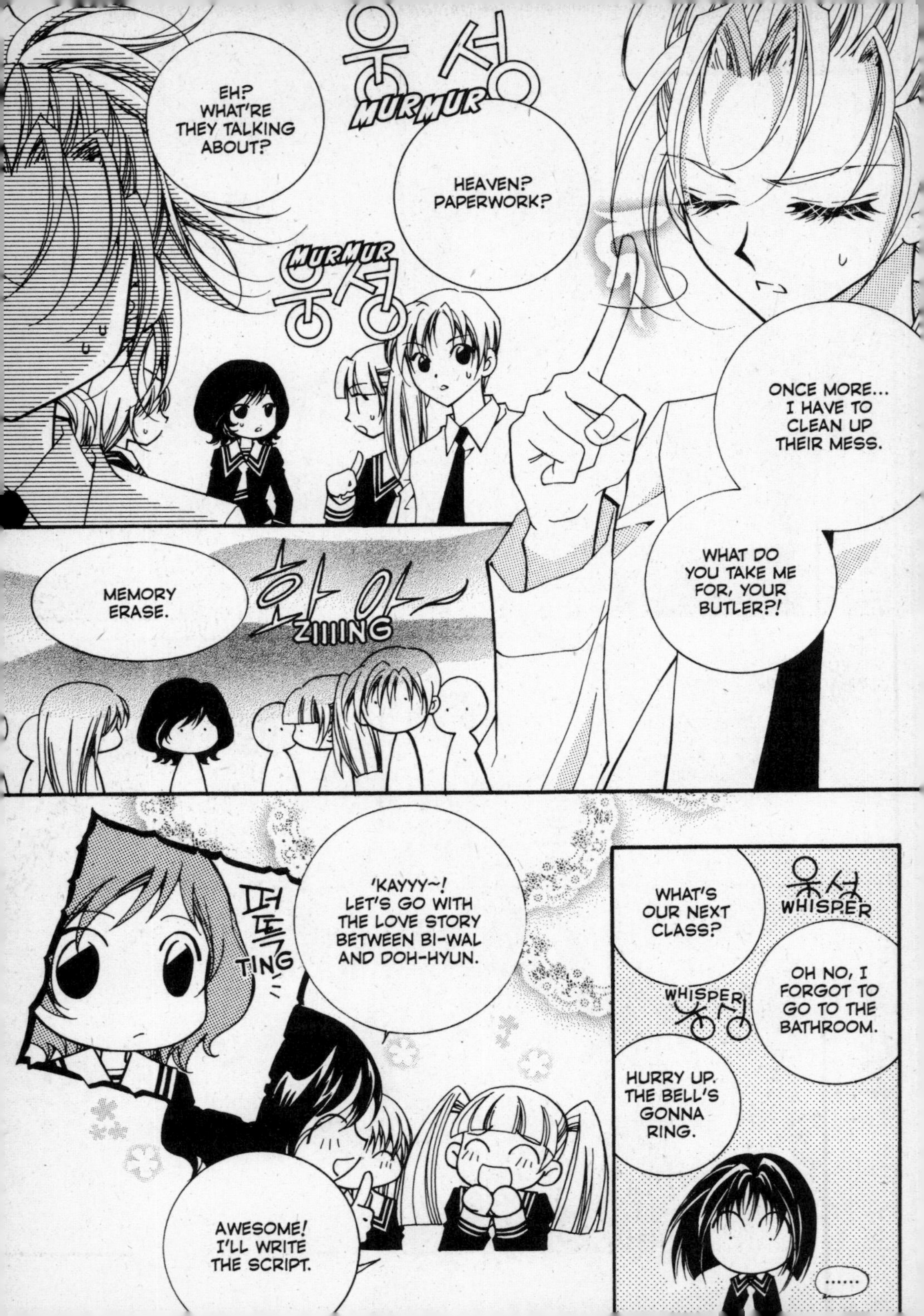
EH? WHAT'RE THEY TALKING ABOUT?
웅성
MURMUR
HEAVEN? PAPERWORK?
MURMUR
웅성
ONCE MORE... I HAVE TO CLEAN UP THEIR MESS.
MEMORY ERASE.
화아~
ZIIIING
WHAT DO YOU TAKE ME FOR, YOUR BUTLER?!
TING
'KAYYY~! LET'S GO WITH THE LOVE STORY BETWEEN BI-WAL AND DOH-HYUN.
AWESOME! I'LL WRITE THE SCRIPT.
WHAT'S OUR NEXT CLASS?
WHISPER
OH NO, I FORGOT TO GO TO THE BATHROOM.
WHISPER
HURRY UP. THE BELL'S GONNA RING.
......

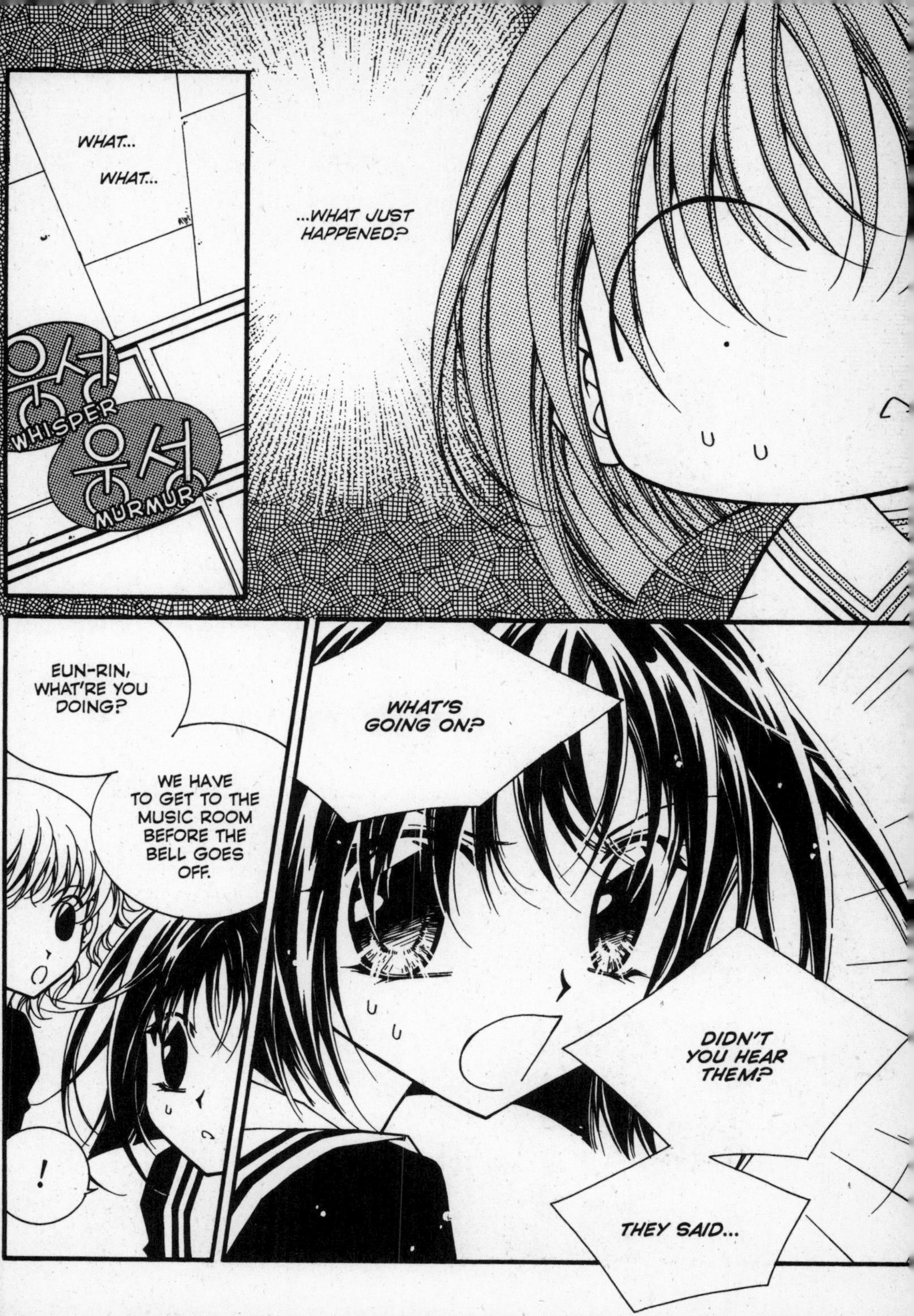
WHAT...
WHAT...
WHISPER
MURMUR
...WHAT JUST HAPPENED?
EUN-RIN, WHAT'RE YOU DOING?
WE HAVE TO GET TO THE MUSIC ROOM BEFORE THE BELL GOES OFF.
WHAT'S GOING ON?
!
DIDN'T YOU HEAR THEM?
THEY SAID...

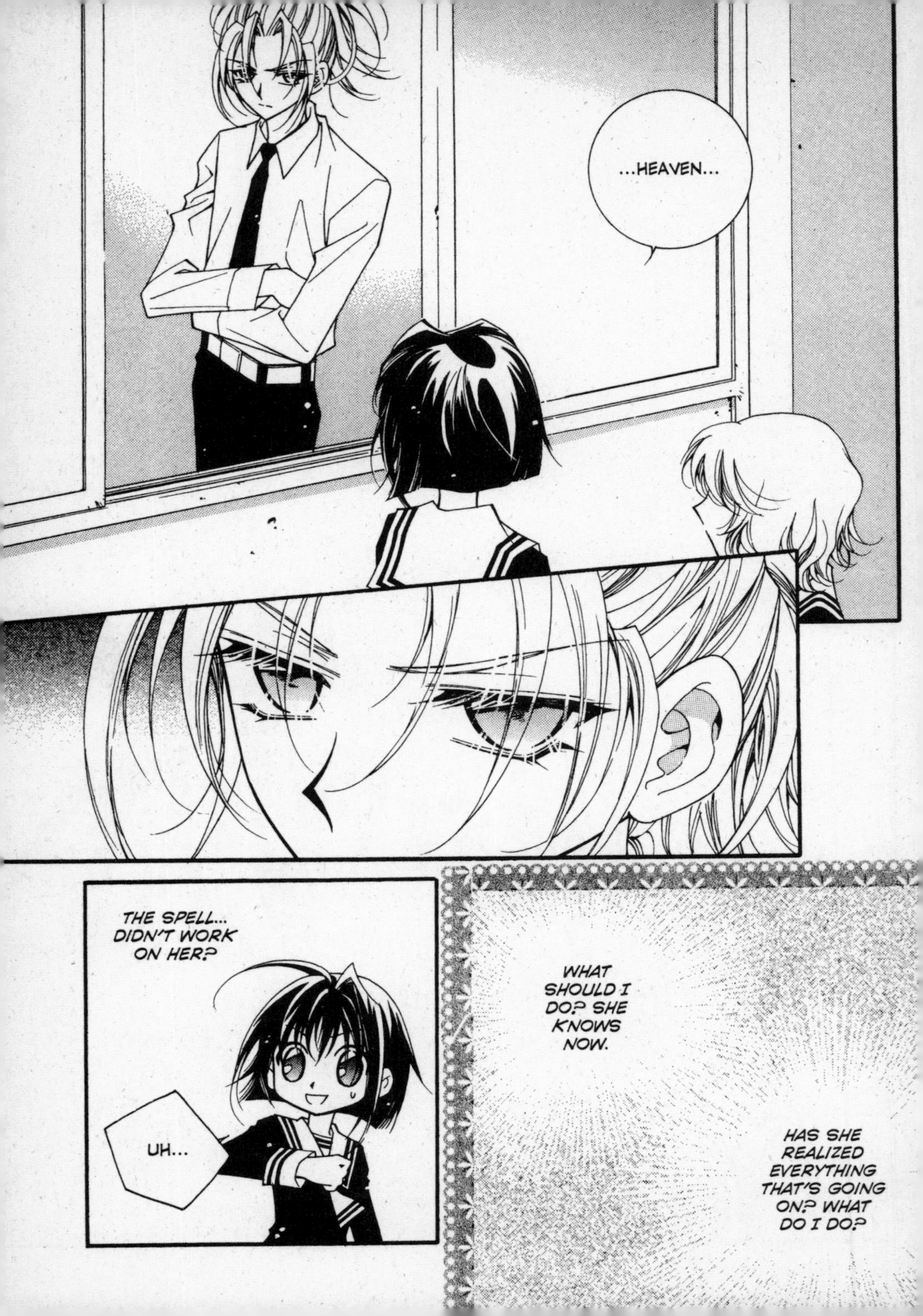
...HEAVEN...
THE SPELL... DIDN'T WORK ON HER?
UH...
WHAT SHOULD I DO? SHE KNOWS NOW.
HAS SHE REALIZED EVERYTHING THAT'S GOING ON? WHAT DO I DO?

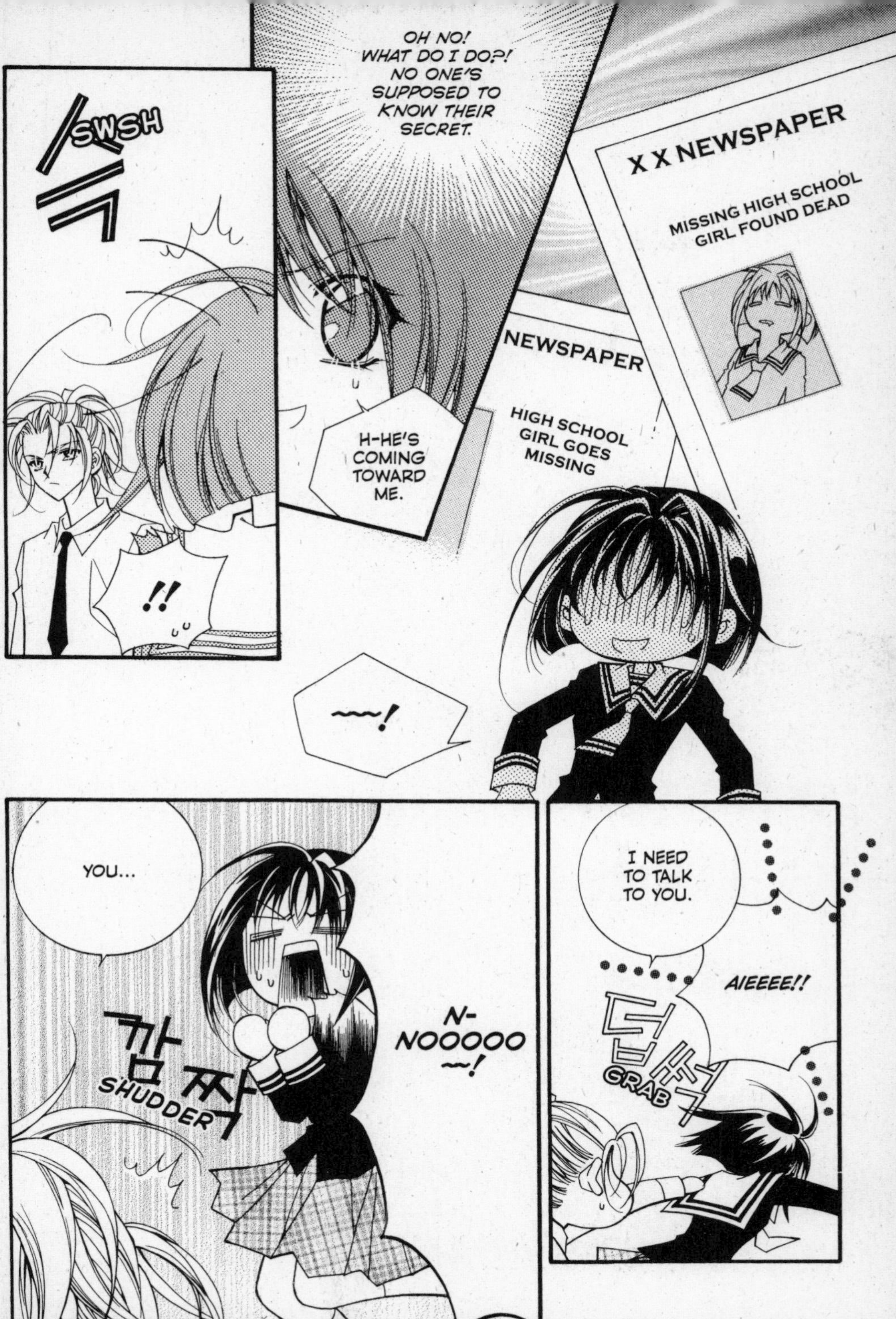
SWSH
!!
OH NO! WHAT DO I DO?! NO ONE'S SUPPOSED TO KNOW THEIR SECRET.
H-HE'S COMING TOWARD ME.
X X NEWSPAPER
MISSING HIGH SCHOOL GIRL FOUND DEAD
NEWSPAPER
HIGH SCHOOL GIRL GOES MISSING
~~~!
YOU...
깜짝
SHUDDER
N-NOOOOO~~!
I NEED TO TALK TO YOU.
AIEEEE!!
덥썩
GRAB
~~~

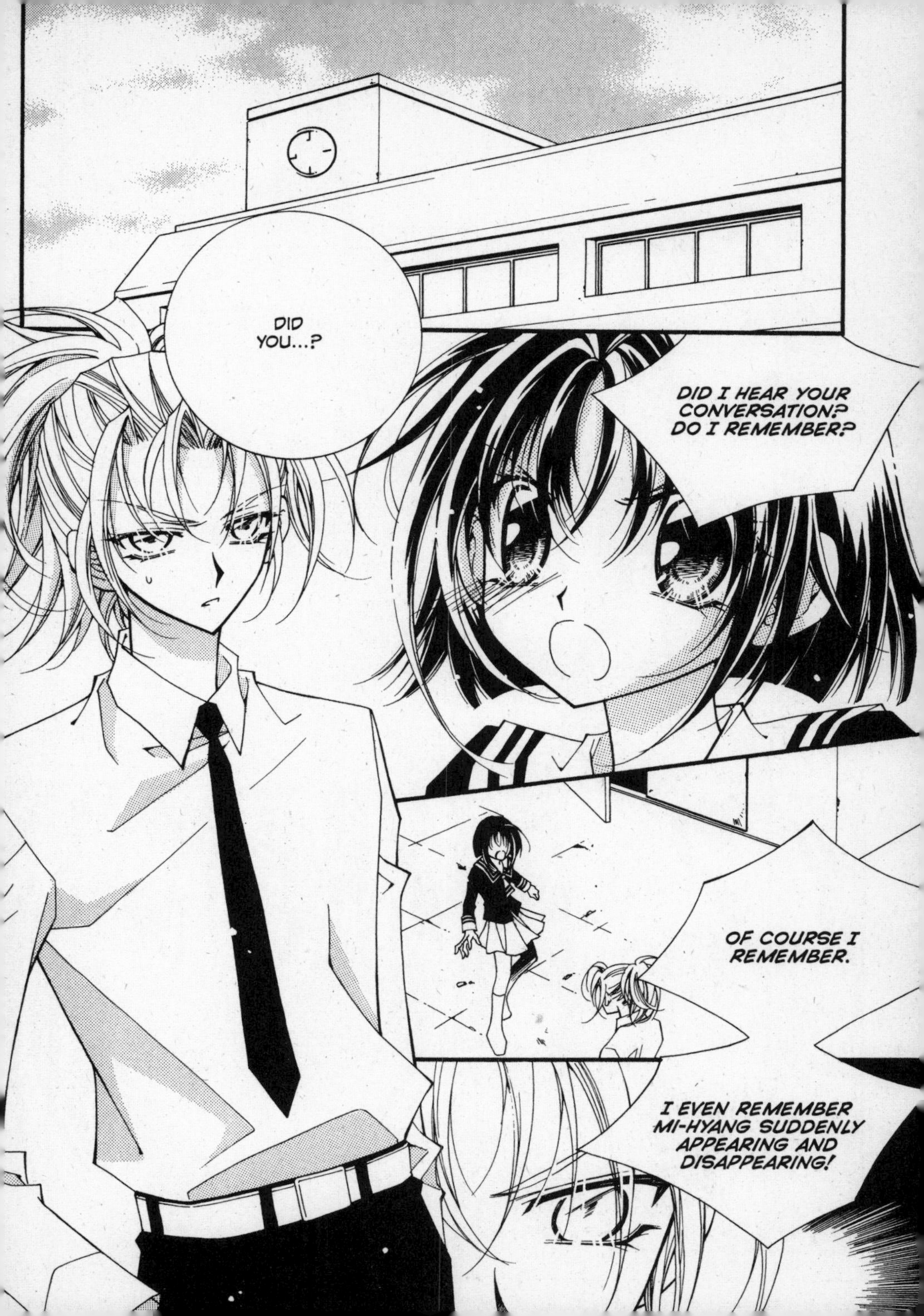
DID YOU...?
DID I HEAR YOUR CONVERSATION? DO I REMEMBER?
OF COURSE I REMEMBER.
I EVEN REMEMBER MI-HYANG SUDDENLY APPEARING AND DISAPPEARING!

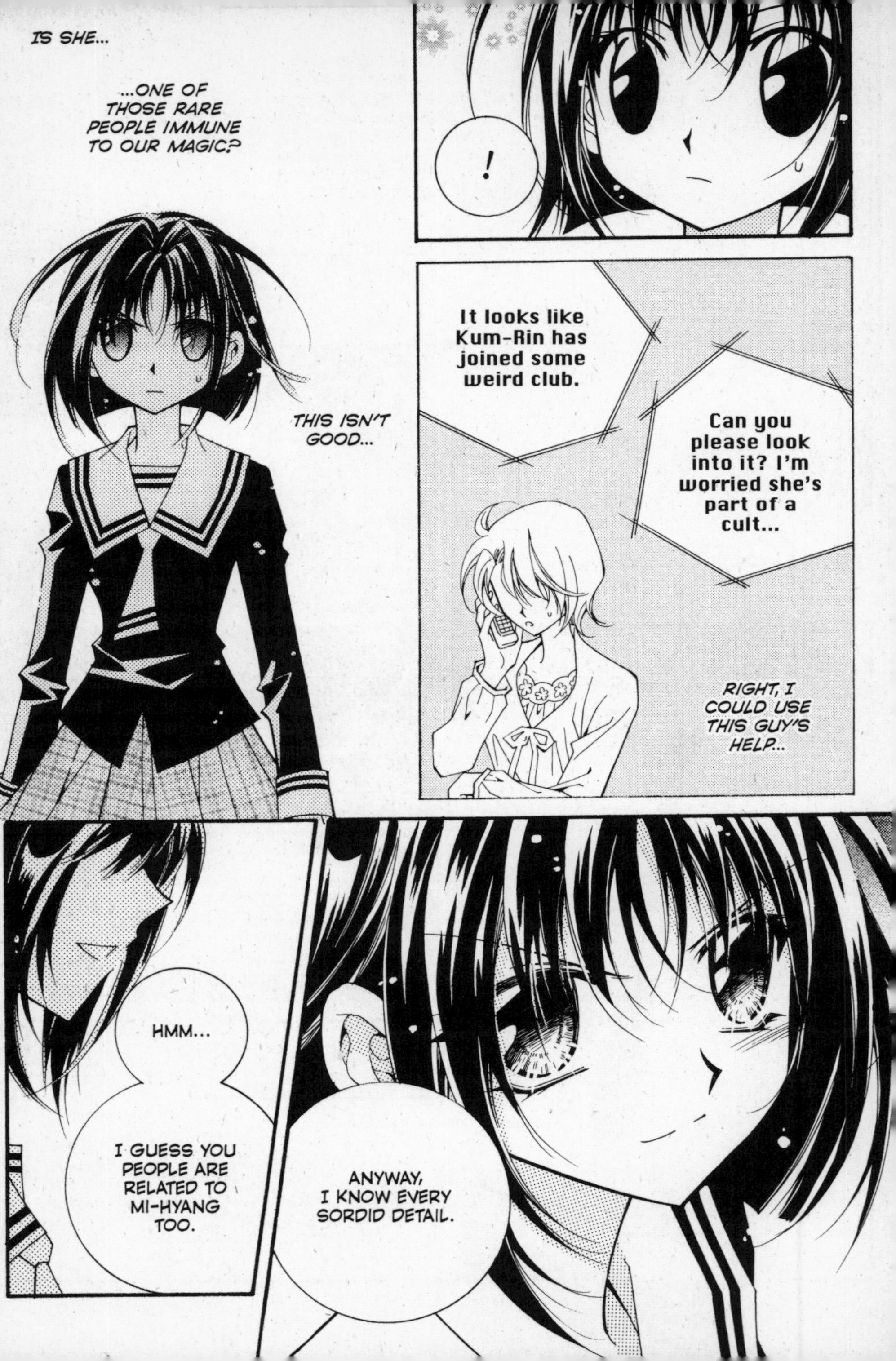
IS SHE...
...ONE OF THOSE RARE PEOPLE IMMUNE TO OUR MAGIC?
THIS ISN'T GOOD...
!
It looks like Kum-Rin has joined some weird club.
Can you please look into it? I'm worried she's part of a cult...
RIGHT, I COULD USE THIS GUY'S HELP...
HMM...
I GUESS YOU PEOPLE ARE RELATED TO MI-HYANG TOO.
ANYWAY, I KNOW EVERY SORDID DETAIL.

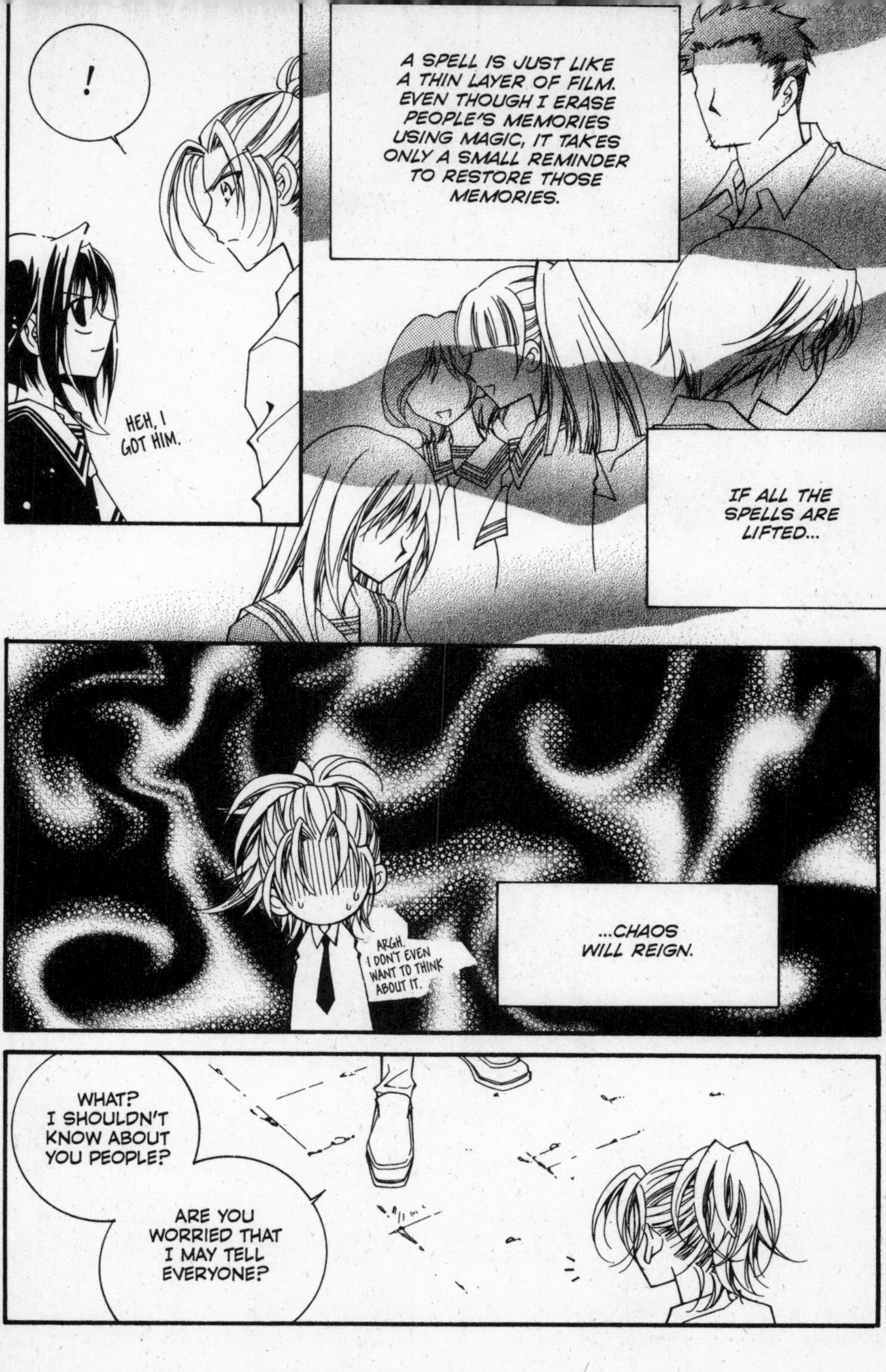
!
HEH, I GOT HIM.
A SPELL IS JUST LIKE A THIN LAYER OF FILM. EVEN THOUGH I ERASE PEOPLE'S MEMORIES USING MAGIC, IT TAKES ONLY A SMALL REMINDER TO RESTORE THOSE MEMORIES.
IF ALL THE SPELLS ARE LIFTED...
ARGH. I DON'T EVEN WANT TO THINK ABOUT IT.
...CHAOS WILL REIGN.
WHAT? I SHOULDN'T KNOW ABOUT YOU PEOPLE?
ARE YOU WORRIED THAT I MAY TELL EVERYONE?

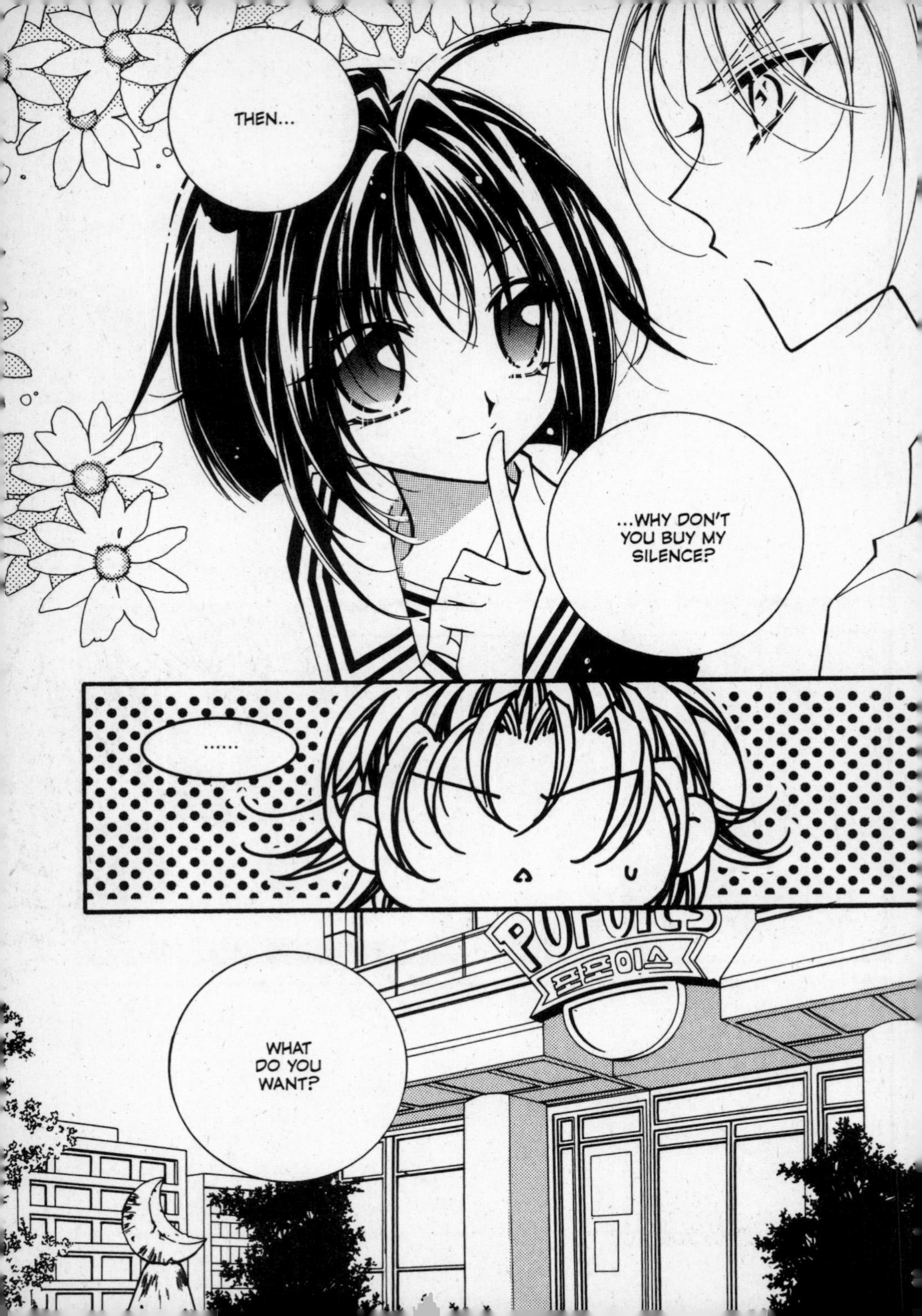
THEN...
...WHY DON'T YOU BUY MY SILENCE?
......
WHAT DO YOU WANT?

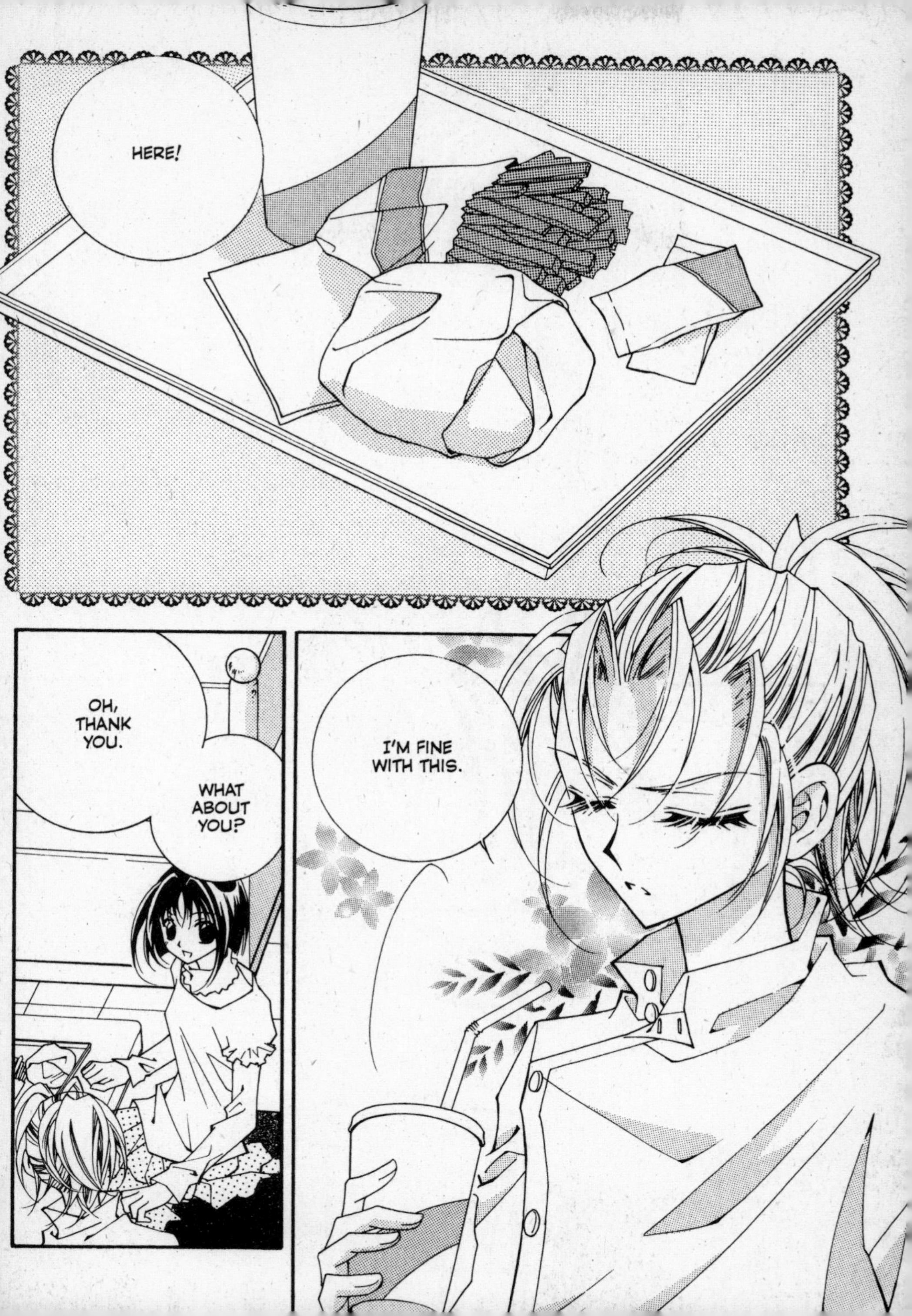
HERE!
OH, THANK YOU.
WHAT ABOUT YOU?
I'M FINE WITH THIS.

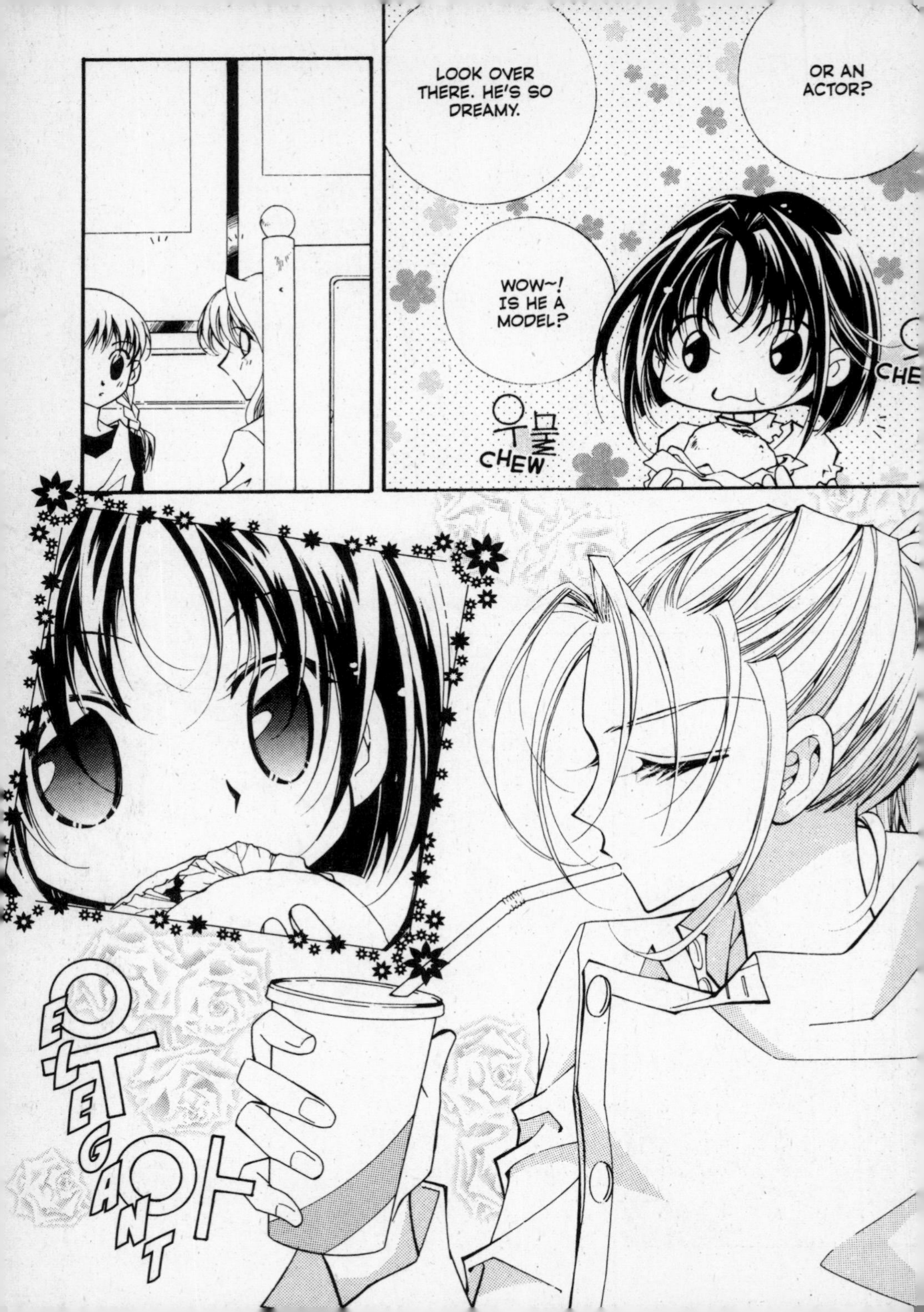
LOOK OVER THERE. HE'S SO DREAMY.
OR AN ACTOR?
WOW~! IS HE A MODEL?
CHE
CHEW
ELEGANT

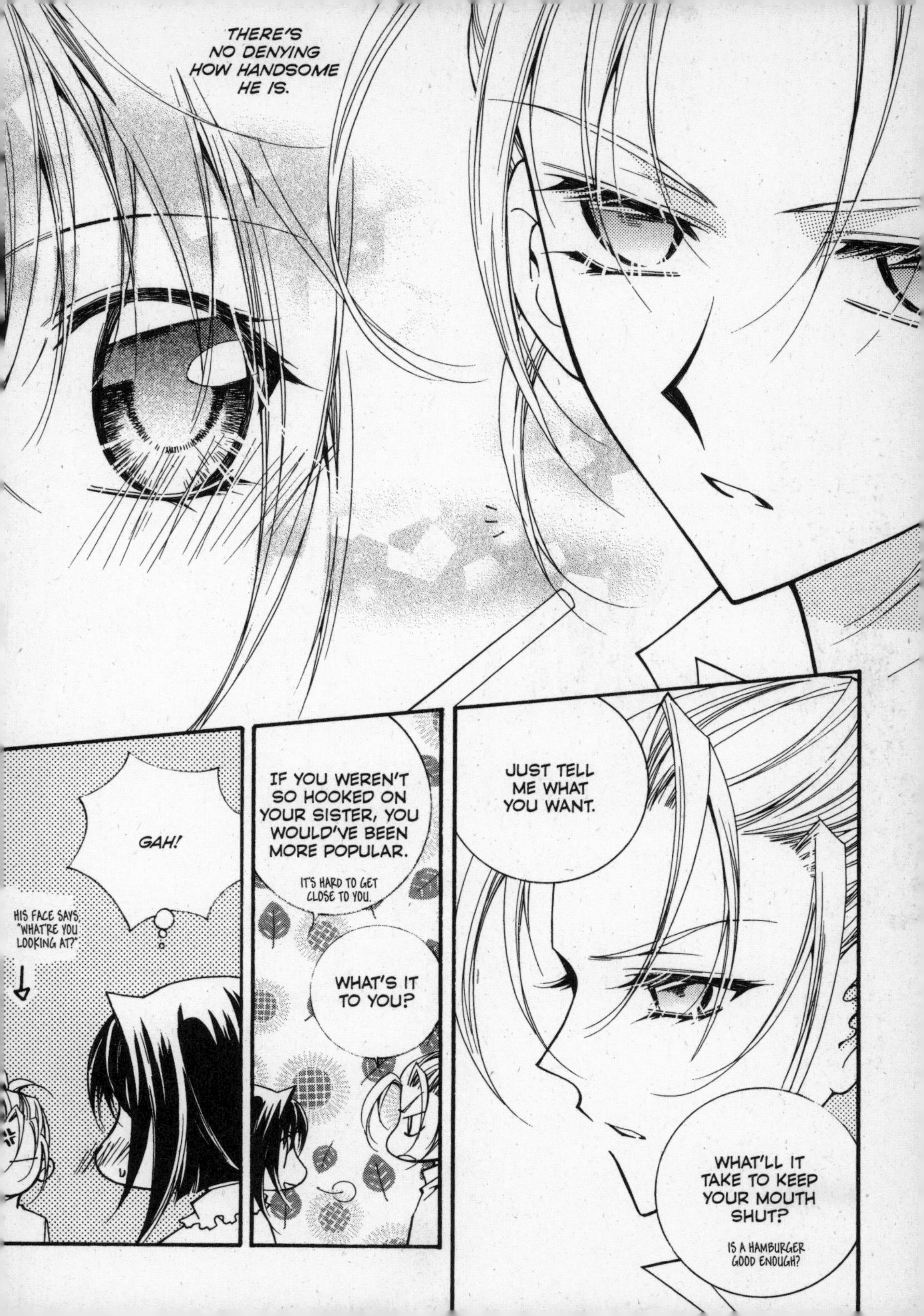
THERE'S NO DENYING HOW HANDSOME HE IS.
GAH!
HIS FACE SAYS, "WHAT'RE YOU LOOKING AT?"
IF YOU WEREN'T SO HOOKED ON YOUR SISTER, YOU WOULD'VE BEEN MORE POPULAR.
IT'S HARD TO GET CLOSE TO YOU.
WHAT'S IT TO YOU?
JUST TELL ME WHAT YOU WANT.
WHAT'LL IT TAKE TO KEEP YOUR MOUTH SHUT?
IS A HAMBURGER GOOD ENOUGH?

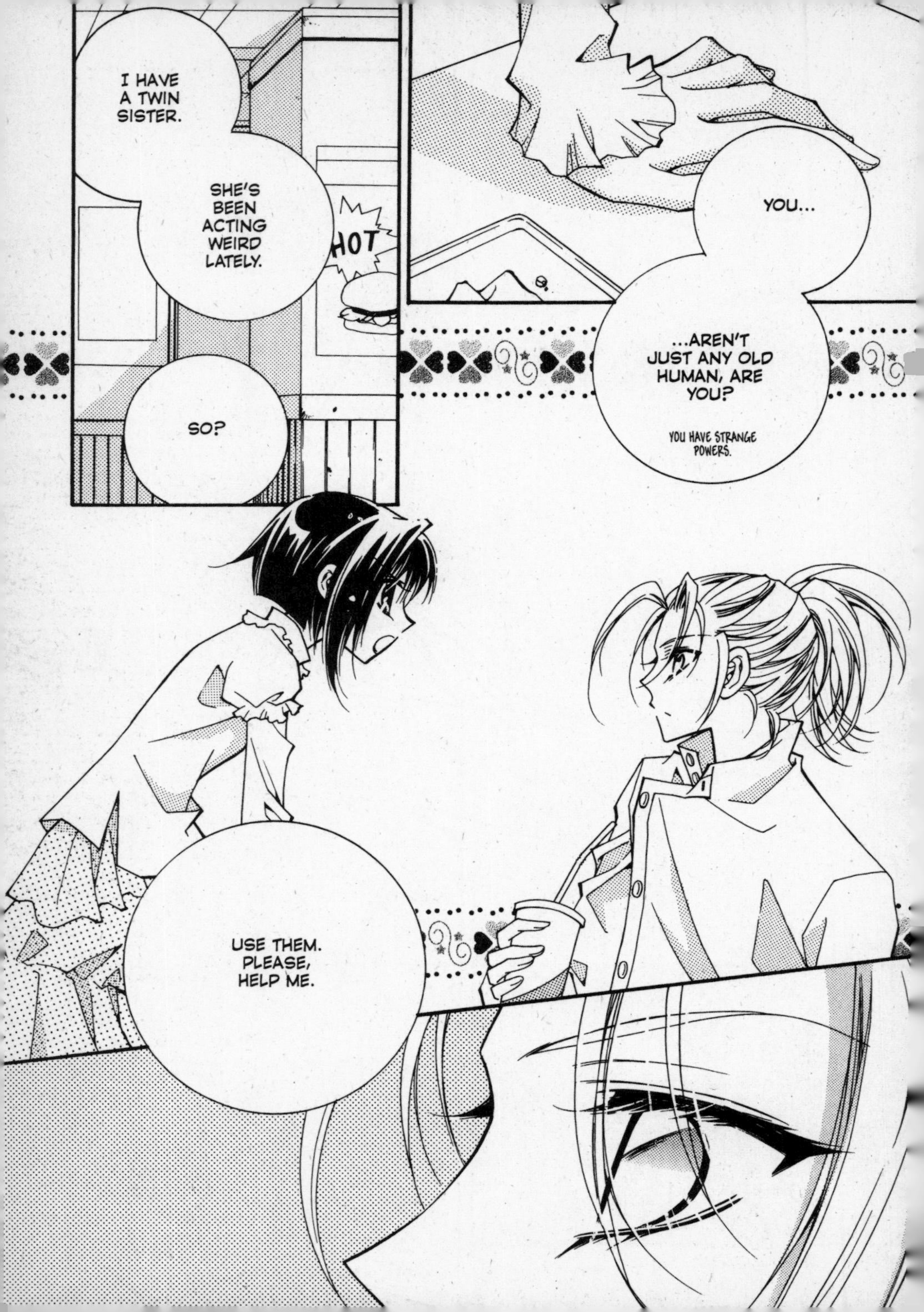

I HAVE A TWIN SISTER.
SHE'S BEEN ACTING WEIRD LATELY.
HOT
SO?
YOU...
...AREN'T JUST ANY OLD HUMAN, ARE YOU?
YOU HAVE STRANGE POWERS.
USE THEM. PLEASE, HELP ME.

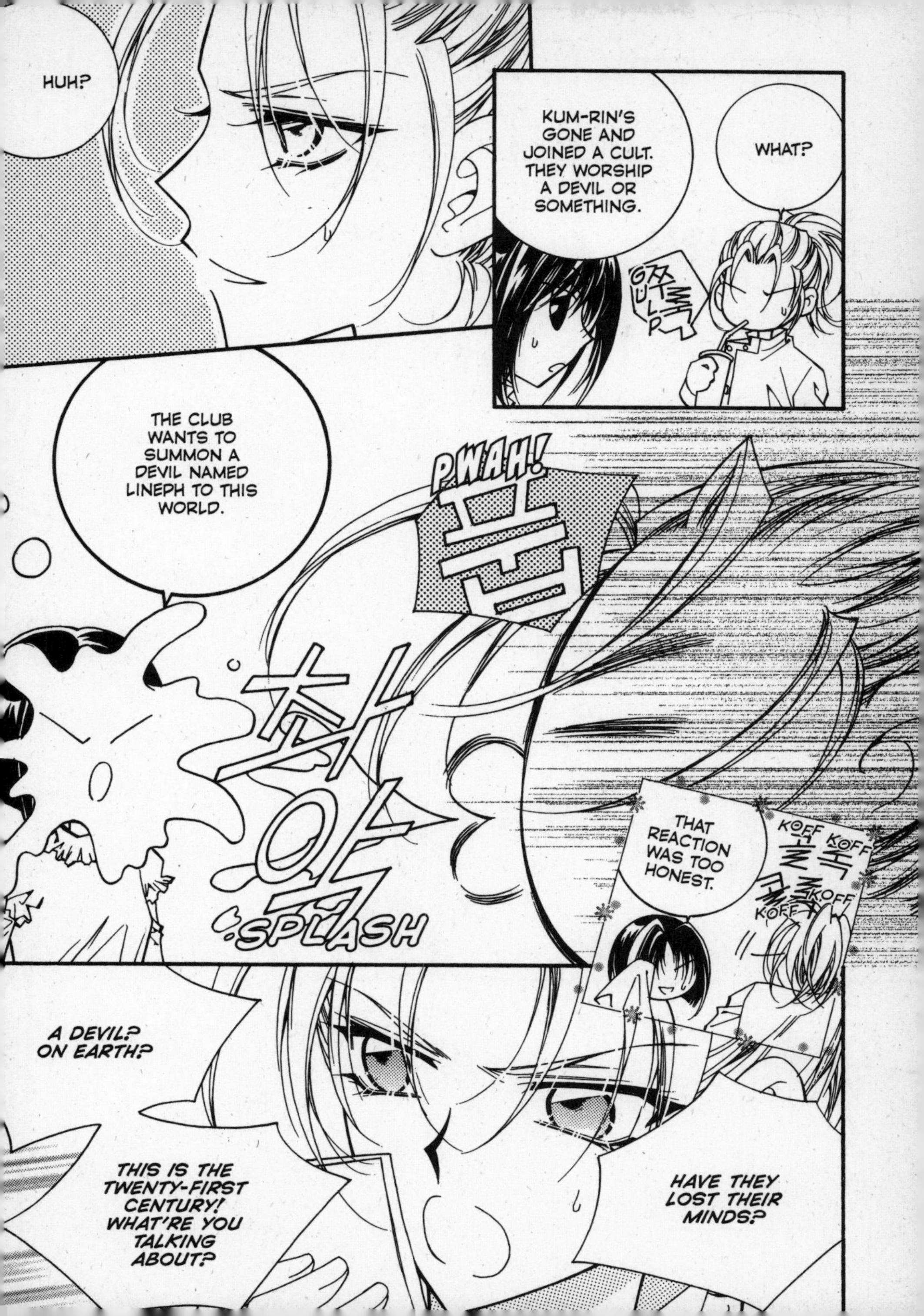
HUH?
KUM-RIN'S GONE AND JOINED A CULT. THEY WORSHIP A DEVIL OR SOMETHING.
WHAT?
GULP
THE CLUB WANTS TO SUMMON A DEVIL NAMED LINEPH TO THIS WORLD.
PWAH!
SPLASH
THAT REACTION WAS TOO HONEST.
KOFF KOFF
KOFF KOFF
A DEVIL? ON EARTH?
THIS IS THE TWENTY-FIRST CENTURY! WHAT'RE YOU TALKING ABOUT?
HAVE THEY LOST THEIR MINDS?

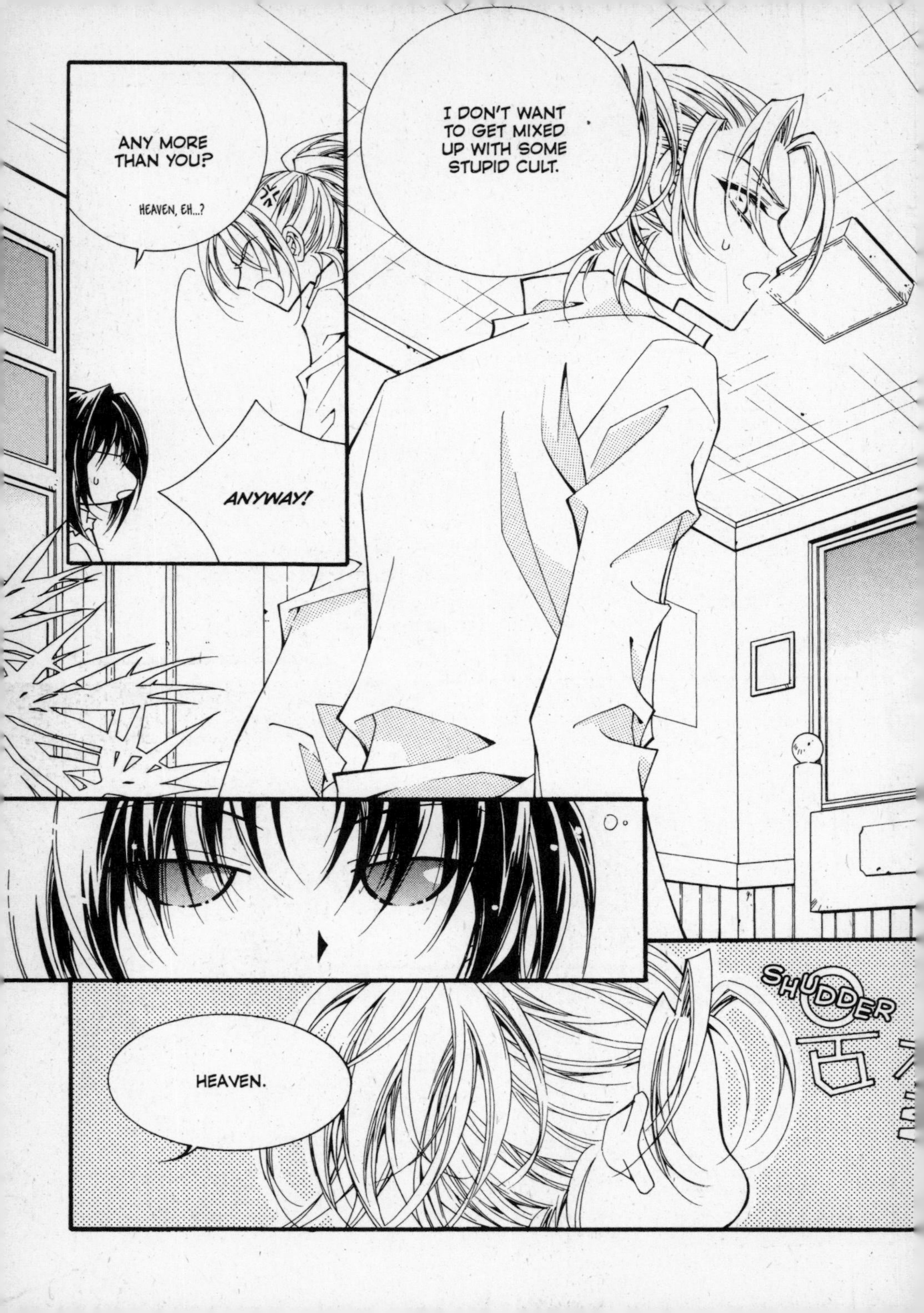
ANY MORE THAN YOU?
HEAVEN, EH...?
ANYWAY!
I DON'T WANT TO GET MIXED UP WITH SOME STUPID CULT.
HEAVEN.
SHUDDER

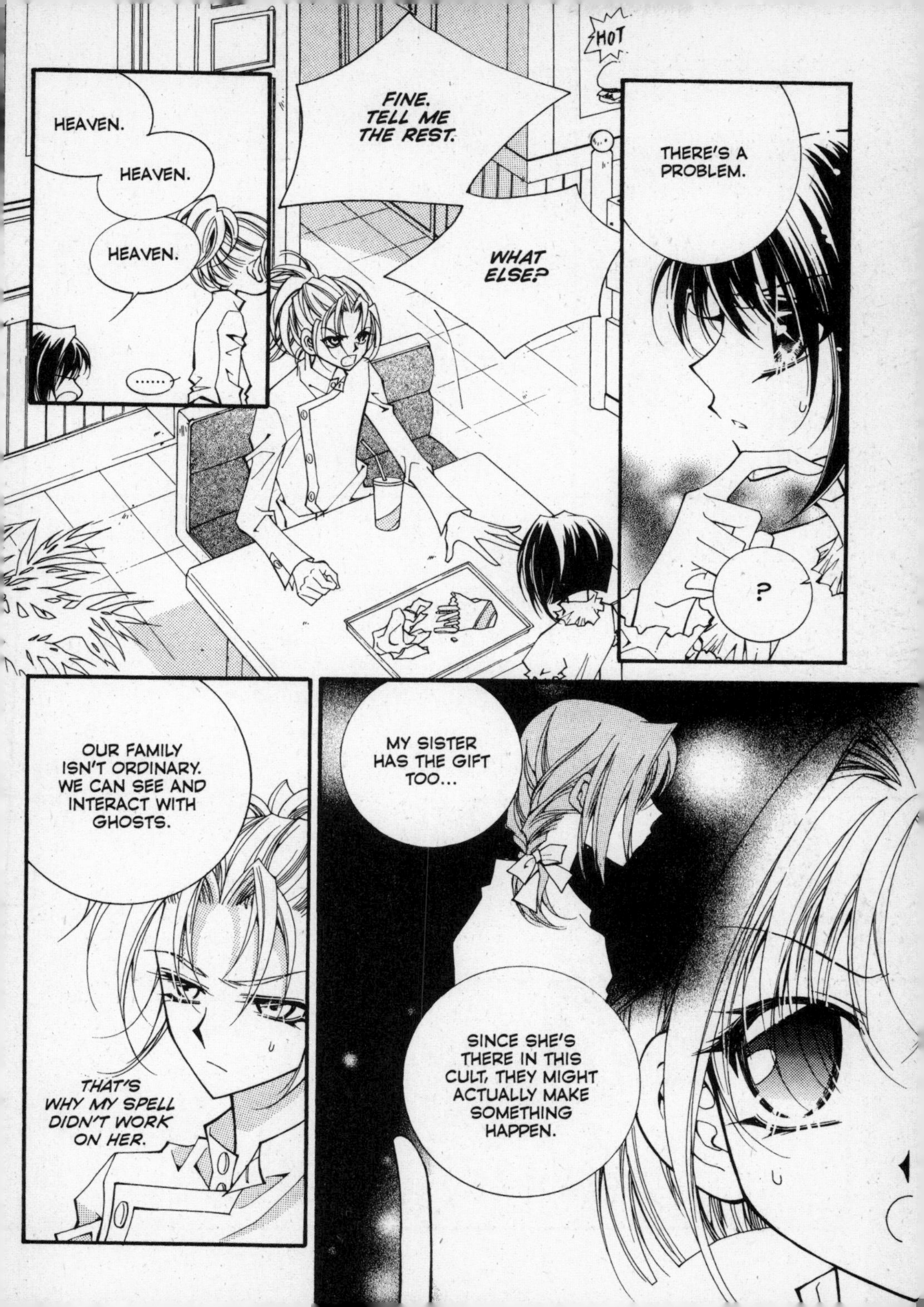
HEAVEN.
HEAVEN.
HEAVEN.
......
HOT
FINE. TELL ME THE REST.
WHAT ELSE?
THERE'S A PROBLEM.
?
OUR FAMILY ISN'T ORDINARY. WE CAN SEE AND INTERACT WITH GHOSTS.
THAT'S WHY MY SPELL DIDN'T WORK ON HER.
MY SISTER HAS THE GIFT TOO...
SINCE SHE'S THERE IN THIS CULT, THEY MIGHT ACTUALLY MAKE SOMETHING HAPPEN.

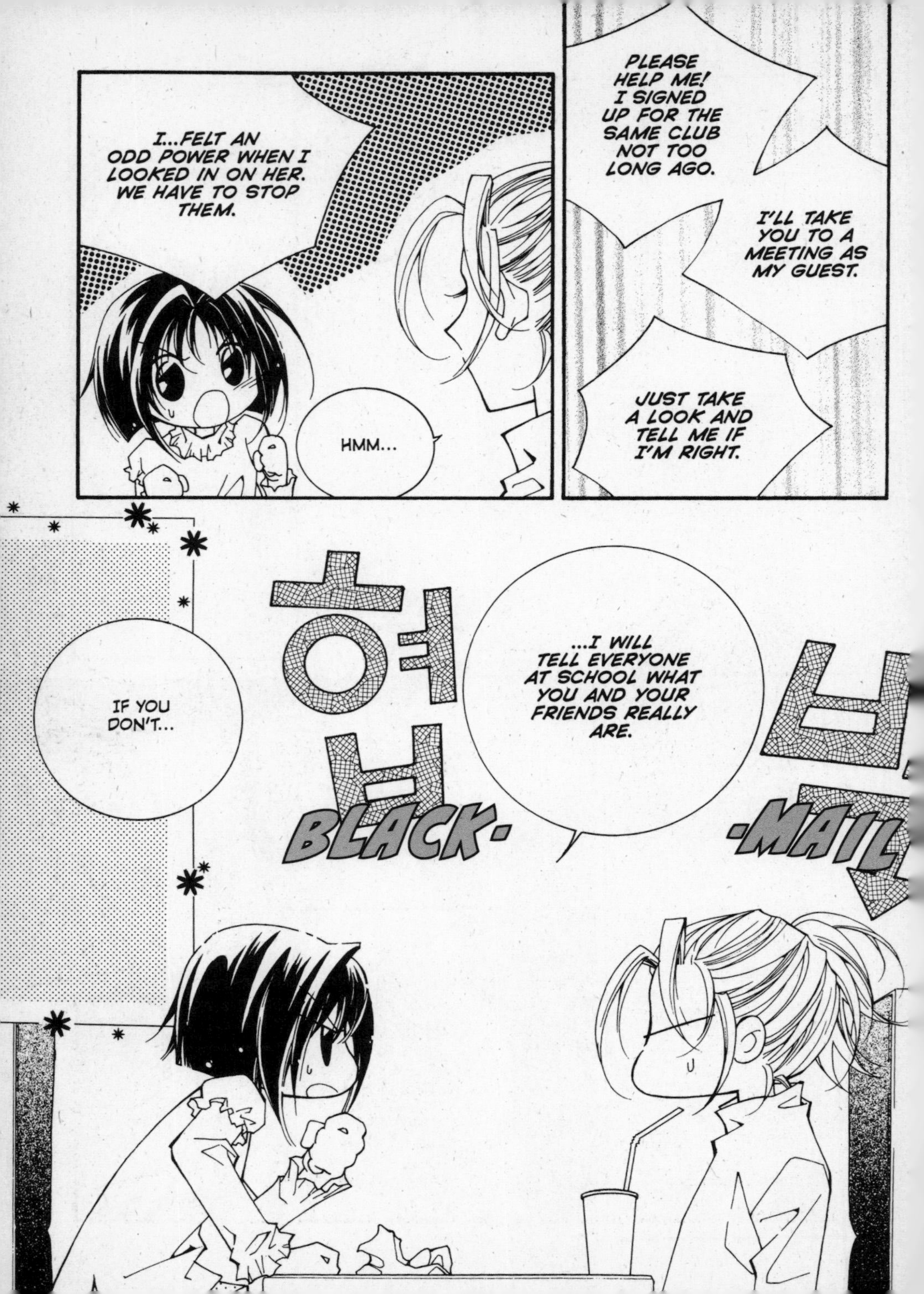
I...FELT AN ODD POWER WHEN I LOOKED IN ON HER. WE HAVE TO STOP THEM.
HMM...
PLEASE HELP ME! I SIGNED UP FOR THE SAME CLUB NOT TOO LONG AGO.
I'LL TAKE YOU TO A MEETING AS MY GUEST.
JUST TAKE A LOOK AND TELL ME IF I'M RIGHT.
IF YOU DON'T...
협
BLACK-
...I WILL TELL EVERYONE AT SCHOOL WHAT YOU AND YOUR FRIENDS REALLY ARE.
-MAIL

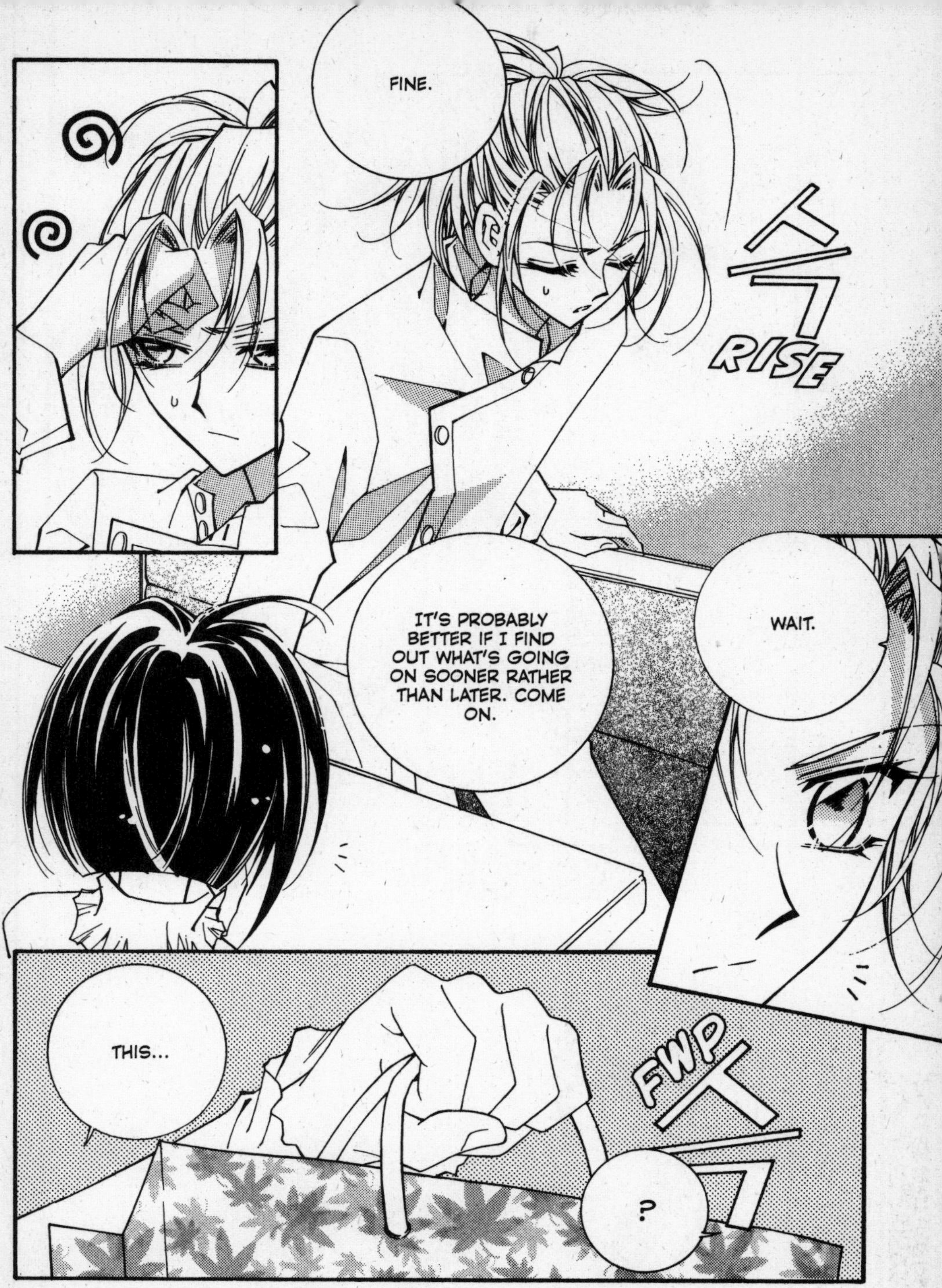
FINE.
RISE
IT'S PROBABLY BETTER IF I FIND OUT WHAT'S GOING ON SOONER RATHER THAN LATER. COME ON.
WAIT.
THIS...
FWP
?

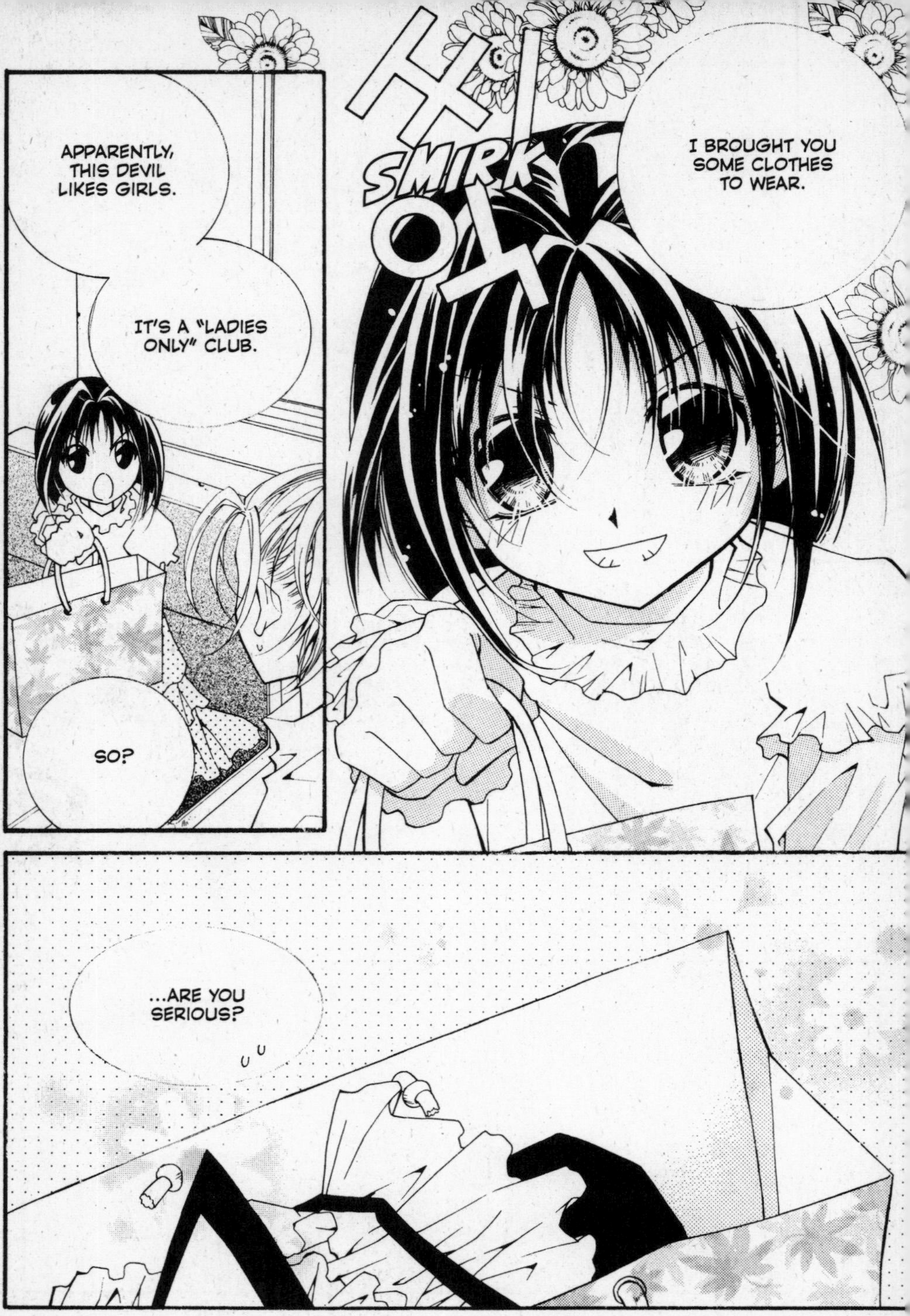
APPARENTLY, THIS DEVIL LIKES GIRLS.
IT'S A "LADIES ONLY" CLUB.
SO?
SMIRK
I BROUGHT YOU SOME CLOTHES TO WEAR.
...ARE YOU SERIOUS?

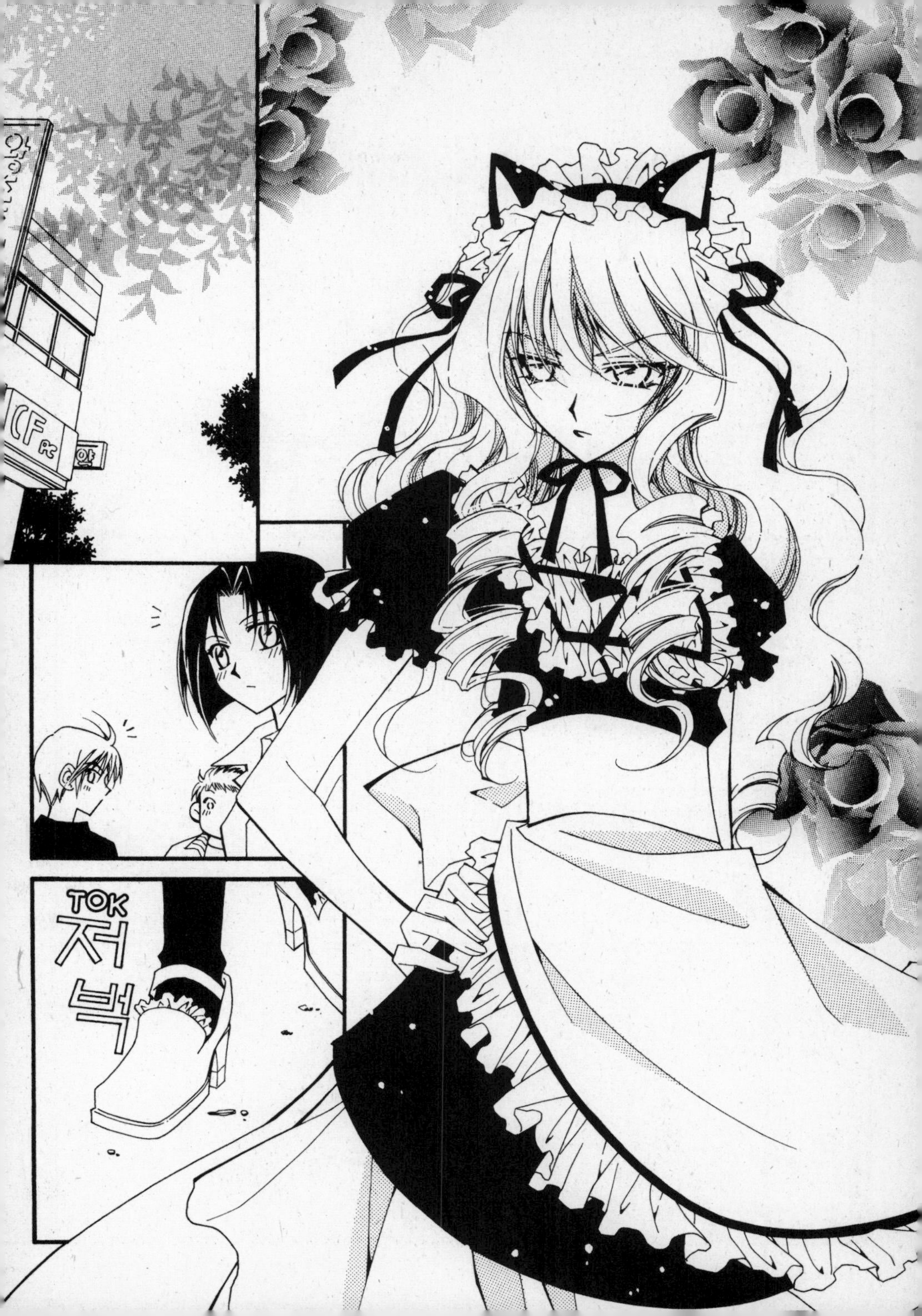
TOK
저벅

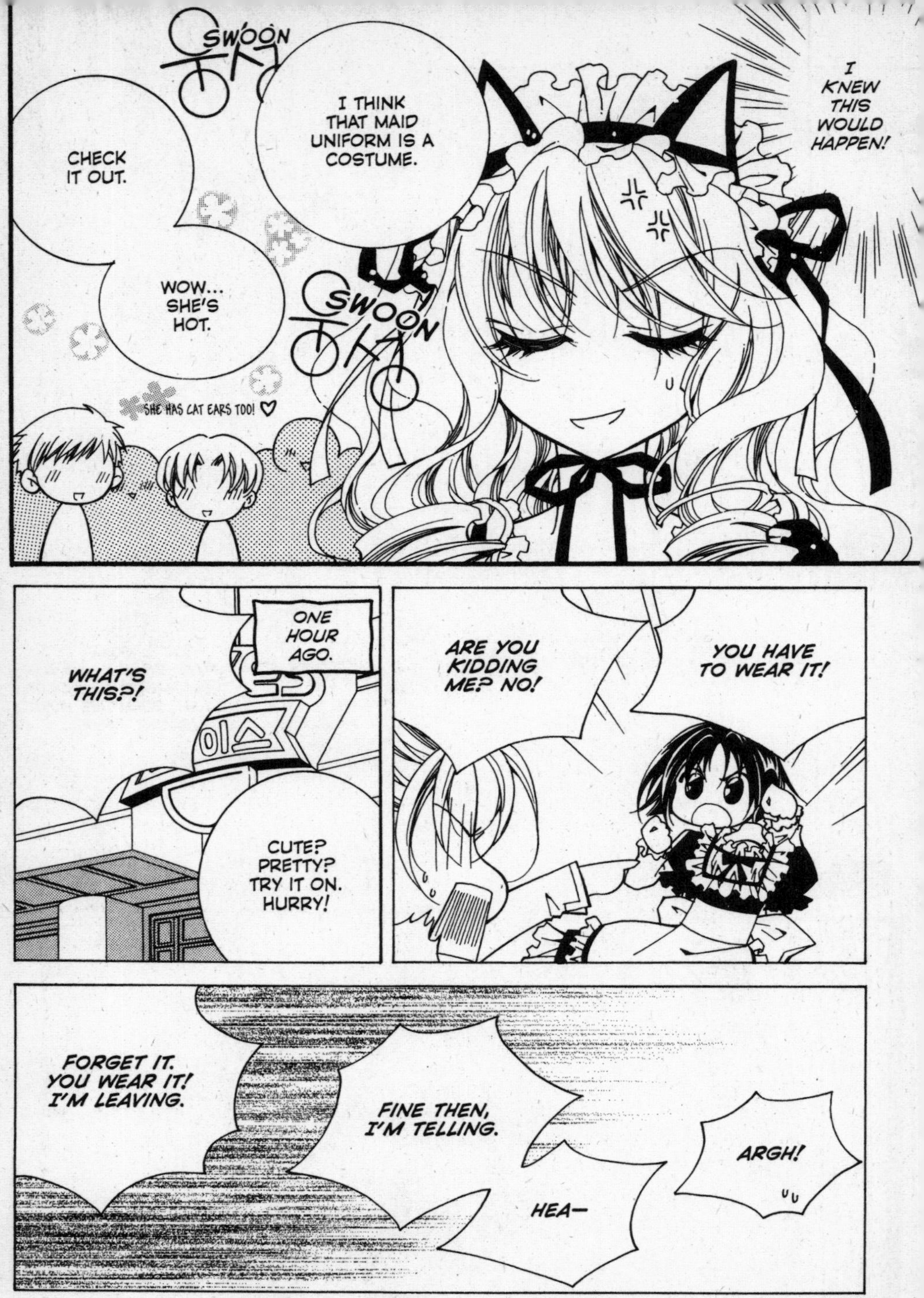
CHECK IT OUT.
WOW... SHE'S HOT.
SHE HAS CAT EARS TOO! ♡
SWOON
I THINK THAT MAID UNIFORM IS A COSTUME.
SWOON
I KNEW THIS WOULD HAPPEN!
ONE HOUR AGO.
WHAT'S THIS?!
CUTE? PRETTY? TRY IT ON. HURRY!
ARE YOU KIDDING ME? NO!
YOU HAVE TO WEAR IT!
FORGET IT. YOU WEAR IT! I'M LEAVING.
FINE THEN, I'M TELLING.
HEA—
ARGH!

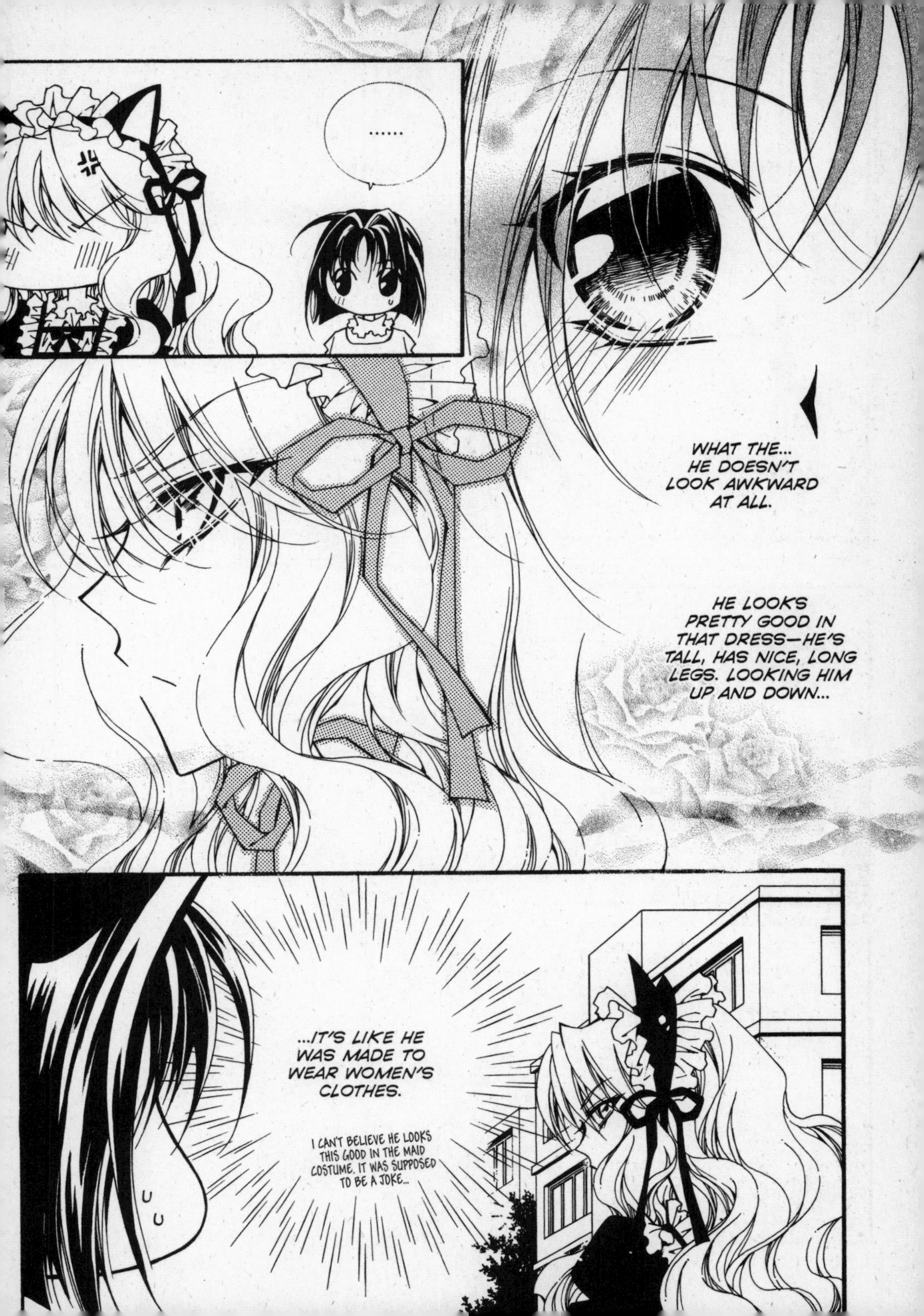
......
WHAT THE... HE DOESN'T LOOK AWKWARD AT ALL.
HE LOOKS PRETTY GOOD IN THAT DRESS—HE'S TALL, HAS NICE, LONG LEGS. LOOKING HIM UP AND DOWN...
...IT'S LIKE HE WAS MADE TO WEAR WOMEN'S CLOTHES.
I CAN'T BELIEVE HE LOOKS THIS GOOD IN THE MAID COSTUME. IT WAS SUPPOSED TO BE A JOKE...

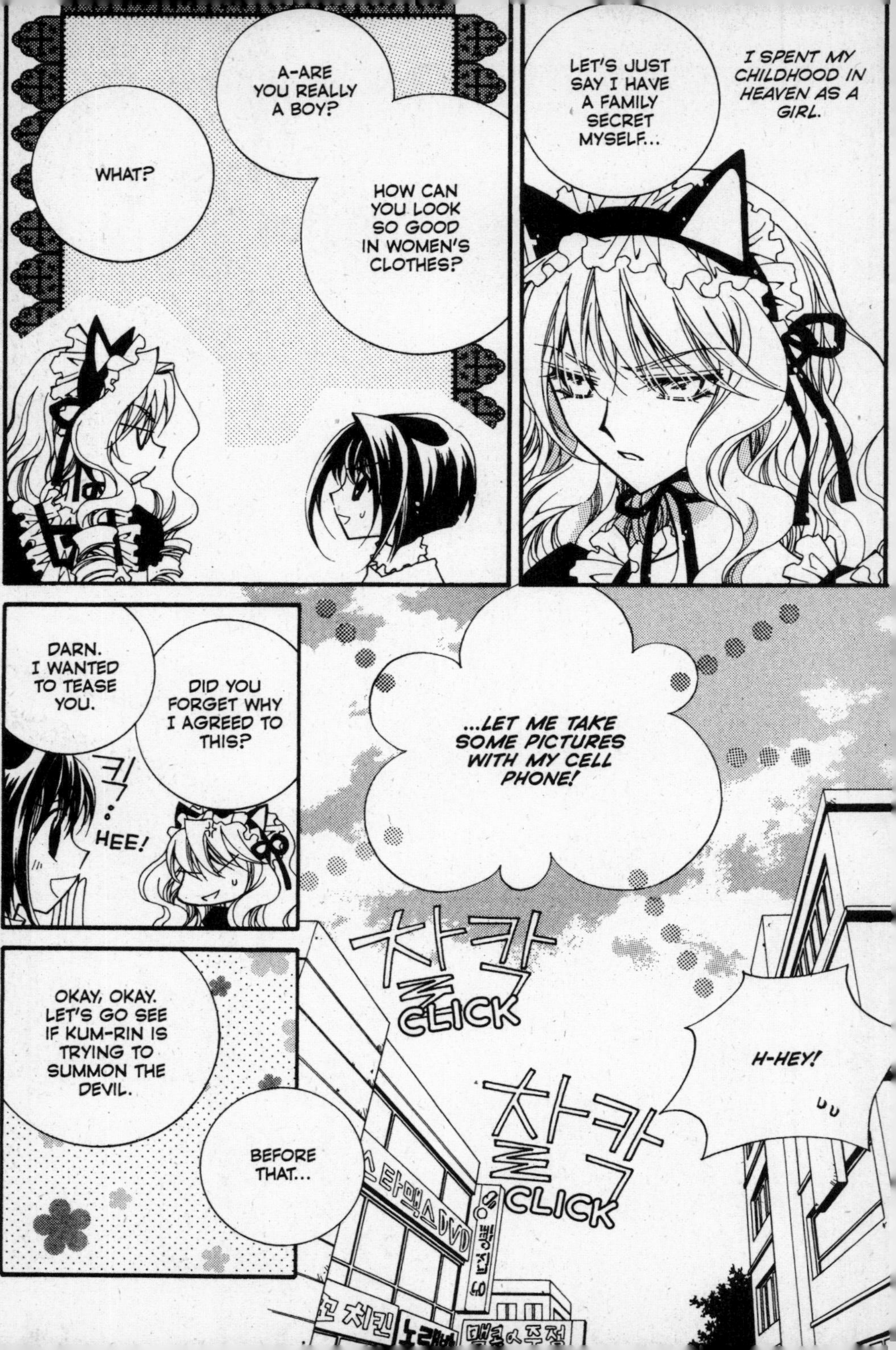
WHAT?
A-ARE YOU REALLY A BOY?
HOW CAN YOU LOOK SO GOOD IN WOMEN'S CLOTHES?
LET'S JUST SAY I HAVE A FAMILY SECRET MYSELF...
I SPENT MY CHILDHOOD IN HEAVEN AS A GIRL.
DARN. I WANTED TO TEASE YOU.
DID YOU FORGET WHY I AGREED TO THIS?
HEE!
OKAY, OKAY. LET'S GO SEE IF KUM-RIN IS TRYING TO SUMMON THE DEVIL.
BEFORE THAT...
...LET ME TAKE SOME PICTURES WITH MY CELL PHONE!
CLICK
CLICK
H-HEY!

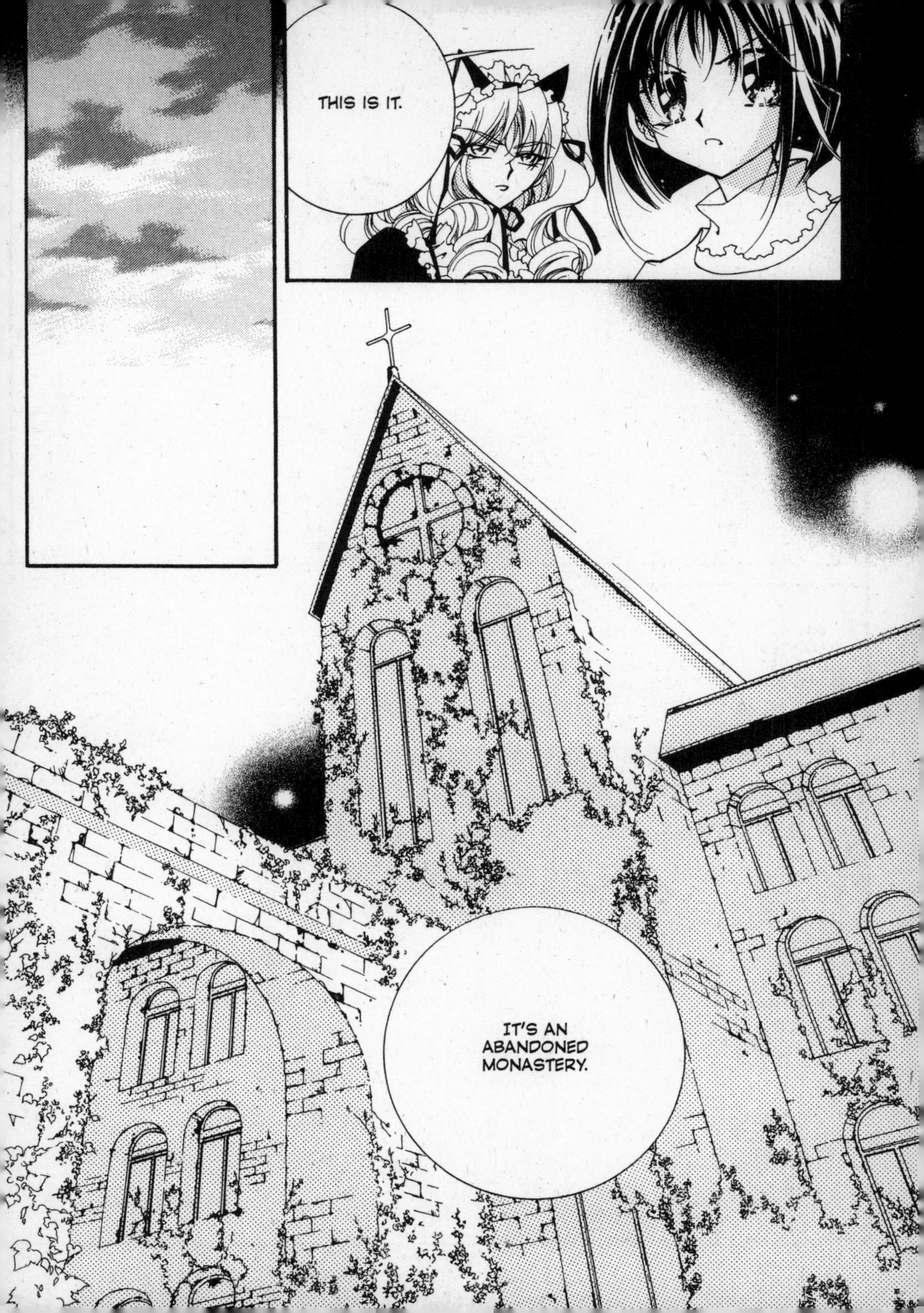
THIS IS IT.
IT'S AN ABANDONED MONASTERY.

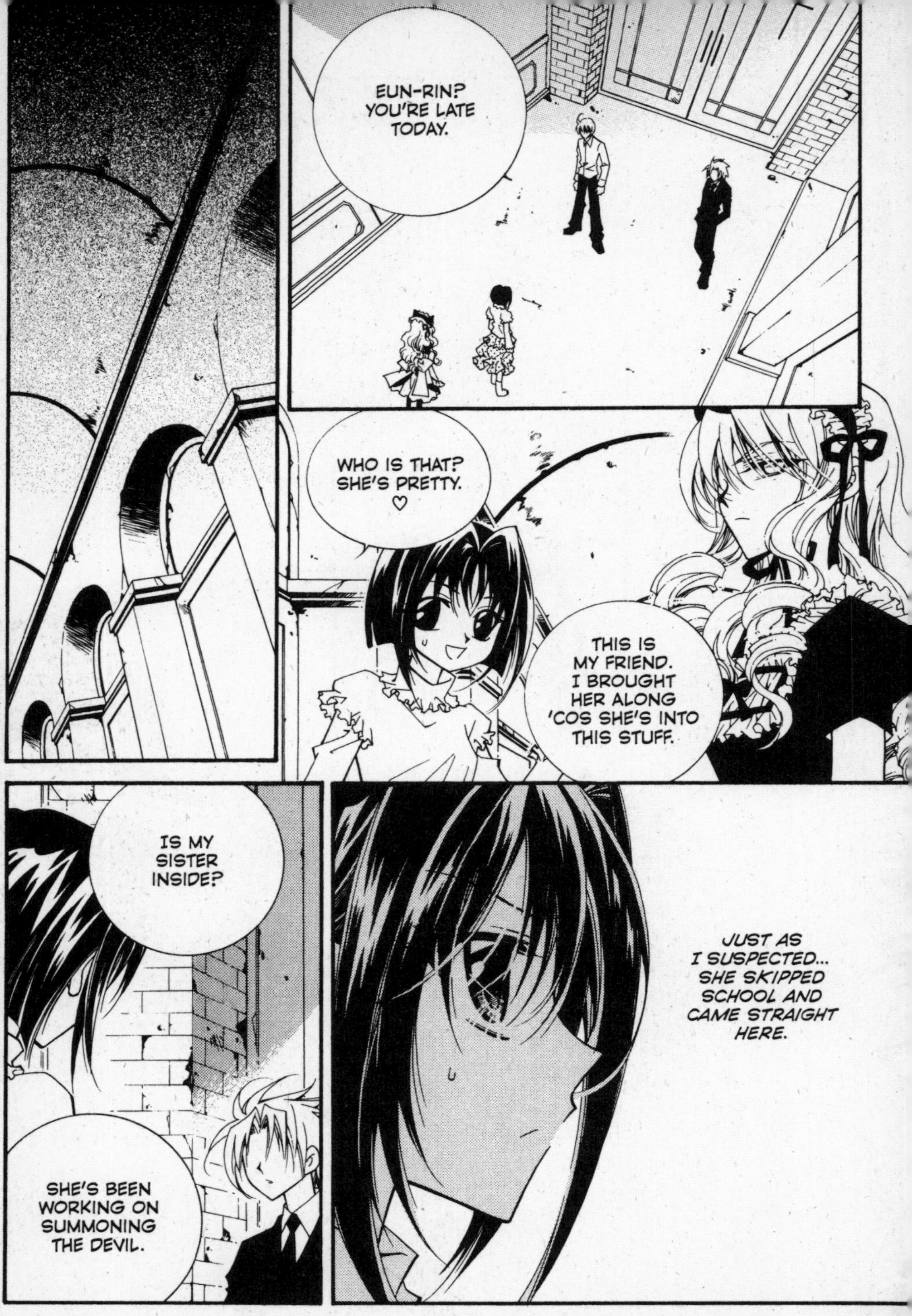
EUN-RIN? YOU'RE LATE TODAY.
WHO IS THAT? SHE'S PRETTY. ♡
THIS IS MY FRIEND. I BROUGHT HER ALONG 'COS SHE'S INTO THIS STUFF.
IS MY SISTER INSIDE?
SHE'S BEEN WORKING ON SUMMONING THE DEVIL.
JUST AS I SUSPECTED... SHE SKIPPED SCHOOL AND CAME STRAIGHT HERE.

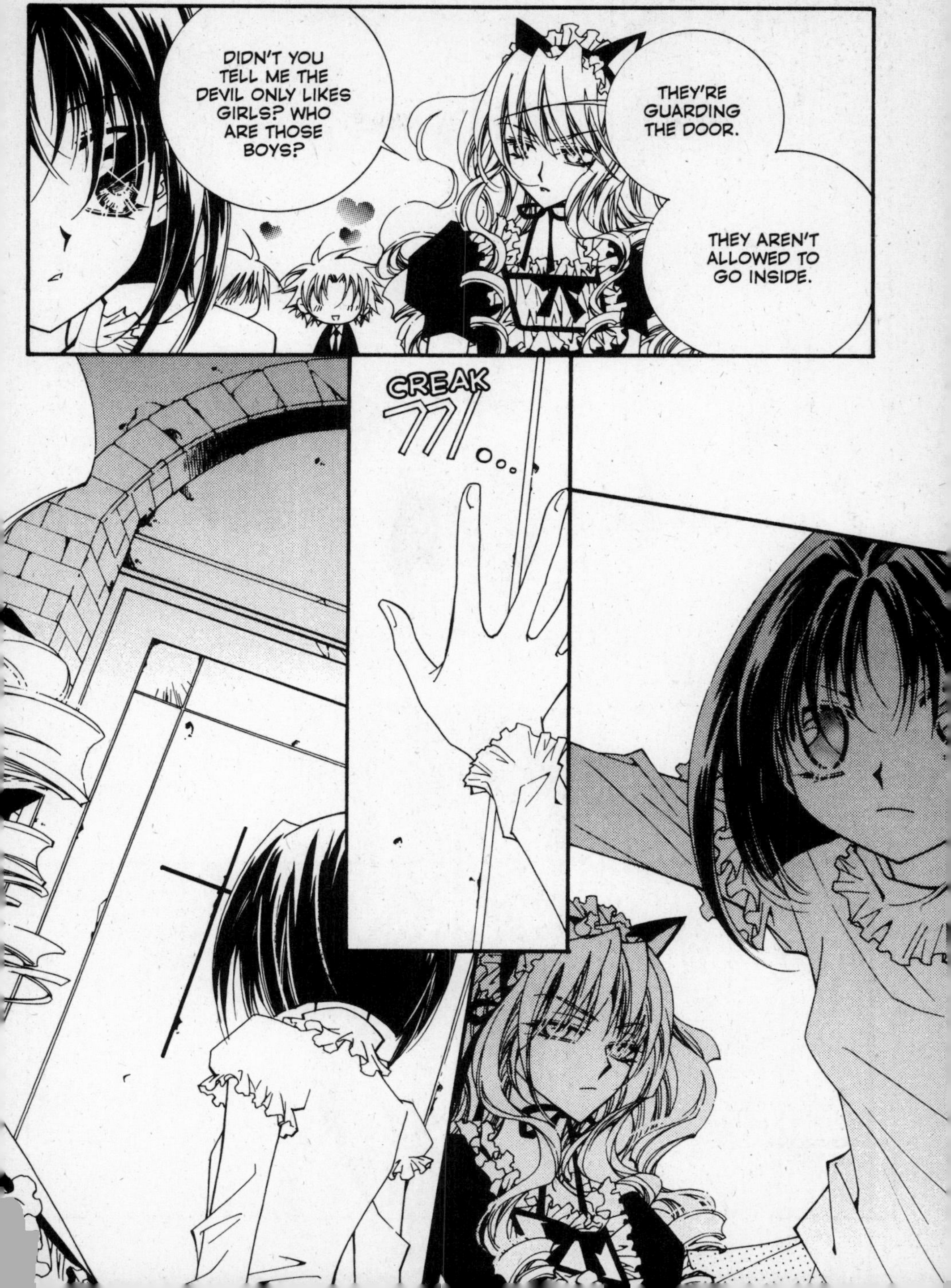
DIDN'T YOU TELL ME THE DEVIL ONLY LIKES GIRLS? WHO ARE THOSE BOYS?
THEY'RE GUARDING THE DOOR.
THEY AREN'T ALLOWED TO GO INSIDE.
CREAK

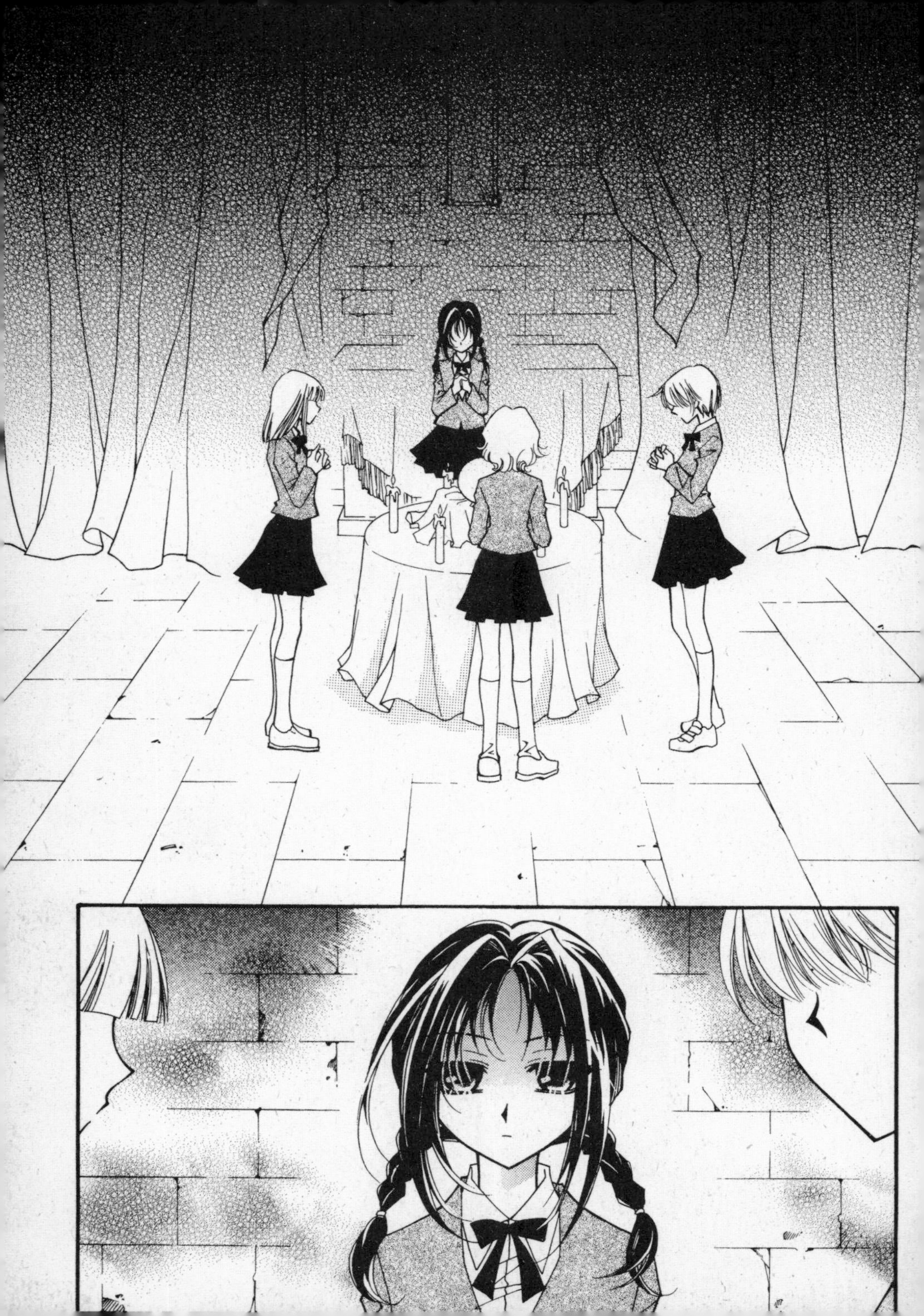

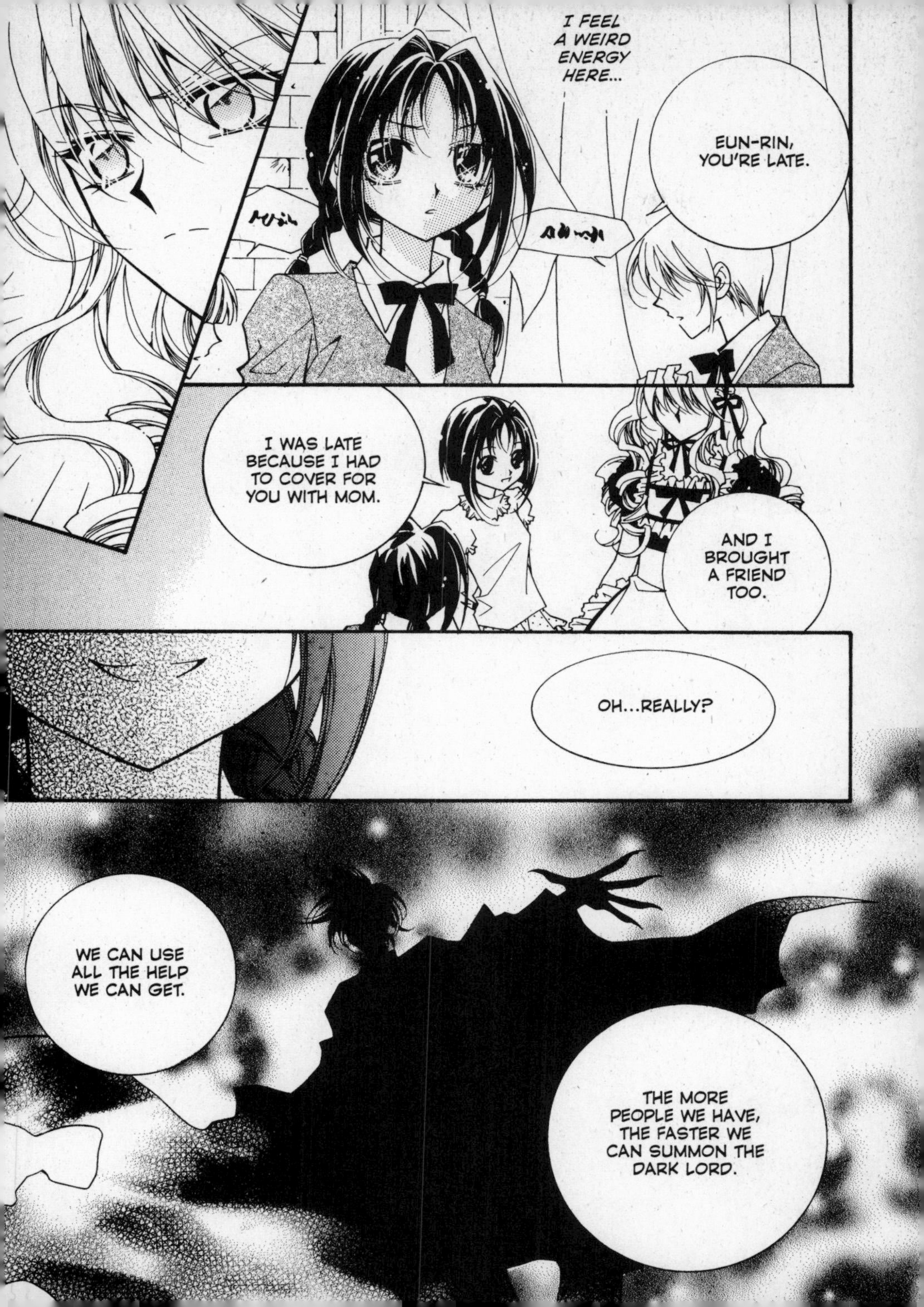
I FEEL A WEIRD ENERGY HERE...
EUN-RIN, YOU'RE LATE.
I WAS LATE BECAUSE I HAD TO COVER FOR YOU WITH MOM.
AND I BROUGHT A FRIEND TOO.
OH...REALLY?
WE CAN USE ALL THE HELP WE CAN GET.
THE MORE PEOPLE WE HAVE, THE FASTER WE CAN SUMMON THE DARK LORD.

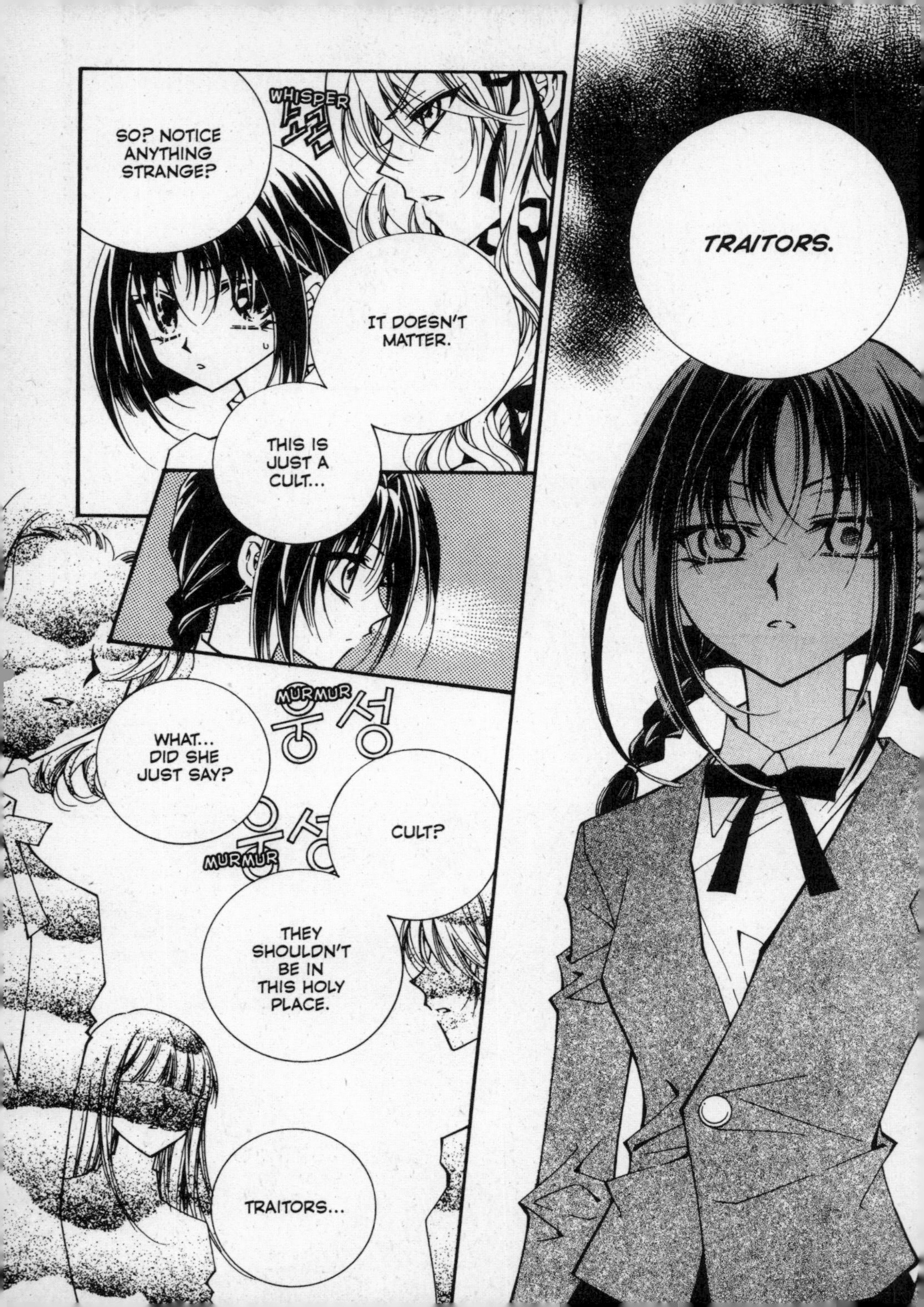
SO? NOTICE ANYTHING STRANGE?
WHISPER
소곤
IT DOESN'T MATTER.
THIS IS JUST A CULT...
MURMUR
웅성
WHAT... DID SHE JUST SAY?
MURMUR
웅성
CULT?
THEY SHOULDN'T BE IN THIS HOLY PLACE.
TRAITORS...
TRAITORS.

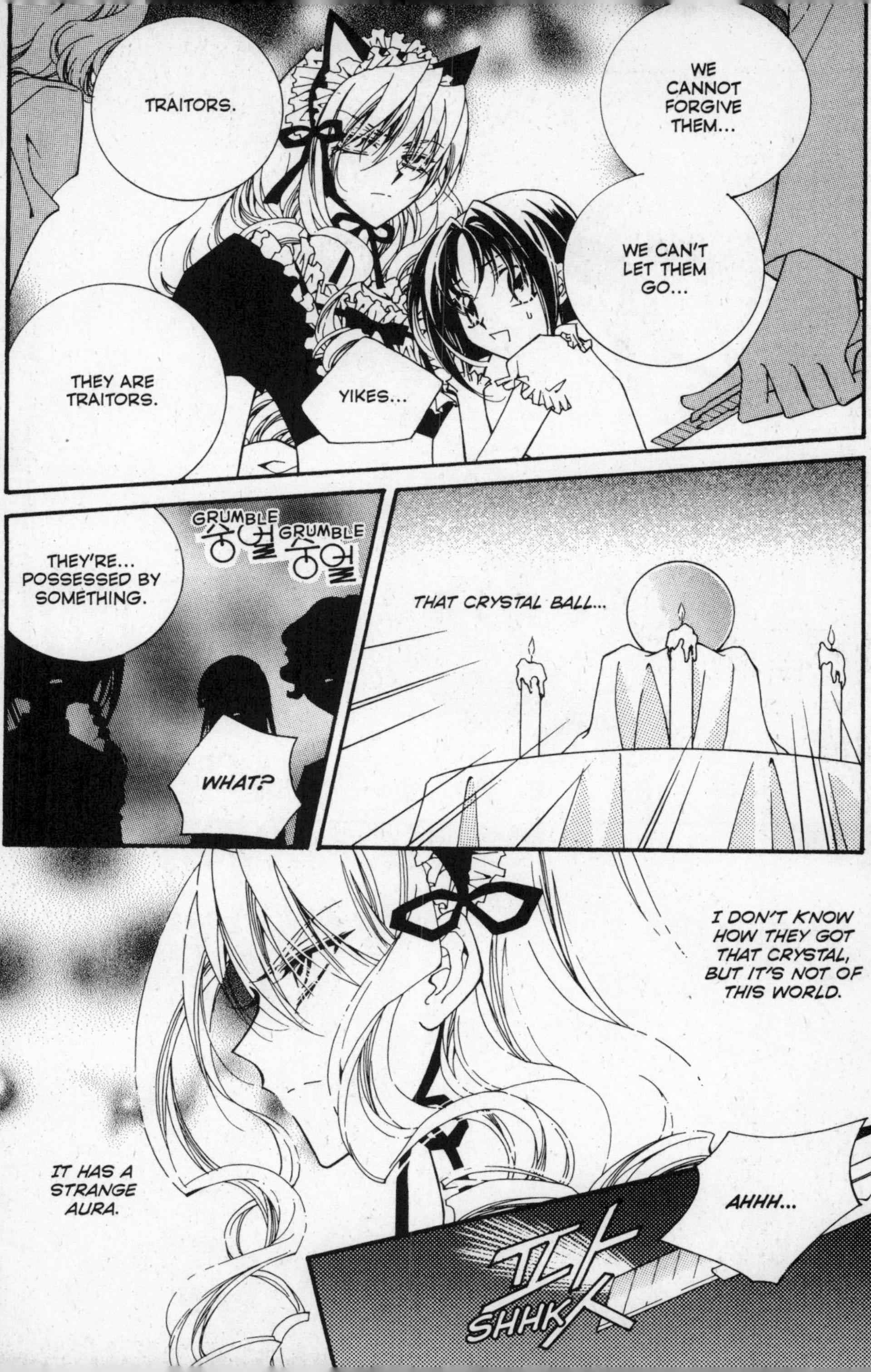
TRAITORS.
WE CANNOT FORGIVE THEM...
WE CAN'T LET THEM GO...
THEY ARE TRAITORS.
YIKES...
THEY'RE... POSSESSED BY SOMETHING.
GRUMBLE
숭얼
GRUMBLE
숭얼
WHAT?
THAT CRYSTAL BALL...
I DON'T KNOW HOW THEY GOT THAT CRYSTAL, BUT IT'S NOT OF THIS WORLD.
IT HAS A STRANGE AURA.
AHHH...
SHHK

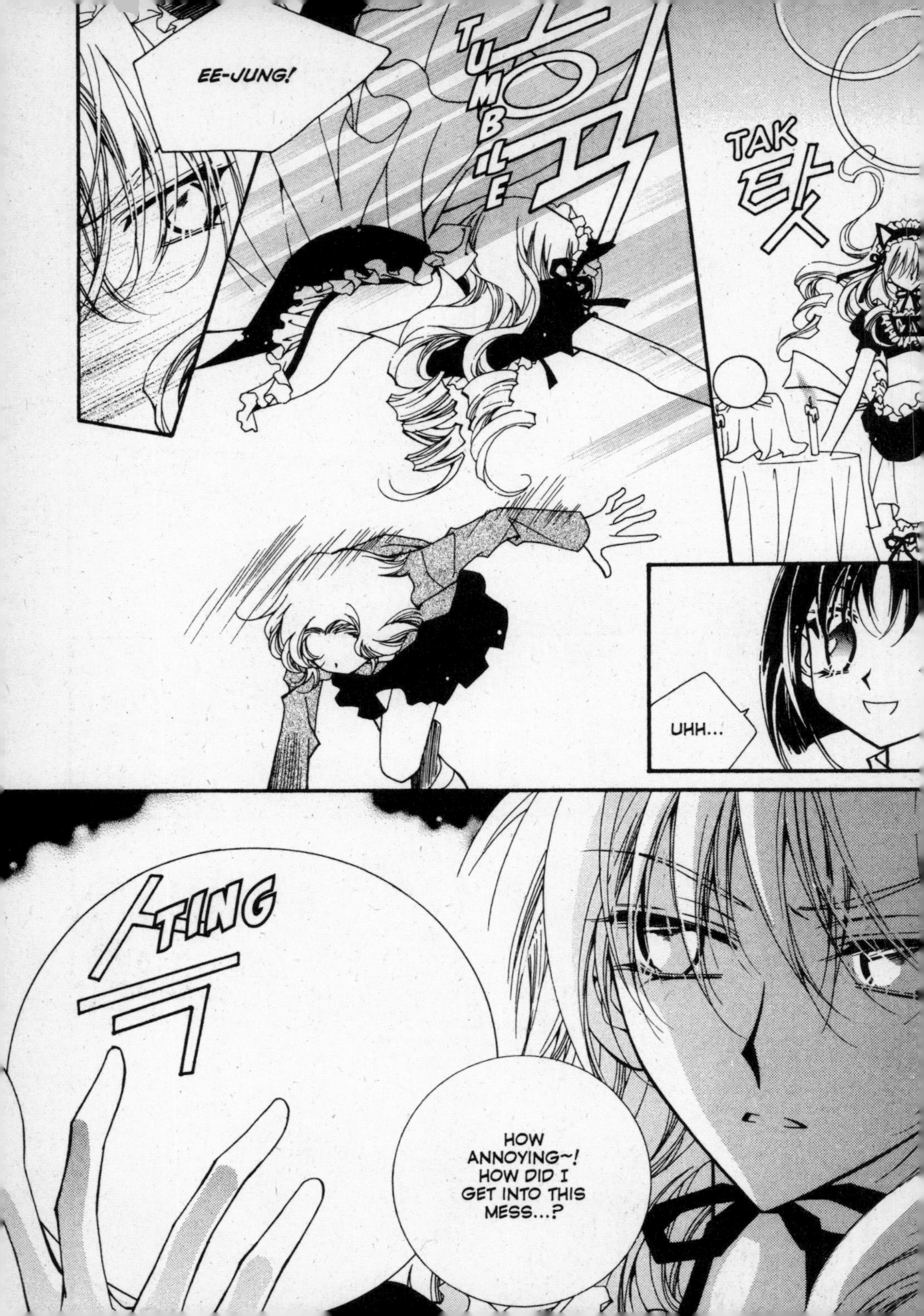
EE-JUNG!
TUMBLE
TAK
UHH...
TING
HOW ANNOYING~! HOW DID I GET INTO THIS MESS...?

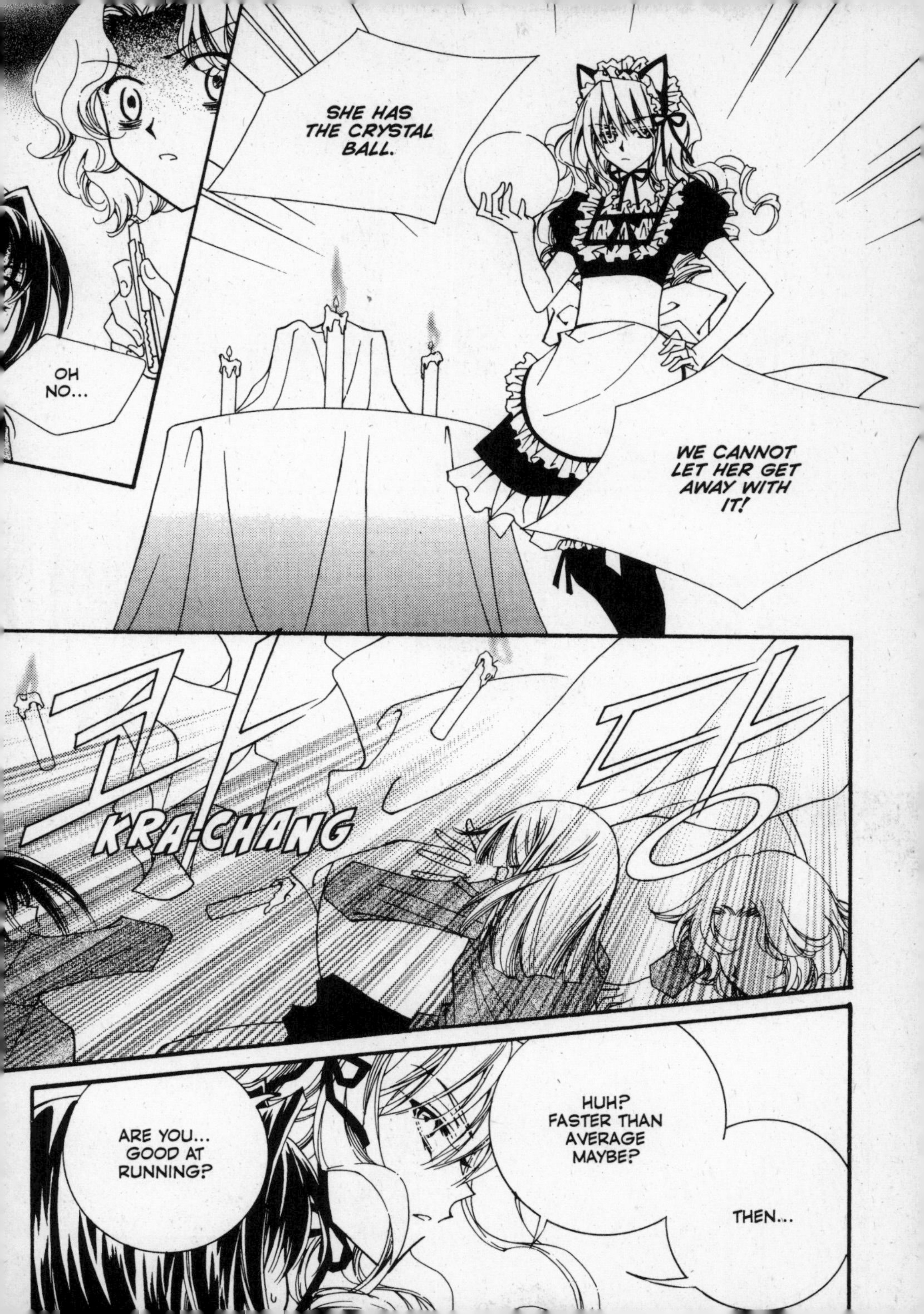
SHE HAS THE CRYSTAL BALL.
OH NO...
WE CANNOT LET HER GET AWAY WITH IT!
KRA-CHANG
ARE YOU... GOOD AT RUNNING?
HUH? FASTER THAN AVERAGE MAYBE?
THEN...

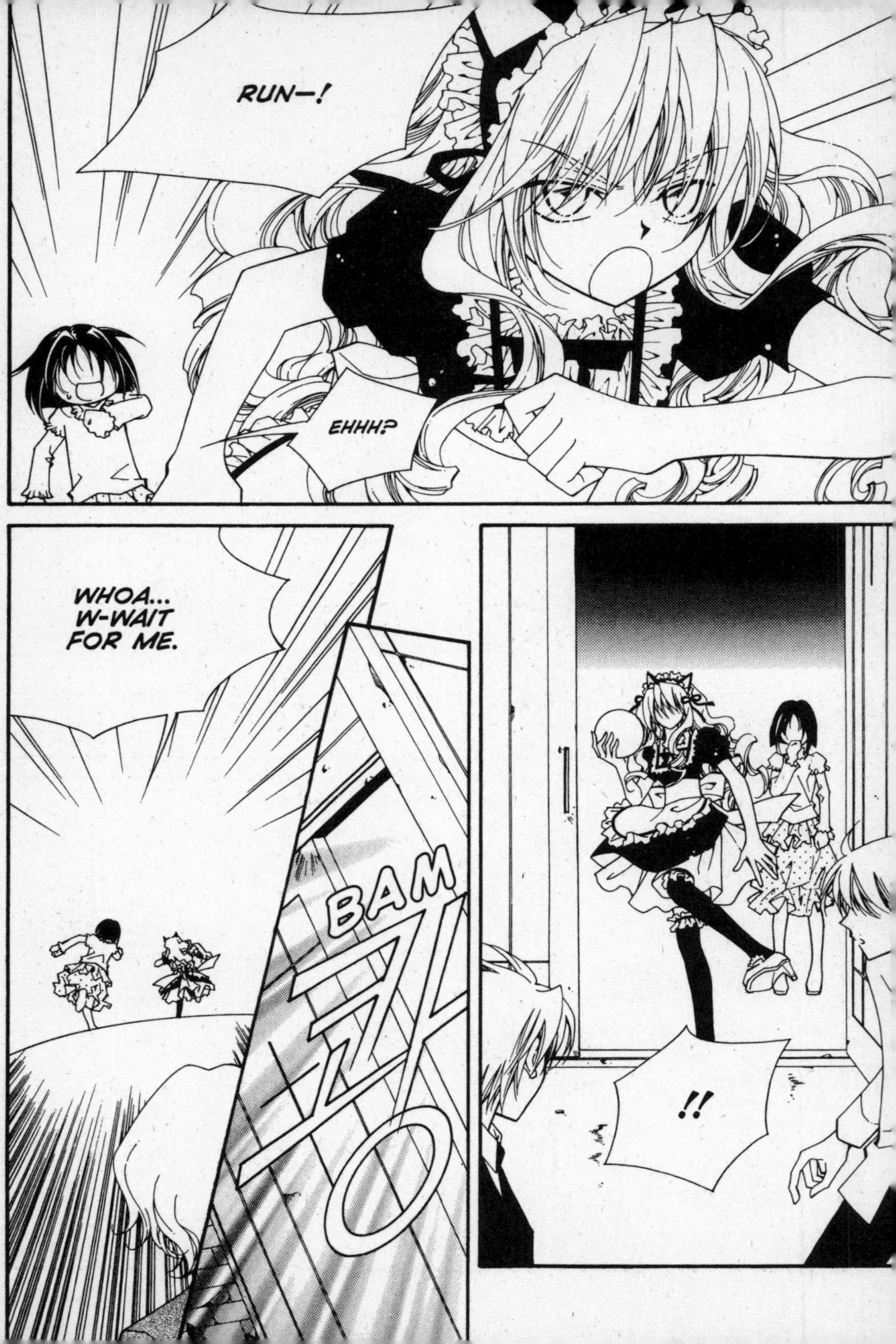
RUN—!
EHHH?
WHOA... W-WAIT FOR ME.
BAM
!!

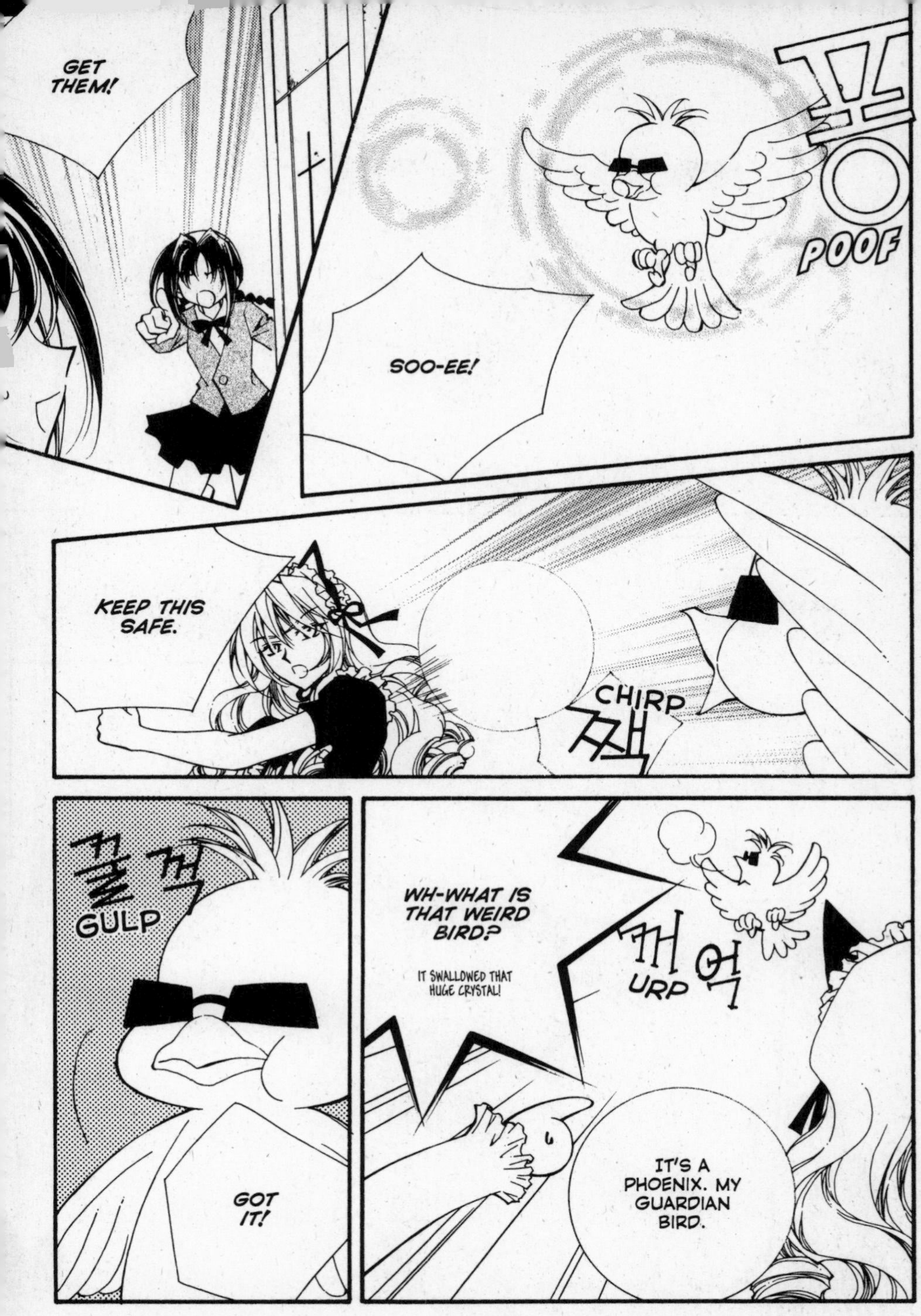
GET THEM!
SOO-EE!
퐁
POOF
KEEP THIS SAFE.
CHIRP
짹
꿀꺽
GULP
GOT IT!
WH-WHAT IS THAT WEIRD BIRD?
IT SWALLOWED THAT HUGE CRYSTAL!
꺼억
URP
IT'S A PHOENIX. MY GUARDIAN BIRD.

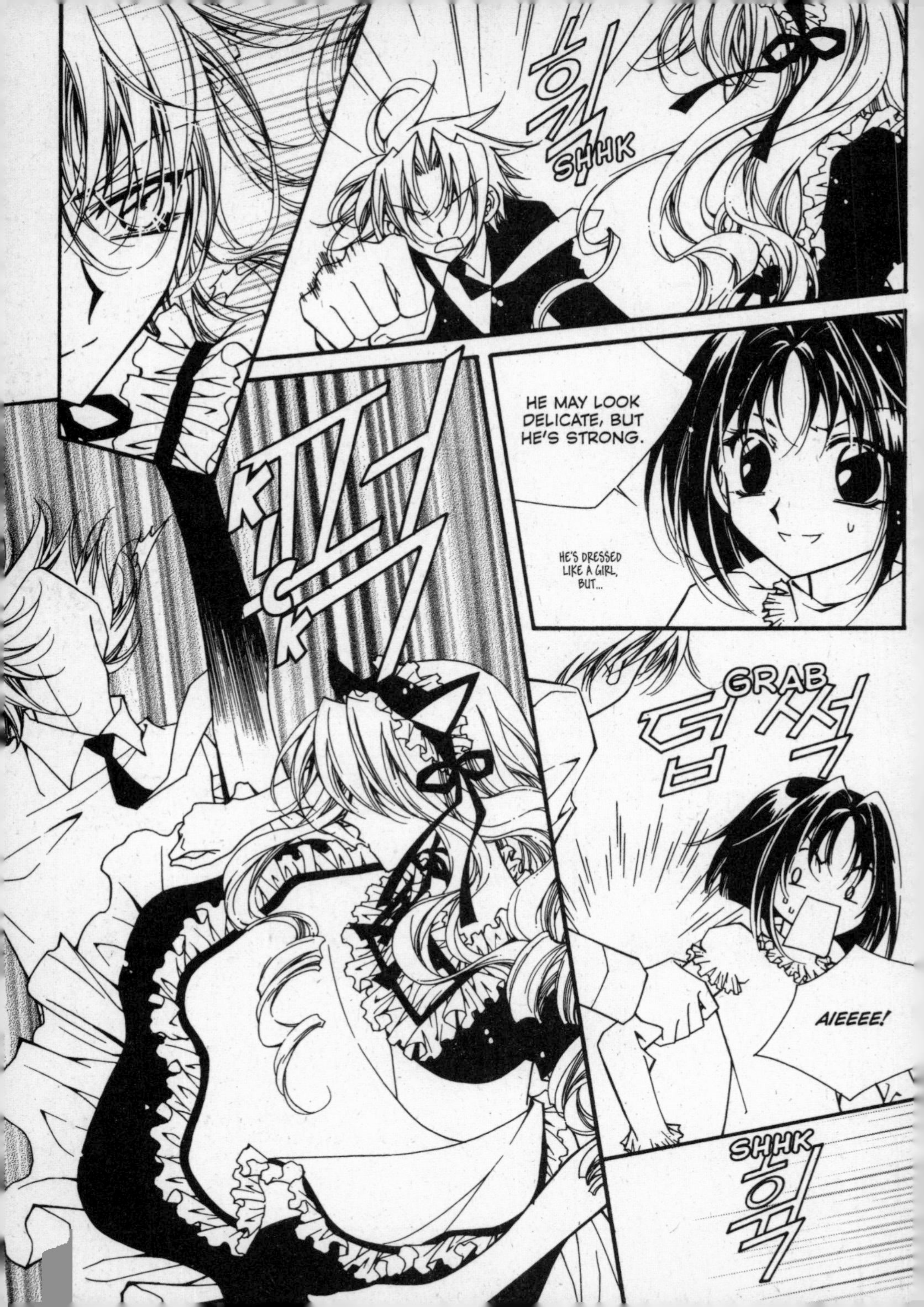
SHHK
KICK
HE MAY LOOK DELICATE, BUT HE'S STRONG.
HE'S DRESSED LIKE A GIRL, BUT...
GRAB
AIEEEE!
SHHK

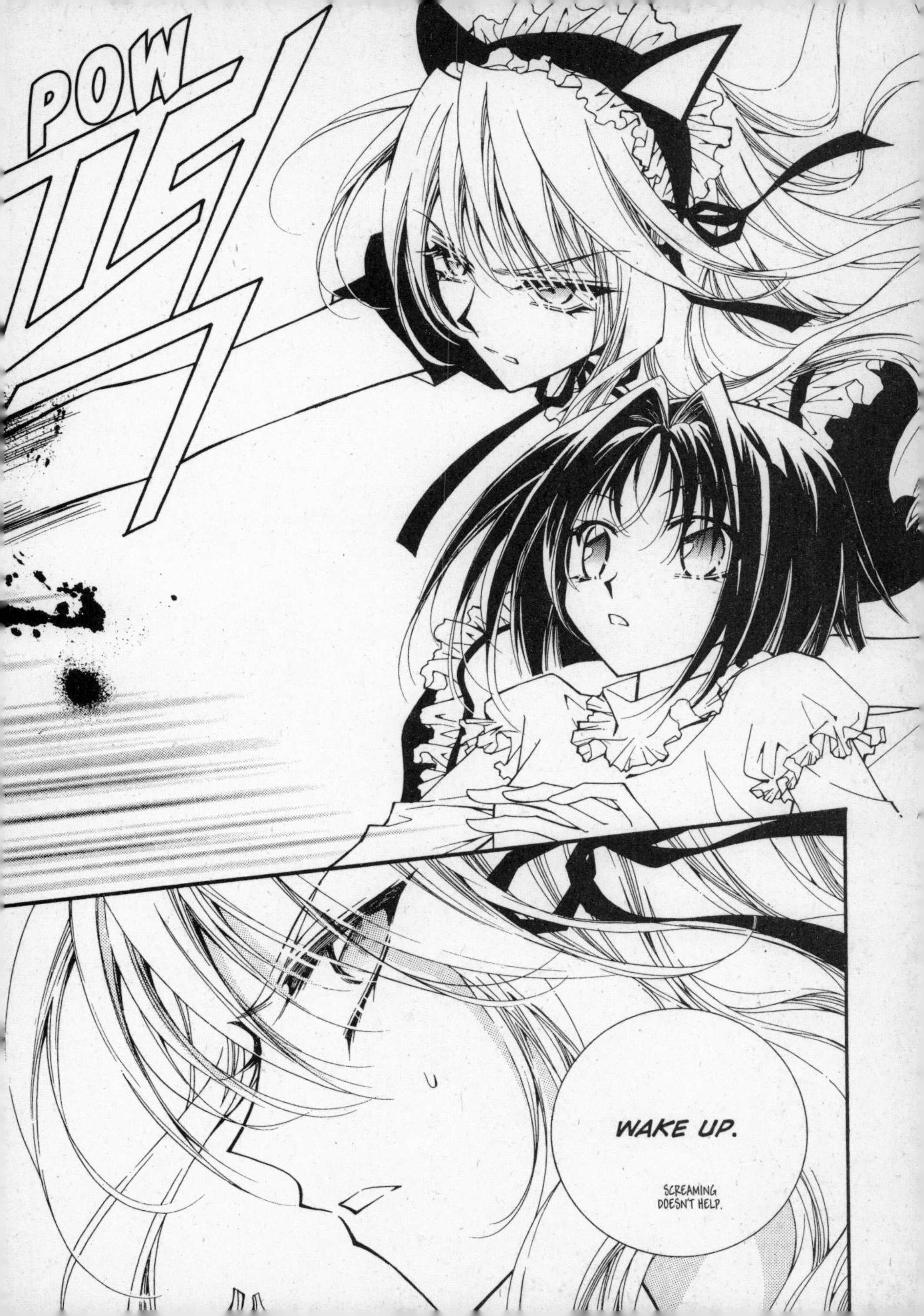
POW
WAKE UP.
SCREAMING DOESN'T HELP.

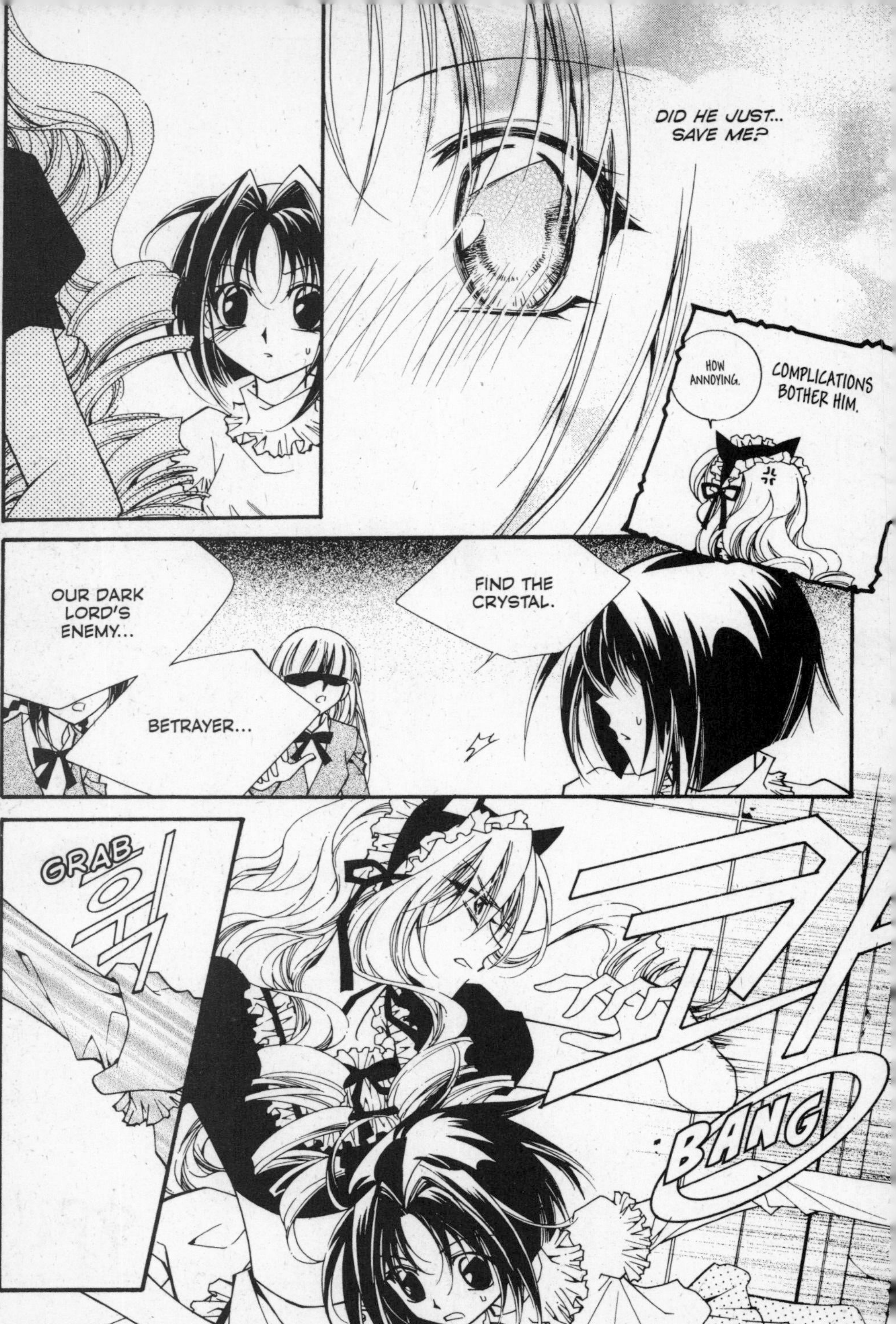
DID HE JUST... SAVE ME?
HOW ANNOYING.
COMPLICATIONS BOTHER HIM.
OUR DARK LORD'S ENEMY...
BETRAYER...
FIND THE CRYSTAL.
GRAB
BANG

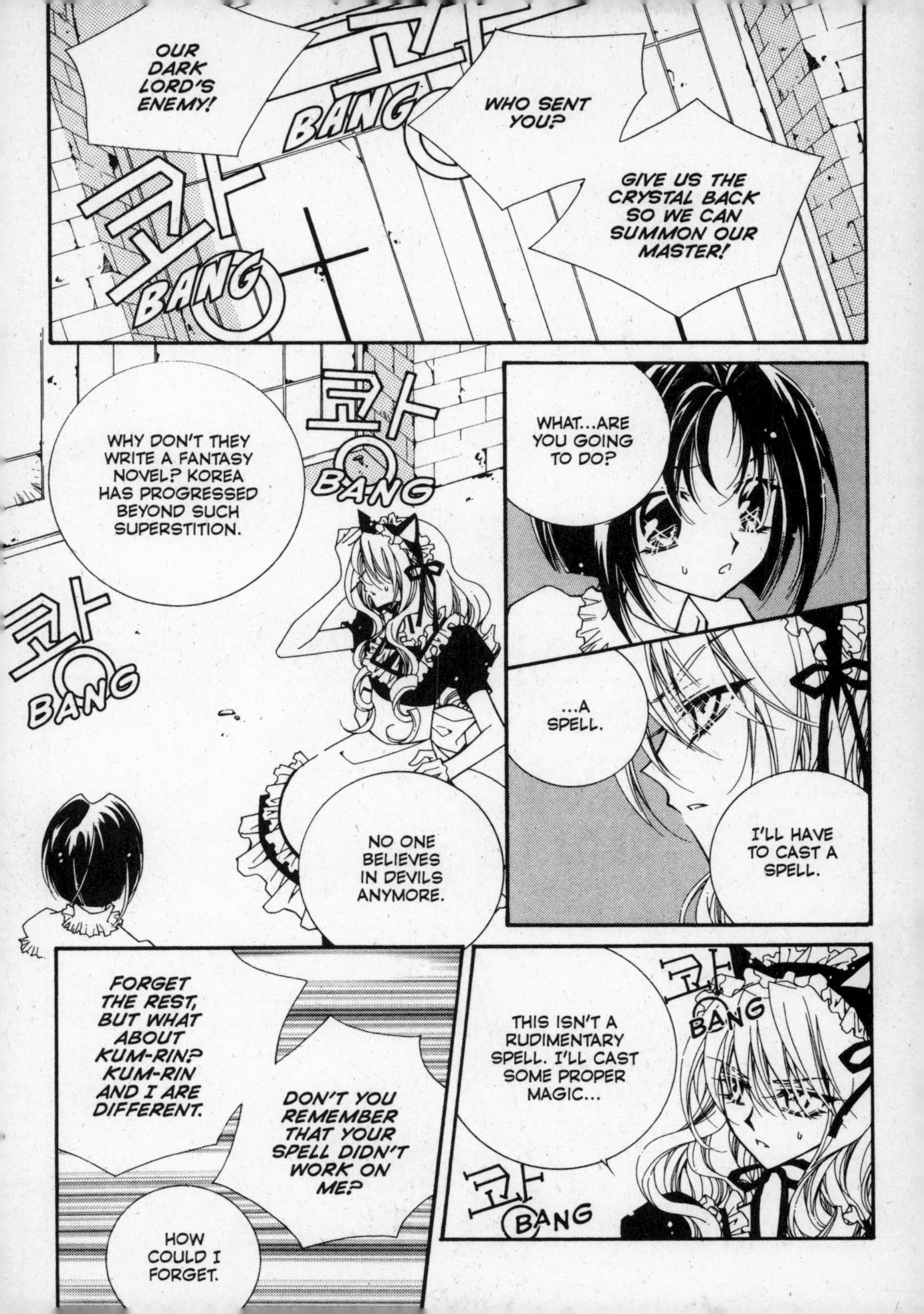
OUR DARK LORD'S ENEMY!
BANG
BANG
WHO SENT YOU?
GIVE US THE CRYSTAL BACK SO WE CAN SUMMON OUR MASTER!
WHY DON'T THEY WRITE A FANTASY NOVEL? KOREA HAS PROGRESSED BEYOND SUCH SUPERSTITION.
BANG
BANG
NO ONE BELIEVES IN DEVILS ANYMORE.
WHAT...ARE YOU GOING TO DO?
...A SPELL.
I'LL HAVE TO CAST A SPELL.
FORGET THE REST, BUT WHAT ABOUT KUM-RIN? KUM-RIN AND I ARE DIFFERENT.
DON'T YOU REMEMBER THAT YOUR SPELL DIDN'T WORK ON ME?
HOW COULD I FORGET.
THIS ISN'T A RUDIMENTARY SPELL. I'LL CAST SOME PROPER MAGIC...
BANG
BANG

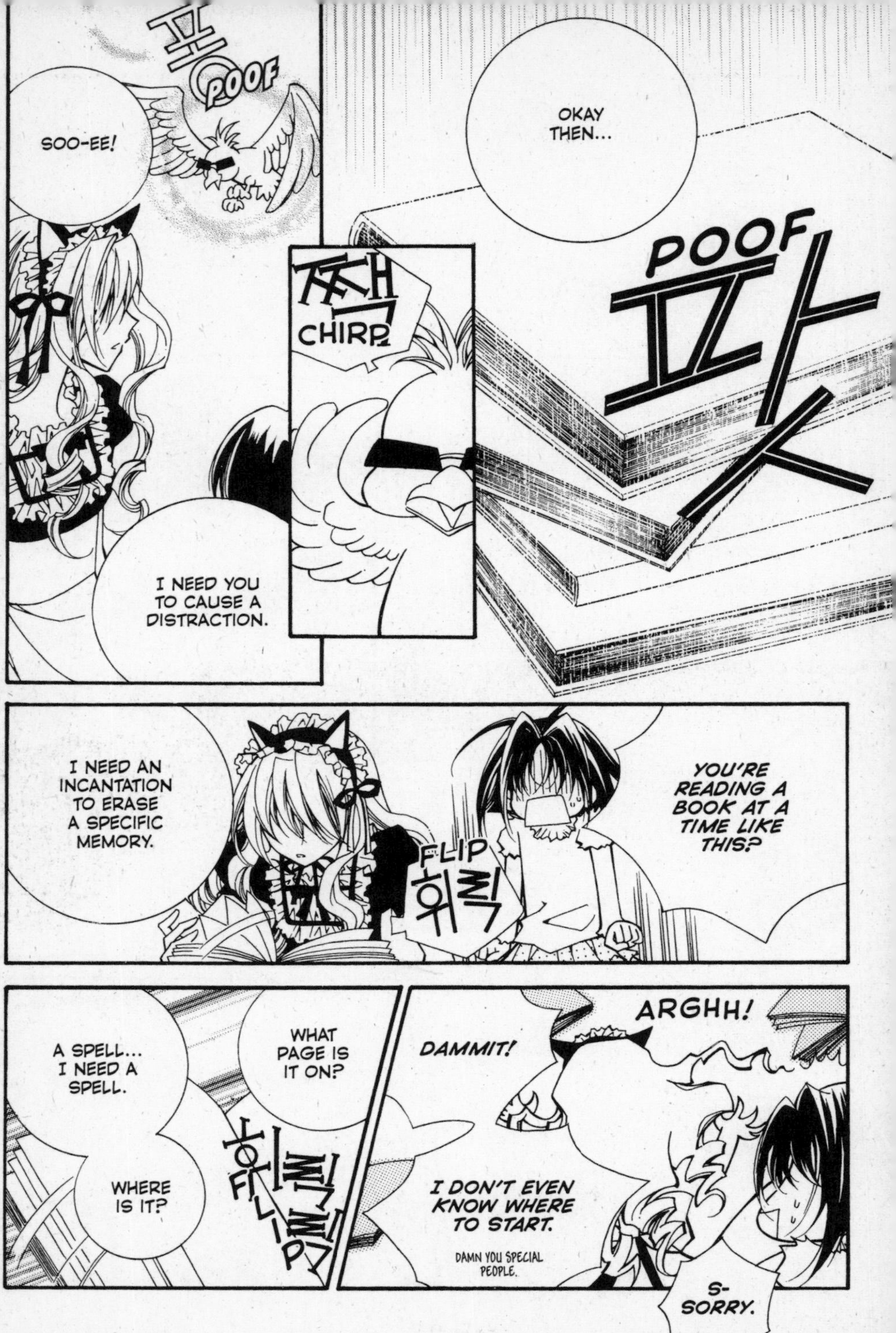
POOF
SOO-EE!
I NEED YOU TO CAUSE A DISTRACTION.
CHIRP
OKAY THEN...
POOF
I NEED AN INCANTATION TO ERASE A SPECIFIC MEMORY.
FLIP
휘릭
YOU'RE READING A BOOK AT A TIME LIKE THIS?
A SPELL... I NEED A SPELL.
WHAT PAGE IS IT ON?
WHERE IS IT?
FLIP FLIP
DAMMIT!
ARGHH!
I DON'T EVEN KNOW WHERE TO START.
DAMN YOU SPECIAL PEOPLE.
S-SORRY.

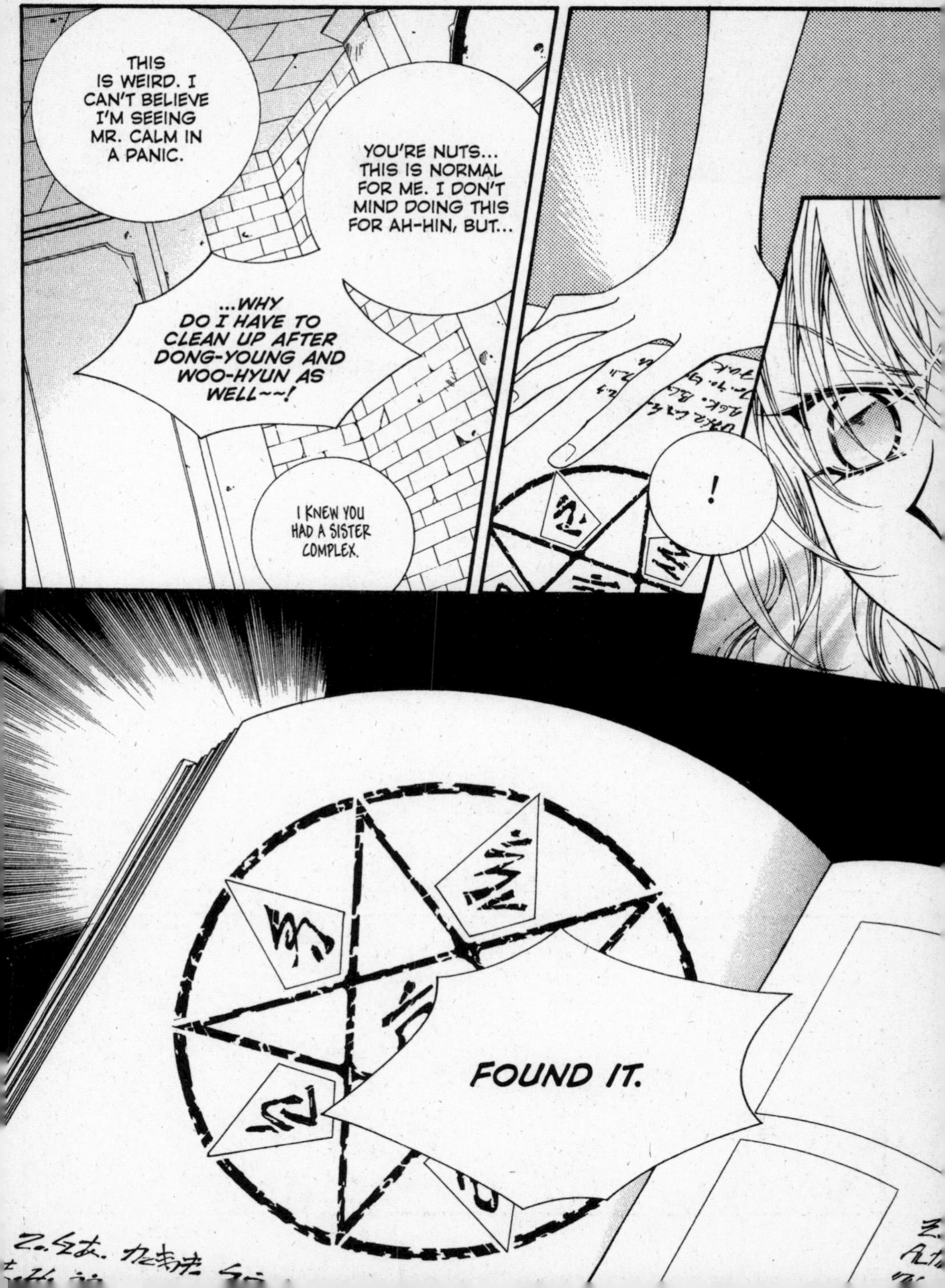
THIS IS WEIRD. I CAN'T BELIEVE I'M SEEING MR. CALM IN A PANIC.
YOU'RE NUTS... THIS IS NORMAL FOR ME. I DON'T MIND DOING THIS FOR AH-HIN, BUT...
...WHY DO I HAVE TO CLEAN UP AFTER DONG-YOUNG AND WOO-HYUN AS WELL~~!
I KNEW YOU HAD A SISTER COMPLEX.
!
FOUND IT.

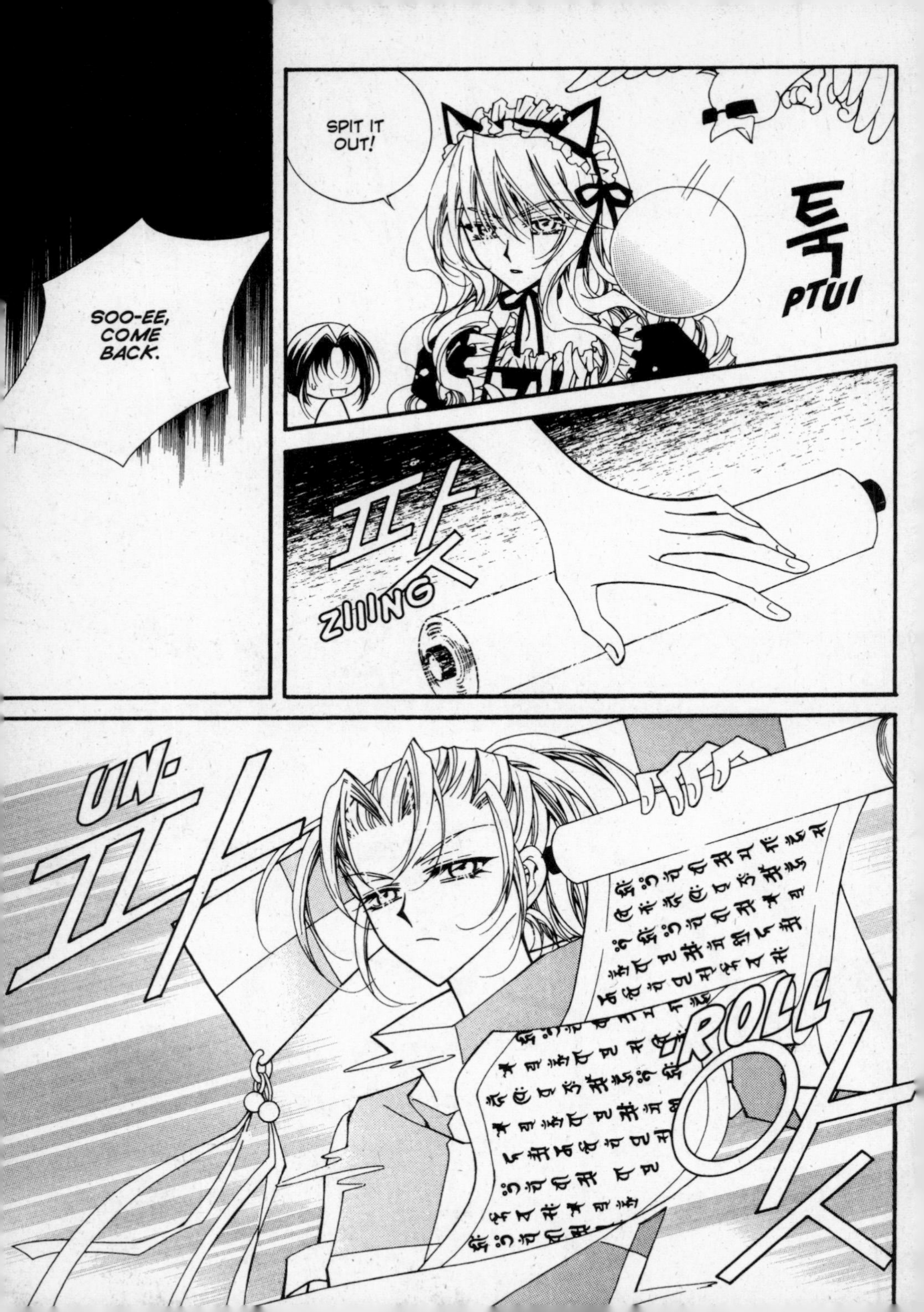

SOO-EE, COME BACK.
SPIT IT OUT!
톡
PTUI
ZIIING
UN-
ROLL

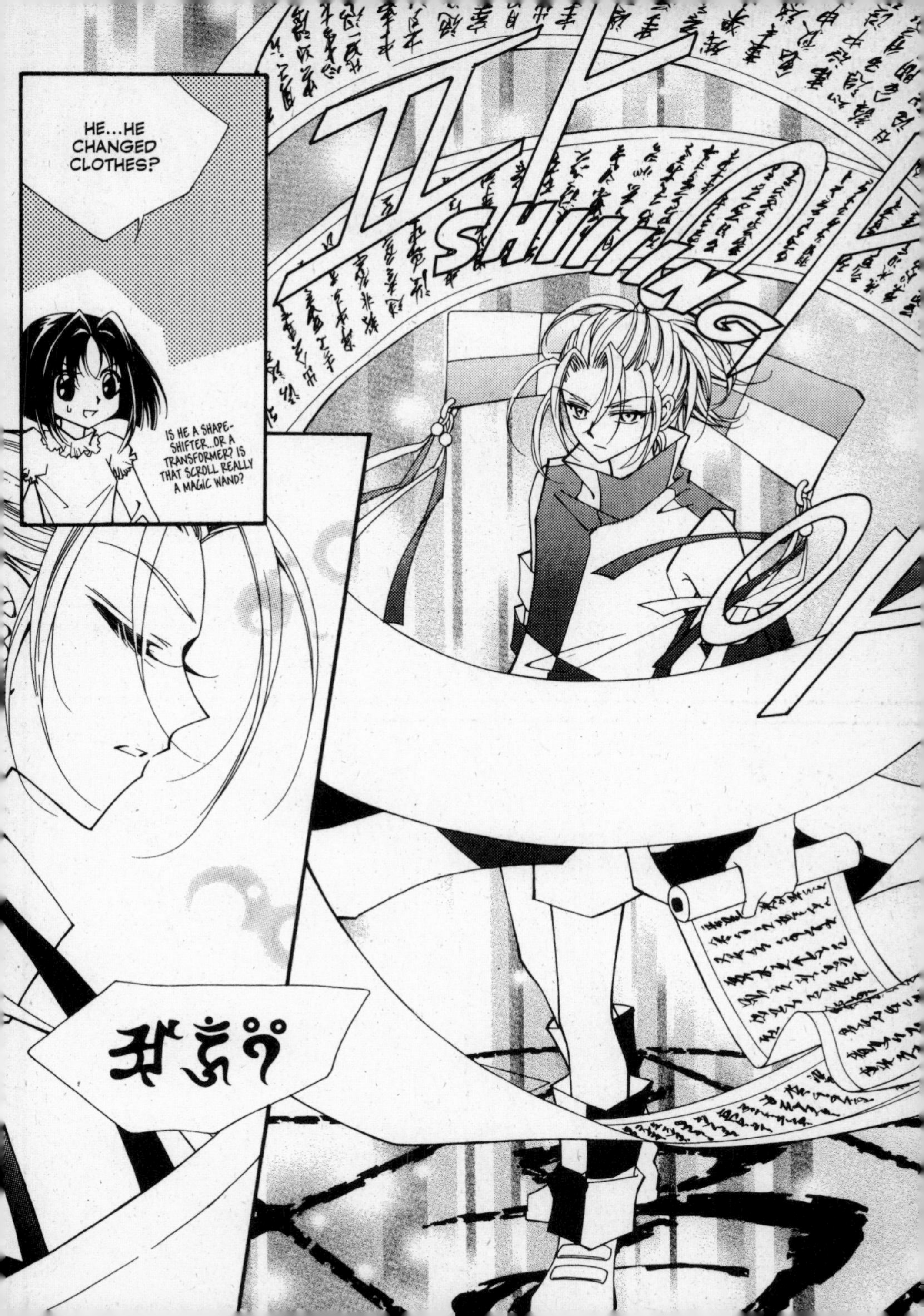
HE...HE CHANGED CLOTHES?
IS HE A SHAPE-SHIFTER...OR A TRANSFORMER? IS THAT SCROLL REALLY A MAGIC WAND?
SHIIIING

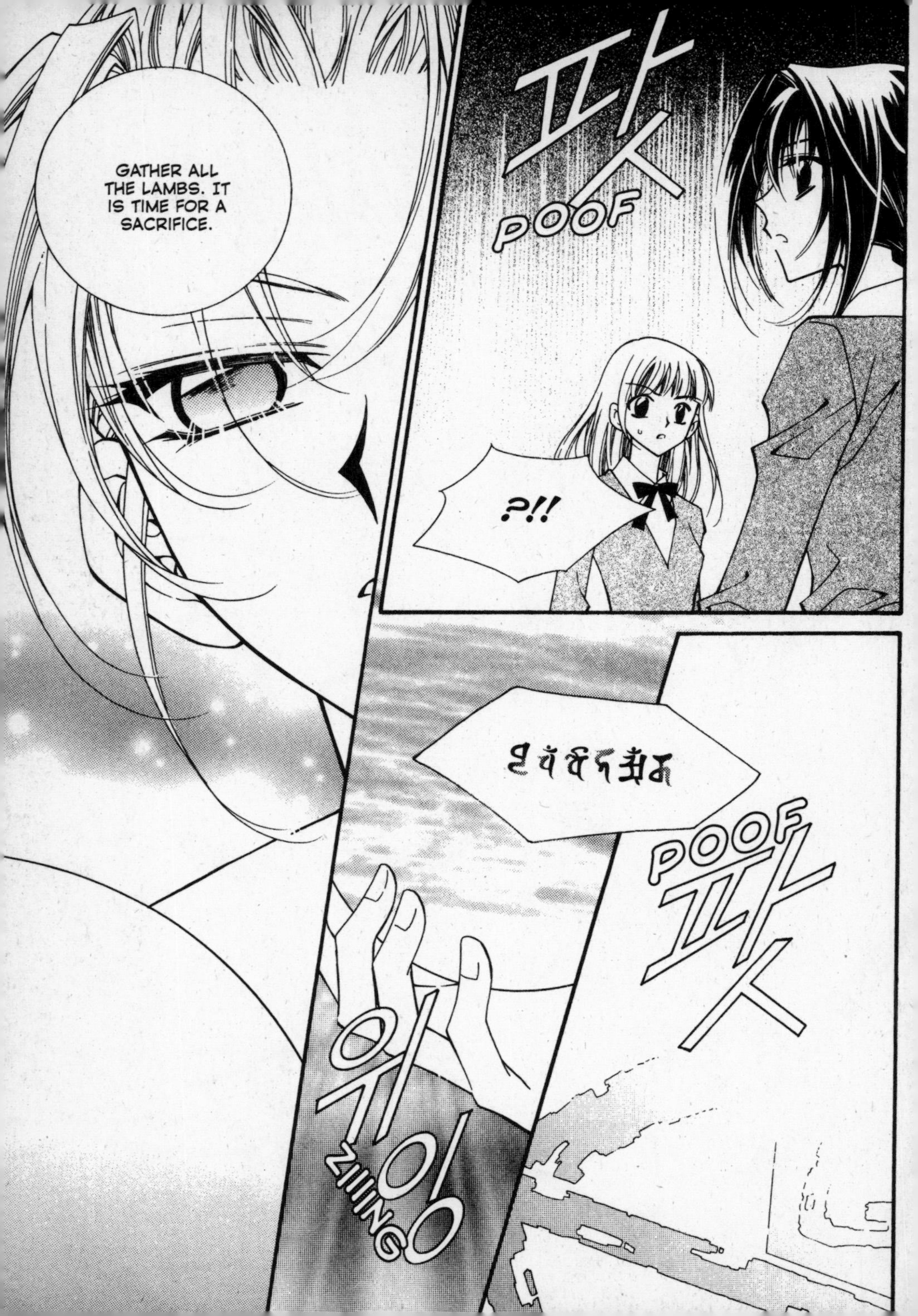
GATHER ALL THE LAMBS. IT IS TIME FOR A SACRIFICE.
POOF
?!!
ZIIING
POOF

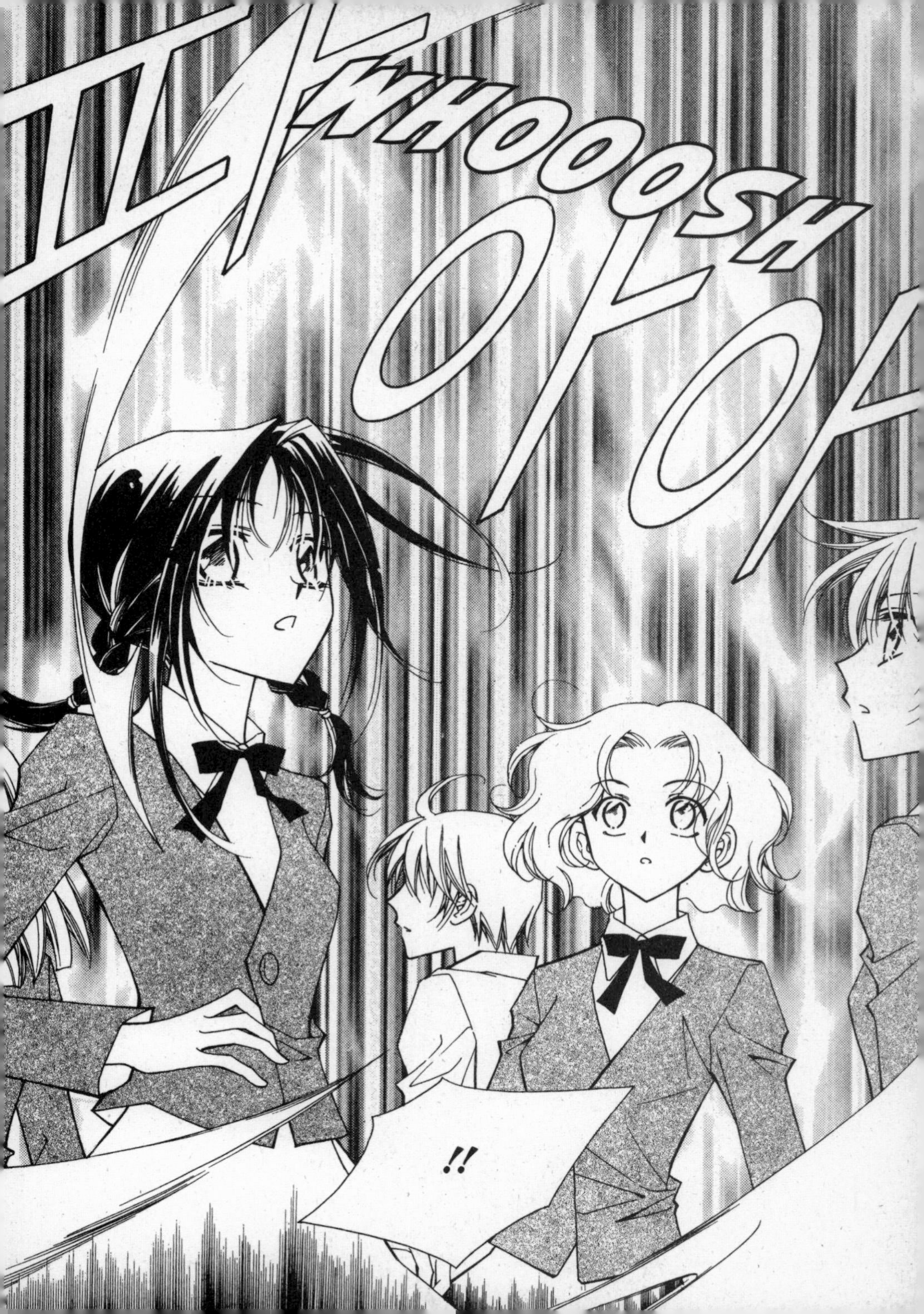
WHOOOSH
!!

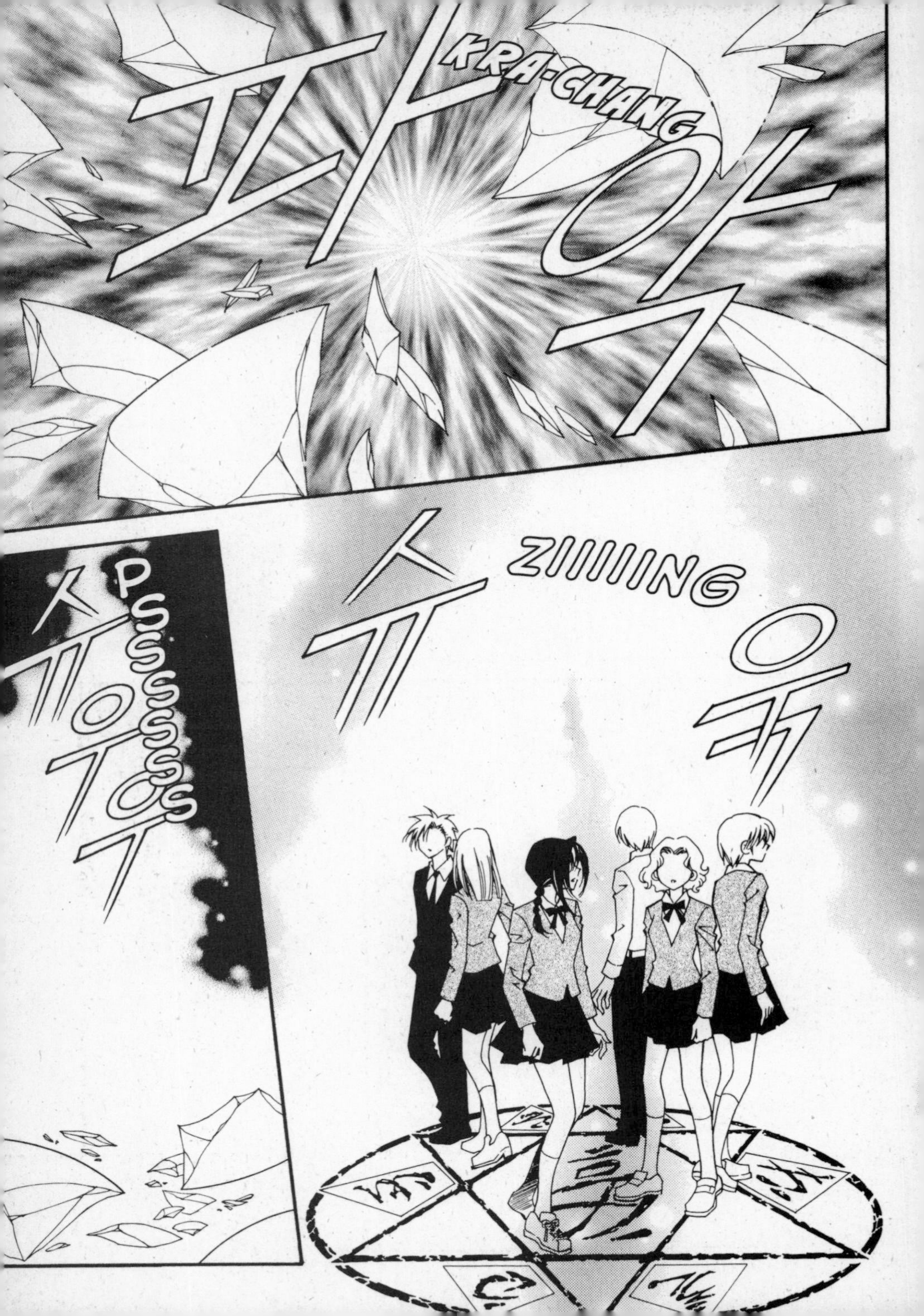
KRA-CHANG
ZIIIIING
PSSSSSS

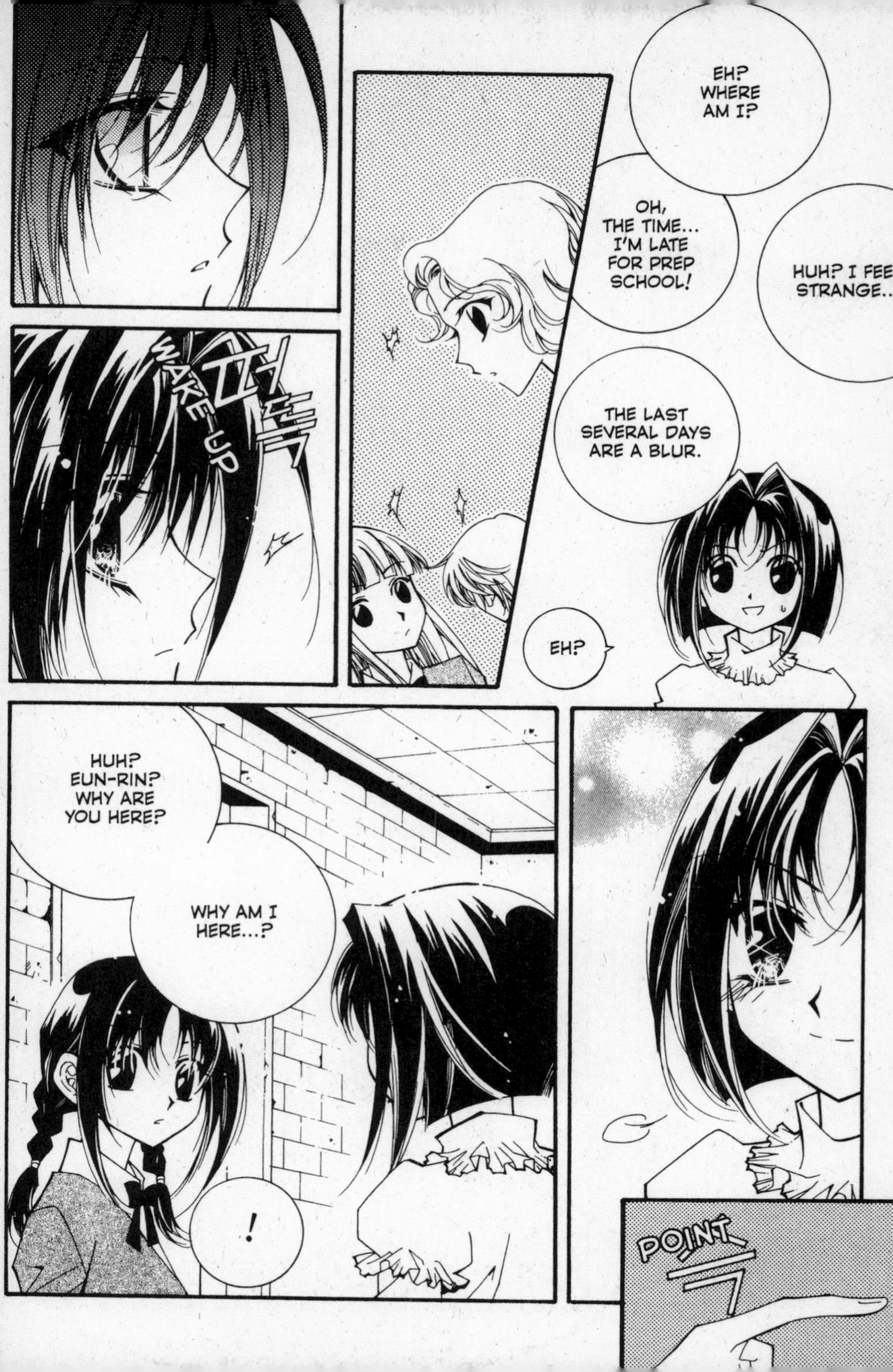
WAKE UP
EH? WHERE AM I?
OH, THE TIME... I'M LATE FOR PREP SCHOOL!
HUH? I FEEL STRANGE...
THE LAST SEVERAL DAYS ARE A BLUR.
EH?
HUH? EUN-RIN? WHY ARE YOU HERE?
WHY AM I HERE...?
!
POINT

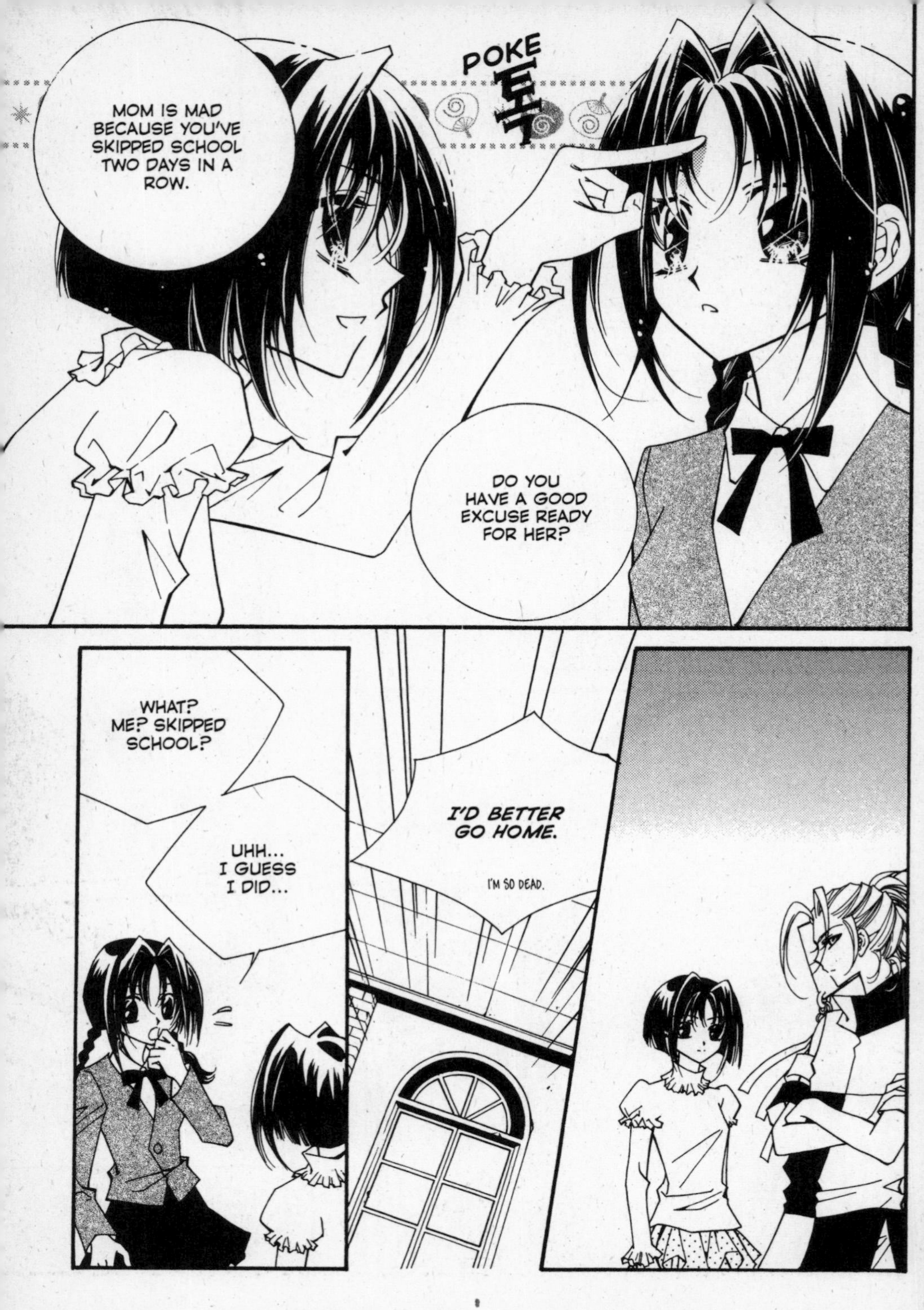
MOM IS MAD BECAUSE YOU'VE SKIPPED SCHOOL TWO DAYS IN A ROW.
POKE
톡
DO YOU HAVE A GOOD EXCUSE READY FOR HER?
WHAT? ME? SKIPPED SCHOOL?
UHH... I GUESS I DID...
I'D BETTER GO HOME.
I'M SO DEAD.

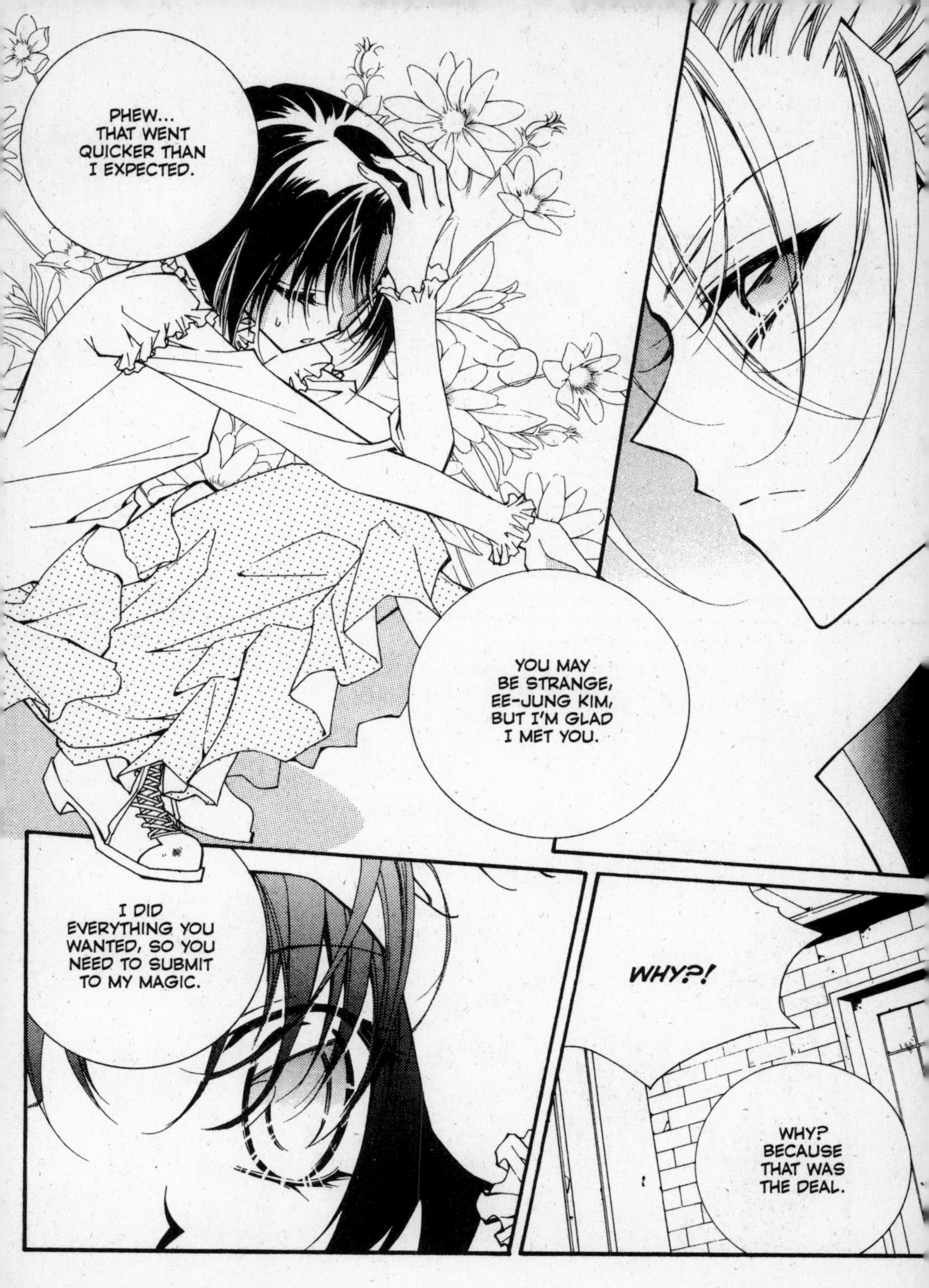
PHEW... THAT WENT QUICKER THAN I EXPECTED.
YOU MAY BE STRANGE, EE-JUNG KIM, BUT I'M GLAD I MET YOU.
I DID EVERYTHING YOU WANTED, SO YOU NEED TO SUBMIT TO MY MAGIC.
WHY?!
WHY? BECAUSE THAT WAS THE DEAL.

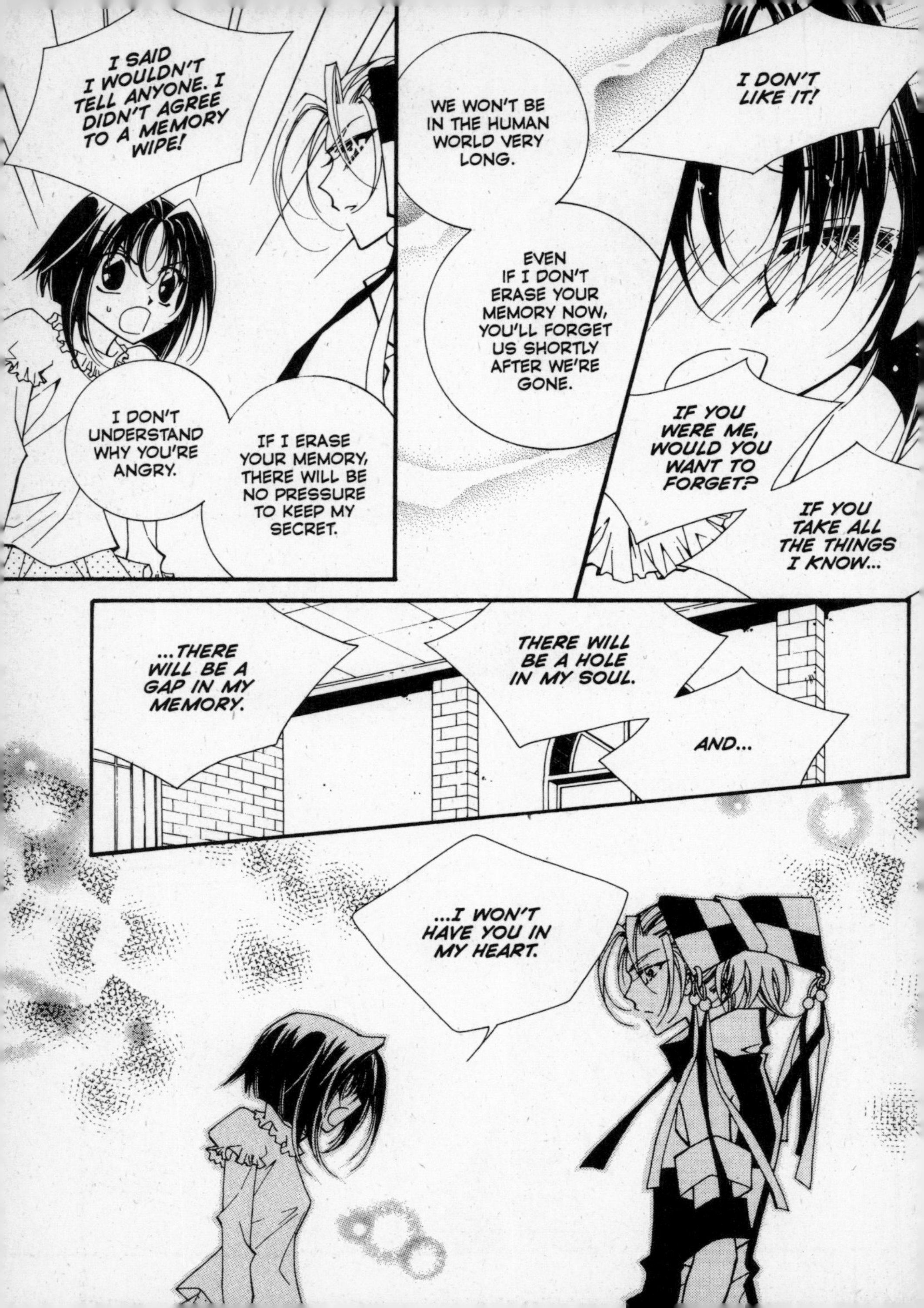
I SAID I WOULDN'T TELL ANYONE. I DIDN'T AGREE TO A MEMORY WIPE!
I DON'T UNDERSTAND WHY YOU'RE ANGRY.
IF I ERASE YOUR MEMORY, THERE WILL BE NO PRESSURE TO KEEP MY SECRET.
WE WON'T BE IN THE HUMAN WORLD VERY LONG.
EVEN IF I DON'T ERASE YOUR MEMORY NOW, YOU'LL FORGET US SHORTLY AFTER WE'RE GONE.
I DON'T LIKE IT!
IF YOU WERE ME, WOULD YOU WANT TO FORGET?
IF YOU TAKE ALL THE THINGS I KNOW...
...THERE WILL BE A GAP IN MY MEMORY.
THERE WILL BE A HOLE IN MY SOUL.
AND...
...I WON'T HAVE YOU IN MY HEART.

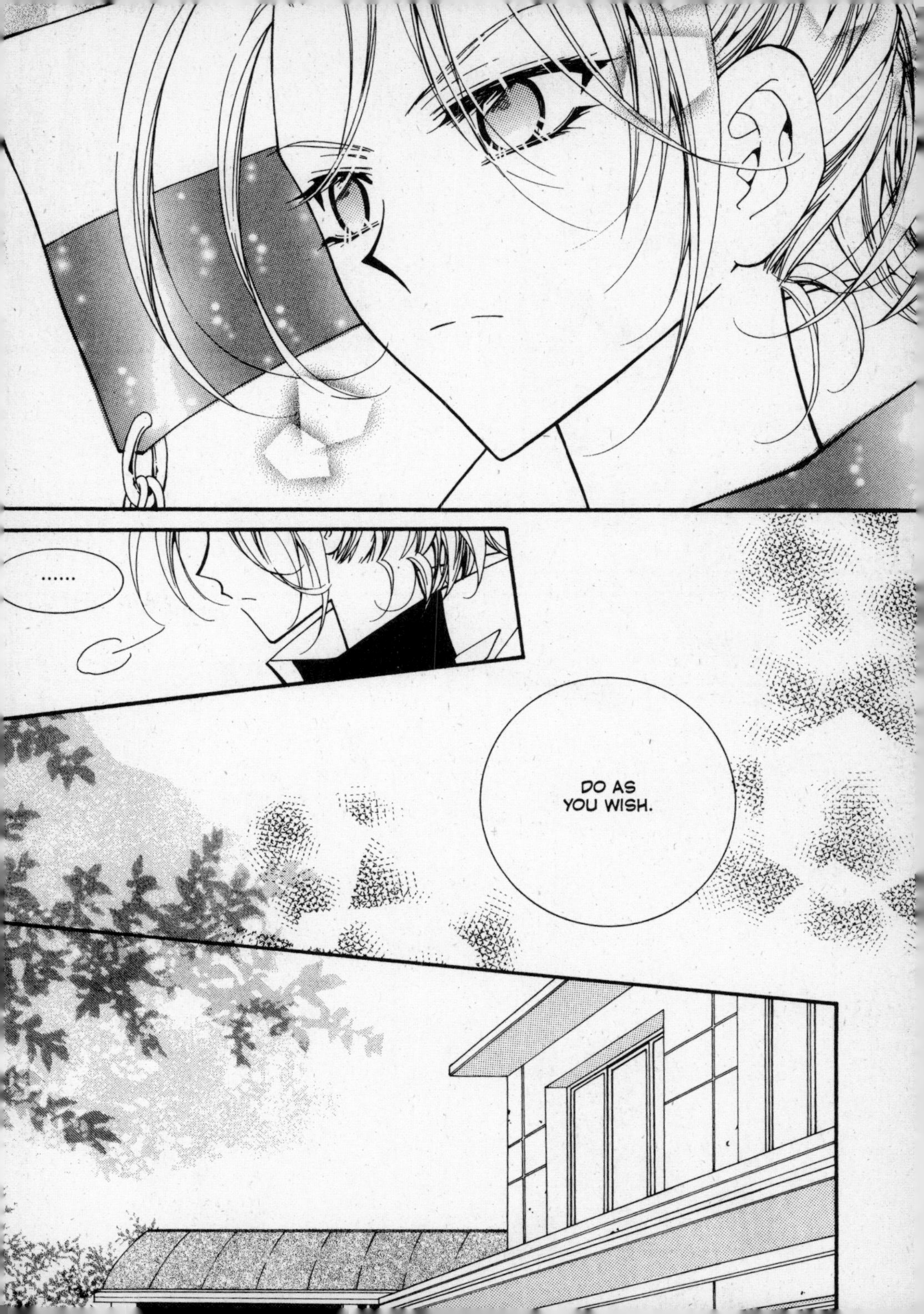
......
DO AS YOU WISH.

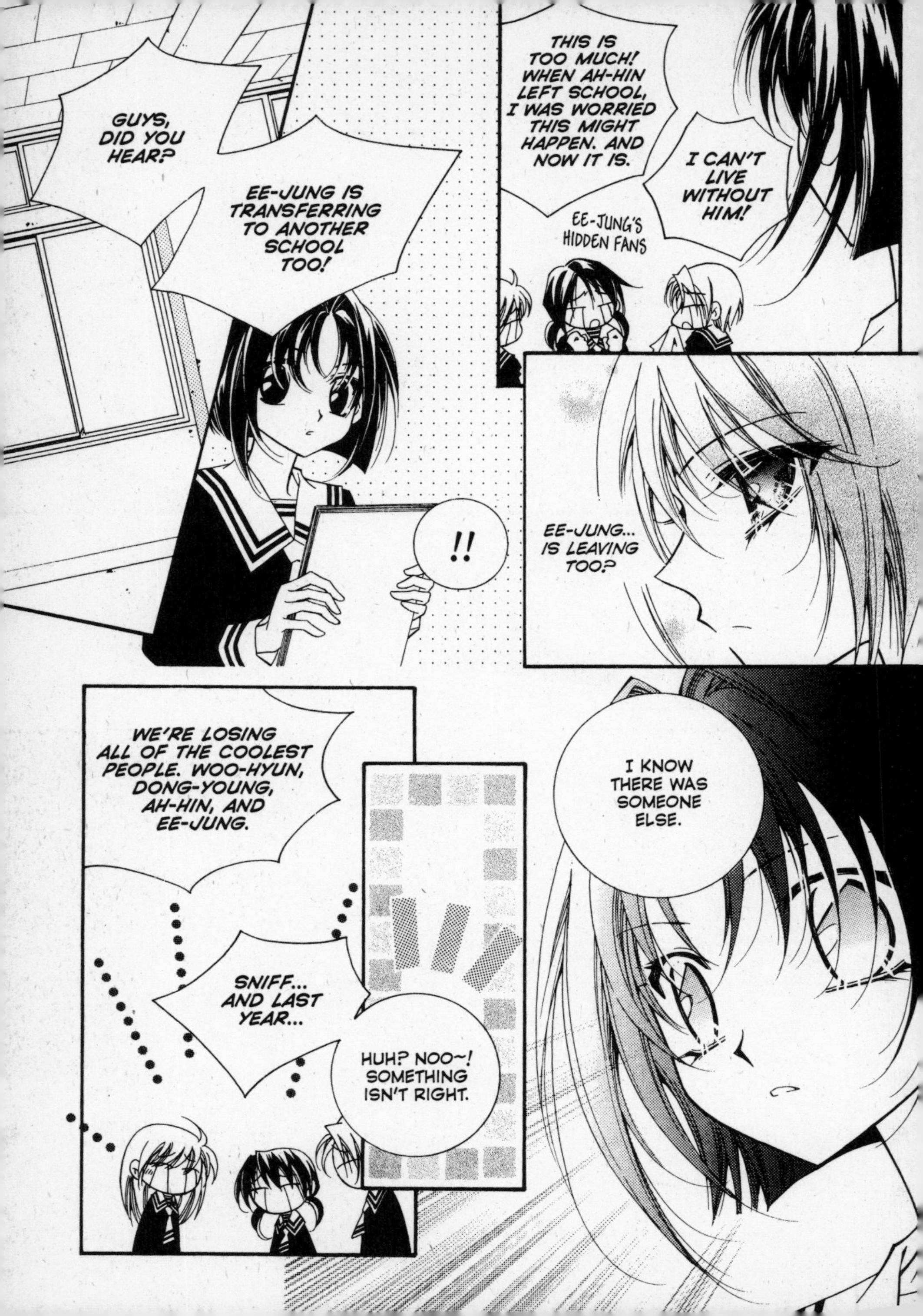
GUYS, DID YOU HEAR?
EE-JUNG IS TRANSFERRING TO ANOTHER SCHOOL TOO!
!!
THIS IS TOO MUCH! WHEN AH-HIN LEFT SCHOOL, I WAS WORRIED THIS MIGHT HAPPEN. AND NOW IT IS.
I CAN'T LIVE WITHOUT HIM!
EE-JUNG'S HIDDEN FANS
EE-JUNG... IS LEAVING TOO?
WE'RE LOSING ALL OF THE COOLEST PEOPLE. WOO-HYUN, DONG-YOUNG, AH-HIN, AND EE-JUNG.
SNIFF... AND LAST YEAR...
HUH? NOO~! SOMETHING ISN'T RIGHT.
I KNOW THERE WAS SOMEONE ELSE.

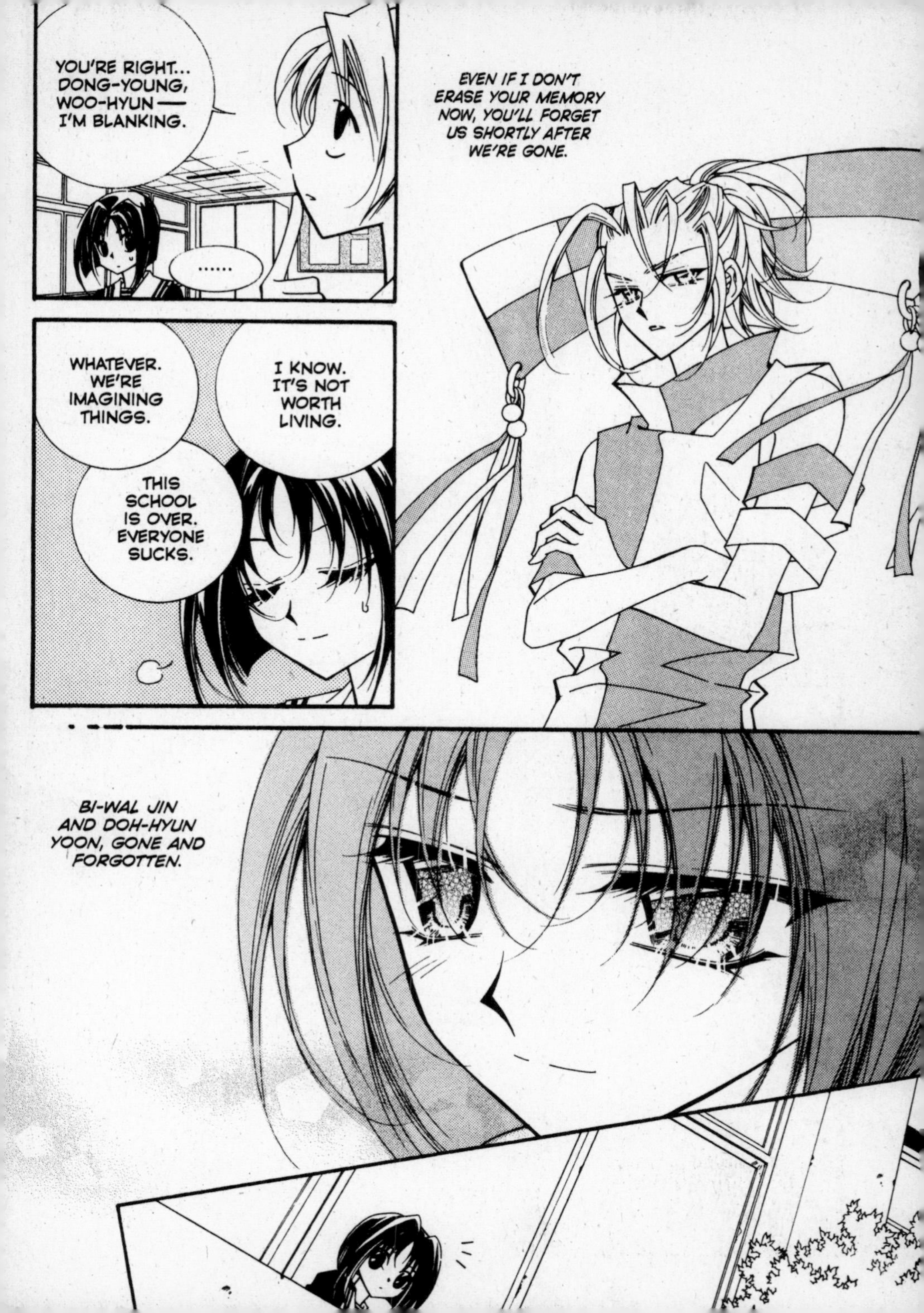
YOU'RE RIGHT... DONG-YOUNG, WOO-HYUN— I'M BLANKING.
......
EVEN IF I DON'T ERASE YOUR MEMORY NOW, YOU'LL FORGET US SHORTLY AFTER WE'RE GONE.
WHATEVER. WE'RE IMAGINING THINGS.
I KNOW. IT'S NOT WORTH LIVING.
THIS SCHOOL IS OVER. EVERYONE SUCKS.
BI-WAL JIN AND DOH-HYUN YOON, GONE AND FORGOTTEN.

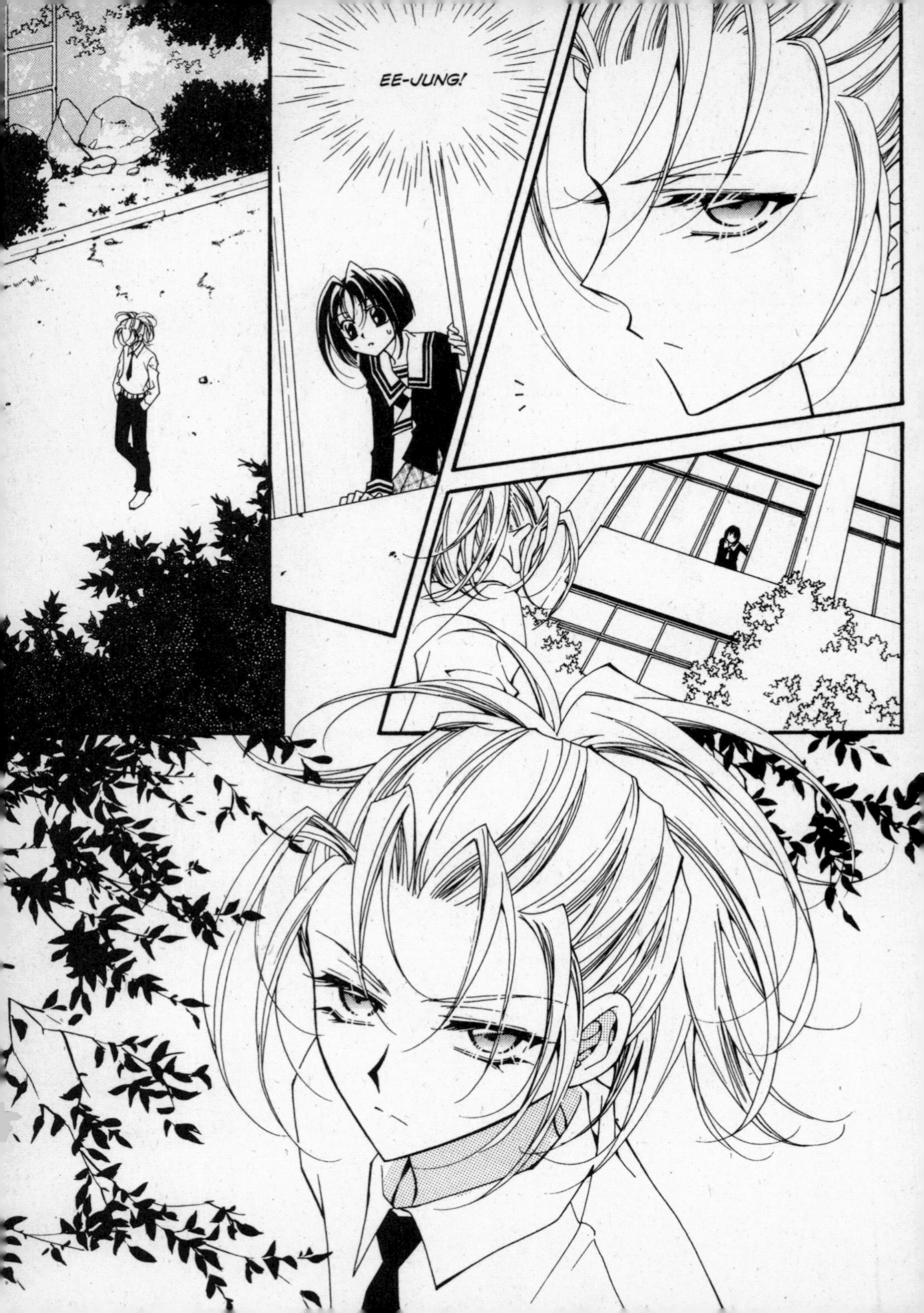
EE-JUNG!

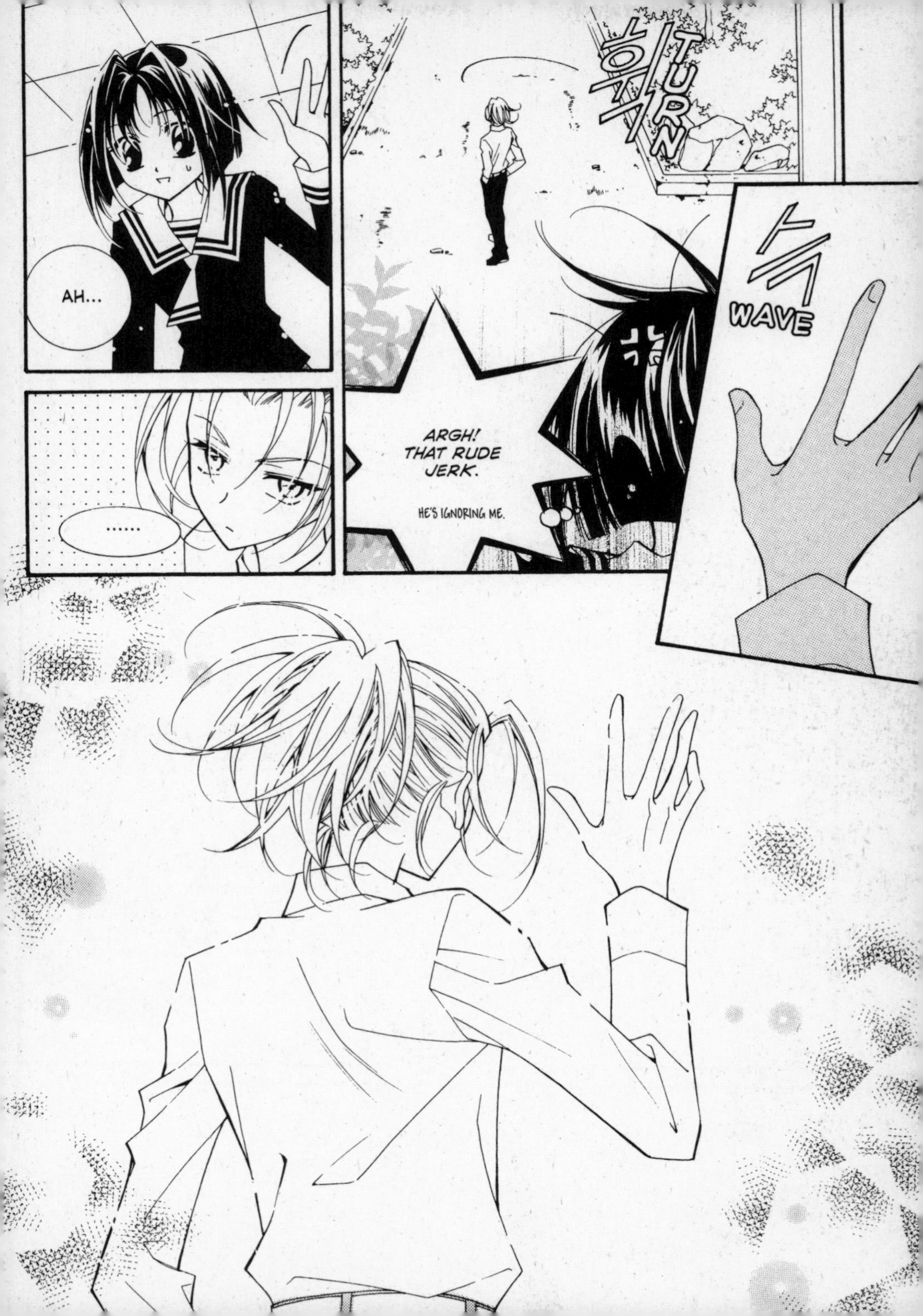
AH...
TURN
......
ARGH! THAT RUDE JERK.
HE'S IGNORING ME.
WAVE

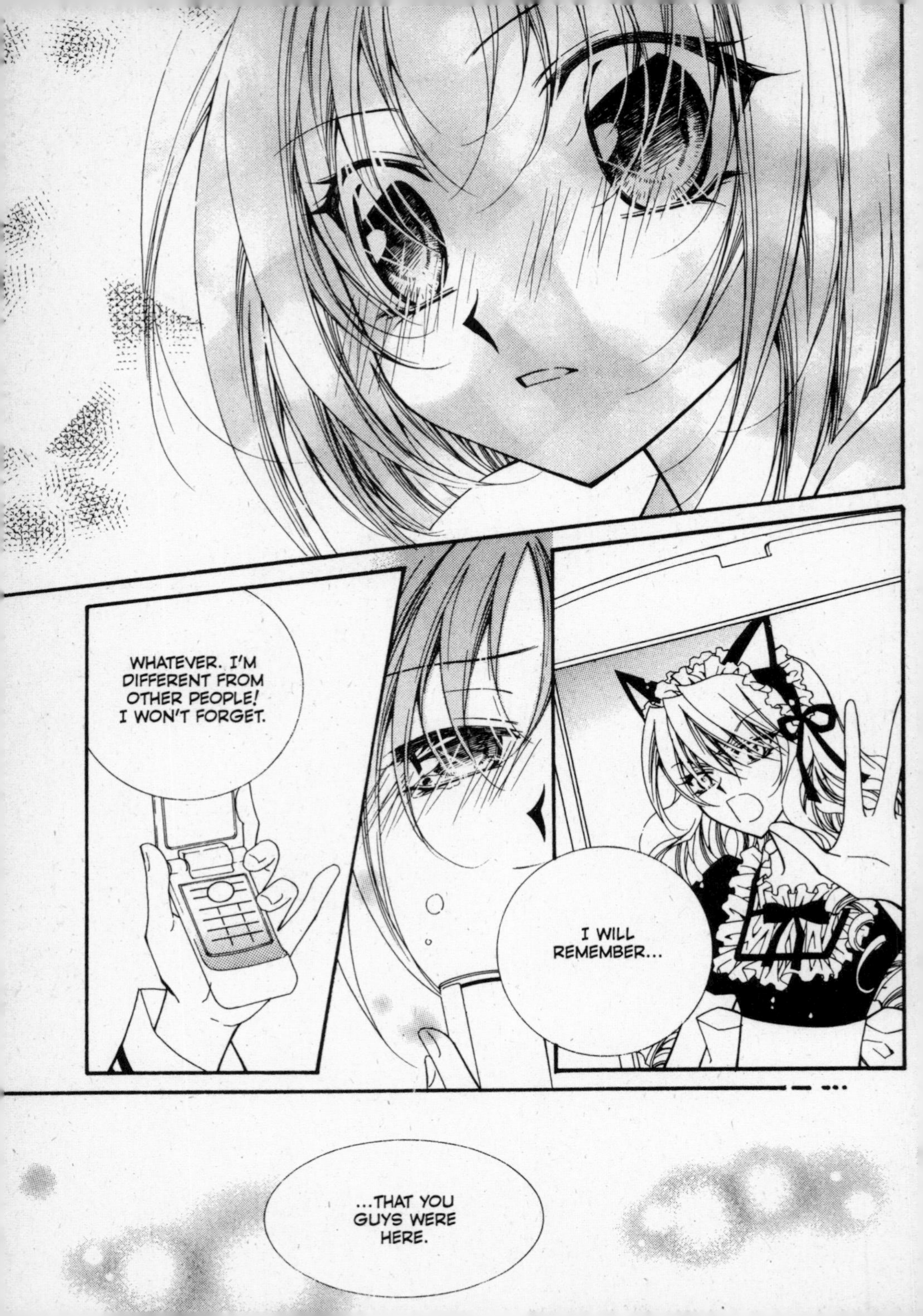
WHATEVER. I'M DIFFERENT FROM OTHER PEOPLE! I WON'T FORGET.
I WILL REMEMBER...
...THAT YOU GUYS WERE HERE.

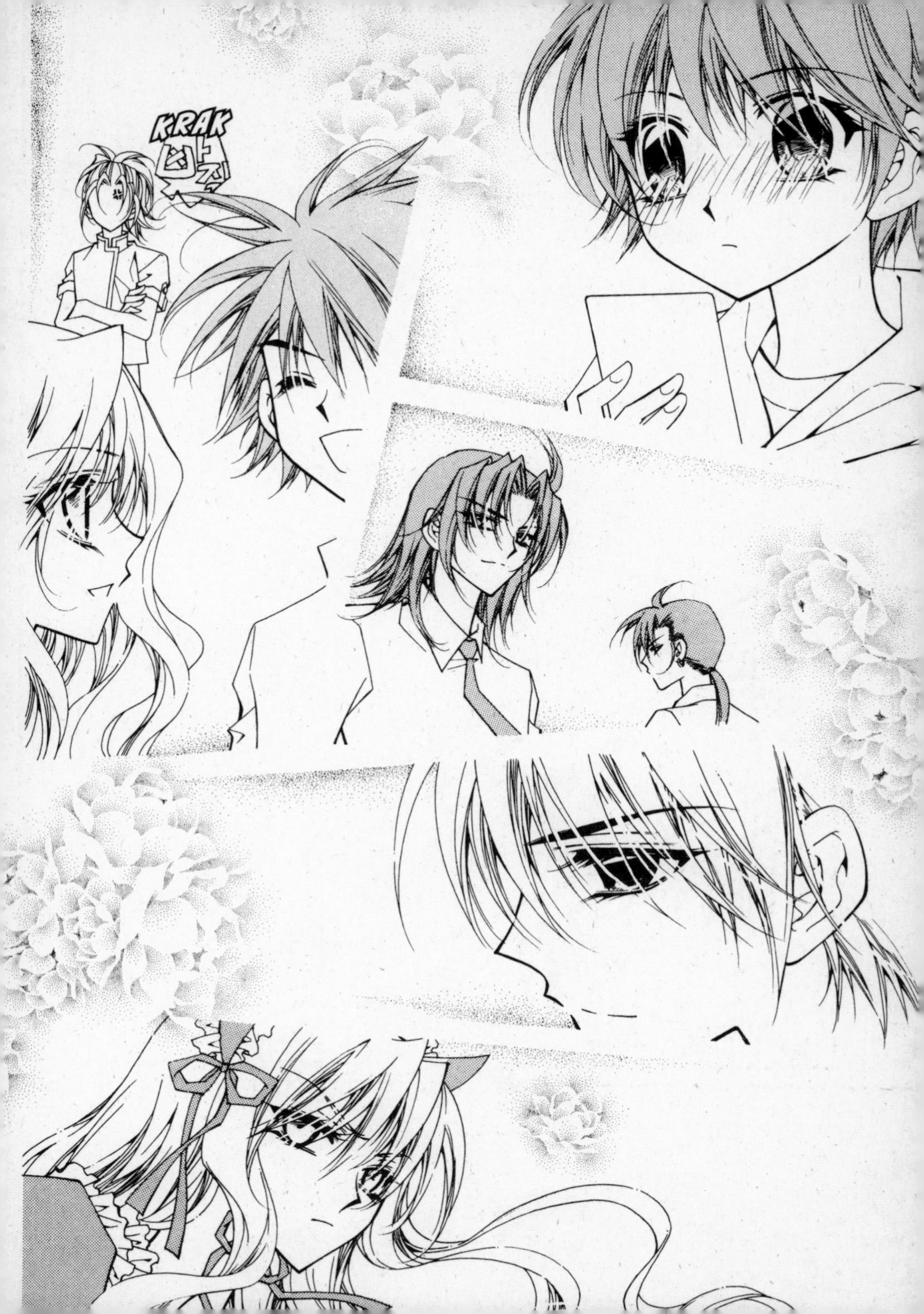
KRAK

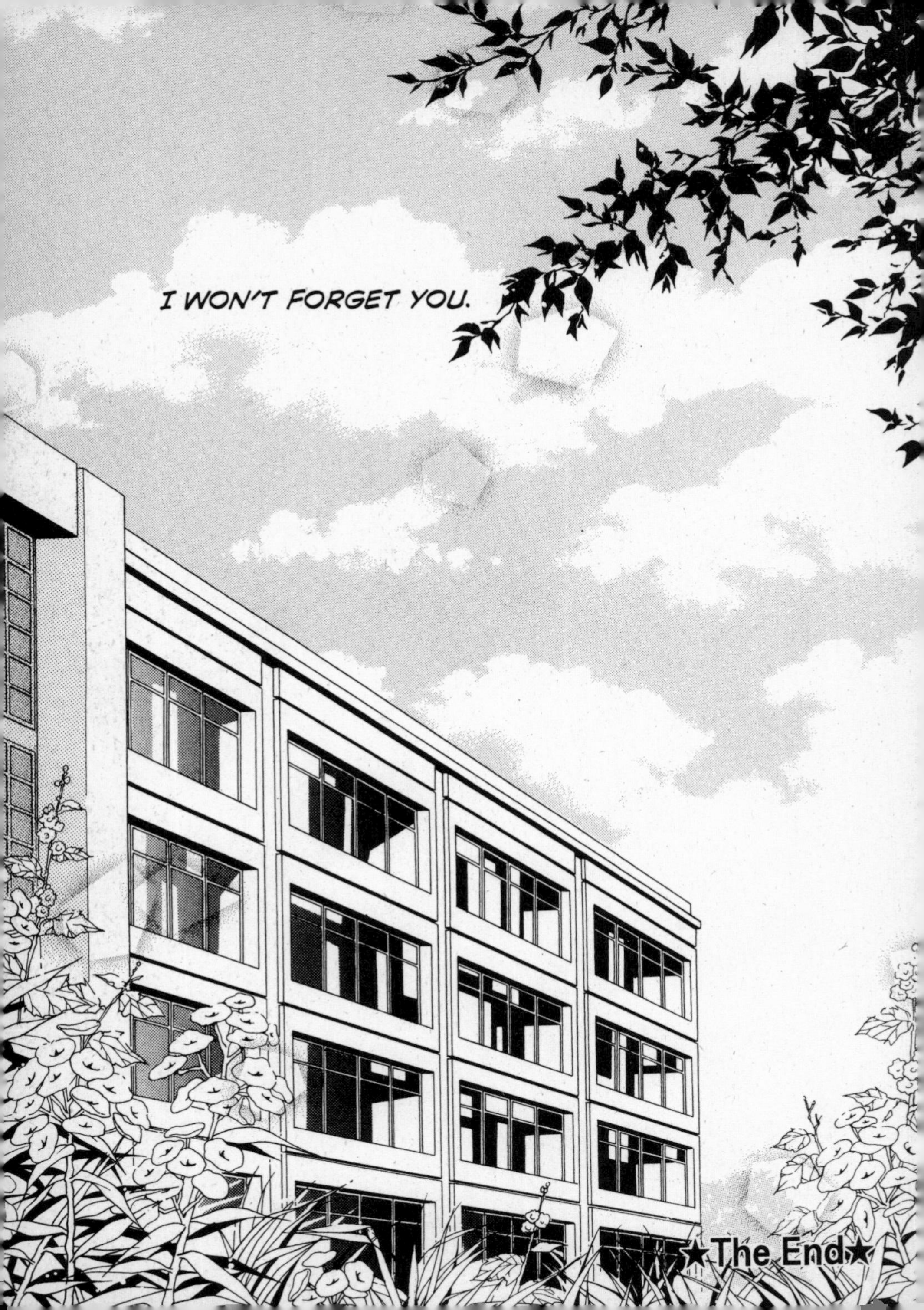
I WON'T FORGET YOU.
★The End★

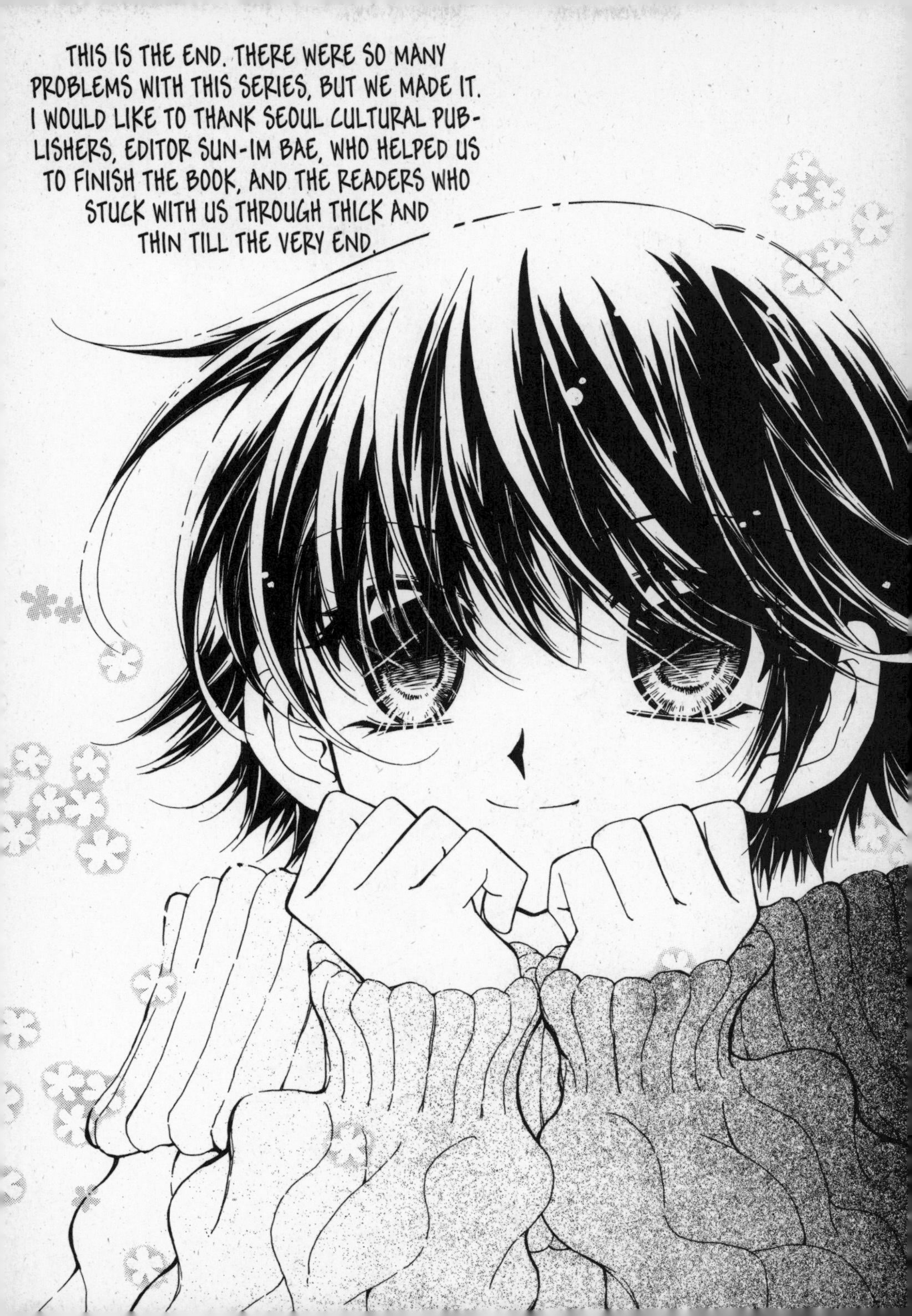
THIS IS THE END. THERE WERE SO MANY PROBLEMS WITH THIS SERIES, BUT WE MADE IT. I WOULD LIKE TO THANK SEOUL CULTURAL PUBLISHERS, EDITOR SUN-IM BAE, WHO HELPED US TO FINISH THE BOOK, AND THE READERS WHO STUCK WITH US THROUGH THICK AND THIN TILL THE VERY END.

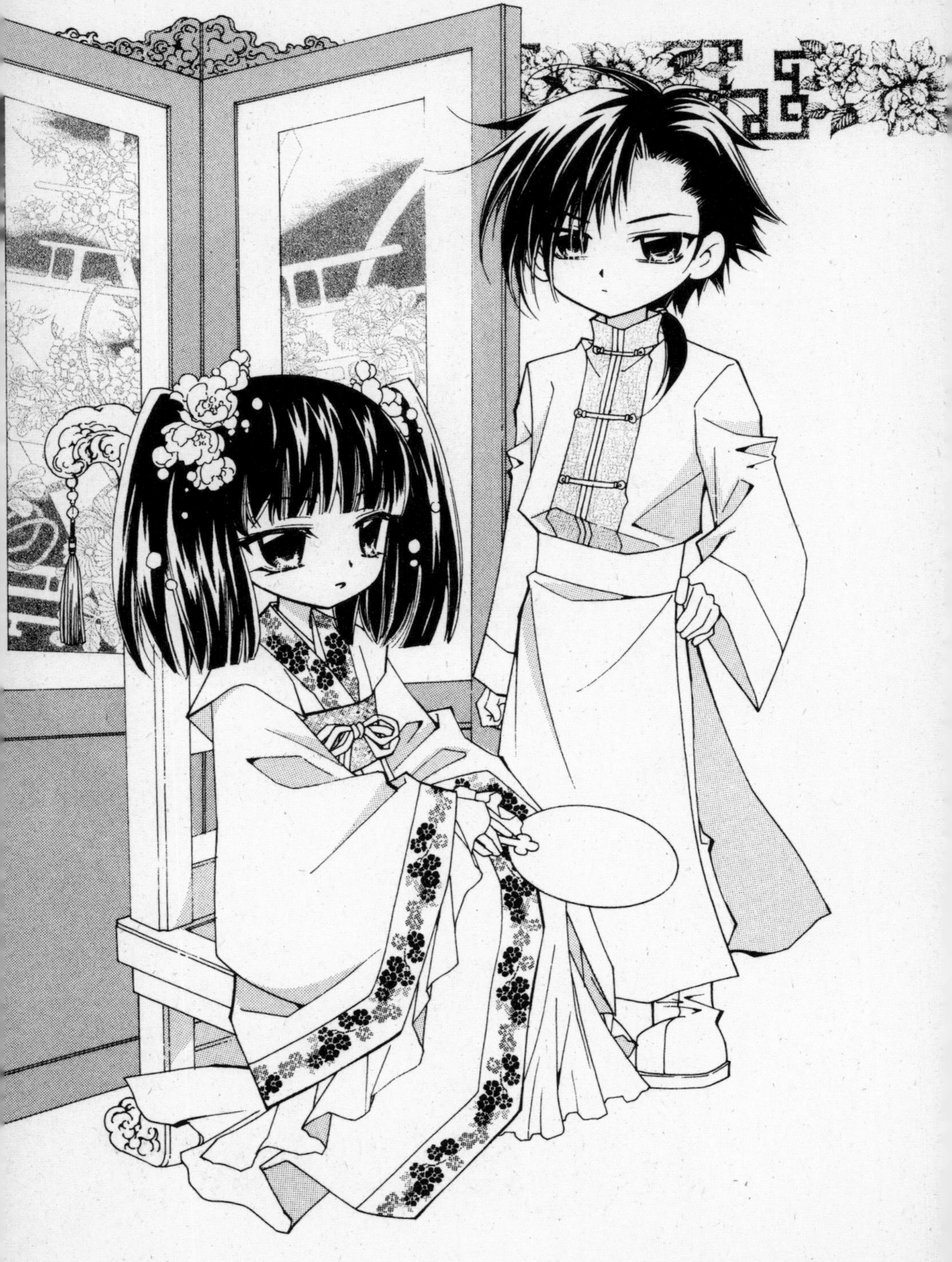

Angel Diary

The newest title from the creators of <Demon Diary> and <Angel Diary>!

Once upon a time, a selfish king summoned the monstrous Bulkirin into the real world. The monster killed half of all human beings, leaving the rest helpless as to what to do. That is, until one day when a hero appeared and defeated the Bulkirin with the legendary "Seven Blade Sword." But···what does all this have to do with 8th grader Eun-Gyo Sung?! First, she gets suspended from school for fighting. Then, she runs away from home. The last thing she needed was to be kidnapped—and whisked into the past by a mysterious stranger named No-Ah!

Available at bookstores near you!

Legend

1-10 COMPLETE

Kara · Woo SooJung

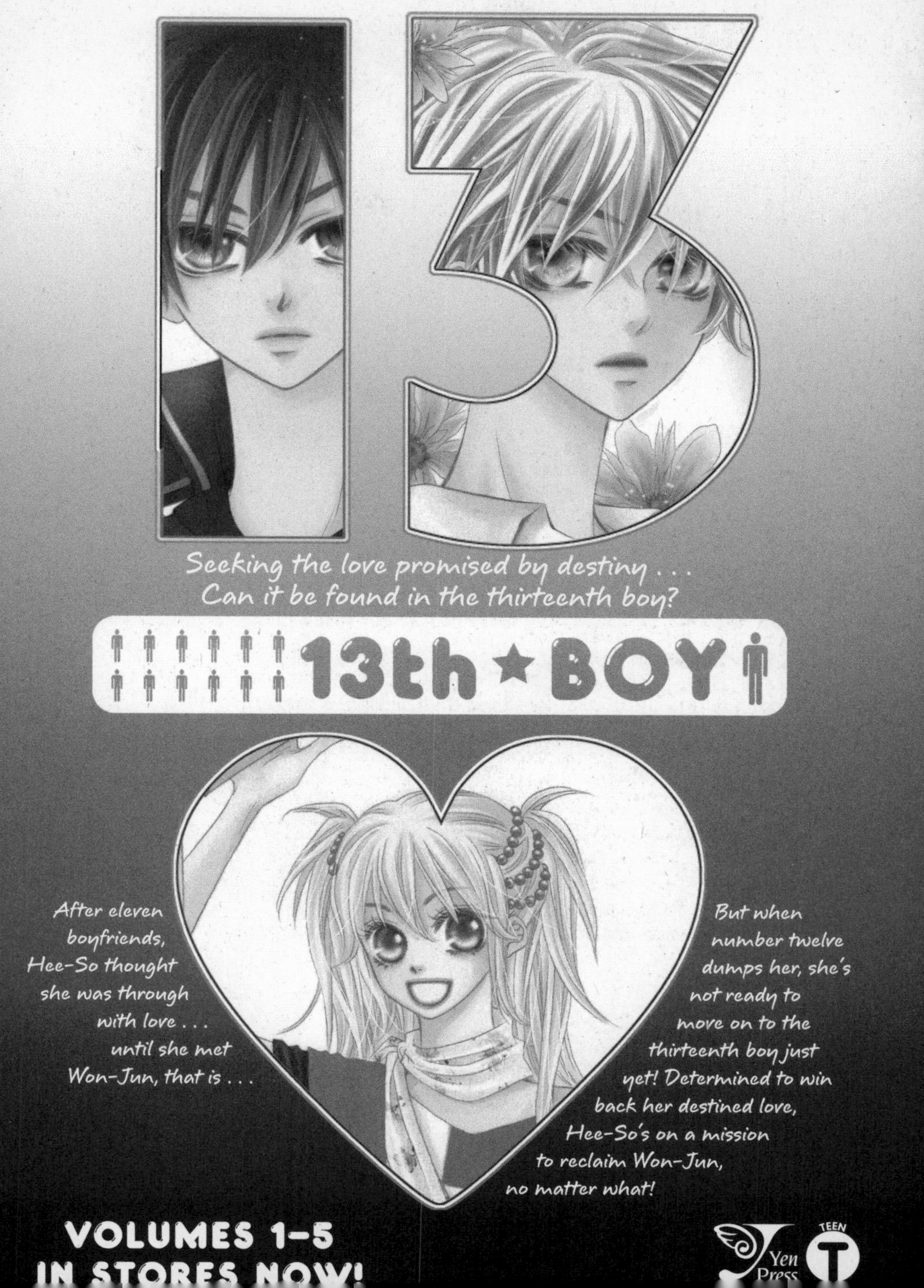
Seeking the love promised by destiny . . .
Can it be found in the thirteenth boy?
13th ★ BOY
After eleven boyfriends, Hee-So thought she was through with love . . . until she met Won-Jun, that is . . .
But when number twelve dumps her, she's not ready to move on to the thirteenth boy just yet! Determined to win back her destined love, Hee-So's on a mission to reclaim Won-Jun, no matter what!
VOLUMES 1–5
IN STORES NOW!
Yen Press
TEEN
T

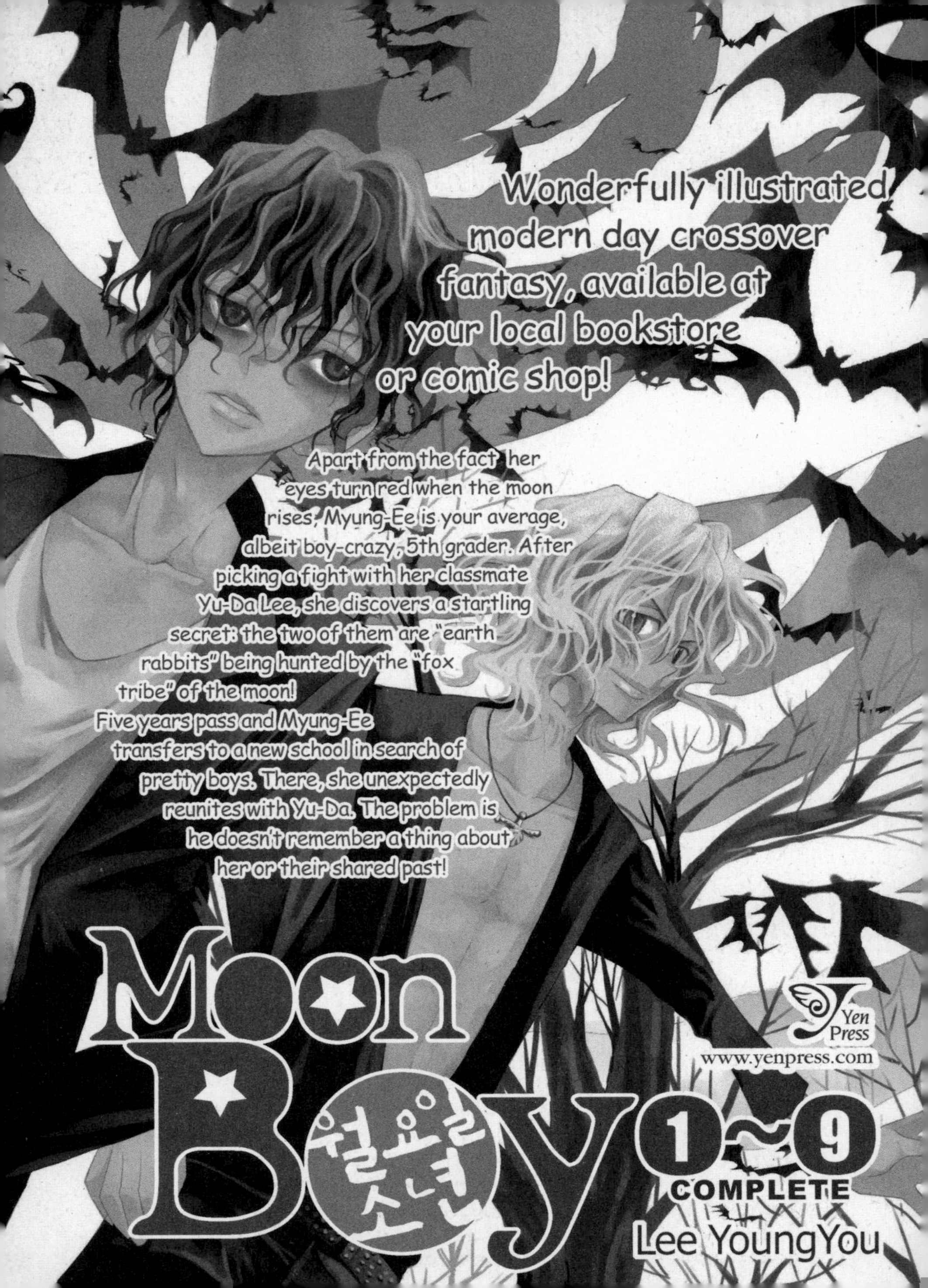
Wonderfully illustrated modern day crossover fantasy, available at your local bookstore or comic shop!
Apart from the fact her eyes turn red when the moon rises, Myung-Ee is your average, albeit boy-crazy, 5th grader. After picking a fight with her classmate Yu-Da Lee, she discovers a startling secret: the two of them are "earth rabbits" being hunted by the "fox tribe" of the moon!
Five years pass and Myung-Ee transfers to a new school in search of pretty boys. There, she unexpectedly reunites with Yu-Da. The problem is he doesn't remember a thing about her or their shared past!
Moon Boy
월요일 소년
1~9
COMPLETE
Lee YoungYou
Yen Press
www.yenpress.com

Becoming the princess... Isn't that every girl's dream?!

Monarchy rule ended long ago in Korea, but there are still other countries with kings, queens, princes and princesses. What if Korea had continued monarchism? What if all the beautiful palaces, which are now only historical relics, were actually filled with people? What if the glamorous royal family still maintained the palace customs? Welcome to a world where Korea still has the royal family living in their everyday lives! Only for this one high school girl, Chae-Kyung, is this a tragedy, since she has to marry the prince — who apparently is a total bastard!

THE ROYAL PALACE
Goong
vol.1 ~ 10

Park SoHee

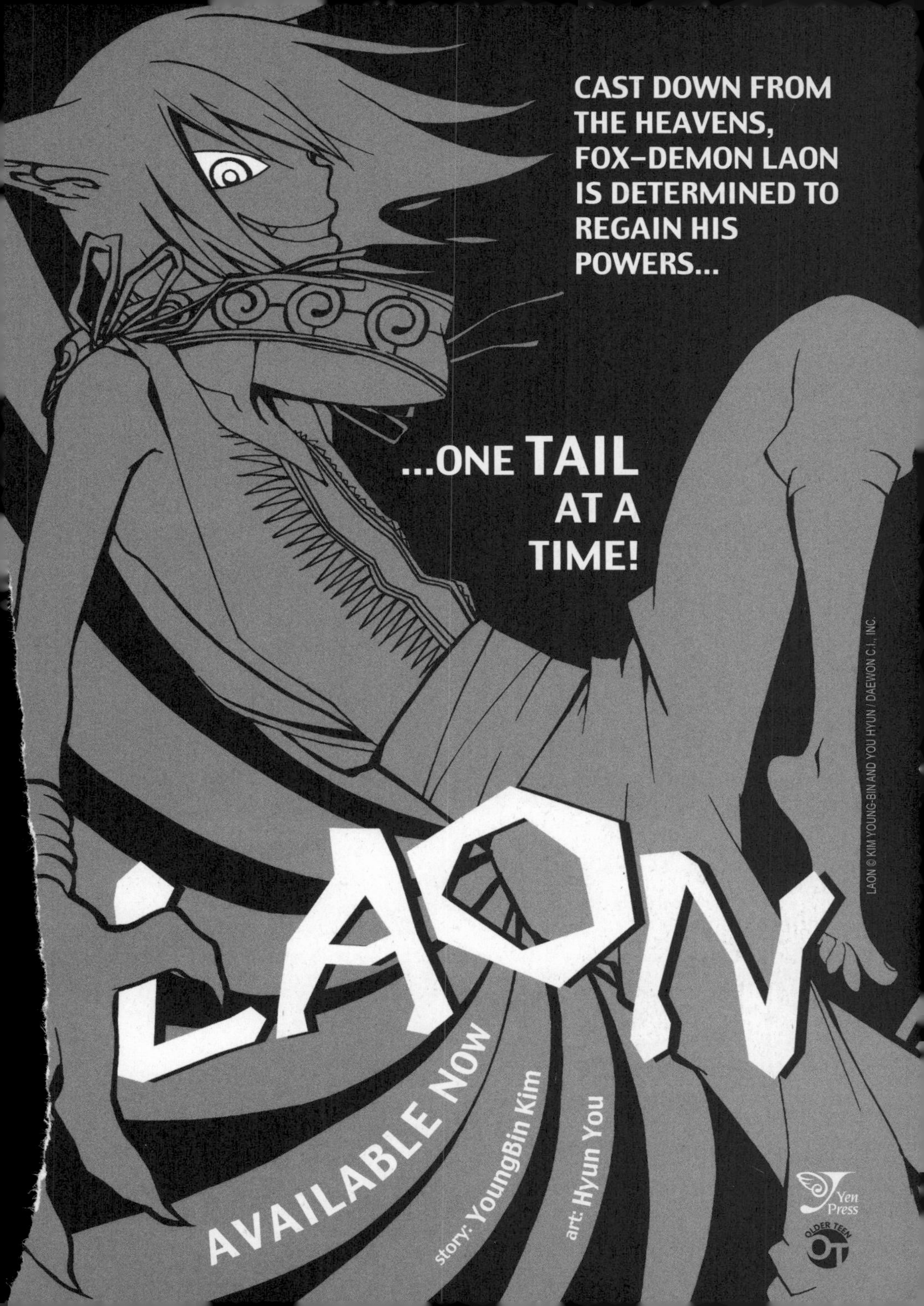
CAST DOWN FROM THE HEAVENS, FOX-DEMON LAON IS DETERMINED TO REGAIN HIS POWERS...
...ONE TAIL AT A TIME!
LAON
AVAILABLE NOW
story: YoungBin Kim
art: Hyun You
LAON © KIM YOUNG-BIN AND YOU HYUN / DAEWON C.I., INC.
Yen Press
OLDER TEEN
OT

Angel Diary vol. 13

Story by YunHee Lee
Art by Kara

Translation: HyeYoung Im
English Adaptation: Jamie S. Rich
Lettering: Terri Delgado

Yen Press
Hachette Book Group
237 Park Avenue, New York, NY 10017

www.HachetteBookGroup.com
www.YenPress.com

Yen Press is an imprint of Hachette Book Group, Inc. The Yen Press name and logo are trademarks of Hachette Book Group, Inc.

First Yen Press Edition: December 2010

ISBN: 978-0-316-09634-8

10 9 8 7 6 5 4 3 2 1

BVG

Printed in the United States of America